PREGNANCY
THE INSIDE GUIDE

PREGNANCY
THE INSIDE GUIDE

A complete guide to
fertility, pregnancy
and labour

PROFESSOR IAN GREER

First published in 2003 by Collins
An imprint of HarperCollins*Publishers*
77–85 Fulham Palace Road, London, W6 8JB

everything clicks at:
www.collins.co.uk

Text © Professor Ian Greer
Original artworks and design © HarperCollins*Publishers*
For a detailed breakdown of artwork and photography credits, see page 304

Project manager: Emma Callery
Designer: Bob Vickers
Copy editor: Kate Parker
Illustrator: Amanda Williams
Indexer: Hilary Bird

For HarperCollins
Managing editor: Angela Newton
Art direction: Luke Griffin
Editor: Alastair Laing

A CIP catalogue record for this book is available from the British Library

ISBN 0007155697

Colour reproduction by Colourscan
Printed and bound in Great Britain by Scotprint

Contents

Foreword 7

Introduction 8

Part 1: Pre-pregnancy 11

Conception & the menstrual cycle 12

Preparing your body for pregnancy 28

Understanding your own health 44

Fertility options 51

Part 2: Pregnancy 63

Discovering you are pregnant 64

Lifestyle in pregnancy 88

First trimester 104

Antenatal care & pregnancy complications 106

Second trimester 162

Your health in pregnancy 164

Third trimester 194

Labour & delivery 196

Part 3: Post-pregnancy 245

Your new baby 246

Your body after delivery 265

Post-delivery special care 277

Glossary 287

Useful addresses 296

Index 300

Acknowledgements 304

To
my wife Lauren,
my children,
and my many patients,
from whom I have learned so much

Foreword

by Professor Robert Winston

Can there be other normal events in life which can cause as much emotional turmoil as having a baby? Humans are amongst the least fertile of all large animals, so getting and staying pregnant is often difficult. Once pregnant, we are taken over in a way that we cannot fully control. As our baby grows inside the womb, pretty well every system in the body changes to accommodate this wonderful, life-giving process. And nature must pull out all the stops as delivery approaches to ensure that the uniquely large human brain is protected adequately. Even after birth this process of extraordinary change continues, for human babies are exceptionally defenceless and dependent on their mother.

But one thing that our uniquely large adult human brain often lacks is sensible, compassionate, accurate information about these life-changing processes. Much of the emotional turmoil that surrounds pregnancy occurs because pregnant women and their partners do not always know what to expect. Above all, they want to find out whether what is happening is normal, and whether, of course, their infant is going to be healthy. People also want to take some control over the processes they are experiencing, to ensure the best start in life for their child. And this requires being properly informed.

No matter how useful the antenatal classes, how good your doctor, or how good the midwives and nurses that care for you in pregnancy, it is impossible to gain all the information in conversations with the medical team. This, of course, is why there are so many pamphlets and books devoted to the subject of having a baby. But few of them, surprisingly, are written by leading practitioners in the field, and even fewer are written in terms that are absolutely clear, understandable and medically accurate, and do not patronise the reader.

Professor Ian Greer is a senior and much respected figure in British obstetrics. The prestigious chair he holds in Glasgow is one of the most distinguished in the British Isles and he carries on a great tradition there with his internationally recognised expertise in all aspects of pregnancy and the management of labour. He is to be congratulated on producing such an informative book and there is no doubt that this *Inside Guide* will remain an important resource for thousands of couples who wish to provide themselves with solid, invaluable information succinctly presented. And all who read this book will feel empowered and reassured to ask the right questions.

This excellent book will, I suspect, replace many others on the same subject on the bookshelves, and will remain a major source of useful information for a very long time to come. It is a pleasure to be associated with it.

Professor Lord Winston, DSc, FRCOG, FRCP, FMedSci
Imperial College, Hammersmith and Queen Charlotte's Hospital, London

Introduction

I spend much of my life talking to women who are or who want to become pregnant, and taking care of them through pregnancy. Often they appear to have insurmountable problems. I try to answer their many questions but sometimes there are no answers and so we work it out together. The course through their pregnancy is not always easy and sometimes uncharted, but we usually get there in the end. When they come to see me, either before or during pregnancy, they have often been searching for some time for the information they need to help them find the right course to take. It became clear to me that the information that women really needed was not readily available and so I wrote this book. With it I hope to share the kind of information that they have found useful. It contains the questions I get asked day in and day out on a wide range of topics. But there are always new questions. While I recognise that this book will not have every answer, I hope that there is something in it that every woman will find useful as she prepares for and journeys through pregnancy to the wonder of delivery of that new life.

Most books on pregnancy health are not written by specialists with expertise and experience in pregnancy care. Furthermore, the majority of books on pregnancy focus on 'normal' pregnancy, labour and delivery and often provide minimal information on the many problems, large and small, that can arise. This can sometimes give pregnant women an unrealistic expectation of how a pregnancy will be and often does not meet their needs when they develop a problem. Few pregnancies are entirely 'normal'. The woman who has absolutely no problems during pregnancy, a straightforward spontaneous labour and normal vaginal delivery is almost the exception rather than the rule. For example:

- Around 25% of conceptions end in miscarriage
- 10–15% of women may develop blood pressure problems with 2–4% being severe
- Around 10% have a baby that is small for dates
- Around 5% have a premature labour and delivery
- Many women have pre-existing medical problems that may increase the risk of pregnancy complications such as epilepsy, thyroid problems, clotting problems and diabetes
- More than 20% of deliveries are by Caesarean section, often as an emergency
- 5–10% of women have a forceps or ventouse delivery.

In addition, many women develop troublesome complaints such as morning sickness, constipation and heartburn. They might wonder why they have developed these symptoms and if it will affect the developing baby.

Whether a problem is big or small, it is important to the woman concerned. Uncertainty often leads to anxiety. Many women find that it is easier to cope with difficulties if they have a clear diagnosis or explanation for a problem coupled with a clear idea of the management options. Negotiating the sea of ever increasing medical information, in books and websites, can be difficult, especially when the information is delivered in medical jargon. This book aims to deliver pregnancy information, addressing not only the issues of 'normal' pregnancy but also an 'inside view' of the problems that can arise and how they are managed in contemporary practice. Such knowledge is important. Knowledge is power.

Embarking on a pregnancy, particularly a first pregnancy, can be an intimidating journey into the unknown. It is established that women who learn about pregnancy and the changes that occur in their body during pregnancy and labour, have a more relaxed pregnancy and a better experience of labour and delivery. They may also feel a greater sense of control and empowerment, making them better able to ask the questions that concern them. They also get the answers that they need to reassure them or help them make the right choices and decisions for their pregnancy care and delivery options. Hopefully, this will make their experience more enriching. There may be parts of this book that may not seem relevant, such as with regard to some pregnancy complications or medical disorders. Sadly, however, these problems do happen to some women and we never know what is ahead of us in life. It is also important to be aware that many problems will be overcome by appropriate advice and management.

Such knowledge and information is not only relevant once conception occurs. Indeed, it is just as critical before conception. This is the time when women are perhaps most able to influence the outcome of their pregnancy. Most women are first seen by a midwife or doctor at around 8–12 weeks of pregnancy. Yet by this time the baby is developing rapidly and opportunities to positively influence the pregnancy may have been missed. Thus it is important to prepare for pregnancy. For example, it is established that taking folic acid vitamin supplements will reduce the chance of a baby having spina bifida, but to be effective this must be taken before seven weeks of pregnancy. So it is best to plan and prepare your body for pregnancy. Bringing a new life into the world is always a source of wonder. The birth of our children is a critical investment in our future, the most critical investment we will ever make. Yet we often approach pregnancy with a degree of naivety or stumble into it with an acceptance that everything will be fine. This investment starts not with pregnancy but before it in our approach to fertility and preparation for pregnancy. Few books address in depth the importance of pre-pregnancy care and this book aims to provide the information you need as well as helping you to overcome any problems you may encounter during and immediately after your pregnancy.

It has been said that there are two kinds of knowledge, either we know the subject ourselves or we know where we can find information upon it. I hope that this book will bring you at least some of the latter, helping make your pregnancy the best experience it can be.

1 Part

Pre-pregnancy

Conception & the menstrual cycle

Most women will take good care of their health when they discover that they are pregnant. But how many are aware that diet and health before pregnancy also play a major role in producing a healthy baby? Doctors have known for a long time that pre-pregnancy care is important, and although women are becoming increasingly health conscious and many now seek specific pre-pregnancy advice, there are many women who don't. Missing your first period is often the catalyst for thinking about your pregnancy, but you will already be two weeks pregnant at this point and it may take a further few weeks before you see your obstetrician. By this time your baby is developing rapidly and you may have missed opportunities to influence the pregnancy positively. The first 12 weeks of pregnancy is the time when all of the major organs are developing in the baby's body. The heart, lungs, liver, kidneys, brain and nervous system are all formed at a time when many women do not even realise that they are pregnant. This is why pre-pregnancy care is so important.

Before getting pregnant: some facts

When is the best time to become pregnant?

There is no 'ideal' time to get pregnant. Fertility varies from person to person, although fertility in both men and women reaches its peak at about the age of

24 years. Many women are now delaying pregnancy until their 30s and even 40s where, once over the age of 35, they are at greater risk of developing complications such as high blood pressure during pregnancy. There is also a higher risk of chromosomal problems in the foetus, such as Down's syndrome *(see p. 17)*. However, the majority of women over 35 will have a successful pregnancy outcome. It is important to keep these extra risks associated with age in perspective, but seek medical advice if you have any particular concerns. The 'best' time to become pregnant will depend largely on what is best for you and your partner, taking into account everything that is going on in both your lives.

How quickly should I conceive?

If you and your partner are having regular intercourse without contraception, statistics indicate that at least 8 in every 10 normal fertile couples will have conceived within 12 months of starting to 'try', and 19 out of 20 such couples will conceive within two years of unprotected intercourse. The chance is actually highest the first month you try: between 1 in 3 and 1 in 4 couples having regular intercourse without contraception will conceive in the first month.

What can reduce my chances of conceiving?

Obviously, you need to have regular sexual intercourse to conceive. If you are having regular sexual intercourse, there are three main factors that can reduce your chances of becoming pregnant:

- Irregular or non-existent ovulation (production of an egg)
- Damaged fallopian tubes (preventing transport of the egg to the womb)
- Reduced numbers of sperm or sperm with reduced ability to fertilise an egg

I have heavy and painful periods. Will this affect my ability to conceive?

Heavy or painful periods should not necessarily affect your ability to conceive, but you may want to check such symptoms with your doctor to rule out causes such as fibroids, endometriosis *(see p. 59)* or pelvic infection. Severe or recurrent pelvic infections may lead to blocked or damaged fallopian tubes that can affect fertility *(see p. 54)*. Irregular or infrequent periods may indicate infrequent ovulation, which can reduce your overall fertility and make it difficult to plan a pregnancy.

Should fibroids be removed before pregnancy?

A fibroid is a benign lump of muscle in your womb. It can sometimes cause your periods to be heavy simply because it makes the womb bigger so that there is more endometrium (the lining of the womb) to shed at each period *(see p. 21)*, and it can increase the risk of heavy bleeding after delivery. If you already have a fibroid, the high levels of oestrogen produced by your body during pregnancy can cause it to grow larger but it is unusual for a fibroid to affect your pregnancy unless it grows very large or obstructs your cervix. It is extremely rare for a fibroid to obstruct labour, however, and in this case a

Caesarean section would be performed. There is not usually any need to remove a fibroid before trying to get pregnant; indeed, the operation to remove fibroids (a myomectomy) carries possible risks to future fertility. A myomectomy might be advised if the womb is very distorted by a large fibroid or multiple fibroid, which leads to recurrent miscarriages, but such cases are very uncommon. However, if you know you have a fibroid, it might be helpful to discuss this with your doctor.

Is it a good idea to get pregnant again soon after a previous pregnancy?

Spacing your pregnancies can also play a role in the outcome. If you have two or more pregnancies in close succession, you are at increased risk of health problems like anaemia and of producing a low-birthweight baby. You may also want to consider that spacing your pregnancies will help with the workload of looking after small children. So timing when you conceive needs to be taken into account when planning a pregnancy.

If I am overweight can this affect my chances of conceiving?

Overweight women can have fertility problems *(see p. 168)*. High levels of body fat, particularly in the abdomen, can disturb the hormones controlling the function of the ovary that produces the egg. Production of oestrogen can be affected, which upsets regular egg development in the ovaries, leading to irregular periods. With weight reduction, the hormonal imbalance is often corrected and a normal menstrual cycle usually ensues, thus improving fertility.

Can stress affect my ability to conceive?

If you have been trying desperately for a baby and you have not conceived, you can end up feeling stressed and anxious, which can have an adverse effect on conception. Having a balanced diet, getting enough sleep and taking regular exercise should help. If you have a very stressful occupation, you might want to consider ways of limiting or avoiding stress at work. *(See also p. 16.)*

I drink a lot of coffee. Will this affect my ability to conceive?

There is no good evidence that drinking up to three cups of coffee a day will reduce your fertility. There is, however, some evidence to show that excessive caffeine intake might reduce your chances of conceiving. It is thought that this may be because caffeine constricts the blood vessels and reduces the blood supply to parts of the body, including the ovaries and the womb, or because it interferes with the metabolism of the female hormone oestrogen. Remember, too, that caffeine is not only found in coffee. There is caffeine in tea and in some soft drinks like cola. If you do drink a lot of coffee, why not switch to a decaffeinated variety?

Should I stop smoking before conceiving?

Research has shown that smoking may triple your chances of not being able to conceive. If your partner smokes, he needs to give up as well. Smoking can

Don't smoke if you want a boy!

Recent research suggests that smoking may influence the sex of the baby. The number of boys relative to the number of girls born has fallen in many Western countries. A recent Scandinavian study investigated whether parental smoking might be a factor that could influence this. It assessed the smoking habits around the time of conception in the parents of almost 12,000 children and found that the more cigarettes that were smoked by both the mothers and fathers, the lower the likelihood of them having a boy. The ratio of boys to girls born was just over 6 to 5 in couples who had never smoked compared to around 4 to 5 when both parents smoked more than 20 cigarettes a day. The reason for this is not clear. Chronic exposure to toxic substances in the environment has been linked to fertility problems in men, but the link between smoking and the sex of the baby is found with both men and women smokers. This effect may be due to the sperm cells that carry a Y chromosome, which lead to conception of a boy, being more sensitive to the effects of smoking than sperm cells that carry an X chromosome, which lead to conception of a girl *(see p. 17)*.

damage his sperm as well as exposing you to passive smoking. In addition, smoking robs the body of vitamins, especially vitamins B and C, and can cause a build up of free radicals in the body. Free radicals are molecules that can damage blood vessels, such as those supplying the placenta, thus reducing the supply of nutrients for the developing baby. Smoking is a powerful addiction and so can be very difficult to stop. However, if you do stop smoking, your fertility will go back to normal. So it is important to stop smoking prior to pregnancy. If your partner also smokes, it would be best if you gave up together.

Can drinking alcohol affect my fertility?

If you drink heavily, this can affect your fertility. Alcohol can upset the production of eggs from the ovary. A Danish study conducted in 1998 found that women drinking four or fewer units of alcohol a week were twice as likely to conceive as those drinking 10 or more units a week. If your partner drinks heavily, this can affect his fertility by upsetting the function of his testicles and their production of both the male hormone testosterone and sperm. Moderate alcohol intake does not seem to cause male fertility problems, but there are some reports that if the father drinks regularly before conception this is associated with a lower birthweight in the baby. The ideal is that you both give up alcohol while you are tying to conceive, or keep your alcohol intake very moderate *(see p. 89)*, as no one knows what the 'safe' level of alcohol is. Remember, too, that if you are trying to get pregnant, you may not know you have conceived until several weeks after conception, and continued heavy alcohol intake could harm your developing baby. In particular, avoid binge drinking, where you take a large amount of alcohol over a relatively short period, as this results in very high levels of alcohol in body. If you generally have a heavy intake of alcohol, it is worthwhile obtaining specialist advice and counselling before trying to get pregnant.

Is where I work relevant when I'm trying to conceive?

If you or your partner has a job that involves working with chemicals, lead, anaesthetics or X-rays, this may affect your chances of conceiving or involve a risk to your unborn baby (see p. 90). Talk to your doctor if you are concerned.

Can I continue to take prescription medicines when I'm trying to conceive?

Certain drugs or medicines can affect your chances of becoming pregnant or could harm the baby in the womb. Equally, you may require medication for your own continued good health. If you take a prescribed medicine on a regular basis, discuss this with your doctor at the pre-pregnancy planning stage.

Do I need a medical check-up before trying to conceive?

No specific check-up is usually necessary if you are healthy, with no previous history of miscarriage, pregnancy complications or a long-standing medical condition. But if you have specific questions or concerns, you should discuss

Checklist for a healthy pregnancy

Are you thinking about becoming pregnant? If so, think now about planning for your pregnancy. It is during those first few weeks of pregnancy, when you might not even know that you are pregnant, that your baby's development can be most easily affected. If possible, plan for your pregnancy at least three months before you try to conceive. Think about the following:

- Are you taking a folic acid supplement?
- Is your diet healthy and varied?
- Are you on the pill?
- Do you smoke or drink?
- Do you have a medical condition that could affect your pregnancy, such as diabetes or epilepsy?
- Do you or your partner have a family history of inherited disease?
- Have you had German measles (rubella) or been immunised against it?
- Does your work bring you into contact with any risk factors that could affect you or your developing baby?

these with your doctor before trying to conceive. You might want to check that your cervical smear tests are up to date, too. If you need treatment for an abnormal smear, this should ideally be carried out before you get pregnant.

Our genetic 'make-up' and how it affects conception

All cells in the body contain DNA (deoxyribonucleic acid), the substance which makes up your genetic code. For this reason doctors sometimes refer to DNA as the 'building blocks' of life. This is what makes you what you are, the blueprint for the structure and function of your body. Everyone has a different genetic code except identical twins. Your genetic code is made up of thousands of genes that are carried on 'chromosomes'. Each of us has 23 pairs of chromosomes in every cell in our body – a total of 46 chromosomes per cell. Of the 23 pairs of chromosomes in every cell 22 pairs are 'general' chromosomes and one is a pair of 'sex' chromosomes.

Sperm and eggs are an exception to this general rule. An egg from a female has only 23 chromosomes; 22 of those chromosomes are 'general' chromosomes and one is a 'sex' chromosome. The sperm from the male also has only 23 chromosomes: 22 general chromosomes and one sex chromosome. When conception occurs and the sperm fertilises the egg, the egg and sperm cells fuse. A fertilised egg therefore has the full complement of 46 chromosomes. The baby that grows from this fertilised egg will have 46 chromosomes in every cell. The sex of the baby conceived is determined by the 'sex' chromosomes – referred to as 'X' and 'Y' chromosomes – and the way these combine determines whether we are male or female. All girls have two X chromosomes and no Y chromosome, while a boy has one X and one Y chromosome. It is the sex chromosome that comes from the father's sperm that determines the sex of your baby. The mother has no power to influence the sex of the baby because she can contribute only an X chromosome, whereas the father can contribute either an X or a Y chromosome.

What are inherited disorders?

Each chromosome contains thousands of genes inherited from your parents. When there is an abnormality or mistake in a gene on the chromosome or an extra or missing chromosome, then abnormalities or changes in the structure and function of the body can occur. These disorders can therefore be passed from parent to child or can arise because of new mistakes occurring in the egg, sperm or fertilised egg. If they are new mistakes there will be no family history of the problem but they can be passed on to future generations.

What is a chromosomal condition?

Each of our cells needs to have 46 chromosomes in 23 pairs to constitute a 'normal' genetic make-up. A chromosomal condition arises when there is a defect in the number of the chromosomes making up each cell. An example of a chromosomal condition is Down's syndrome. It usually occurs when an egg or a sperm is being formed and accidentally acquires an extra chromosome. The pairs of chromosomes making up the sperm or unfertilised egg are numbered 1–22 (leaving out the sex chromosomes). In Down's syndrome, for some reason the baby receives an extra chromosome from either the sperm or the egg, and it is always chromosome number 21 that is the extra one. This means there are three number 21 chromosomes instead of the more usual two in every cell of the baby's body, creating 47 pairs of chromosomes in each cell, instead of the normal 46.

What is a genetic condition?

You receive chromosomes from your mother and father and with them the genes that make up your genetic code. A genetic condition is due to a mistake or mutation in the genetic code on a chromosome. In addition, the gene can be passed from parent to child. An example of a genetic condition is sickle-cell anaemia, in which there is an abnormality in the gene controlling the formation of the red blood cells that carry oxygen around the body. *(See also p. 49.)* Thalassaemia is another genetic condition in which there is an abnormality in the gene controlling the production of red blood cells, leading to varying degrees of anaemia. Another example of a genetic condition is cystic fibrosis, in which the mucus produced by the lungs is abnormally thick and difficult to clear, leading to recurrent chest infections. In this condition there is also abnormality of the pancreas, affecting its ability to produce enzymes to break down food in the gut and thus leading to malabsorption of food.

Some genetic conditions are 'dominant', others are 'recessive'. Sickle-cell anaemia, like cystic fibrosis, is a so-called 'recessive' condition because for a baby to be affected it needs to inherit two sickle-cell genes, one from each parent. Each parent will pass the gene to the child at conception. If one parent passes on the sickle-cell gene and the other passes on a normal gene, this is not sufficient to cause the condition. To pass on the two sickle-cell genes necessary to produce the disease each parent will have to be either affected by the disease or be a carrier of it. A carrier has one normal gene and one abnormal gene. Carriers do not usually have the disease, but have the potential to pass this gene on to a child. They are unlikely to know that they have the gene unless there is a family history of the disease.

Occasionally the abnormal gene can be 'dominant', however, as in the case of brittle bone disease and Huntingtons chorea (in which brain cells degenerate, leading to jerky, involuntary movements and progressive dementia). This means that if the baby has one abnormal gene it will be affected even if the other gene is normal. In dominant conditions only one parent need carry and pass on the gene. This doesn't just relate to disease, of course. Probably the most common example of a dominant gene is that for eye colour. The brown eye-colour gene is dominant over the blue eye-colour gene. So if a baby receives a 'blue' gene from its mother and a 'brown' gene from its father, it will have brown eyes. If it gets a 'blue' gene from both parents, it will have blue eyes. Another example of a dominant condition occurs in some forms of dwarfism. If the baby has one dwarfism gene, it will have dwarfism even if the other gene is normal.

Some genetic disorders are carried on the X chromosome, the best known being haemophilia. This is an X chromosome recessive condition which boys suffer from and girls carry. It causes recurrent, often severe bleeding problems. A girl has two X chromosomes, so if a haemophilia gene is present on one chromosome and a normal gene on the other, she will not be affected as it is a recessive condition, but she will be a carrier. A boy has only one X chromosome, the other sex chromosome being Y. So if he has the haemophilia gene on his X chromosome, he will be affected by haemophilia, for there is no normal gene to protect him, as there is in a 'carrier' girl. When a man with haemophilia has children, his sons will be normal as they get the Y chromosome from their father and a normal X chromosome from the mother. All his daughters, however, will be carriers as they get the X chromosome with the haemophilia gene from their father and a normal gene on the X chromosome they get from their mother.

Do I need genetic counselling?

Genetic counselling is aimed at determining the risk you run of passing on an inherited disease to your child. You may need advice if you are over the age of 35 or if you or your partner are carriers of a genetic or chromosomal disorder which could be passed onto your child.

What happens when I go for genetic counselling?

You will usually be asked about your health and your family background. Some blood tests may be required to determine whether you or your partner are carriers for an inherited disease. Based on this information, the counsellor will help to assess the degree of risk. This can help couples make an informed decision when deciding whether to proceed with a pregnancy. The counsellor can also advise if there are tests available to determine whether your unborn baby is affected by specific inherited conditions.

Genetic counselling: who can benefit?

- If you have a previous child born with a congenital problem like spina bifida or a heart abnormality
- If you have a previous child born with a genetic disorder (e.g. cystic fibrosis, Down's syndrome or sickle-cell anaemia
- If there is a family history of an inherited problem such as haemophilia or sickle-cell anaemia
- If there is a blood relationship between you and your partner
- If you have a history of repeated miscarriage

If I have a genetic condition, is there anything that can be done before pregnancy to tell if the baby will be affected?

Strictly speaking, until conception occurs it will not be possible to determine whether the baby might have inherited the genetic condition you have. However, a new technique, using assisted conception technology, is becoming available which allows diagnosis of some genetic conditions before the embryo is implanted. Essentially, the mother undergoes in-vitro fertilisation (IVF) *(see p. 57)*, then the resulting embryos are tested before they are placed into the mother's womb. When a fertilised egg has developed to a four- or eight-cell stage, one of these cells is taken from the early embryo using special microscopic techniques. This single cell is tested for the genetic condition. If the embryo is not affected by the condition, it is then transferred to the mother's womb. The removal of a single cell for testing at this very early stage does not upset the development of the baby.

I am over 35 and I am worried about the risk of having a Down's syndrome baby. What should I do?

While women over the age of 35 are at increased risk of having a Down's syndrome baby, that does not mean that younger mothers never have a Down's syndrome baby. There is no predictor other than age pre-pregnancy unless there is a family history of Down's syndrome. If you have a family history of Down's syndrome, you should seek specific genetic counselling prior to pregnancy as there is one form that can be passed on even if the mother is unaffected, because of a change in the structure of the chromosomes. After you have become pregnant there are tests that can assess your risk of having a Down's syndrome child *(see pp. 120–4)*.

Immunity to German measles (rubella)

Why is rubella immunity important in pregnancy?

Rubella, probably better known as German measles, is a very common infection in children and most children either contract it in childhood or are immunised against it. German measles, if caught, particularly in the first three months of pregnancy, can cause malformations in your baby *(see p. 149)*. However, it can only be caught if you are not immune to it.

How do I know if I have immunity to German measles?

Your family doctor should have a record of your immunisations. In addition, your mother or father may remember if you had German measles as a child. Once you have had rubella or been immunised against it, you should be immune to it. It is rare to lose immunity. If there is any doubt, immunity to German measles can be checked with a simple blood test. If a woman is not immune, she should be immunised before trying to become pregnant.

Can immunisation affect the unborn baby?

Immunisation cannot be given during pregnancy, as the vaccine is live and could also potentially cause problems for the baby. After being immunised, it is essential to use effective contraception for three months.

The menstrual cycle

What happens during the menstrual cycle?

Regular menstrual bleeding is controlled by a complex system. The brain controls the release of 'signalling' molecules (follicle-stimulating hormone, or FSH, and luteinising hormone, or LH) from the pituitary gland at the base of the brain. FSH and LH stimulate the ovaries to produce and release a mature egg (ovulation) and female hormones (oestrogen and progesterone) each month. Oestrogen and progesterone control the growth of the lining of the womb (the endometrium) and keep it in a condition suitable for the fertilised egg to implant. If a fertilised egg does not implant, the production of hormones from the ovary falls. As these hormone levels fall, the endometrium is shed and results in the bleeding which we know as a period. The whole process then starts over again.

How frequently should periods occur?

The normal interval between menstrual periods is most commonly around 28 days, but it may range from 21 to 35 days. As ovulation (production of a mature egg) is essential for a regular menstrual cycle, women who do not regularly ovulate have irregular and usually infrequent periods.

How long should menstrual bleeding last?

Periods usually last for 5–7 days. No matter whether periods are light or heavy, most of the blood is lost in the first three days of the period. The average monthly blood loss with periods is between 30–40 ml (1–1^1/2 fl oz).

When does ovulation occur?

The time of ovulation depends on the length of your cycle. As the graph on p. 22 shows, if you have a 28-day cycle, ovulation will occur at around day 14. If you have a 21-day cycle, ovulation will occur at around day 7. If you have a 35-day cycle, ovulation will occur at around day 21. This is because the time taken to mature an egg and ovulate can vary from woman to woman. The part of the cycle during which the egg develops is called the follicular phase as the egg develops in a small 'follicle' or cyst in the ovary. The time from ovulation to a period (if fertilisation does not occur) is fixed at around 14 days. This is called the secretary phase of the cycle as the ovary makes and 'secretes' progesterone, a hormone essential for pregnancy. Provided your cycle is regular, you will be able to estimate the time that you ovulate.

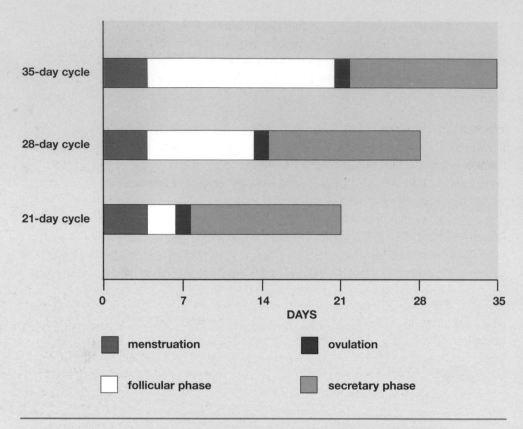

The phases of the menstrual cycle and approximate time of ovulation for different cycle lengths.

Some women know when they are ovluating because they feel lower abdominal pain at the time when the egg is released from the ovary. The pain is quite normal and is referred to as 'Mittelschmerz' (from German words for 'middle' and 'pain' – hence pain felt mid-cycle). As the egg develops at the beginning of the menstrual cycle, the follicle that contains it will reach about 2 cm (3/4 in) in diameter before it ruptures, releasing the egg, at the time of ovulation. This is what produces pain in some women. The small cyst that remains after release of the egg is necessary for normal menstrual function, as it secretes progesterone, the hormone that is essential for preparing the lining of the womb for pregnancy. If a fertilised egg does not implant then this small cyst will shrink down and disappear at the end of a cycle. If pregnancy occurs it will persist for a few weeks longer as progesterone is needed to maintain the pregnancy in the first few weeks.

When should I stop contraception when trying to get pregnant?
This depends on the type of contraception you are using. Barrier methods do not disturb ovulation or the menstrual cycle and you can simply stop at any time. There is no need to delay attempts at conception provided you have no other menstrual or medical problems. If you use an intrauterine contraceptive

device, or 'coil', for contraception then this must be removed before you try to conceive. It is probably best to delay conception until at least the next cycle as the coil may have disturbed the lining of the womb. So, after the doctor has removed the coil, you should use another technique such as barrier contraception until you are ready to conceive.

When should I stop taking the pill?

If you use the oral contraceptive pill or an injectable contraceptive, your normal menstrual cycle and ovulation will be disrupted. If you wish to get pregnant, it is best to stop taking the oral contraceptive pill, or injectable contraceptive, and wait until your normal menstrual cycle resumes before trying to conceive. As this may take about three normal menstrual periods, you might want to use a technique such as barrier contraception until your cycle has stabilised. If you become pregnant before the regular rhythm of your periods has become established, this can make it difficult to predict your delivery date.

Can the date of ovulation be worked out if I have just stopped taking the pill?

No. The pill suppresses ovulation and, after you have stopped taking it, it will usually take 2–3 cycles before your own regular pattern is established. The time from stopping the pill to ovulating is extremely variable. Estimates of the time of ovulation are based on the date when the next natural (not pill-induced) period is expected. So it is impossible to estimate when ovulation will occur after you stop the pill.

At what time in the menstrual cycle am I fertile?

Your fertile time can be worked out by estimating when ovulation occurs. That is 14 days before the first day on which the next period is due. So just subtract 14 days from the date you expect your period to arrive. For example, let's say that your period is due to start on August 24. Take 14 days from August 24 and this is the date around which you ovulate. In this example it will be the August 10. Once an egg is released, it remains viable for around a day. Allow a day or so on either side of this for minor variations in the time of ovulation. Sperm can remain viable in the woman's body for around two days. Therefore the fertile time is estimated as being from 2–3 days before the estimated time of ovulation to two days after the estimated time of ovulation. This is the best time to try to conceive.

Are there other signs of ovulation?

Yes. Changes in temperature and the vaginal mucus can help tell you when ovulation is occurring.

How does temperature help me to know when I am ovulating?

Your body temperature should fall slightly before ovulation then rise quickly afterwards. It is worth noting, however, that sometimes the fall prior to ovulation is absent. If you want to use this technique to find out when you are ovulating

Conception & the menstrual cycle

then you should take your temperature with a thermometer in the morning before getting up out of bed. You need to take your temperature at the same time every day. This should be repeated for each cycle that you want to check for ovulation, but if you have a very regular cycle, ovulation is likely to occur at around the same time during each cycle. If an oral temperature reading is to be used, remember to check your temperature before drinking anything hot or cold, to avoid confusion.

Why is there an increase in temperature?

The increase in temperature occurs in response to the progesterone that is produced after ovulation occurs. Progesterone levels and the body temperature remain elevated until a day or so before the next period occurs. If pregnancy occurs, the temperature rise (and elevated progesterone levels) will persist. The typical change seen would be a body temperature of, say, 36.6–36.8°C (97.9–98.2°F) which falls to 36.2–36.4°C (97.2–97.5°F) before ovulation. The temperature would then increase to, say, 37.0–37.1°C (98.6–98.8°F) by around 36 hours after ovulation. If you regularly chart your temperature then you will see a pattern developing *(see below)*.

Can I use any thermometer?

Any medical thermometer that can measure in tenths of one degree centigrade can be used. Thermometers (including electronic ones) and temperature charts can be purchased from pharmacies.

How effective is this method of predicting ovulation?

Waiting for a rise in temperature before you have intercourse can be an ineffective course of action as your temperature rise occurs *after* ovulation and by the time the temperature has risen the egg may no longer be viable. If you

A typical pattern of temperature rise when ovulation occurs around day 14.

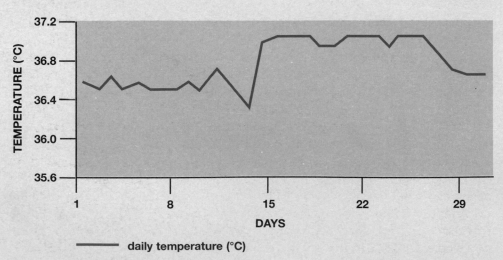

daily temperature (°C)

have a regular menstrual cycle, however, the time of ovulation may be anticipated based on a well-recorded pattern in temperature rise. This allows intercourse to be timed to coincide with ovulation.

How do changes in my vaginal mucus help show when I am ovulating?

The consistency of your vaginal mucus can help predict the fertile phase as the character of the discharge varies through the menstrual cycle. Just after a period it is scant, sticky and thick. Just before the time of ovulation, when oestrogen levels are high, the amount of mucus increases and it becomes watery, stringy and clear – a bit like raw egg white. If you collect the mucus on your finger at this time and try and stretch it between your thumb and forefinger, it will stretch for several inches without breaking. After the fertile time the mucus again becomes thicker. Sperm can survive particularly well in the thinner, 'fertile' mucus, which also makes it easier for the sperm to get through the cervix and into the womb. Hence charting the pattern of changes in your vaginal mucus can help work out when you are ovulating.

Are there other methods for telling when I am ovulating?

If you want to know when you are likely to be most fertile, you could buy an ovulation prediction kit. These kits, which are available from pharmacies, measure the amount of luteinising hormone (LH) in your urine – the hormone that stimulates the release of eggs from your ovaries each month. The kit identifies a surge in this hormone that precedes ovulation by around 12 hours. This can help establish the fertile days in your cycle. Ovulation prediction kits are a little more accurate than temperature charts and avoid the need for regular temperature assessment, but they are more expensive.

Conception

How does conception occur?

Sperm cells are formed in the testicles and mature sperm cells are released at the time of ejaculation. Normally a minimum of 60–100 million are released and often well in excess of 200 million. Although some will be lost from the vagina, many will make their way through the cervix (helped by the thin, watery mucus produced at this time) into the womb and up into the fallopian tubes. The egg, having been released from the ovary, will be picked up by the finger-like ends of a fallopian tube. It will then be transported down the tube. Fertilisation of the egg occurs about one-third of the way down the fallopian tube. The egg is surrounded by sperm and one sperm will succeed in penetrating the outer layer of the egg. This is the point of conception after which no other sperm can penetrate the egg.

After conception the genetic material (chromosomes) of the sperm and egg cells merge with each other and then the fertilised egg, which starts off as a single cell, divides to form two cells then four and then eight and so on

Conception & the menstrual cycle

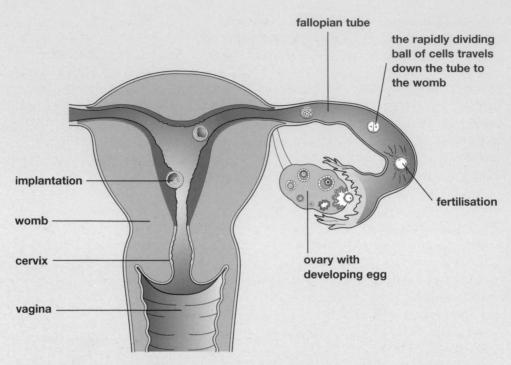

fallopian tube

the rapidly dividing ball of cells travels down the tube to the womb

implantation

womb

cervix

vagina

fertilisation

ovary with developing egg

The journey of an egg – fertilisation. The egg matures in a small cyst, which develops in the ovary. At ovulation the egg is released from the cyst and 'picked up' by the fallopian tube. The cyst persists in the ovary and makes the hormone progesterone. The sperm travel all the way from the vagina, through the cervix and womb, to meet the egg in the fallopian tube. Once fertilised, the egg cell starts to divide and travels down the tube to the womb. Three to four days after conception the ball of cells that will eventually form the baby and the placenta, reaches the womb. A cavity forms within the ball of cells and then, by seven days after conception, it implants into the lining of the womb.

The journey of an egg – cell division. The fertilised egg starts as a single cell, then divides to form two cells, then four (left) and then eight (right), and so on until a ball of cells is formed. This ball of cells will continue its journey down the fallopian tube to the womb, where it will stay for around three days, before it implants in the womb about seven days after ovulation.

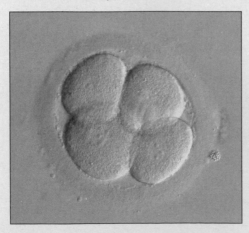

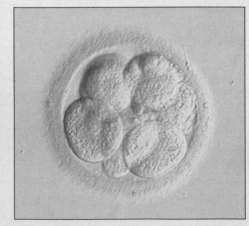

until a ball of cells is formed. This ball of cells will continue its journey down the fallopian tube to the womb, where it will stay for around three days, bathed in secretions from the womb. It will implant about seven days after ovulation into the wall of the womb, whose lining has been prepared by the production of progesterone from the ovary *(see above)*. Another hormone, known as human chorionic gonadotrophin (hCG), is produced by the developing placenta. This maintains the production of progesterone from the ovary to help to support the early pregnancy. The ball of cells, once implanted, organises itself into two different layers of cells, one that will become the embryo and the other the placenta.

Does sexual position influence conception?

Provided intercourse is comfortable and semen is deposited at the top of the vagina, the sexual position should not influence conception. However, it is perhaps best for the woman to avoid more upright positions after the man ejaculates to prevent some of the semen draining out of the vagina. Equally, there is no truth in the old wives' tale that you can't get pregnant if you have intercourse standing up.

When is the best time of the month to try and get pregnant?

The best time for you to have intercourse is in the days immediately before ovulation and on the day of ovulation itself. However, even with temperature charts or prediction kits, it is often difficult to identify the precise time of ovulation in advance. So, from a practical perspective, you should have intercourse several times around the estimated time of ovulation. Generally, there is no need to restrict intercourse at other times of the month. Indeed, the best plan is to have intercourse regularly every couple of days throughout the cycle. This avoids putting pressure on you both to identify the fertile time, obliging you to make love according to the calendar rather than by desire.

How often should we have intercourse?

If you have intercourse every couple of days throughout the cycle, this is usually sufficient for conception to take place. Sperm will persist in the woman and be capable of fertilising an egg for around two days following intercourse, especially during her most fertile time.

What is the chance of getting pregnant each month?

Humans are not highly efficient when it comes to fertility. The chance of getting pregnant for a normal fertile couple in the first month of trying is around 1 in 3 or 30%. This might be because highly fertile couples conceive quickly and so the statistic is relatively high for the first month. After the first month, the likelihood decreases, reaching around 1 in 10 by 12 months. Even with entirely normal couples, 10% of them will take more than a year of trying before they manage to conceive.

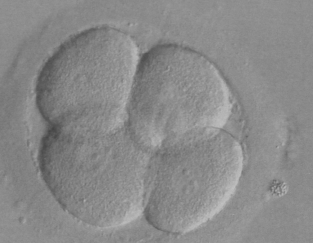

Preparing your body for pregnancy

Keeping healthy and eating well are important when you are pregnant. Did you know that it is also important to be healthy *before* you become pregnant? So, if you are thinking about trying to conceive, a critical part of your healthcare planning is your diet. It has been said that you are what you eat, and of course your baby will be too. Indeed, eating a well-balanced diet before you conceive is one of the most important things you can do for your baby. In addition, if you are overweight, it is best to reduce your weight before trying to conceive. This is because not only does being overweight reduce your chances of conceiving, but it will also put both you and your baby at greater risk of complications. If you are a smoker, you should know that smoking can reduce your fertility, make you more prone to miscarriage, and ristrict foetal growth *(see p. 14)*. As it may take you some time to give up smoking, it is again best to try to stop several months before attempting to conceive. Indeed, there is no better incentive for you and your partner to stop smoking than when you are trying for a baby.

Vitamins and iron

What type of vitamin supplements do you need when preparing for pregnancy?

If you are planning a pregnancy, it makes sense to be as healthy as possible. When you are pregnant you need the same healthy diet and balance of nutrients

Vitamins and minerals in a pre-pregnancy diet

Vitamin / mineral	Recommended pre-pregnancy daily allowance for vitamin supplements	Typical food source
Beta-carotene (precursor of vitamin A)	800 mg	Carrots, spinach, red peppers
B vitamins	Vitamin B6: 2 mg Vitamin B12: 1 mcg	Bread, cereal, cheese, eggs, meat, oily fish, green leafy vegetables
Folic acid	400 mcg	Broccoli, Brussels sprouts, peas, green beans, chickpeas, spinach, breakfast cereals
Vitamin C	60 mg	Fruit, vegetable, fruit juice
Vitamin D	5 mcg	Eggs, oily fish (e.g. mackerel, sardines), fortified margarine
Calcium	800 mg	Cheese, milk, yoghurt
Iron	14 mg	Beans, bread, red meat, breakfast cereals
Zinc	15 mg	Bread, pasta, hard cheeses, milk

that you need when you are not pregnant. Remember that your body will make adjustments in how it handles certain nutrients so that it can cope with the extra demands of pregnancy. If you have a balanced and healthy diet and no nutritional or medical problems, then there is probably only one vitamin supplement you need to take. This vitamin is folic acid. If you have any doubts about your vitamin requirements, however, it is worth discussing these with your family doctor. Equally, it is a good idea to consult your doctor or pharmacist before taking vitamin supplements other than folic acid. If you have a well-balanced diet (see overleaf), this should provide you with all the other vitamins and minerals you need.

What is folic acid?

Folic acid is an important member of the B vitamin family (vitamin B9) although it is occasionally referred to as vitamin M. It is soluble in water and is stored mainly in the liver. Folic acid is essential for the production of healthy red blood cells, which carry oxygen round the body. We are constantly making and replacing our red blood cells: it has been estimated that on average an adult will make more than 120 million new red blood cells every minute. Hence deficiency of folic acid means that insufficient red blood cells are produced, leading to problems such as anaemia. An adequate folic acid intake is also essential for the formation of the developing baby as a deficiency can result in neural tube defects *(see overleaf)*.

Does folic acid occur naturally in the body?

Vitamins like folic acid are substances that are essential in small quantities for normal body metabolism. In general, they are substances that the body cannot produce and folic acid is one such vitamin that does not occur naturally in your body. You need to obtain it from other sources such as your food or by means of vitamin supplements.

Which foods contain folic acid?

Folic acid is found in fresh dark green vegetables like broccoli, Brussels sprouts, peas, green beans, chickpeas and spinach. It is also present in oranges. Peanuts are rich in folic acid but salted peanuts should be avoided if possible. In addition, if you or your family have a history of peanut allergy

Folic acid is found in fresh dark green vegetables like broccoli, Brussels sprouts, peas, green beans, chickpeas and spinach, as well as fortified breakfast cereals.

Foods high in folic acid

Food source	Folic acid content (approximate)
Breakfast cereal	70–140 mcg per 100 g (3$^{1}/_{2}$ oz) serving
Brussels sprouts	110 mcg per 100 g (3$^{1}/_{2}$ oz)
Yeast extract	50 mcg spread over a slice of bread
Oranges	45 mcg per orange
Fortified bread	35 mcg per slice
Wholemeal bread	15 mcg per slice

or other allergic conditions, like asthma and hay fever, it is recommended that you avoid peanuts in pregnancy. Many breakfast cereals have added folic acid (it will tell you on the label) and milk and yoghurt also contain it. Wholemeal and wholegrain breads are high in folic acid, as are wheatgerm, brewer's yeast and yeast extract. Folic acid is largely destroyed by cooking, so make sure that you eat salads and stir-fry or steam vegetables lightly rather than boiling them.

If I eat a balanced diet, do I need to take folic acid tablets?

Many women with a good diet may have a sufficient folic acid intake for pregnancy simply from their food without the need for supplementation. But folic acid deficiency commonly arises in pregnancy due to the extra demands the baby places on the mother's body. Even women who have an adequate diet may have insufficient folic acid because the body is not absorbing it efficiently from food. Folic acid supplements are therefore recommended for every woman trying to conceive to be sure that her intake is sufficient. In pregnancy the kidneys filter folic acid from the blood at four times the normal rate, which is another reason why supplements are recommended. If you decide not to take folic acid supplements, however, you should ensure that you have a good intake of folic acid in your diet by good quantities of the foods listed in the table above on a daily basis.

Why are folic acid supplements recommended when trying to conceive?

Folic acid is known to reduce the risk of certain abnormalities in the baby known as neural tube defects, of which spina bifida is perhaps the best known. All babies are potentially at risk of spina bifida, or other neural tube defects such as hydrocephalus, whatever the mother's age and whether or not this is a first or a subsequent pregnancy. Interestingly, in the USA folic acid has been added to all flour for bread and pasta from 1998. Since that time the number of babies with neural tube defects has fallen by almost 20%. There is also some evidence to suggest that adequate folic acid intake might help prevent problems such as small-for-dates babies *(see p. 124)*. In addition, it will help prevent anaemia in the mother, which can result from a shortage of folic acid in pregnancy. However, there is one relatively uncommon form of anaemia due to deficiency of vitamin B12 that folic acid supplements could make it difficult for routine blood tests to pick up. If you have a history of anaemia due to vitamin B12 deficiency, check with your doctor before taking folic acid.

What are neural tube defects?

The neural tube is the part of the developing baby that will eventually become the brain and the spinal cord. It forms at about four weeks after you have conceived or about two weeks from the time of your missed period. Research has shown that sufficient folic acid in the mother's blood is essential for normal formation of the neural tube. However, disorders such as spina bifida, which in its severe form can be seriously handicapping for the baby, are caused by neural tube defects.

What are spina bifida and hydrocephalus?

In babies with spina bifida there is a defect in which part of one or more vertebrae, the bones making up the spine, fails to develop completely, leaving a portion of the nervous tissue in the spinal cord exposed, which leads to damage of the nerves. This defect can occur anywhere in the baby's spine but is most commonly seen in the lower back. The condition varies in severity and much depends on where the defect is and how much of the nervous tissue is exposed. Mild cases may have no major disability but in more severe cases there can be paralysis of the legs, loss of sensation and incontinence due to loss of bladder control.

Hydrocephalus is where there is an excess of fluid in chambers within the brain. This often arises because the flow of fluid through these chambers is obstructed. The excess fluid builds up in the chambers and the pressure causes them to enlarge, which can damage the brain tissue *(see p. 284)*. Hydrocephalus may occur with spina bifida or on its own.

Am I more at risk if I have already had one child with spina bifida?

Women who have had a child with spina bifida are more at risk than women who have had a child without the condition. In such instances it would be worthwhile obtaining specific pre-pregnancy advice before conceiving again, and you should consult your doctor.

When should I start to take folic acid when preparing for pregnancy?

Ideally, you should start taking folic acid supplements 2–3 months before you start trying to conceive. Make this part of your pre-pregnancy planning.

How much folic acid do I need and how long do I need to take it?

The recommended daily allowance of folic acid for adults is 200 mcg. Prior to becoming pregnant it is recommended that you double this intake to 400 mcg a day. You can obtain folic acid tablets from all good pharmacies. If you do not like taking tablets, you could try folic acid milk, available from pharmacies; one carton usually represents the daily requirement. You should continue to take 400 mcg during at least the first 12 weeks of your pregnancy. Remember always to follow the instructions on the pack: some prescription medicines can be affected by taking folic acid, for instance. If you are taking prescribed medicines, check with your doctor before taking the supplements.

When can I stop taking folic acid during pregnancy?

Some doctors are happy for you to stop at 12 weeks while others recommend that you take it throughout pregnancy. This is because folic acid is a vitamin that can help prevent health problems such as anaemia in the mother. There is no hard and fast rule after 12 weeks, however; seek your doctor's advice if you are in any doubt.

What if I become pregnant and have not taken folic acid tablets?

Many women become pregnant without taking folic acid supplements, but you shouldn't worry if you haven't. Most women obtain enough folic acid from their normal diet to prevent neural tube defects occurring. Your grandmothers and possibly even your mothers were not advised to take folic acid supplements, after all. If you realise you are pregnant within 12 weeks of conception and you have not taken folic acid supplements then you should start immediately. It is worth starting even if you are a bit late.

Are there any risks involved in taking folic acid supplements?

There are no known risks and the only problem of taking supplements is the possible masking of the symptoms of B12 deficiency anaemia, described above. If you feel strongly that you do not want to take any supplements, make sure that your diet is rich in the foods that are known to contain folic acid.

Do I need to take vitamin supplements other than folic acid before pregnancy?

You will need a good source of vitamins C and D. Vitamin C is important as it helps you absorb iron (see p. 35) and also because it is needed for the production of the red blood cells that carry oxygen round the body. You will get this from the fresh fruit and vegetables in your diet. Vitamin D is essential for the good development of bones and you will get this from eating dairy products. However, specific vitamin supplements, of these or other vitamins, are not usually required prior to pregnancy unless you have particular medical or nutritional problems, in which case you will need to seek advice from your doctor. If you are vegetarian or vegan, you may need specific supplements of vitamins and minerals. These will require individual advice from your doctor.

Foods high in vitamin A

Food source	Vitamin A content (approximate)
Cooked lamb's liver	22,200 mcg of retinol per 100 g (3$^{1}/_{2}$ oz)
Liver pâté	7330 mcg of retinol per 100 g (3$^{1}/_{2}$ oz)
Carrot	1700 mcg of retinol per carrot
Full fat milk	300 mcg of retinol per $^{1}/_{2}$ litre (pint)
Eggs	110 mcg of retinol per egg

Should I avoid a high intake of vitamin A?

Vitamin A is a fat-soluble vitamin that is stored in your liver and is vital for the maintenance of good eyesight, healthy skin, hair and nails. In the developing baby it is essential for tissue growth. Vitamin A occurs in two main forms in our diet: the first form is 'retinol' – the 'real' vitamin A; the second is the 'carotenoids', which your body converts into retinol (vitamin A).

Beta-carotene is a carotenoid and is converted into retinol only when it is required. It acts as an antioxidant in the body (helping prevent damage to blood vessels caused by free radical molecules) and is the pigment that gives the green, yellow or orange colour to vegetables and fruit. The brighter the vegetable, in fact, the more beta-carotene it contains. Fresh liver is a particularly rich natural source of vitamin A, as animals, like humans, store vitamin A in their livers.

Very high intakes of 'true' vitamin A – 'retinol' – have been linked with an increased risk of foetal abnormalities during pregnancy. Such high levels are likely to be far in excess of those you would find in your normal diet, however. The amount of retinol linked with foetal abnormalities is in excess of 3300 mcg per day. This level is very high: you would need to eat 30 eggs in one day, for example, to get that much vitamin A. At the same time, you should not take supplements containing vitamin A in the retinol form or eat foods that are rich in retinol, such as liver or liver products like pâté, when you are planning to become pregnant. Fish liver oils (e.g. cod liver oil) should also be avoided.

Is iron important when I am trying to become pregnant?

Iron is a mineral rather than a vitamin. It is stored in your liver, spleen and in the centre of certain bones. Maintaining an adequate iron intake is important both before and during your pregnancy. Your developing baby will need iron for the formation of several important proteins. In particular, iron is needed for the formation in the red blood cells of haemoglobin, the substance which

Iron is found in foods such as baked beans, red meat, sardines, eggs and wholemeal bread, as well as breakfast cereals and pulses.

transports oxygen around your body. If you have an adequate intake of iron in your diet before and during your pregnancy, you will usually be able to meet your own and your developing baby's needs quite adequately. Iron supplements are not routinely required when planning a pregnancy. However, there are some women who will be more likely to have low iron stores *(see box, below)* and will therefore need to take supplements. Your doctor will be able to advise you about this.

Which foods contain iron?

You find iron in foods such as baked beans, bread (fortified white, as well as brown and wholemeal), breakfast cereals, pulses such as lentils and red kidney beans, red meat (but avoid liver because of its high vitamin A content – *see*

Women who are likely to have low iron stores

- Vegans and vegetarians
- Those who have had two or more pregnancies close together
- Those who have suffered from anaemia
- Those with heavy periods

Foods high in iron

Food source	Iron content (approximate)
Breakfast cereal	2–9 mg of iron per 30 g (1 oz) serving
Steak	3.4 mg of iron per 100 g (3$\frac{1}{2}$ oz)
Baked beans	1.5 mg of iron per 100 g (3$\frac{1}{2}$ oz)
Green leafy vegetables	1.5 mg of iron per 100 g (3$\frac{1}{2}$ oz)
Eggs	1 mg of iron per egg
Wholemeal bread	1 mg of iron per slice

table, above) and tinned sardines and pilchards. The recommended daily intake pre-pregnancy is 14 mg.

A healthy pre-pregnancy diet

Your baby's health depends to a great extent on the health of not only you but also your partner at the moment of conception. You will increase your chances of conceiving a healthy baby if you both eat a healthy, varied diet. Ideally, your diet needs to be low in animal fats and should include a good selection of fresh vegetables and raw fruit (taking care to wash them thoroughly). You should also try to reduce your salt and sugar intake.

What foods should I eat when I'm trying to conceive?

The key to preparing for pregnancy is a well-balanced, healthy diet to ensure that your body is prepared for pregnancy, including a good daily supply of vitamins and minerals. Your diet should include foods rich in protein, such as lean meat, fish, poultry, eggs and beans; foods rich in calcium, such as milk, cheese and yoghurt; fruit and vegetables to provide vitamins and fibre; and cereals, bread, pasta and potatoes to provide carbohydrates and additional fibre. Keep your intake of foods rich in fat and sugar to a minimum. It is also sensible to combine this with a good fluid intake, and water, several glasses a day, is better than coffee, tea or sugar-rich drinks such as cola. Eat regular meals with a wide variety of healthy foods that you enjoy. If you get your diet right before conception, you will have established an ideal pattern for your pregnancy.

Is fish an important part of the diet when thinking about pregnancy?

Fish is an excellent source of protein. In addition, oily fish like salmon and herring provide a rich source of essential fatty acids (so-called omega 3 essential fatty acids), which are important for the development of the baby's nervous system. Moreover, a high fish intake is associated with a reduced risk of pregnancy complications such as premature labour or a low-birthweight baby. So fish is a valuable component of a healthy diet in pregnancy.

Are there any fish that should be avoided?

Yes. A US food and drug administration panel have recently recommended that pregnant women should limit their consumption of fish such as tuna, and avoid completely swordfish, shark, tilefish and king mackerel. This is because of concerns that these particular fish may contain levels of mercury that could be harmful to people, especially developing babies. Mercury enters the sea environment through pollution and virtually all fish contain tiny amounts of mercury. Long-lived fish that are predators, such as shark or swordfish, accumulate the greatest amounts of mercury and so might be harmful to people who eat them regularly. The safe level of tuna intake with regard to the effects of mercury in pregnancy has not been established, but in the meantime it has been recommended that pregnant women should eat no more than two 170 g (6 oz) cans of tuna each week.

What other foods should be avoided in pregnancy?

There are certain foods that are best avoided when you are trying to conceive and also in pregnancy *(see box below)*. This is because of risk of infection or because they contain potential toxins. For example: unpasteurised milk, soft cheeses and pâté can contain a type of bacteria called listeria that can cause miscarriage and premature labour; raw and uncooked cured meats (such as ham, prosciutto) and unwashed (soil-covered) vegetables may carry toxoplasma, an organism that can cause abnormalities in the baby *(see p. 153)*; liver, as we have seen, contains high quantities of vitamin A; and raw meat,

Foods to avoid eating in pregnancy

- Unpasteurised milk and milk products like soft and mould-ripened cheeses
- Pâté
- Raw and uncooked cured meat
- Unwashed fruit, vegetables and salads
- Raw or partially cooked eggs
- Raw shellfish
- Liver
- Liver sausage
- Dietary supplements rich in vitamin A, e.g. cod liver oil
- Shark, swordfish, king mackerel

poultry and eggs can carry salmonella, a type of bacteria that causes food poisoning. Remember when storing or preparing food to keep raw meat and poultry separate from cooked and pre-prepared foods and use separate utensils for them. In addition, always wash you hands thoroughly after handling raw meat and poultry.

Is a vegetarian diet sufficient when preparing for pregnancy?

More and more people are turning to vegetarian or vegan diets. Some vegetarians eat dairy products and others eat dairy products but avoid eggs. Vegans avoid all animal products including meat, fish, dairy products, eggs and honey. Because a few micro-nutrients occur naturally only in animal products, planning a balanced vegetarian or vegan diet requires a little extra effort. There are not usually any problems with a well-balanced vegetarian diet before and during pregnancy, however. Such a diet will provide sufficient protein, vitamins and minerals to meet the needs of most women, although sometimes iron supplements are required to help prevent anaemia caused by the extra demands of the unborn baby on the mother's stores of iron. Some very strict vegan diets contain no food at all that is derived from animal sources, including dairy products. Women following such a diet may need extra vitamin supplements and should discuss this with their family doctor. If you are vegan, you may be prescribed supplements of calcium and vitamins D and B12.

Can I eat processed food?

Try if possible to avoid convenience foods that have been highly processed, such as canned foods and packet mixes. These often have added sugar and salt as well as a high fat content. They also contain chemicals in the form of artificial flavourings, colourings and preservatives. Additives in food can usually be identified by looking at the label.

How much food should I eat?

How much you eat depends on your body weight and whether or not you are overweight. However, if your weight is satisfactory you should aim for a balanced and healthy diet. For example, a woman weighing 60 kg (9$^1/_2$ st) should consume each day:

- 1–2 portions of lean meat
- 6 portions of fruit and vegetables each day
- 5 slices of wholemeal bread each day
- 1–1$^1/_2$ portions of rice or pasta
- 1 portion of breakfast cereal

In addition, she should try to eat a portion of fish every other day.

Why do I need carbohydrates in my diet?

Carbohydrates are essential for giving us energy. Many women worry about carbohydrates being related to weight gain and thus cut down on all carbohydrates when trying to become pregnant. There are 'good' and 'bad' carbohydrates, however.

- Starchy carbohydrates such as pasta, wholemeal bread, breakfast cereal and potatoes are 'good'
- 'Bad' carbohydrates are those foods that are sugar-laden, such as cakes, biscuits and sweets

Cut down on the 'bad' carbohydrates and think about increasing your intake of starchy carbohydrates instead.

How do I increase starchy carbohydrates in my diet?

You should eat wholemeal bread each day, and include a portion of potatoes, pasta or wholegrain rice with each main meal. For breakfast you should have porridge or a high-fibre or wholegrain breakfast cereal, avoiding cereals with a high sugar content.

How do I increase fruit and vegetables in my diet?

You should try eating more salads using a wide range of fresh vegetables, and try to take two portions of vegetables with each meal. Avoid overcooking vegetables as this will break down many of the vitamins they contain; try steaming them instead. Then have fresh (not canned) fruit for dessert – and for snacks during the day – and drink fruit juices.

How do I reduce fat in my diet?

It is best to avoid fried food and foods with a high fat content like meat pies, sausages and pastries, if possible. If you want to fry food, however, use an unsaturated vegetable oil such as olive oil, or try grilling it instead, especially if you are going to eat sausages. You should always try to choose lean meat, too, and trim off any excess fat before you cook it. Chicken with its skin removed is the leanest form of meat that you can eat.

How do I reduce salt in my diet?

You do not want or need to eliminate all salt from your diet. As with most foods, moderation is the key: try not to put extra salt on the foods you eat and minimise the salt you add during cooking, as well as eating fresh foods rather than processed or tinned products, which are often high in salt. Remember that meat extracts and soy sauce are high in salt, too, so keep intake of these products to a minimum.

How do I reduce sugar in my diet?

You want to avoid high levels of sugar in your diet. Try to avoid or at least minimise your consumption of sweets and chocolate and also sugar-rich soft drinks. It is easier said than done, but try to eat fruit for a snack instead, and drink mineral water.

Preparing your body for pregnancy

Body weight and preparation for pregnancy

Does my weight matter when I am trying to conceive?

If you are trying to conceive and you are seriously overweight or underweight, discuss this with your doctor. Extremes of weight are associated with an increased risk of problems in pregnancy. Underweight mothers are more at risk of having problems such as a small-for-dates baby or going into premature labour. Overweight mothers are at risk of problems such as chronic high blood pressure and pre-eclampsia – a serious pregnancy condition related to high blood pressure *(see opposite)*, which can lead to kidney upset and risk to the baby. In addition, both extremes of weight can be associated with fertility problems. You don't want to have to contemplate dieting when you are pregnant, so it is important to think about reducing your weight prior to trying to get pregnant.

When I stop smoking I just gain weight. What should I do?

Weight gain is common after stopping smoking as your appetite usually increases and metabolic rate decreases, so your diet may have to be modified to prevent excessive weight gain. For your general health, you should know that stopping smoking ought to be given a higher priority than weight loss, even in very overweight people.

Is there an ideal weight to achieve before becoming pregnant?

There is no 'ideal' weight for pregnancy. Your own individual 'ideal' weight will depend on you as an individual and it is not based on what you weigh when you stand on the scales. The way to work out if your weight is satisfactory is to calculate your body mass index (BMI). This is probably the best guide to weight as it gives a better indication of body fat content than weight alone, both in pregnant and non-pregnant women. It also takes into account your height, which obviously influences what you should weigh.

How do I calculate my body mass index?

Your BMI is calculated by taking your body weight in kilograms and dividing it by your height squared (height multiplied by height). For example, if a woman weighs 60 kg ($9^1/_2$ st) and is 1.5 m (4 ft 11 in) tall, her BMI is calculated as follows:

$$\frac{\text{Bodyweight (kg)}}{\text{Height x height (metres)}} = \text{BMI}$$

e.g. A woman who weighs 60 kg and is 1.5 m tall would be:

$$\frac{60}{1.5 \times 1.5} = \frac{60}{2.25} = 26.66$$

Gradings of BMI

Category	Body mass index
Underweight or low	Less than 20
Normal	20.0–25.9
Overweight	26.0–30.9
Obese	31.0–40.9
Extremely obese	41 or more

Does my body shape matter?

Yes. It is not just the quantity of fat you have in your body that matters, but also where it is in your body. Women who are 'pear-shaped', with fat principally on their buttocks and thighs, seem to be at less risk of problems than those who are 'apple-shaped', carrying fat on their abdomen. These problems include a risk of pre-eclampsia when you are pregnant and also heart disease in later life. Your waist circumference will give a measure of this. Measure round your waist without any clothes on and do not pull the tape tight; let it just rest on the skin.

Can my waistline influence the chance of developing high blood pressure in pregnancy?

In the last 10 years or so it has become clear that waist circumference, which reflects the amount of fat in the abdomen, is a risk factor for heart disease. The greater the size of your waist, the greater the risk. Indeed, measuring waist circumference has been advocated as a health screening test. Pre-eclampsia is a high blood pressure problem that affects 2–4 of every 100 pregnant women. It causes damage to the blood vessels and can affect not only the mother, but also the baby through damage to the placenta. It has some similarities to the underlying disturbance in blood vessels seen in heart disease. *(See pp. 136–41.)*

Calculating the ideal waist circumference for women

Ideal	Increased risk	Higher risk
Waist less than 80 cm (31^1/$_2$ in)	Waist 80–87 cm (31^1/$_2$–34 in)	Waist more than 88 cm (34^1/$_2$ in)

It has been shown that women who subsequently developed pregnancy-related high blood pressure or pre-eclampsia had a 3–4 cm (1–1$^1/_2$ in) greater waist circumference compared to those who did not. It has been calculated that a waist circumference of 80 cm (31$^1/_2$ in) or more in early pregnancy almost doubles the risk of high blood pressure and almost triples the risk of pre-eclampsia. So getting your waistline into shape before pregnancy, with a good diet and regular exercise, might not only be good for your figure but also for the health of you and your baby.

Are many women overweight?

Yes, the proportion of people who are overweight in developed countries is increasing. In Western society at least 30% of women are overweight and as many as 15% have a BMI over 30.

Which BMI categories are associated with pregnancy problems?

The low and obese BMI categories are associated with fertility and pregnancy problems. Although it is probably best to be in the normal range before pregnancy, the overweight range is not usually associated with major problems, provided there is no excessive weight gain in pregnancy. However, miscarriage rates do increase by around a third when the BMI is in excess of 25.

If I am significantly overweight, should I correct this before becoming pregnant or can I diet to lose weight in pregnancy?

Dieting to lose a lot of weight is not advisable either when trying to get pregnant or during pregnancy. This is because you may disturb your nutritional balance at crucial stages of your baby's development. However, limiting weight gain in pregnancy is important for women who are overweight. This can be achieved by carbohydrate restriction. Limiting weight gain will reduce the risk of pregnancy complications such as high blood pressure and also help prevent having a very large baby. As being overweight can also influence fertility, it is important to reduce weight, with a proper programme of exercise and nutrition, before trying to get pregnant.

Do I have to reduce my weight to the 'normal' BMI range to get benefit?

No, substantial benefits can be obtained by modest reductions in weight and by preventing further weight gain. Indeed, most people trying to lose weight find it difficult to sustain weight loss for more than 3–4 months. However, it has been estimated that losing 10 kg in weight (around 22 pounds) will result in a 10% fall in cholesterol, a significant reduction in blood pressure and a 20% reduction in risk of death!

How do I lose weight?

Ideally, specialist advice is required to provide you with an individualised assessment and management plan. Specific help from dieticians and support groups is invaluable in losing weight and maintaining it. It is valuable to consult your doctor for a full health assessment if you are overweight. This will identify any additional or associated problems like high blood pressure or high blood lipids (fats), which might need specific treatment. When losing weight, a realistic target should be set for you over a period of around three months. A programme of a weight-reducing diet specific to your needs should be implemented, along with an increase in your physical activity. In the longer term a change in eating patterns or lifestyle, to include a healthy diet and exercise, should be established to maintain a steady weight and avoid further increases.

Is exercise important for weight loss?

Exercise is indeed important for weight loss. Your weight depends on the balance between the food you take in and the energy you burn up with exercise. If you take in more energy from your food than you burn up with exercise, you will gain weight. If you burn up more energy with exercise than you take in with your food, you will lose weight. If you do not take much regular exercise, you should build up gradually before you get pregnant.

If possible, find a form of exercise you enjoy and make it part of your routine. For example, this could be walking, jogging, swimming, cycling or aerobics. The important thing is to do it regularly. Thirty minutes of moderate exercise three times a week or more will make a big difference to your fitness. You should also increase your exercise as you go about your daily activities. Walk wherever possible and take the stairs instead of the lift. Regular exercise is also good for reducing stress and will make you feel more energetic, as well as increasing your sense of well-being. However, you must make the time for regular exercise, trying to make it a part of your day. If you have any medical problems or are overweight, your doctor can advise you on suitable forms of exercise for you.

Understanding your own health

Women with pre-existing medical problems can and do become pregnant and have successful deliveries. It is worth remembering, however, that many medical problems can influence your pregnancy and that pregnancy can have an effect on your medical condition. If you have poorly controlled diabetes before pregnancy, for instance, this carries a higher risk of abnormalities occurring in the baby than if your diabetes is well controlled. If you have had a previous thrombosis (clots in the leg or lung), there is an increased risk of further thrombosis in pregnancy. If you need to take medicinal drug therapy, pregnancy can influence the effectiveness of some of your medication, while some medication can have potentially harmful effects on the unborn child.

Specific problems that might give concern in pregnancy

If I have a pre-existing medical condition, should I seek specific medical advice before conceiving?

If you have a medical condition or are on long-term drug therapy, you should discuss the implications of your condition, and any drugs used to treat it, with your doctor before conceiving. Depending on the condition, you may require specialist help, which your doctor can usually arrange. This will allow optimal planning and treatment of your condition before and during pregnancy. In particular, it is best to make sure that any chronic illnesses or disorders are well controlled prior to embarking on pregnancy. It is also important to ensure that any drug therapy you are taking is appropriate for pregnancy. Some medication can be safely continued, other medication requires modification or discontinuation. As this can be a complex issue, it is essential to seek medical advice prior to pregnancy, before altering any treatment. Ill-advised or unnecessary changes in treatment may precipitate problems not only for your baby, but also for your own health. Some of the more common medical conditions are discussed in this chapter and information for many others can be found in *Your health in pregnancy (page 164)*, which also provides full details on some of the conditions described below – diabetes, asthma, venous thrombosis, high blood pressure, heart disease, epilepsy, SLE – and how they can be managed in pregnancy.

I am diabetic. What factors should I bear in mind before trying to conceive?

Insulin is a hormone produced by the pancreas, a gland in the abdomen, and is essential for regulating blood-sugar levels. When your pancreas produces insufficient insulin, blood-sugar levels rise and diabetes mellitus occurs. Women with diabetes frequently do become pregnant and have successful, untroubled pregnancies. Equally, pregnancy does not necessarily make diabetes worse, but your insulin requirements and your blood-sugar regulation will need to be

Checklist for the diabetic mother

- Ensure you obtain pre-pregnancy advice on diabetes from your doctor or obstetrician
- Get your blood-sugar levels under really good control before you become pregnant
- Keep careful records of your blood-glucose levels and insulin dosage
- Be aware of the problems that can occur during pregnancy and the need for increased vigilance
- Hypoglycaemia (very low blood sugar) is a relatively common occurrence when you are trying to get blood-sugar levels under good control; you and your partner should learn how to deal with hypoglycaemia, just in case *(see p. 180)*
- Take folic acid supplements
- Ensure that any diabetic complications are under control or have been assessed before pregnancy

altered. In pregnancy, hormones produced by the placenta have an anti-insulin effect, which can increase your insulin requirements. It is therefore important that insulin-dependent diabetic women have their condition well under control before conception. Adequate regulation of blood-sugar levels prior to and during the early weeks of pregnancy is essential to avoid or minimise the risk of congenital abnormalities. Folic acid supplements should also be taken to reduce the risk of some of these abnormalities *(see p. 29)* and diet will need to be carefully controlled.

I have asthma. Do I need to alter my therapy when I am tying to get pregnant?

Asthma is very common in young women, and mild asthma should not cause any problem in pregnancy. However, it is important to continue with your asthma medication when you are trying to conceive and during pregnancy as uncontrolled severe asthma can be associated with problems for the developing baby due to lack of oxygen. You should discuss your medication with your doctor before trying to conceive.

I suffer from high blood pressure. What problems can this cause in pregnancy?

Most non-pregnant women with high blood pressure have what is called 'essential hypertension'. Since high blood pressure is associated with an increased risk of having pre-eclampsia and a small-for-dates baby – one that has not grown as big as it should have for the stage it has reached in pregnancy *(see p. 124)* – you will require a little more antenatal care. However, the majority of women with high blood pressure will have a successful pregnancy. If you take anti-hypertensive medication, this needs to be reviewed so that you can avoid medication that may have harmful effects on the pregnancy. This is obviously best considered prior to pregnancy and you should consult your doctor.

I have a past history of venous thrombosis (blood clot) in my leg. Is this important to bear in mind for pregnancy?

Your risk of developing a blood clot is greater if you have had a previous clot or if you have an inborn tendency of your blood to clot (thrombophilia). If you have a previous history of thrombosis or a family history of blood clots, you should consult your doctor for pre-pregnancy advice about this as treatment might be needed in pregnancy to reduce the risk. If you have a personal or family history of thrombosis, many doctors believe that you should be screened for thrombophilia. This is best done before conception. All that is required is some details of any family clotting problems that may exist and a simple blood test. Interestingly, recent research suggests that certain thrombophilia conditions might be associated with pregnancy complications such as pre-eclampsia, possibly due to increased clotting upsetting the function of the placenta.

Risk factors for pre-eclampsia

- Chronic high blood pressure
- Previous severe pre-eclampsia or a small-for-dates baby
- Kidney disease
- Diabetes
- Connective tissue disease such as SLE
- First pregnancy
- Migraine
- Overweight when starting pregnancy
- A family history of pre-eclampsia on mother's side (genetic component)
- Age less than 20 or more than 35 years

Might I be at risk of pre-eclampsia in pregnancy?

Pre-eclampsia is a potentially serious condition that occurs only when you are pregnant. It causes high blood pressure and upset to your kidneys, which results in protein leaking into the urine. *(See pp. 136–41 for full details on pre-eclampsia in pregnancy.)* If you have had severe problems with pre-eclampsia in a previous pregnancy, such as a premature delivery or a small-for-dates baby, then pre-pregnancy advice may be helpful. Your doctor can advise you on these areas. As pre-eclampsia is so variable in its presentation and severity, the risk of recurrence has to be assessed individually, taking all factors into account *(see box above)*.

I have heart disease. Is it safe for me to get pregnant?

Women with relatively mild levels of heart disease are unlikely to have major problems during a pregnancy, but if you have a heart problem and are considering pregnancy, it is important to obtain specific advice from your doctor.

I was born with a heart defect that was corrected by an operation when I was a child. Can I get pregnant without risking my health?

More and more women who were born with a heart abnormality are choosing to have children. This reflects the enormous success of surgery to correct heart abnormalities in childhood. Because there are so many types of abnormality, individual advice is required about pregnancy if you have had such a problem, although for the women concerned pregnancy is not usually associated with serious problems or complications. However, it is best to discuss these matters with your doctor prior to becoming pregnant.

I have epilepsy. How could this affect pregnancy?

The majority of women with epilepsy will have a successful pregnancy with a healthy baby at the end of it, but there is a higher risk of certain antenatal

Pre-pregnancy checklist for women with epilepsy

- Plan your pregnancy and use reliable contraception until you are ready to conceive
- Note: The effectiveness of the contraceptive pill is reduced by some anti-epileptic drugs, which increase the speed of breakdown of the hormones in the pill
- Discuss your anti-epileptic therapy with your doctor before you try to get pregnant
- Do not alter your therapy without first consulting your doctor
- Take folic acid supplements in the dosage prescribed by your doctor
- Seek antenatal advice and care as soon as possible after you are aware that you are pregnant

complications. In particular, there is an increased risk of foetal abnormalities associated with anti-epileptic drugs. If you suffer from epilepsy, you might want to think about the timing of your pregnancy and have your medication reviewed prior to conception. You should talk to your doctor about these problems and how to minimise any extra risk before you try to try to conceive. Folic acid supplements are especially important for the woman with epilepsy wishing to get pregnant and should ideally be taken for at least three months before trying to conceive. For women who are on anti-epileptic medication, many doctors recommend they take a higher dose of folic acid supplements, 5 mg a day, than is usually given to women without epilepsy wishing to become pregnant (400 mcg).

I have multiple sclerosis. Can I consider getting pregnant?

Multiple sclerosis affects up to 1 in 1000 of the population in the UK and tends to first present between the ages of 20 and 40. In this condition the insulating material around nerve fibres (like the insulating material around electrical wires) is damaged so upsetting the function of the nerves. While the cause of multiple sclerosis is unknown, it tends to be a relapsing and remitting condition with damage to the nerves occurring in different parts of the brain and nervous system at different times. Alternatively, it can be a chronic progressive disorder.

Women with multiple sclerosis can consider a pregnancy – their fertility is not usually affected. The condition is unlikely to present for the first time during pregnancy. It is also less likely to relapse during pregnancy. Those women whose bladders are affected (where the function of the nerves controlling the bladder are upset) may be prone to recurrent cystitis (bladder infections), so their urine should be examined for infection at each antenatal check. Sometimes antibiotics are prescribed to prevent recurrent bladder infections. Almost half of women with multiple sclerosis will experience a temporary worsening of their multiple sclerosis in the six months after delivery. However, there are no long-term detrimental effects of pregnancy or breast-feeding on the course of multiple sclerosis. Similarly, multiple sclerosis tends not to have an effect either on pregnancy or on the developing baby. If you take drugs for your multiple sclerosis, you should discuss this with your doctor before becoming pregnant.

Should I have pre-pregnancy counselling if I have SLE?

SLE (systemic lupus erythematosis) is a connective tissue disease in which inflammation can attack various parts of the body. It is associated with particular problems in pregnancy, such as miscarriage, premature delivery, a small-for-dates baby, worsening of SLE, pre-eclampsia and thrombosis. As there are risks for you as a prospective mother and for your unborn baby, specialist pre-pregnancy counselling is essential to take account of all the factors that might affect you. This will allow you to decide, on an informed basis, whether or not to become pregnant and, if so, when to try. It is best if you try to conceive when your SLE is not active and where medication is minimal. Your medication may have to be modified before and during pregnancy as some drugs used in SLE are best avoided when you are pregnant. Ideally, you need to obtain advice from a physician or obstetrician with specific expertise in SLE about drug therapy before you become pregnant.

I have a family history of sickle-cell anaemia. What are the implications for pregnancy?

Sickle-cell anaemia is a condition that affects the red blood cells and is most commonly found in people of African origin. It is so called because the red blood cells, which carry oxygen around the body, are crescent-shaped instead of disc-shaped, as they would be normally. When there is a shortage of oxygen or when there is an infection in the body, these red blood cells clump together and so prevent the smooth flow of blood. As well as causing chronic anaemia, the condition can give rise to bone pain, kidney upset and lung problems. It may also increase the risk of thrombosis (blood clots).

Sickle-cell anaemia is a genetic disorder and so can be inherited (see p. 17). If you carry the trait you will not usually develop anaemia, but you will be more prone to kidney and bladder infections. Where there is a family history of the condition, it is a good idea to have a blood test prior to getting pregnant to check whether you have sickle-cell trait. Indeed, if you were found to be a carrier, you partner may wish to be tested prior to conception to see whether the baby would be likely to inherit sickle-cell disease (which requires an abnormal gene from each parent). Sickle-cell anaemia in the mother carries a higher risk of giving birth to premature and low-birthweight babies. During pregnancy a woman with sickle-cell anaemia will need folic acid supplements and sometimes a blood transfusion. Iron supplements are not routinely required, however, and are only given when iron stores are low.

Specialist antenatal care will be needed as treatment has to be tailored to each individual woman's needs. Whether you have sickle-cell anaemia or could be a carrier, it is important to discuss all this with your doctor before becoming pregnant.

I am HIV positive. Do I need pre-pregnancy advice?

Yes, because this is a problem that could not only affect you but also your baby. HIV (human immuno-deficiency virus), sometimes referred to as the AIDS virus, is a virus that attacks the body's immune system, weakening its resistance to infection. HIV infection is not usually worsened by pregnancy, though, and there is no evidence of pregnancy increasing the risk of progression to AIDS. If you have advanced disease, however, you will be at high risk of deterioration, whether or not you are pregnant. Although this risk might not be influenced by pregnancy, pregnancy is usually best avoided in this situation.

HIV infection is also associated with a higher risk of you having an abnormal cervical smear test. It is a good idea, therefore, to have a smear test before you try to conceive, so that any treatment necessary can be carried out before pregnancy. Because there are so many issues to consider that can have an impact on pregnancy – such as a higher risk of miscarriage, premature delivery and a low-birthweight baby – it is vital that you obtain specialist advice from an HIV expert before trying to conceive, so that you get the correct up-to-date information for your particular situation. This should include advice on anti-viral therapy to reduce the risk of infection being transmitted to the baby at birth. *(See also p. 153 for a fuller discussion on HIV infection during pregnancy.)*

I carry the hepatitis virus. Will this affect my pregnancy?

If the disease is transmitted to the baby in the womb, either of the two main types of hepatitis, B or C, can cause hepatitis and the baby may become a carrier of either. The risk of transmission varies in each case, but in neither instance does it give rise to any other pregnancy complications. However, it is best to get information on the type of hepatitis you carry and the risk of transmission to the baby in your own particular situation. Hence a pre-pregnancy discussion with your doctor is recommended. *(See p. 155 for full details on hepatitis during pregnancy.)*

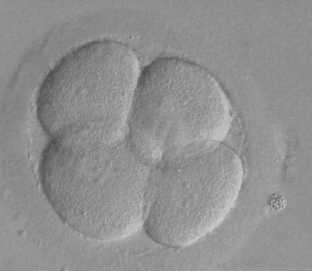

Fertility options

Many couples take fertility for granted, yet natural human fertility is relatively low compared with that of many animals. Indeed, 1 in 6 couples will need investigation and treatment because of difficulties conceiving. When couples encounter a fertility problem, this can be a very distressing and emotional experience. The ensuing difficulties and disappointments can dent your confidence and lead to feelings of frustration and anger as well as a sense of failure. However, although distressing, it is important to remember that fertility problems are common. You should also know that if you encounter a fertility problem, help is available. While not all problems can be solved, a great many can be helped owing to advances in our understanding and knowledge of fertility problems. This is further aided by advances made in the technology that can assist conception.

Assessing potential fertility problems

How long do couples usually take to conceive?

Between 80 and 90% of normal fertile couples will conceive within a year of regular unprotected intercourse. This rises to 95% after two years of unprotected intercourse. So do not be alarmed if you do not get pregnant within the first few months of trying. Infertility is usually defined as an inability to conceive after a minimum of 12 months of unprotected intercourse. Doctors would not usually investigate for a fertility problem unless you had been trying unsuccessfully for at least a year. This is because many 'normal' couples take at least this long to conceive.

How many couples have difficulty conceiving?

Fertility problems affect around 1 in 6 couples – that is, about 15%. So this is a common problem.

Why do some couples have difficulty conceiving?

The main causes that lead to difficulty conceiving can be due to problems in producing eggs (25%), problems with the fallopian tubes preventing transport of the egg (20%), or problems with the quantity or quality of the sperm (30%). Sometimes, in around 15% of couples, there may be more than one factor. In most other cases no obvious reason is found and this is termed 'unexplained' infertility (25%). When investigating infertility it is essential to assess both the woman and her partner. Other factors associated with fertility problems include being underweight or overweight, rapid weight loss and smoking.

Is age important?

The age of the woman is important as fertility wanes especially after 40, but age has much less of an effect with regard to male fertility. Women over 40 are likely to produce fewer eggs and the eggs they produce may not have as good an ability to implant into the womb as they did at a younger age. The risk of miscarriage increases in women over 40 and there is also an increased risk of other pregnancy complications, such as the baby being affected by Down's syndrome (see p. 17).

We have been trying for a baby for more than a year. What should we do?

You should seek medical advice and, ideally, you and your partner should be seen together. Remember that it is common for causes of infertility to be found in both partners. The doctor will take a detailed history from you both, including your age, how long you have been trying to conceive, how often you have intercourse, previous contraception, whether you have any problems with intercourse, the presence of chronic medical conditions or long-term medication, and details of any previous pregnancies (including any with previous partners). You will be asked about menstrual problems and any history of pelvic infection or abdominal surgery. Your partner will be asked about his occupation, any past medical problems, surgical operations or trauma to the testicles and any infections affecting the genitals, such as mumps. He will also be asked about any regular medication as this can sometimes upset sperm function and about any sexual difficulty. The doctor will also want to know if either of you smoke and how much alcohol you each drink. You both may be examined as well.

What will the doctor tell us to do?

The doctor will tell you if there are any obvious problems and whether a specialist referral is required. You will be given general advice such as the need to take folic acid, stop smoking, cut down or stop drinking alcohol, and asked about your immunity to rubella *(see p. 149)*. Your doctor may check whether you are anaemic and if you carry hepatitis or HIV, as testing is needed prior to assisted conception as these conditions may have implications for the baby *(see p. 108)*. If you are overweight your doctor will advise about the need to reduce weight or limit weight gain. It is unlikely that you will be asked to use temperature charts or ovulation prediction kits *(see p. 24)* in the first instance as there is little evidence to show that they improve success over regular intercourse occurring every couple of days throughout the cycle.

What investigations will be performed?

Your initial investigations can be performed by a family doctor, but more detailed assessment and treatment requires referral to a specialist. There are three key questions to be answered:

- Do you produce an egg (ovulate) regularly?
- Is your partner's sperm production satisfactory?
- Is there any problem with your fallopian tubes that could prevent transport of the egg?

How is ovulation assessed?

If you have regular periods with a cycle of 21–35 days, this suggests that you are ovulating regularly. If you experience Mittelschmerz (mid-cycle pain associated with ovulation), changes in your cervical mucus and increased temperature mid-cycle, these features also suggest that you are ovulating *(see pp. 21–5)*. The key medical investigation is to measure the concentration of progesterone in a blood sample taken seven days before your expected period is due. If you have an irregular cycle then several samples may be required, each taken a few days apart. Progesterone is only produced in high quantities after ovulation, so a high level means that you have ovulated. If you are not ovulating, further hormonal assessments will be required to identify the cause.

How are sperm problems assessed?

The male partner will be asked to produce a semen sample by masturbation after abstaining from intercourse for at least two days. He should not collect the sample in a condom – most condoms have spermicidal lubricants that will make analysis impossible. Nor should the sample be collected by coitus interruptus (withdrawal during intercourse) as much of the sample can be lost – remember that some semen is often released prior to ejaculation proper, which the man may not be aware of. The sample should be collected in a wide-mouthed plastic specimen pot and promptly transported, avoiding extremes of temperature, to the laboratory. As there is marked variation in semen from day to day and week to week, at least two specimens should be

Fertility options

assessed. A normal semen sample has a volume of 2.5–5 ml with more than 20 million sperm in each millilitre. Fifty per cent of the sperm cells should be able to move forward and more than 15% of the sperm cells should have a normal form. As it takes around 70 days for sperm to mature, it is usual to allow 2–3 months between samples so that any temporary upset in sperm production will be rectified.

How is the function of the fallopian tubes assessed?

Several investigative methods are available for assessing tubal function, of which diagnostic laparoscopy is considered by many gynaecologists as the method of choice. During the procedure, which usually requires general anaesthesia, a laparoscope (a telescope-like instrument) is inserted below the navel (umbilicus) so that the surgeon can view the womb, fallopian tubes and ovaries *(see illustration below)*. Blue dye is injected through the cervix using an instrument placed in the cervix through the vagina. This dye flows through the womb and fallopian tubes and, if the tubes are open, spills into the abdomen. If the tubes are blocked then the dye will not spill from the ends. Using the laparoscope, the surgeon can watch the progress and spillage of dye from within the abdomen.

Cross-sectional view of the vagina, womb, ovary, fallopian tube and bladder. When the fallopian tubes are being investigated a laparoscope is used to view the womb, fallopian tubes and ovaries (see above).

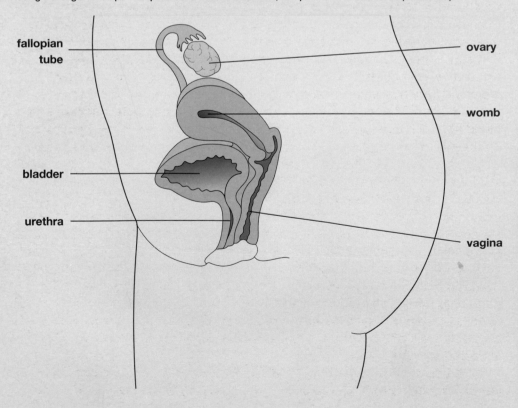

X-ray assessment can also be used. Special dye that appears white on an X-ray is injected through the cervix. An X-ray is then taken and the outline of the womb and tubes will be seen. If the dye is seen spilling into the abdomen on X-ray then the tubes are open. Ultrasound can also be used in a similar way to assess tubal function.

As infection is the most common cause of tubal damage, a test to look for evidence of past or current infection, which can affect the fallopian tubes, may also be performed.

Treatment of fertility problems

If I am not ovulating, how can this be treated?

The treatment of disturbance of ovulation depends on the reason causing the disturbance. Irregular or infrequent periods are most commonly due to a hormonal disturbance affecting the ability of the ovaries to produce eggs. Sometimes the cause is not directly linked to the hormones controlling the ovaries, but to other hormones that have a knock-on effect. For example, upsets in your thyroid or adrenal glands can also disturb ovarian function. Obviously if you have a specific problem, such as thyroid disease, this should be treated. However, a disturbance in the balance of hormones controlling the ovaries is the usual cause of irregular ovulation and this can be treated with medication that stimulates the ovaries to produce eggs. Success of the treatment in inducing ovulation can be checked by measuring progesterone levels in the blood. One drawback of this therapy, however, is that sometimes the ovaries will produce more than one egg in response to stimulation so that there is an increased risk of conceiving twins or even triplets. Where this is considered a significant risk, the response of the ovaries to the drugs will be monitored by the gynaecologist using techniques such as blood hormone measurement or ultrasound to visualise the eggs developing on the ovaries.

What is the treatment if my fallopian tubes are blocked?

Infection in the womb and fallopian tubes, such as that which can occur after miscarriage or giving birth, or abdominal problems, such as appendicitis, that are associated with infection and inflammation in the pelvis, can lead to damage to the fallopian tubes, blocking the access of the sperm to the egg. In the worst cases both tubes can be blocked. An added complication is that sometimes the ovaries are covered by adhesions, preventing release of the egg *(see Endometriosis, p. 59)*. One episode of pelvic infection can lead to infertility in up to 15% of women. The more episodes of infection a woman has had, the greater the risk of tubal damage. It is therefore important that pelvic infection is treated promptly.

The best treatment if you have tubal blockage is in vitro fertilisation (IVF) *(see p.57)*. Alternatively, you could have tubal surgery to release the blockage, but this is not usually as effective as IVF. In addition, the greater the level of fallopian tubal damage, the lower the likelihood of successful surgery and subsequent pregnancy.

My partner has a problem with his sperm count. How can this be treated?

In cases where there is no sperm in the seminal fluid, the task is to determine whether there is a problem with production or whether the tubes connecting the testicles to the penis are blocked. Blockage can be treated surgically. If absolutely no sperm is being produced, this implies a problem with the testicles or hormones controlling sperm production and specialist help is required. It is, however, very rare for a man to have absolutely no sperm. More commonly, the sperm count will be low or there will be reduced sperm function, such as reduced ability of the sperm to move.

As yet, no effective treatment has been proven to increase male fertility where the sperm function is impaired. The treatment is usually by assisted conception *(see p. 55)*, although conception may still occur spontaneously. The alternative is to use semen from a donor *(see p. 58)*. The decision to embark on this line of treatment requires careful consideration and counselling from specialist clinics.

What is unexplained infertility?

Unexplained infertility is diagnosed after the other causes of infertility have been excluded. It accounts for about a quarter of all cases of infertility.

Is there no chance of conception with unexplained infertility?

If you have unexplained infertility and have been trying to get pregnant for less than three years, your chances of falling pregnant without treatment is as much as 5–10% per month. However, if you have unexplained infertility and have been trying to get pregnant for more than three years, your chances of getting pregnant without treatment is around only 1–2% each month. If this is you position, you will probably want to consider some sort of specialist treatment as soon as possible.

What treatment can we get for unexplained fertility?

For younger women a 'wait and see' policy can be adopted as some will conceive naturally, particularly if they have been trying to get pregnant for less than three years. Where you are older or the infertility has been present for more than three years, other options should be considered. The treatments are to stimulate your ovaries with drugs to produce more eggs or use assisted conception techniques like IVF. Each of these methods is described fully over the following pages.

What is assisted conception?

Assisted conception is the use of techniques to bring sperm and egg together and so facilitate pregnancy.

Fertility options

Types of assisted conception

The main techniques are in vitro fertilisation (IVF), intracytoplasmic sperm injection (ICSI) and donor insemination (DI).

What is in vitro fertilisation (IVF)?

IVF was developed to treat tubal blockage but it is now also used for couples with unexplained infertility and in some couples where there are problems with the sperm count. IVF involves stimulation of the ovaries with hormones called gonadotrophins to stimulate multiple egg production. The response of the ovaries to stimulation is checked by ultrasound, and sometimes also by measuring hormone levels in the blood. When the eggs have reached maturity, they are retrieved. This is done by passing a needle through the vagina into the ovary, while the woman is under sedation. The needle is guided into position using an ultrasound scan, then the eggs are sucked down the needle and collected. The eggs are incubated with sperm from the woman's partner. Fertilised eggs are transferred to the womb through the cervix two days later. Usually no more than two fertilised eggs are put back to reduce the risk of multiple pregnancy, which can lead to problems such as a high risk of premature delivery.

In vitro fertilisation (IVF). The ovary is stimulated with medication (gonadotrophin hormones) to produce several eggs. When the eggs are mature they are retrieved by a long needle, which is passed through the top of the vagina into the ovary. The needle is guided into position by an ultrasound scan, which is carried out with the ultrasound probe in the vagina.

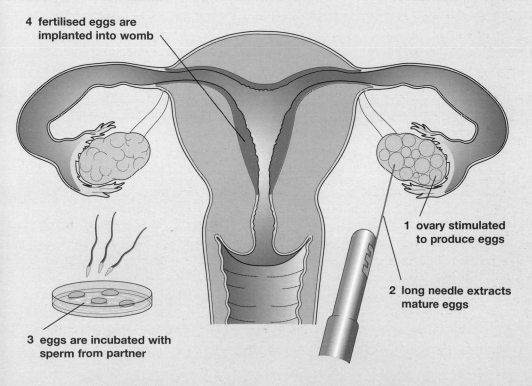

4 fertilised eggs are implanted into womb

1 ovary stimulated to produce eggs

2 long needle extracts mature eggs

3 eggs are incubated with sperm from partner

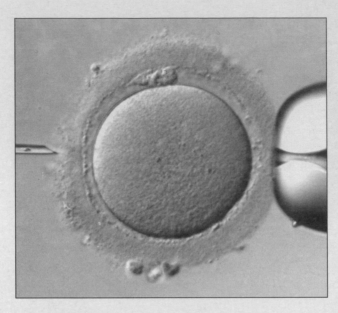
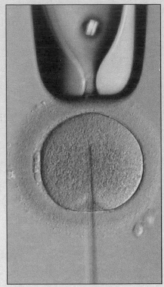

Intracytoplasmic sperm injection, or ICSI for short, involves the direct injection of a single sperm into the egg. On the left, the single sperm cell is in the needle and on the right the needle has been inserted into the egg to inject the sperm cell.

What is intracytoplasmic sperm injection (ICSI)?

ICSI has revolutionised the treatment of male-factor infertility. Until ICSI was developed success in the treatment of this type of infertility was very limited. ICSI is the direct injection of a single sperm into the egg. As with IVF, eggs are obtained by stimulation of the ovaries with hormones called gonadotrophins to bring about multiple egg production and the eggs are collected in the same way. ICSI is the best treatment in cases where the sperm count is very low or where the sperm fail to move properly. Where there is an obstruction to sperm getting to the penis, sperm can be taken surgically from the testicles and used in ICSI. Thus it is a technique of great value when infertility is associated with sperm problems. Around 70% of eggs injected with a sperm will fertilise successfully using ICSI. As with IVF, up to two fertilised eggs are put into the womb two days after the eggs have been collected and fertilised.

What is donor insemination (DI)?

In DI, donated semen is placed at the cervix or inside the womb at the time of ovulation. It can be used where the male partner has no sperm production or severe sperm problems. The semen comes from a donor, who is usually anonymous and who has been checked for health problems and infections. The donor can be matched for physical characteristics with the male partner. Donor sperm is usually stored frozen in special sperm banks. At the woman's fertile time, the sperm is defrosted and injected into either the vagina around the cervix, or directly into the womb. If the woman has more than one pregnancy using DI, then the same donor can be used.

How successful are assisted conception techniques?

First of all, you should remember that normal conception rates are around only 20% per month on average. If you compare this with the rates for assisted conception techniques, you can see that these techniques are often as good or sometimes better than natural rates. You should also remember that the woman's age is important both in natural and assisted conception, and that fertility starts to fall after age 35, becoming quite marked after age 40. Results vary from one fertility clinic to another and also depend on the type of patients treated. In the UK the overall live birth rate after IVF and ICSI is currently around 24% per embryo replaced. The rate is slightly higher, around 27%, where the woman is under 38 years of age. With donor insemination, the live birth rate is around 11–12% for each treatment cycle.

Endometriosis

What is endometriosis?

Endometriosis is a condition where tissue similar to the tissue found in the lining of the womb (endometrium) occurs in small patches in sites outside the womb. It can sometimes be found in the muscle of the womb when it is termed adenomyosis. Where it is found at other locations in the body, it is termed endometriosis. The most common sites are on the ovaries, fallopian tubes and the ligaments in the pelvis that support the womb. Often it produces no symptoms, but sometimes it can cause problems. These problems happen because each month, when a period occurs, the small patches of endometriosis also bleed. This blood cannot escape from the body and it irritates and inflames the surrounding tissues and causes pain. Chronic irritation of these tissues can lead to scarring and adhesions in the pelvis where tissues stick together. This can sometimes cause problems with fertility due to the tubes being obstructed by adhesions or the ovaries being caught up with adhesions, preventing release of the egg. The main symptoms of endometriosis are pain in the abdomen and pelvis, pain with periods (dysmenorrhea) and pain deep in the pelvis during intercourse. Endometriosis affects around 5 in 100 women and is more common in women with infertility.

Why does endometriosis occur?

Many theories have been proposed to explain why endometriosis occurs but doctors don't really know the answer. One view is that endometriosis results when fragments of the tissue lining the womb (endometrium) 'escape' down the fallopian tube and into the abdomen during a menstrual period. These fragments then 'seed' onto the tissues in the abdomen and patches of endometriosis form. These patches behave as though they were in the womb, producing a 'period' each month. The endometriosis tissue needs the female hormone oestrogen to survive, so endometriosis is not found in girls before puberty or in women after the menopause when oestrogen levels are low.

How do I know if I have endometriosis?

Your doctor might suspect you have endometriosis from your symptoms (outlined above), but diagnosis requires visual identification of the endometriosis tissue, usually via a laparoscopy. As when assessing tubal function, a laparoscope is inserted into the abdomen through a small cut, usually below the navel. The surgeon can then see the womb, fallopian tubes and ovaries as they lie in the pelvis. Patches of endometriosis appear like blue or black spots and sometimes scar tissue and adhesions are seen.

Does endometriosis cause infertility?

Endometriosis can sometimes cause infertility. If you have severe endometriosis, with damage to the fallopian tubes or where your ovaries are trapped in adhesions preventing release of the egg, this will obviously reduce your fertility. Doctors are uncertain whether mild endometriosis, where the tubes and ovaries remain normal, actually causes infertility. However, it is certainly more common in women with infertility. If mild endometriosis does reduce fertility, the underlying mechanism is not clear. Many possibilities have been suggested including inflammatory changes in the pelvis which might upset egg development, transport and fertilisation.

Does endometriosis increase my chance of having a miscarriage?

There is no good evidence to suggest that endometriosis will increase your risk of miscarriage.

How is infertility treated if I have endometriosis?

Where your tubes are damaged or where your ovaries are trapped in adhesions preventing release of the egg then surgery can sometimes correct this damage. Alternatively, you can be treated by in vitro fertilisation. Where there is no tubal damage and the ovaries are not trapped through endometriosis, and where there is no sperm problem, you should receive similar treatment to that offered for so-called 'unexplained' infertility.

Is treatment available for pain due to endometriosis?

Yes, these symptoms can be treated with medication or by surgery. Medication is used to reduce pain and to stop the growth of the endometriosis tissue. Common approaches are to give high doses of progesterone, which stop the growth of the endometriosis, or by the use of medication that reduces the production of oestrogen. Without oestrogen, endometriosis will die out. Medication is often given in courses of around six months' duration. Unfortunately, it is not unusual to get recurrence of endometriosis after treatment stops. Surgery can also be used. In the most severe cases hysterectomy (removal of the womb) and removal of the ovaries may eventually be required. If the ovaries are removed, you will need hormone replacement therapy to prevent menopausal symptoms. Obviously, hysterectomy must be avoided until your family is complete.

2

Part

Pregnancy

Discovering you are pregnant

Finding out you are pregnant can be an exhilarating but anxious time. Very quickly you will notice changes as your body rapidly starts to adapt to meet the needs of your developing baby. But this transition is not just physical, it is also emotional. The pregnancy hormones affect how your brain functions, so that your emotions are heightened, with more extreme reactions to happy and sad events. On learning that you are pregnant, your emotions may be mixed: a combination of the joy and excitement of pregnancy, and, with your first baby, the pangs you might feel about the changes in your lifestyle and the increased responsibility that a baby brings. Share your feelings with your partner and friends. Talk to other mothers-to-be; you will probably find that despite their confident and happy exterior, inside they have the same whirl of emotions as you.

Establishing a pregnancy

What symptoms might make me think that I am pregnant?

You might suspect that you are pregnant before you miss a period or do a pregnancy test. This is because you may be aware of the changes made by pregnancy in your body, which start from very early in pregnancy. They will include breast changes, tiredness and the feeling that you need to pass urine more often. You may experience morning sickness or feel faint or dizzy. In addition, it is common to feel irritable or emotional and sometimes you may find that you have difficulty making decisions.

If I miss a period, does that mean I am pregnant?

Often the catalyst for doing a pregnancy test is when you miss a period. So if you normally have a regular cycle and miss your period, you should always think about the possibility of pregnancy and perform a pregnancy test.

Apart from pregnancy, are there other reasons why my period could be late?

Your period can be delayed by stress, such as that due to a bereavement or to exam pressure, jet lag or sudden weight change, but don't just assume that a factor like stress is the reason for your late period. If pregnancy is possible, take a pregnancy test! If you are concerned about late or irregular periods, you should discuss this with your doctor.

How do I confirm that I am pregnant?

The easiest way to confirm your pregnancy is to purchase a pregnancy test kit – available from all pharmacies. Alternatively, you could visit your doctor, who will arrange to perform a pregnancy test for you.

How do pregnancy tests work?

Pregnancy tests measure a specific pregnancy hormone, secreted only by the placenta (the organ that supports the baby in the womb) and known as human chorionic gonadotrophin (hCG). This hormone passes from the placenta into the bloodstream. It then passes through the kidneys and is detectable in urine in early pregnancy.

Are pregnancy tests reliable?

Modern pregnancy tests are very reliable – more than 95% accurate – and easy to use. The best results are obtained from urine obtained as soon as you get up in the morning, as is it in its most concentrated form at this time. Some tests are more sensitive than others and are able to detect very low concentrations of hCG in the urine. These more sensitive tests may give a positive reading even before your period is missed and will provide an accurate result based on any sample of urine, in which case you can take the test at any time of day.

How soon after I miss a period can I perform a pregnancy test?

Generally, you can check as soon as you know your period is late. Pregnancy tests will usually give a positive reading by that time. If it is negative, however, wait a few days; if your period has still not started, repeat the test. Your doctor can confirm the result and will arrange appropriate antenatal care for you.

How do you do a pregnancy test?

Doing a pregnancy test is straightforward. The precise instructions vary from brand to brand, but all work on the same principle. You either collect some of

Discovering you are pregnant

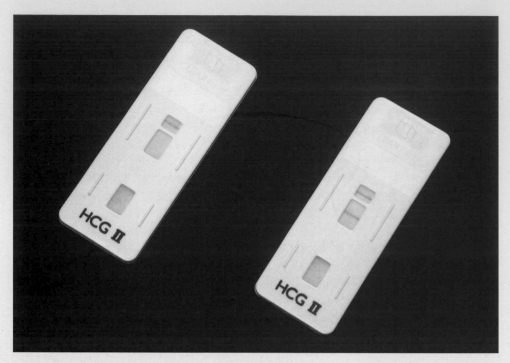

When a pregnancy test is positive the result is displayed in the window of the test stick as two lines (right) that will appear blue. When a test is negative only one blue line appears (left).

your urine and drop it onto the test stick or you hold the stick under your stream of urine. You will have to wait for about five minutes to see the result, which, if positive, may be displayed in the 'window' of the test stick as two blue lines or as a red cross or two pink dots. Again, this varies from brand to brand. Because the tests vary in the way they are performed, it is essential that you read the manufacturer's instructions carefully and follow them precisely. Sometimes your doctor will measure the pregnancy hormone hCG in your blood to confirm that you are pregnant.

Will my breasts change?

Your breasts will get bigger often before your period is missed and they will feel tender. You will probably notice that your bra is beginning to feel a bit tight. You may have a tingling sensation in your breasts or feel that your nipples are sore. The veins on your breasts can become very obvious, especially if you have pale skin. This is because of an increase in blood supply to prepare them for breast-feeding. Your nipples will also enlarge and become darker in colour, as well as exquisitely sensitive to touch. The pigmented skin round each nipple, the areola, will develop small raised glands known as Montgomery's tubercles (Montgomery was an 18th-century gynaecologist who first described these glands). These little glands produce an oily secretion that lubricates and protects the skin of the nipples during breast-feeding. Your breasts may feel lumpy to touch and may get extremely itchy. It is important to wear a bra that fits properly to minimise the discomfort. Remember that breast size will change in pregnancy and you may need to be re-measured.

I feel tired. Is this normal?

It is common to feel very tired in the early stages of pregnancy. It is not unusual to feel that you have to sleep in the afternoon or early evening, even when you would not normally do this. The reason you feel tired is because your body is adapting to meet the demands of your developing baby. If you are worried about tiredness, or it continues or is severe, you should consult your doctor. Occasionally, tiredness can be due to anaemia *(see p. 171)*, which can be checked by a simple blood test and is subsequently easily treated by iron and vitamin supplements.

I can't stand the taste of coffee any more and often feel sick. Why is this?

It is very common to go off certain foods and drinks during pregnancy. You may find that you don't like the taste of alcohol when you are pregnant or can't drink coffee. Many women describe a metallic taste in their mouth. Your sense of smell may also become more sensitive, such that the smell or taste of certain foods can make you feel nauseous. You might feel nauseated and vomit, especially in the morning – hence the term 'morning sickness'. Doctors don't know why women 'go off' certain foods or drinks but it is possible that this is nature's way of protecting the baby from potentially harmful substances like alcohol at a critical stage in the baby's development.

Do all pregnant women experience nausea or morning sickness?

About half of all pregnant women experience morning sickness. Nausea and morning sickness usually start a few weeks after conception, although some women will not suffer from these at all.

What causes morning sickness?

Doctors don't know precisely what causes morning sickness but it is probably related to the hormonal changes in your body due to the implanting pregnancy. It is usually most severe when the levels of hCG, the pregnancy hormone, are highest in the first three months of pregnancy and resolves as levels decline in the second three months.

Is morning sickness confined to the morning?

Morning sickness is a misleading name as it can occur at any time of day. It may be worse when your stomach is empty, hence the association with morning. It can also be worse when you are tired.

How long is my morning sickness likely to last?

Your morning sickness will usually pass by the 14th week of pregnancy. However, for a small number of women it can persist for much longer. In fact, some women can experience it throughout the pregnancy.

Hyperemesis gravidarum

Hyperemesis gravidarum is the medical name for a very severe form of morning sickness. The condition is uncommon, occurring in less than 1% of pregnancies. It usually starts between six and eight weeks from the last menstrual period and tends to continue until about 20 weeks. Occasionally it can last throughout the pregnancy. Morning sickness becomes hyperemesis when you have persistent nausea with vomiting several times a day, leading to dehydration, with biochemical upset in your body and inadequate nutrition, leading to weight loss. Unfortunately, it tends to recur in subsequent pregnancies, so if you have had it once you are likely to have it again. Sometimes there is also a mild upset of liver function.

Doctors don't yet know why hyperemesis occurs. However, it is known that there is a link with high levels of hCG. This may be why hyperemesis is more common in twin pregnancies as, with two placentas, the level of hCG will be much higher than with a single baby. High levels of hCG occur in the first three months of pregnancy then levels start to decline; morning sickness and hyperemesis occur over this same period. These high levels of hCG in the blood can cause the thyroid gland to become slightly overactive on a temporary basis, which might partially account for all the nausea and vomiting. Another possible cause is stomach infection with the bacterium *Helicobacter pylori*, known to cause stomach ulcers. A psychological component to hyperemesis has also been proposed.

Hyperemesis gravidarum can be a very serious condition if not adequately treated. Complications such as deficiency of B vitamins, dehydration and malnutrition can occur as a result of severe vomiting. In addition, there is a higher risk of blood clots in the vein as the result of being confined to bed for long periods. Such complications can be dangerous for the mother but, despite the severe metabolic upset, there is no evidence of an increased risk of abnormality in the developing baby. However, in particularly severe cases, where a woman loses more than 5% of her body weight, there is a higher chance of the baby being small compared with uncomplicated pregnancies or pregnancies where morning sickness is mild.

Women with hyperemesis gravidarum are usually admitted to hospital. Treatment includes fluids given through a vein to rehydrate the mother, medication to reduce the nausea and vomiting and vitamin supplements to replace lost nutrients. Steroid medication has been shown to be effective in severe cases. Occasionally, intravenous feeding is required and medication can also be given to reduce the risk of blood clots. If you have severe morning sickness or think that you have hyperemesis gravidarum, you should seek advice from your doctor or midwife as treatment can improve the situation and will reduce the risk of complications.

Will morning sickness harm my baby?

Your baby will not be harmed by morning sickness. Indeed, morning sickness is thought to be a sign of a well-established pregnancy. It can lead you to lose weight in early pregnancy, but the baby's growth will not be affected. Your baby will get all the nourishment it needs from your body's stores.

Is there anything I can do to alleviate the symptoms of morning sickness?

Obviously, you should avoid any foods that make it worse, but take frequent snacks so that your stomach is not empty. Many women find dry biscuits or dry toast are good, especially in the morning, and they keep some by the bed so that they can eat as soon as they wake up. Indeed, it is often best to eat something before you get out of bed in the morning.

Do not take any drugs to combat morning sickness. If you are not coping very well, keep a record of how much food and fluid you are managing to keep down and get help from your doctor. Severe morning sickness can lead to dehydration that can make you ill. Do try and take your folic acid vitamin supplements *(see p. 29)* even if you feel sick; you may have to adjust the time you take your tablets. If you are on iron tablets to prevent anaemia, these may aggravate the condition and need to be withheld until the morning sickness settles. Some women find that acupressure on a point on the wrist (known as the 'Neiguan point') relieves nausea. Wrist bands used for travel sickness put pressure on this point and may be worth trying if you have morning sickness that is particularly troublesome.

If morning sickness is very severe, should I seek medical help?

If your morning sickness is very severe and you are unable to keep down fluids, then you must seek medical advice to avoid becoming ill through dehydration. Medical help, including intravenous fluid replacement, may be required and this would usually require hospitalisation *(see box, opposite)*.

Why do I need to pass urine more frequently?

When you are pregnant, it is common to need to pass urine more often that you would have before. This is due to the pressure of the enlarging womb (uterus) on your bladder. Although urinary frequency is normal, pain on passing urine is not and could indicate a bladder infection (cystitis), which should be treated promptly, especially in pregnancy. If pain is present on passing urine then you must see you doctor at once.

I have a vaginal discharge. Is this normal?

Vaginal secretions increase in pregnancy. This is due to the increase in blood flow in your pelvis. The discharge is normally clear or white in colour. If it is yellow, green or bloodstained, smells offensive or is accompanied by itching, discomfort or ulceration, then you must tell your doctor. A bloodstained discharge may indicate a threatened miscarriage, for instance. An abnormal discharge in pregnancy is most commonly due to a yeast infection called thrush

Discovering you are pregnant

(candida infection). It causes itching and irritation round the vulva and vagina and often has a thick white or yellow discharge that can be described as 'curd-like'. It is easily treated by a course of pessaries or creams. The infection is confined to the skin alone and will not affect the baby or harm the pregnancy.

I have noticed that there is a dark line running down the middle of my abdomen. Is this normal?

As well as darkening of the nipples, other pigment changes will occur in your body. This is because high levels of oestrogen, the female hormone produced in increased quantities when you are pregnant, increase the ability of your skin to produce pigment. These changes are normal. The thin line that appears in pregnancy running from your pubic area to the navel (umbilicus) is called the 'linea nigra'. If you have freckles, these will often darken in pregnancy. You may notice that any recent scars and even your genital area become more pigmented. In darker-skinned people, pigmented vertical lines can appear on the fingernails in pregnancy. You will also find that you tan more readily in the sun although your tan may be more patchy than usual. Patchy pigmentation can also occur on the face around the chin, forehead and nose and mouth; this is known as chloasma, the so-called 'mask' of pregnancy. It probably affects about half of all pregnant women to a greater or lesser degree and is more common in brunettes than in blondes. It can also occur in women taking the combined (oestrogen-containing) contraceptive pill. To help reduce pigmentation, you should use a high-protection sunscreen when exposed to the sun. Any changes can usually be camouflaged with cover-up cosmetics. If the changes are marked and cause you concern, you should seek specialist medical advice. Once the baby is born, they will fade and your skin will usually go back to normal.

My skin feels greasier. Is this due to the pregnancy?

The changes in your hormones in pregnancy often lead to more oil production by the skin. Your skin, especially that of the face, will tend to feel greasier. Regular use of a clarifying lotion can help, along with a moisturising cream that is designed for oily skin. If you use make-up, find one with an oil-free base. If you find you get troublesome acne or 'spots' along with increased 'greasiness', you should consult your doctor. Do not take any medication for acne without discussing it with your doctor as some acne preparations might harm the baby.

Sometimes my gums bleed after I brush my teeth. This did not happen before I got pregnant.

Changes in your gums are probably related to the hormonal changes of pregnancy. Some softening of the gums together with increased blood supply can make your gums more likely to bleed after brushing as well as more prone to gingivitis – inflammation of the gums. Such changes are common in pregnancy, affecting around a third of pregnant women, and can appear early in the pregnancy. Dental decay can also worsen in pregnancy. It is important, therefore, to brush and floss your teeth regularly, and it is usually advisable to see your dentist at least once during pregnancy.

My palms appear redder and I have little, red 'spider-like' blood vessels on my skin. Is this normal?

Such changes to the skin are normal in pregnancy. They are due to the high oestrogen levels and increased blood flow to the skin. Over 10% of white women will have vascular 'spiders' by the second month of pregnancy and two-thirds will have them by term. They are less common in black women, however, affecting fewer than 15% by term. Over half of all women will develop red palms in pregnancy, referred to by doctors as 'palmer erythema'.

Calculating when your baby is due

How do doctors calculate when my baby is due?

The estimated date of delivery (EDD) is calculated as 40 weeks (280 days) from the start of your last menstrual period. Conception usually occurs two weeks after the last period and the duration of the pregnancy is 38 weeks (266 days) from conception. But this only applies if:

- You have a regular four-week cycle
- The first day of the last period is certain
- There has been no bleeding since your last period
- No contraception was being used (if you conceived after coming off the pill then the last menstrual period is not reliable for calculating your dates)

My menstrual cycle is regular but isn't 28 days long. Can my EDD still be calculated from my periods?

If you have a menstrual cycle that is longer than 28 days – say, 35 days – but regular, then the estimated date of delivery can be calculated by adding 41 weeks to the first day of your last period. Conversely, if you have a regular 21-day cycle, the estimated date of delivery is calculated by adding 39 weeks to the last day of the menstrual cycle. This is because ovulation and conception occur almost 14 days before year next period is due, regardless of the length of your cycle. If you have an irregular cycle or a cycle longer than 35 days, the EDD cannot be estimated reliably from starting date of your last period.

How do doctors confirm the stage of my pregnancy?

It is critical to have a good assessment of the stage of your pregnancy in case complications arise. It is best, therefore, to confirm your dates by an ultrasound scan. Especially where there is uncertainty about your menstrual dates, ultrasound is very reliable at dating the pregnancy in its early stages. Convention has always related gestation to the first day of the last menstrual period, so for women who know the date of conception, such as those undergoing assisted conception, the duration of pregnancy from conception is

Discovering you are pregnant

Naegele's formula

This is a formula that doctors use as a quick way to calculate when a baby is due. It is based on the date of the last menstrual period. It only works when the start date of the the woman's last menstrual period is known, where there is a regular 28-day cycle, and where no contraception was being used prior to conception.

How the formula is calculated
- Add seven days to the starting date of your last menstrual period
- Subtract 3 from the month
- Add 1 to the year

Here are two examples:

Your last menstrual period began on 8 May 2003 (8.5.2003)
- Add seven days to the day: 7 + 8 = 15
- Subtract 3 from the month (May being the fifth month): 5 – 3 = 2 (February 2003)
- Add 1 to the year: 2003 + 1 = 2004
- So the estimated date of delivery is: 15 February 2004 (15.2.2004)

Your last menstrual period began on 15 January 2003 (15.1.2003)
- Add seven days to the day: 7 + 15 = 22
- Subtract 3 from the month: three months earlier than January 2003 is October 2002
- Add 1 to this year: 2002 + 1 = 2003
- So the estimated date of delivery is: 22 October 2003 (22.10.2003)

38 weeks rather than 40. While every woman is given an estimated date for delivery, very few women will deliver on that day, however. It is normal for you to go into labour at any time between 37 and 42 weeks.

How soon can my baby be seen on ultrasound scan?
You will probably be eager to see your baby on the scan and watch its heart beating. Ultrasound scan is the final confirmation of the presence of a viable pregnancy in the womb and is usually carried out at your first visit to the obstetrician. It may be performed by the obstetrician or by a radiologist (a medical specialist in imaging), an ultrasonographer (a specialist ultrasound technician) or a midwife. Most women feel very reassured by seeing their developing baby on the scan. A scan carried out through the abdomen will usually reveal a pregnancy in the womb by six weeks after the missed period. The pregnancy may be detected slightly earlier if the scan is carried out through the vagina.

How big is my developing baby in early pregnancy?

At four weeks from the last menstrual period (14 days from fertilisation) the gestation sac – the bag of fluid in which the baby grows – is approximately 3 mm ($^1/_{10}$ in) in diameter and the embryo would be just about visible to the naked eye.

At six weeks the gestation sac is around 2 cm ($^3/_4$ in) in diameter and the umbilical cord is formed. The embryo is less is 4–6 mm ($^1/_6$–$^1/_4$ in) long and cylindrical in form with a head and tail end present. Ultrasound can usually show the foetal heartbeat at this stage. The age of the embryo is assessed by measuring the crown–rump length, the length from the top of the head to the bottom of the embryo.

At eight weeks the gestational sac is 3–5 cm ($1^1/_4$–2 in) in diameter and the embryo is approximately 15–18 mm ($^3/_5$–$^3/_4$ in) in length. The limbs are well formed, toes and fingers are present. The age is again assessed by measuring the crown–rump length of the embryo.

At 10 weeks the foetus is over 3 cm ($1^1/_4$ in) long. The head is taking on a more recognisably human shape. The internal organs have all formed and the limbs are becoming well defined. The age of the foetus at this stage is still assessed by measuring the crown–rump length.

At 12 weeks the gestational sac is 10 cm (4 in) in diameter and the foetus is approximately 5–6 cm (2–$2^1/_4$ in) long. At this stage ultrasound will determine the age of the foetus by measuring the diameter of the head. The skull bones can be seen clearly on the scan. At this stage the face will have formed and finger- and toenails will be starting to develop.

What is the difference between an embryo and a foetus?

The developing baby is known as an embryo up until the eighth week of pregnancy. In this first eight weeks the body and major organ systems are rapidly developing from the ball of cells that implanted seven weeks earlier. By the eighth week, the outward appearance of the foetus is recognisably human and from this stage until delivery it is known as a foetus.

Can doctors tell the sex of the baby on the first ultrasound scan?

Before 12 weeks it is not possible to identify clearly the sex of your developing baby. There will be a swelling in the genital region but it is only after 12 weeks that this will form a penis in a boy. Doctors usually wait until around 16–18 weeks, when the baby is bigger, before trying to determine the sex using an ultrasound scan.

If the baby has any abnormalities, will this show up on the first scan?

It is very unusual to see abnormalities on the first scan if this is carried out early in pregnancy, at 6–12 weeks. Ultrasound at this stage will confirm that the baby is alive by showing the heartbeat and help assess the stage of the

Ultrasound scans during the first three months

Ultrasound scan showing the ▶ developing embryo in the bag of fluid within the womb at 5–6 weeks of pregnancy. The age of the embryo is measured by assessing the length of the embryo from the crown of its head to its bottom, the so-called crown-rump length (shown by the white crosses).

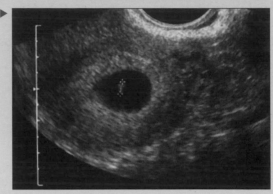

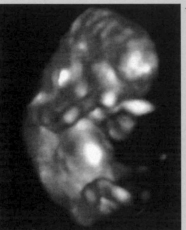

◀ Three-dimensional ultrasound scan of the developing baby at approximately 7–8 weeks of pregnancy. The bumps on the foetus are due to the fact that it is moving in the womb making some bones more prominent than others.

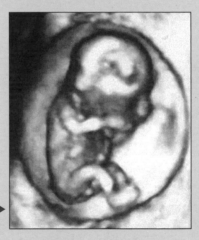

Three-dimensional ultrasound scan of the developing ▶ baby at approximately 10 weeks of pregnancy.

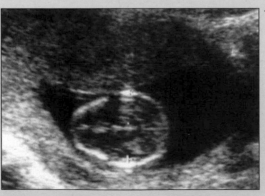

◀ At around three months the age of the foetus is assessed by measuring the diameter of the head. This is a two-dimensional ultrasound showing a cross section across the head of the developing baby and the placenta. The bone of the skull can be clearly seen. The crosses on the scan show the measurement taken to assess the so-called biparietal diameter. This baby is just over 12 weeks gestation. The placenta is to the left of the head.

pregnancy by measuring the size of the developing foetus. Where scans are being performed to exclude abnormality in the baby, they are usually carried out later in pregnancy, at 16–18 weeks, when the baby has developed further and is large enough for the organs to show up adequately. A scan at this stage will assess very carefully the anatomy of the baby.

What is the placenta?

The placenta is essential as it acts as the interface between foetus and mother. A disc-shaped organ, it consists of a rich network of blood vessels derived from the foetus that implants into the wall of the womb very early in pregnancy. The placenta is linked to the foetus by the umbilical cord and is therefore the means by which the foetus is physically attached to the mother. The placenta 'invades' the mother's blood vessels and so becomes bathed in the mother's blood, from which it is able to extract oxygen and nutrients. These are then transported to the foetus through its bloodstream. The blood going from the foetus to the placenta contains the carbon dioxide and waste products produced by the foetus. These are transferred to the mother's blood and the mother then excretes these for the foetus through her lungs and kidneys.

What is the umbilical cord?

The umbilical cord connects the foetus to the placenta. It contains three major blood vessels: two umbilical arteries that carry blood and waste products from the foetus to the placenta, and one umbilical vein which carries blood, rich in oxygen and nutrients, from the placenta back to the foetus. These vessels are encased in a jelly-like substance (the medical term is 'Wharton's jelly'), which in turn is covered in a tough outer coating. The umbilical cord is often coiled so that there is plenty of 'give' to allow foetal movement in the womb.

Where does the amniotic fluid come from and what does it do?

In early pregnancy the amniotic fluid comes from the membranes encasing the foetus and placenta. In late pregnancy the fluid is actually produced by the developing baby's kidneys and excreted as 'urine' (waste products still pass through the placenta to the mother who filters them out through her kidneys). Well-nourished babies produce lots of urine so there is plenty of amniotic fluid. This helps cushion the baby from any injury and allows it to move within the womb until 32 weeks or so when the size of the baby will make it difficult for the baby to move around. In a baby who is not receiving a good supply of nutrients, usually because the placenta is not working as well as it should, the amount of fluid will be low. Marked reductions in amniotic fluid, which are usually assessed by ultrasound (see p. 115), are an important indication that the baby may have a problem.

Discovering you are pregnant

Complications in early pregnancy: miscarriage

Why does vaginal bleeding occur in early pregnancy?

Any bleeding that occurs in early pregnancy is not due to a period, as commonly believed (ovulation cannot take place following the fertilisation of an egg, so is not possible for periods to continue in pregnancy), but bleeding can occur as the pregnancy implants into the womb. The main problem associated with bleeding in early pregnancy is threatened or actual miscarriage, although it is important to exclude ectopic pregnancy (in which the pregnancy implants outside the womb, most commonly in the fallopian tube – *see p. 83*). Occasionally, bleeding may come from a lesion at the neck of the womb, such as a polyp, a fold of friable tissue on the skin that bleeds easily, but this will not affect the pregnancy.

What is a miscarriage?

A miscarriage is the spontaneous loss of a pregnancy before the 24th week. When the foetus is younger than 24 weeks, it is generally not capable of sustaining life outside its mother. The vast majority of miscarriages occur before weeks 10–12 of pregnancy

Why do miscarriages occur?

First of all, you should know that miscarriages are common and occur in up to 25% of all pregnancies. There are several known causes of miscarriage *(see box, p. 79)* but, despite this, doctors can often find no cause and the majority of miscarriages remain entirely unexplained, though at least some may be 'nature's way' of dealing with a problem in the pregnancy. There is usually nothing that anyone can do, particularly you, to prevent a miscarriage.

What should I do if I have vaginal bleeding in early pregnancy?

You should call your family doctor or the hospital immediately, particularly if pain is associated with the bleeding.

Because problems with miscarriage are so common, many hospitals have specialised early-pregnancy assessment units, usually staffed with specially trained doctors and midwives, which can provide rapid assessment and management of problems in early pregnancy problems. Often this is carried out on an outpatient basis.

Causes of bleeding in early pregnancy

- Threatened miscarriage
- Complete or incomplete miscarriage
- Ectopic pregnancy
- Bleeding from the neck of the womb (cervix) such as from a polyp

What will the doctor do?

To find out what is happening, the doctor will ask you certain questions, examine you and usually arrange an ultrasound scan within 24 hours or so. It can sometimes also be useful to repeat your pregnancy test. The doctor will be trying to establish several key pieces of information:

- Confirm that you are definitely pregnant
- Confirm that your pregnancy is within the womb (and not ectopic)
- Determine whether your pregnancy is still viable (which will usually require an ultrasound test)
- Determine how far advanced your pregnancy is
- Establish when the bleeding occurred; for example, whether it came on after intercourse, which would suggest a local problem such as a polyp
- Establish how heavy your bleeding was, whether there was any pain and whether any tissue was passed along with the blood
- Find out whether you have had miscarriages before.

This last is to identify if you have a problem with recurrent miscarriage. It is unusual to find a cause for miscarriage in a woman who has had a single miscarriage. However, women with recurrent miscarriages are often found to have an underlying cause and should therefore be investigated. Some causes of recurrent miscarriage can be successfully treated (see p. 80).

Are there different types of miscarriage?

Yes. Some types, such as a threatened miscarriage, need have no effect on the pregnancy while others will lead to loss of the pregnancy. The doctor will determine what type of miscarriage you are having, based on the clinical features and the findings of the ultrasound scan (see box, p.79).

How does ultrasound help in the diagnosis of miscarriage?

Ultrasound has allowed doctors to make a more accurate diagnosis of some types of miscarriage by allowing them to see what is happening to the pregnancy inside the womb. This has led to the identification of two additional types of miscarriage: a 'blighted ovum' and a 'missed miscarriage'.

What is a blighted ovum?

A blighted ovum is where placental tissue develops in the womb but no embryo or foetus is ever found. Doctors do not know the reason underlying the failure of the embryo to develop. However, without an embryo or foetus, a pregnancy obviously cannot continue. Therefore a blighted ovum will eventually progress to an inevitable miscarriage, with bleeding and pain, and in turn to an incomplete or complete miscarriage. A blighted ovum should only be diagnosed when serial ultrasound scans, conducted at least one week apart, confirm that no embryo is developing. It is important that serial ultrasound scans are carried out in case the dates of the pregnancy are wrong. If the pregnancy is earlier than thought, the ultrasound findings could be misinterpreted. In this situation the size of the pregnancy will not be consistent with the mother's dates. If the dates are wrong,

The known causes of miscarriage

Genetic abnormalities: 'Mistakes' in the genetic blueprint for development may arise at around the time of conception and are a common cause of miscarriage. Such mistakes can mean that the pregnancy will never succeed as the pregnancy does not have the correct information in order to develop properly. In fact, some studies have found such abnormalities in at least 50% of miscarriages. Very occasionally, some genetic abnormality in one or other parent can be involved in a miscarriage.

An abnormal-shaped womb: Examples of an abnormal-shaped womb are a bicornuate uterus, where instead of having a triangular cavity the womb is shaped in the form of two 'horns', or a unicornuate uterus where the womb is shaped like a single horn. However, many women with these abnormalities have successful pregnancies so it is difficult to establish whether this is actually a genuine cause of miscarriage or just a coincidental finding.

A weak cervix (neck of the womb): Up until labour occurs, the cervix must remain tightly closed to keep the baby safely in the womb and to prevent any infection reaching the developing baby. Weakness of the cervix, known as 'cervical incompetence', may be due to a problem that you are born with or can be due to the cervix being damaged during surgery or childbirth. With cervical incompetence, recurrent miscarriage will occur, with minimal pain. Usually the womb has to contract powerfully, and very painfully, to deliver the baby. With cervical incompetence, the cervix is weak and so opens without contractions – hence the absence of pain. Miscarriage because of cervical incompetence will initially be in the middle of pregnancy, with subsequent miscarriages occurring earlier and earlier. The condition is treatable, however *(see p. 83)*.

Infection: An infection within the womb or affecting the foetus can lead to miscarriage, but this is very uncommon. You should bear in mind that most of the common causes of vaginal discharge in pregnancy, such as thrush, are not associated with miscarriage.

Medical conditions: A medical condition in the mother can sometimes cause miscarriage, such as untreated thyroid disease, chronic kidney disease, and conditions where the mother has a tendency to form blood clots that can damage the placenta.

Hormonal disturbance: Disturbance of the hormones controlling ovulation and early pregnancy has been linked to miscarriage, but correcting these problems does not appear to prevent miscarriage.

the pregnancy may not have reached the stage when ultrasound can visualise the developing embryo. Ultrasound carried out through the vagina at six weeks or earlier allows visualisation of the embryo at an earlier stage than a scan carried out through the abdomen.

What is a missed miscarriage?

A missed miscarriage, sometimes called a delayed miscarriage, is diagnosed via ultrasound. Here the embryo or foetus is clearly seen but the foetal heart is not beating. This indicates that the pregnancy has ended some time before. With a missed miscarriage you will not usually have had pain or bleeding. Often you will have stopped feeling pregnant. Just as with a blighted ovum, this will eventually progress to an inevitable miscarriage and in turn to an incomplete or complete miscarriage. Should the size of the embryo be consistent with a very early stage in pregnancy (in which the heartbeat wouldn't be detectable), the ultrasound scan is repeated to confirm that no change has occurred in case the dates are inaccurate.

The different types of miscarriage

Threatened miscarriage: This is painless vaginal bleeding from the site of the placenta in your womb. The bleeding is often not severe enough to trouble the pregnancy; it can settle spontaneously and the pregnancy will continue normally. When you are examined, the doctor will find that the neck of the womb (cervix) is closed. However, sometimes a threatened miscarriage will progress, with further bleeding and pain, to an inevitable miscarriage.

Inevitable miscarriage: With an inevitable miscarriage there is usually 'cramping' pain, which is often severe, accompanying the bleeding. The cervix is usually open – which the doctor will check when you are examined – due to uterine contractions attempting to expel the pregnancy from the womb. The contractions are the reason for the cramping pain that frequently occurs with inevitable miscarriage.

Incomplete and complete miscarriage: An inevitable miscarriage may progress to become an incomplete miscarriage, where part of the pregnancy has been expelled but there is some tissue, usually placental, remaining in the womb. The cervix is usually found to be open when the doctor examines you, which is due to the womb trying to expel the remaining pregnancy tissue. Complete miscarriage is where the whole pregnancy has been expelled from the womb and so the uterus will be empty. With a complete miscarriage, the cervix is usually closed.

2

What else can the ultrasound show?

An ultrasound can can also confirm a continuing pregnancy, such as in the case of a threatened miscarriage, by showing the heartbeat of the embryo or foetus. Ultrasound can therefore be very reassuring if you have had a problem such as bleeding in early pregnancy. For women who have miscarried, an ultrasound scan can also allow the doctor to determine whether a miscarriage is incomplete (tissue will be seen inside the womb) or complete (the womb will be empty).

How is miscarriage treated?

Threatened miscarriage is treated by nothing more specific than reassurance and follow-up ultrasound scans to check that everything is going well. Traditionally, bed rest was recommended, but doctors now know that this is no more beneficial than reassurance and demonstration to the mother, using ultrasound, that the pregnancy is continuing. Thus there is no need for you to be admitted to hospital or confined to bed if you have a threatened miscarriage, although it is sensible to avoid excessive physical stress.

A complete miscarriage can only be diagnosed after vaginal bleeding, which is usually associated with pain, and where there has been good evidence of a pregnancy, such as positive pregnancy tests or ultrasound confirmation of pregnancy, followed by the finding of an empty womb on ultrasound. The doctor will be careful to exclude an ectopic pregnancy, in which the womb is empty but a continuing pregnancy is present outside the womb, usually in the fallopian tube. The treatment of complete miscarriage is reassurance – that miscarriage is common, it may not happen again, nothing could have been done to prevent it, and no further action is needed.

Will I need an operation if I have a miscarriage?

In cases of incomplete miscarriage, blighted ovum and missed miscarriage, the pregnancy has ended and the treatment is to proceed to empty the womb either medically (with drugs) or surgically – a procedure known as 'evacuation of the uterus'. It is important to ensure that your womb is empty, as dead tissue retained in the uterus can lead to bleeding and infection *(see opposite)*. Infection can cause you to become very ill, or even threaten your future fertility by damaging the fallopian tubes that carry the eggs from your ovaries to the womb.

How is evacuation of the uterus carried out?

Surgical evacuation of the uterus is usually carried out under general anaesthesia. Your cervix is often open following an incomplete miscarriage, which allows the surgeon access to the womb. If the cervix is not already open, it is stretched open using instruments called dilators. This can be made easier by the use of special pessaries given before the operation to soften the cervix before the dilatation. Dilators gradually stretch the neck of the womb until it opens wide enough (usually no more than 8–10 mm, less than half an inch) to allow any remaining tissue to be removed, either by the surgeon's fingers or with surgical instruments. The wall of the womb is usually scraped with a special instrument called a curette to ensure that it is empty and no pieces of tissue still adhere to the uterus. Drugs are given to make the womb contract as contractions minimise any bleeding during and after the evacuation.

An alternative to surgical evacuation, and more appropriate in certain cases, such as missed miscarriage or incomplete miscarriage, is medical evacuation using drugs. In this instance, drugs consisting of prostaglandins are usually given vaginally, causing your womb to contract strongly so expelling any tissue. The womb can be checked with ultrasound after medical evacuation to ensure that it is empty. If it is not empty then surgical evacuation may be required, but this is not often necessary.

What complications can occur with a miscarriage?

The most common complications that are encountered after miscarriage are haemorrhage and infection, both of which are often due to retained pregnancy tissue. In cases of severe haemorrhage, drugs are given to contract the womb and reduce bleeding while awaiting surgical evacuation. The risk of infection is reduced by prompt evacuation of the uterus to remove any remaining dead tissue, which acts as a fertile breeding ground for bacteria. Infection can cause you to have abdominal and pelvic pain and tenderness, a high temperature, and often an offensive vaginal discharge. In addition, it can sometimes cause heavy bleeding from the womb.

If there is a possibility of infection in the womb, the doctor will take bacteriological swabs, in the form of long cotton buds, from any discharge at the top of the vagina and inside of the cervix. The swabs are then sent to the bacteriology laboratory for analysis to determine what, if any, bacteria are causing the infection. Antibiotics suitable for dealing with the majority of bacteria that cause infection in the womb should be given as soon as possible.

My blood group is rhesus negative. Does this matter if I have bleeding in early pregnancy?

The fact that your blood group is rhesus negative will not cause you to bleed in early pregnancy. However, to prevent problems with rhesus disease in future pregnancies, you may require an injection of anti-D immunoglobulin, usually referred to as anti-D. Your doctor can advise you about this. Generally, anti-D should be given when a susceptible mother has had a threatened or confirmed miscarriage after 12 weeks. If she has a miscarriage at less than 12 weeks, requiring an evacuation of the womb, anti-D should also be given. Sometimes anti-D is not needed for uncomplicated threatened miscarriages at less than 12 weeks. If there is any doubt about whether or not anti-D is needed then anti-D is usually given to be on the safe side. *(See p. 147 for full details on rhesus disease and its effects on pregnancy.)*

How do women feel after a miscarriage?

Inevitably, many women, and their partners, feel completely devastated and heart broken after a miscarriage. The majority describe a feeling that a part of

Discovering you are pregnant

them has died. The loss of a pregnancy is therefore a very distressing experience. More than half of all women suffering a miscarriage want something to remember their baby by, such as an ultrasound scan photograph. Often women feel they have failed or have a sense of guilt or anxiety. Others react with anger. These are all normal reactions to grief and bereavement. Many women feel a sense of loneliness after a miscarriage. Anxiety about the ability to conceive successfully in the future, and indeed persisting through subsequent pregnancies, is common. So a great deal of support is required, not just after a miscarriage but also in any future pregnancy.

Depression is common after a miscarriage and the emotional problems can cause difficulties in relationships. Patience, understanding and support from partners is required. It is important to talk about the problem with partners, families or friends. Some women find it especially useful to discuss the situation with someone who has experienced a similar problem or someone who can explain how miscarriages occur and answer the questions that arise. The appropriate emotional support varies from woman to woman; however, there are several support groups who can provide such information and support. Your family doctor or obstetrician and gynaecologist can also provide specific medical information and support.

Do women frequently blame themselves after a miscarriage?

Almost three-quarters of women worry that they might have caused the problem leading to their miscarriage. They think back on the pregnancy and try to identify something that they have done or not done which could have caused the problem. This is, at least partly, because doctors can usually give them no specific medical reason for the miscarriage. The truth, however, is that it is exceptionally rare for there to have been anything that the mother could have done or not done which would have caused or prevented the miscarriage. Knowing this may not help to alleviate the sense of loss or bereavement, but it may help her to understand that the miscarriage was not preventable and therefore not her fault.

How soon after a miscarriage is a further pregnancy advisable?

From a physical point of view, it is usually reasonable to try to conceive after the menstrual cycle has returned to normal following an uncomplicated miscarriage. Perhaps more important to consider, however, is whether you are ready emotionally to deal with another pregnancy. Only you and your partner can really determine this. If you have had a miscarriage, you should try and avoid pregnancy until you and your partner feel able to cope with the anxiety that a pregnancy will inevitably generate.

What if miscarriages recur?

Miscarriages are common; they are the most common complication in pregnancy. So it is not unusual for a woman to have more than one. Indeed, recurrent miscarriage is a problem that affects around 1 in 100 women. As noted earlier, it is very unusual to be able identify a specific cause for a miscarriage. However, where recurrent miscarriage occurs, it is important to perform investigations to exclude the known causes of recurrent miscarriage, some of which are treatable. Many doctors will not perform such investigations until three miscarriages have occurred, unless there are special considerations or a strong suspicion of an underlying medical problem. This is because the majority of miscarriages are unexplained. Indeed, the medical definition of recurrent miscarriage is the loss of three or more consecutive pregnancies. However, some doctors prefer to investigate women after experiencing two consecutive miscarriages.

In the first instance, it is important to check the genetic make-up of the parents (and, if possible, of the pregnancy that miscarried), which is done by a simple blood test. In 3–5% of cases one or other parent is shown to carry a genetic abnormality. It is also important to screen for specific medical conditions. In particular, 15% of women with recurrent miscarriage will be shown to have antiphospholipid antibody syndrome *(see p. 177)*, a condition that predisposes the mother to develop blood clots that can damage the placenta and lead to pregnancy loss. This condition can be treated, however, using drugs to inhibit clotting. Another treatable cause of miscarriage is cervical incompetence, which is treated surgically with a stitch to support and reinforce the cervix.

What if no cause for recurrent miscarriage is found?

In many cases of recurrent miscarriage no cause is found. However, while this is unsatisfactory in terms of explaining the problem, it does not mean the situation is hopeless. In such cases, three-quarters of women will go on, with supportive care alone, to have a successful pregnancy.

Ectopic pregnancy

What is an ectopic pregnancy?

Ectopic pregnancy occurs when the fertilised egg implants in a location other than the womb. This happens in around 1 in 300 pregnancies. The most common site for ectopic pregnancy is the fallopian tubes as over 95% occur there. However, it can also occur at the junction of the tube and the womb (the so-called 'cornua' of the uterus), on the ovaries, in the abdomen or even on the cervix. As the fallopian tube is not designed to allow a pregnancy to develop, the tube will eventually rupture as the pregnancy grows. This will lead to serious bleeding inside the abdomen that can be life-threatening. It is unusual for a tubal pregnancy to proceed beyond 8–10 weeks – either it will resolve or lead to symptoms indicating the need for medical intervention.

Why do ectopic pregnancies occur?

Ectopic pregnancy is becoming increasingly common in the West, with a several-fold increase over the last 20 years. This is due to an increasing

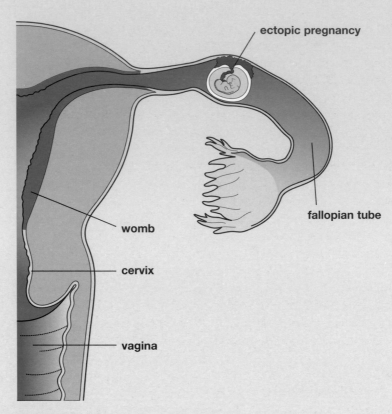

Ectopic pregnancy in the fallopian tube.

incidence of pelvic inflammatory disease, causing infection of the womb and fallopian tubes and leading to tubal damage, in addition to the effects on the tubes of surgery, including sterilisation and its reversal. Such damage to the fallopian tubes can slow the progress of the fertilised egg as it journeys down the tube to the womb. If this process is delayed, the pregnancy will implant in the tube. In addition, the rising incidence of ectopic pregnancy may reflect improvements in the ability of doctors to diagnose the problem. There are now very highly sensitive pregnancy tests and high-quality ultrasound scans that can identify a pregnancy at a much earlier stage than was possible years ago. This allows the early identification of ectopic pregnancies that in the past may have resolved without any treatment (see p. 86), before they reached the stage when they would cause a clinical problem.

Does the 'coil' lead to ectopic pregnancy?

In the unlikely event that a pregnancy occurs while a coil is in place in your uterus, the risk of ectopic pregnancy relative to a normal pregnancy in the womb is slightly increased. Thus if pregnancy occurs while you have a coil in place, it is slightly more likely to be an ectopic pregnancy. Because of this, it is important to see your doctor as early as possible if you think you have conceived with a coil in place.

Do ectopic pregnancies affect future fertility

An ectopic pregnancy does damage the fallopian tube and will inevitably affect future fertility. Unfortunately, more than half of women who have had an ectopic pregnancy will have difficulty in becoming pregnant again without assisted conception (techniques such as in vitro fertilisation – *see p. 57*), and 12–18% of women who have had an ectopic pregnancy will have a further ectopic pregnancy.

What are the symptoms and signs of ectopic pregnancy?

If you have an ectopic pregnancy, the most common signs are pain in the lower abdomen, usually on one side, and vaginal bleeding in early pregnancy. The pain may be present over several days or come on suddenly. It may lead to you to collapse due to pain or to blood loss into the abdomen. Occasionally there is pain in the shoulder tip, due to irritation of the diaphragm caused by the bleeding into the abdomen. The diaphragm is the large sheet of muscle that separates the abdomen from the chest. Its nerve supply is linked to the nerve supply to the shoulder. So if the diaphragm is irritated or damaged, pain is felt at the shoulder. Because of the serious implications of ectopic pregnancy, you must see a doctor urgently if you have any of these symptoms.

How is ectopic pregnancy diagnosed?

The two key features in the diagnosis are to confirm that you are pregnant and to determine whether the pregnancy is inside the womb. If you have a positive pregnancy test and there is no pregnancy in the womb, the pregnancy must be somewhere else and must therefore be an ectopic pregnancy. After the doctor has confirmed that the pregnancy test is positive, the next step is to determine if the pregnancy is inside the womb, which is done with ultrasound scanning. Thus a positive pregnancy test coupled with a uterus found to be empty on ultrasound scan implies an ectopic pregnancy. An abnormal mass of tissue or free fluid in the pelvis (possibly due to bleeding into the abdomen) is highly suggestive of ectopic pregnancy if you have the characteristic symptoms and signs. As previously noted, ultrasound scans performed through the vagina provide a better image in early pregnancy and therefore better potential for early detection of ectopic pregnancy. Sometimes the actual ectopic pregnancy can be seen on ultrasound. It can be directly confirmed by laparoscopy – a surgical procedure, usually performed under general anaesthesia *(see p. 54)*. Blood in the pelvis from a ruptured fallopian tube or the ectopic pregnancy will be revealed by the lapararoscope.

> ## Ectopic pregnancy is increasing
>
> Ectopic pregnancy rates doubled from around 5 per 1000 pregnancies in 1970 to almost 10 per 1000 pregnancies in 1992.

Discovering you are pregnant

Sometimes it is difficult to distinguish an ectopic pregnancy from a very early pregnancy that is in the womb. With a normal pregnancy in the womb, the concentration of hCG in the blood doubles approximately every two days. Doctors can measure this by taking several blood samples. In ectopic pregnancy, however, the doubling rate is much slower. There is also a level of hCG at which a pregnancy would definitely be seen in the womb using ultrasound. If this level has been reached and no pregnancy is seen in the womb then the pregnancy must be ectopic.

How is ectopic pregnancy treated?

The classic treatment of ectopic pregnancy is using surgery. The abdomen must be opened surgically and the fallopian tube with the ectopic pregnancy removed to arrest or prevent serious bleeding as a result of its rupturing. Increasingly, doctors are leaving the tube in place if it has not ruptured. They do this by opening the tube surgically and removing the pregnancy but not the tube. Although the tube is damaged, future prospects for a successful pregnancy may still be more favourable if the tube is left in place. There is also the increasing use of minimal-access or 'keyhole' surgery to deal with ectopic pregnancy, whether to remove the tube or to open the tube and remove the ectopic pregnancy alone. Keyhole surgery, being less invasive, allows a faster recovery and shorter time in hospital than conventional surgery and might reduce the risk of a further ectopic pregnancy in the future. Where the tube has ruptured and there is bleeding into the abdomen, immediate surgery is required and the tube removed together with the pregnancy.

Is surgery always necessary?

Sometimes ectopic pregnancy will not require any surgery. If you are clinically stable and at a very early stage in pregnancy with a small unruptured ectopic pregnancy then sometimes doctors will simply monitor you to determine whether any specific treatment is necessary. This is because some early ectopic pregnancies may end without leading to haemorrhage or tubal rupture. Doctors use a combination of ultrasound scans and serial measurements of hCG to monitor ectopic pregnancies. Treatment with drugs to stop the pregnancy growing is also being explored as an alternative to surgery.

Cysts on the ovary in pregnancy

When I had my first ultrasound scan in pregnancy, the doctor found a cyst on my ovary. What does this mean?

It is relatively common for small cysts on the ovary to be found by chance during ultrasound scan in early pregnancy. The cyst most commonly found in pregnancy is the 'corpus luteum' cyst *(see p. 21)*. The presence of a corpus luteum cyst is normal and it will shrink as the pregnancy advances and the placenta takes over the production of essential hormones. Sometimes a simple, fluid-filled cyst is found and occasionally dermoid cysts are detected. These can contain a whole variety of tissues such as skin, sweat glands, teeth and thyroid tissue. They form because the tissue of the ovary gets 'confused' and manufactures the wrong type of tissue.

What treatment will I need if I have a cyst?

Simple small cysts that do not produce symptoms, including corpus luteum cysts, frequently resolve without treatment. Your doctor will usually repeat the ultrasound examination to check that the cyst is disappearing. If the cyst causes pain, is large (greater than 5 cm/2 in in diameter) or solid then it should be removed surgically. If it is not removed, there is a risk of complications such as twisting of the cyst or the cyst rupturing. Removal is necessary as the cyst could cause not only severe pain and require emergency surgery, but also miscarriage or premature labour. So if you have an ovarian cyst requiring treatment, it is often best that the surgery be performed while you are pregnant before any complications should arise. Your doctor will advise you about this and discuss the procedure, its risks and benefits, with you.

The best time for surgical removal of a cyst in pregnancy is usually between 15–20 weeks. This will minimise the risk of miscarriage following the operation, avoid exposure of the developing foetus to anaesthetic medications in the first 12 weeks, when the baby's organs are being formed, and also allow sufficient time for the scar on your abdomen to heal prior to labour. The most worrying complication is perhaps that the operation on the ovary might trigger a miscarriage. This is uncommon, however, but drugs are sometimes given following surgery to stop the womb contracting as surgery in the abdomen and pelvis can sometimes irritate the uterus, which in turn might lead to a miscarriage.

Lifestyle in pregnancy

When you are pregnant you will invariably have questions about your lifestyle and whether this might influence the pregnancy. There may be factors that you wish to change or that you are concerned or anxious about. These questions frequently relate to diet, work environment, exercise and sex during pregnancy. There are some factors, such as whether you smoke, that you would be better to change while you are pregnant, and others that you can be reassured will not influence the pregnancy.

Potential lifestyle changes

Is drinking coffee harmful in pregnancy?

Caffeine crosses the placenta and blood levels in the developing baby are similar to those found in the mother's blood. Moderate coffee drinking (up to 4–5 cups of coffee a day) does not appear to cause problems in pregnancy. There is no good evidence to suggest that caffeine ingested in moderate amounts will harm the developing baby or cause problems such as miscarriage or premature birth. However, large amounts of caffeine are not recommended in pregnancy as they *might* be associated with problems such as miscarriage, so you should avoid drinking more than 4–5 cups of coffee a day. The combination of high caffeine intake together with smoking may have a more injurious effect on the baby's growth than smoking on its own, which is known to be linked to impaired growth of the developing baby.

What about drinking alcohol in pregnancy?

There is no doubt that women who consume large amounts of alcohol in pregnancy can damage their developing baby. On the other hand, small amounts of alcohol do not appear to cause serious problems, although no one knows what the 'safe' level of alcohol in pregnancy is. Many women find that they lose the taste for alcohol in pregnancy, but if you do enjoy the occasional glass of wine, it's worth knowing that there is no good scientific evidence to prove conclusively that drinking less than two glasses of wine a day during pregnancy will cause a problem. Generally, it is recommended that you drink no more than two glasses of wine (or its equivalent in alcohol content) once or twice a week, to be on the safe side. Drinking more than 15 glasses of wine a week (or its equivalent) can be associated with a reduction in the baby's birthweight. Drinking more than 20 glasses of wine a week can be associated with intellectual impairment in the baby.

During the first two months of pregnancy, the developing baby appears to be particularly vulnerable to the effects of alcohol and it is best to avoid alcohol at this time. In particular, avoid binge drinking, where you take a large amount of alcohol over a relatively short period, as the effects of this on the foetus are not yet clear. But if you are usually a light drinker and generally healthy, there appears to be very little chance that if you got drunk once early in your pregnancy that it will it have harmed your baby. The only way to be absolutely certain that alcohol will not affect your developing baby is to give it up altogether while you are pregnant.

What is foetal alcohol syndrome?

Extremely high consumption of alcohol on a regular basis in pregnancy can lead to so-called 'foetal alcohol syndrome'. This condition is rare, however, affecting between 1 in 300 and 1 in 2000 pregnancies. The full syndrome affects only about a third of babies whose mothers drink around the equivalent of three bottles of wine a day in pregnancy. The fact that only a third of these babies are affected suggests that other factors such as poor nutrition, genetic make-up or drug abuse need to be present, in addition to heavy alcohol intake, for the syndrome to develop. Foetal alcohol syndrome has several features: the baby will be small; there may be abnormalities in the brain and nervous system, affecting development and intellectual ability; and there may also be physical abnormalities such as a short, up-turned nose, receding forehead and chin, and asymmetrical ears, causing a characteristic facial deformity.

Should I stop smoking in pregnancy?

If you continue to smoke after you become pregnant, you are putting yourself at an increased risk of miscarriage, or of your baby being small for dates *(see p. 124)*, which can lead to problems during pregnancy. Passive smoking in pregnancy may also be harmful, so if your partner smokes too, it is best that you both stop. Your doctor can provide advice or support to help you come off cigarettes. Even after pregnancy it is important not to smoke. This is because the baby will be more prone to 'cot death' *(see p. 254)* and to breathing problems.

Is where I work relevant to my pregnancy?

If you work with certain chemicals, lead, anaesthetics or X-rays, this may involve a risk to your unborn baby. Talk to your doctor about it. In the past, it was suggested that computers, VDUs (visual display units) and copying machines gave off harmful rays, but there is no scientific evidence to suggest that they present any risk to pregnant women or their babies. In fact, there have been a number of quite large research studies on VDUs, none of which have identified a risk. Studies on 4000 women who experienced miscarriage and over 30,000 women who did not have shown there was *no* link between miscarriage and VDU exposure. Other studies on over 1500 women who delivered small babies and 30,000 who delivered normal-sized babies have likewise identified that there is *no* link between VDU exposure and low birthweight. In addition, other large studies have looked at whether VDUs might be linked to congenital abnormality or premature birth, but again *no* link was found. So if you work with a VDU, there is no need to be concerned or to take any special precautions when you are pregnant.

Can I continue to take prescription medicine in pregnancy?

If you take regular prescription medicine, you need to discuss this with your doctor as certain drugs can affect the baby in the womb.

Can street drugs affect pregnancy?

If you are pregnant, you should not take street drugs as they are all potentially harmful to your baby. Some, like cocaine, can lead to birth abnormalities; others, such as heroin, methadone, amphetamines and marijuana, can affect the growth of your unborn baby so that it will be small. There is also an increased risk of premature delivery, bleeding from the placenta and an increased risk of infant death. The baby may also suffer after delivery from drug withdrawal symptoms as these drugs cross into the baby's body while it is in the womb. The baby's later development in childhood can also be impaired. In addition, there is a much higher rate of complications to the woman in pregnancy, such as anaemia, infection (hepatitis B and C, HIV and septicemia – from infected needles) and thrombosis (blood clots).

I have heard that keeping a cat can be dangerous in pregnancy. Is this so?

It is not so much your cat as its litter tray that presents a risk to you because cat's faeces can contain an organism known as toxoplasma, which can give you an infection and cause abnormalities in the unborn baby. *See p. 153* for other sources of infection and what measures you should take to avoid being infected.

Can I have a massage during pregnancy?

Massage in pregnancy can be a terrific way to help you relax, ease backache and give you a general feeling of well-being. You should, however, avoid vigorous massage of your pregnant abdomen. Massage oils are great for enhancing the experience but some of the aromatic essential oils, distilled from flowers, trees and herbs, need to be avoided in pregnancy. Before using any of these, you should check with an experienced aromatherapist or, if you have any remaining doubts, your doctor. Aromatherapy can also be useful in pregnancy for relaxation and treatment of some ailments like nausea and it can also help with pain relief in labour. Again, you should consult an experienced aromatherapist before you use aromatherapy for any of these purposes.

Sex during pregnancy

Should I have intercourse while I am pregnant?

There is absolutely no reason to stop having intercourse simply because you are pregnant. Indeed, you can enjoy sex right up until you go into labour. It is a good way to exercise and relax as well as helping keep you and your partner physically and emotionally close. There are only a few conditions where your doctor is likely to advise you to avoid intercourse while you are pregnant, including vaginal bleeding due to placenta previa (see pp. 143–6), in case this provokes more bleeding and in some cases of recurrent miscarriage. In addition, if your membranes rupture prior to labour (usually in late pregnancy, though it could occur much earlier), intercourse should be avoided as this could encourage infection to get to the baby, which is normally protected by the enclosed bag of amniotic fluid.

Will intercourse harm the baby?

The baby will not be harmed by intercourse in an uncomplicated pregnancy even if your partner is on top. Your baby is well protected and cushioned in the amniotic sac.

If I have an orgasm, will this upset the baby?

There is no evidence to indicate that orgasm causes harm to the baby. However, you may feel or be more aware of tightening of the womb after having an orgasm in late pregnancy.

Will intercourse trigger my labour?

The physical stimulation to the neck of the womb and semen coming into contact with the top of the vagina and cervix can stimulate contractions, especially in late pregnancy. Physical stimulation encourages chemicals called prostaglandins to be produced by the neck of the womb and semen also contains prostaglandins, which play a role in encouraging softening of the cervix prior to labour and also in stimulating contraction of the womb. Indeed, doctors

Lifestyle in pregnancy

use synthetic prostaglandins to induce labour. However, do not worry that intercourse will put you into premature labour. Intercourse, while it can stimulate contractions at any time during pregnancy, will only encourage labour when you body is ready to go into labour itself.

Will intercourse feel the same when I am pregnant?

Many women find that the sensations from intercourse are heightened in pregnancy. This is because the blood flow to the pelvis and genitals is increased and the tissues are swollen, making them more sensitive. Your breasts will also be more sensitive, making physical arousal easier. You will probably feel more lubricated because of the increased vaginal secretions associated with the increased blood flow. In addition, your orgasm may be more intense and last longer. In early pregnancy, when you feel tired and nauseated, you may not feel like making love. Usually the tiredness and nausea diminish by the 14th week, however, and you will start to feel more sexual again.

What positions are best for intercourse in pregnancy?

In early pregnancy there is no need to change the positions in which you like to have intercourse. In later pregnancy the missionary position can become uncomfortable, though, and you may need to adapt to ensure that the positions you use are comfortable for you both. There is no 'best' position. Experiment to find the positions that suit you best. In late pregnancy, for instance, you could try being on top during intercourse, which will avoid putting any weight on your abdomen and give you good control over the depth of penetration. Lying side by side with your partner can often be comfortable, too, or try a sitting position with you on your partner's lap. Your partner entering you from the rear while you are on all fours will also keep pressure off of your abdomen.

Travel during pregnancy

Can I fly when I am pregnant?

Flying is not usually a problem in pregnancy, although most airlines will not accept you after around 34–36 weeks, mainly in case you go into labour while airborne. If you are expecting twins or have specific problems like diabetes, thrombosis, heart disease, vaginal bleeding or a history of premature labour, you should check with your doctor before flying. Flying in the pressurised cabin of a commercial airliner presents no risk to your developing baby, but some airlines request a doctor's letter to indicate that you are not at risk of premature labour before accepting you as a passenger after around 28 weeks of pregnancy. It is clearly best to check with the airline well in advance to avoid arriving at the airport and finding you are not allowed to fly.

Are there any precautions I should take if I am flying?

Long-distance airline travel is recognised to raise slightly the risk of blood clots in the leg (deep vein thrombosis), due to several factors including immobility, low cabin pressure and dehydration (often exacerbated by excessive consumption of alcohol and caffeine on the flight). Prolonged periods of immobility, whether or not on an aeroplane, increase the risk of thrombosis in the legs, as does pregnancy itself *(see p. 191)*, although the overall risk is very low, at around 1 in 1000 pregnancies. It is not yet known how great the risk of developing a blood clot is in pregnant women on long-haul flights. However, the more risk factors a woman has for blood clots, the greater the chance of a clot forming. So it makes sense to think about this risk when planning to travel long distances by air. The main risk factors to bear in mind are being very overweight, a medical condition that increases the risk of clotting, having had a blood clot before or a family history of blood clots (suggesting that there may be an inherited factor that makes the woman more likely to have a clot).

Official guidelines are beginning to be published on this issue. It is suggested that if the pregnant woman has no additional risk factors then for a flight lasting three hours or less she should simply avoid dehydration, minimise her intake of alcohol and coffee, perform calf-muscle exercises and move around the cabin whenever possible.

For flights of over three hours' duration she should also wear special support or 'compression' stockings. These are very effective at preventing leg swelling, which can be quite marked when you fly during pregnancy. Avoid support tights, however, as these can make you very warm, which will encourage thrush infection. You need to put on these special stockings before going aboard the aeroplane. Comfortable, fairly loose-fitting shoes, such as trainers or slip-on sandals, are also recommended as it is often difficult to get your shoes on at the end of a flight because of swelling.

Women with additional risk factors, such as having a history of blood clots or being very overweight, should obtain specific medical advice. They may need to take specific medication to prevent clotting, especially on long-haul flights, in addition to following all the advice outlined above.

How to prevent deep vein thrombosis when flying

- Do stretching exercises with your legs while sitting
- Take plenty of fluids, avoiding caffeine and alcohol
- Take frequent walks up and down the aisle
- Wear compression stockings
- If you have a history of thrombosis, obtain specialist medical advice before flying

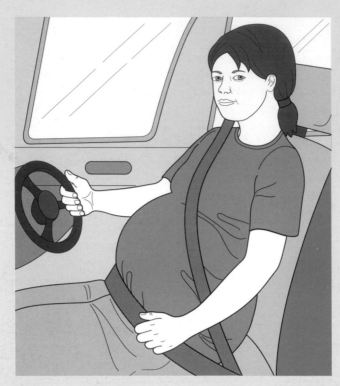

Correct use of a seat belt in pregnancy. The lap belt should be as low as possible beneath the 'bump'. The shoulder belt should pass above the 'bump', running between the breasts. If necessary, adjust the seat belt to fit snugly.

Is it safe to wear a seat belt when I am travelling by car?

It is important to continue wearing a seat belt while travelling by car. Automobile accidents can happen when you are pregnant, after all. The risk of dying in an automobile accident is around 1 in 3 for pregnant women thrown from the car (not wearing a seat belt) and just over 1 in 20 for those not ejected (wearing a seat belt). The risk of the unborn baby being killed is around 50:50 for women thrown from a car and around 1 in 10 for those not ejected. As seat belts will usually restrain drivers and passengers, they reduce the risk of death and major injury, whether in pregnancy or not.

The correct positioning of the seat belt is to place the lap belt as low as possible beneath your bump, so that it rests on the upper thighs. The diagonal shoulder strap should be placed above your bump lying between your breasts. A three-point restraint is still necessary in pregnancy. It used to be considered that a lap belt was sufficient, but in fact research has shown that this is worse for the unborn baby. The risk of the unborn baby dying is less with a three-point restraint than with a lap belt because both mother and child are less likely to sustain internal injuries.

Should I continue to drive when I am pregnant?

There is no reason for you to stop driving if you have an uncomplicated pregnancy. After 36–37 weeks, however, it is best not to drive anywhere alone for anything other than short distances, just in case you go into labour.

Diet in pregnancy

When you are pregnant you need to continue with the same healthy diet and balance of nutrients that you needed when you were preparing for pregnancy and the detailed advice given in *Preparing your body for pregnancy (p. 28)* applies equally during pregnancy.

What type of vitamin supplements do I need for pregnancy?

The requirements for protein, iron, calcium, vitamins B, C, D and E increase in pregnancy, but a well-balanced diet will usually provide you with enough protein, vitamins and minerals to meet these extra demands. As when preparing for pregnancy, the only vitamin supplement you need is folic acid.

Why do I need extra folic acid?

As we saw in *Preparing your body for pregnancy*, folic acid is essential for the formation of the developing baby and for the production of healthy red blood cells. In pregnancy there is a significant increase in the number of red blood cells in your body, around 25% on average by 32 weeks of pregnancy. So there is an extra demand for folic acid not just for the baby but also for you. *See pp. 29–33* for a fuller discussion of the benefits of folic acid and how to ensure you get enough during pregnancy.

Do I need vitamin supplements other than folic acid during pregnancy?

Other vitamin supplements are not usually required in pregnancy. If you have specific medical or nutritional problems, you may need additional vitamins and should discuss this with your doctor. As when trying to conceive, you should avoid a high intake of vitamin A *(see p. 34)*.

Is iron important when I am pregnant?

Maintaining an adequate iron intake is equally important during your pregnancy as it was when planning your pregnancy *(see p. 34)*. If you have an adequate intake of iron in your diet before and during your pregnancy, you will usually be able to meet your own and your developing baby's needs. However, there are some women who will be more likely to have low iron stores in pregnancy, such as those expecting twins or triplets *(see also box on p. 35)*. If you are at risk of having low iron stores, you might need iron supplements.

You can maximise the absorption of iron if you take the iron tablet with a citrus drink like fresh orange juice, which is rich in vitamin C (important for treating anaemia).

If you suffer from heartburn or indigestion, do not take your iron supplements at the same time as your antacid medicine as this will reduce the absorption of iron. Iron supplements are often combined with folic acid, frequently in the same tablet. As folic acid, like iron, is essential for the formation of red blood cells, you will require both to prevent or treat anaemia. Your doctor will be able to advise you about this.

How much more food do I need during pregnancy?

Despite the old adage about eating for two in pregnancy, there is actually no need to increase substantially your food intake as your body becomes much more efficient in its use of food and energy when you are pregnant. In late pregnancy your energy intake should be increased by about 10%, which amounts to an additional 200 calories for the average woman. This amount of calories can be gained by eating a large bowl of cornflakes with semi-skimmed milk, or two medium slices of wholemeal bread, very lightly buttered, although the amount can be spread out over several smaller meals if a large portion cannot be eaten in one sitting at this stage of pregnancy. *(See table opposite for recommended quantities of different types of food.)*

What foods should I avoid in pregnancy?

There are certain foods that are best avoided when you are pregnant, chiefly because of the risk of infection, and these are discussed in detail in Preparing your body for pregnancy *(p. 37)*. Remember, too, that while fish can be an excellent source of essential fatty acids, important for the development of the baby's nervous system, certain sea fish should be avoided because of their high mercury content *(see p. 37)*.

Do I need to increase my fluid intake?

It is a good idea to increase your fluid intake in pregnancy. You should aim to drink around six glasses of water a day. Along with an increase in fibre in your diet, this will help to prevent constipation, which is common in pregnancy. Water is better than coffee, tea and soft drinks, such as cola. Fizzy drinks often have a high sugar (and calorie) content and can exacerbate heartburn, a common problem in pregnancy.

Why do I need fibre in my diet in pregnancy?

Fibre or roughage is found in foods derived from plants. Fibre cannot be digested and absorbed by our bodies and so it stays in the bowel, providing roughage. It can be broken down to some extent by bacteria in the large bowel and some of these breakdown products can be absorbed and used as a source of energy. Because it provides roughage for the bowel – aiding the process of peristalsis by which the food is pushed through the gut – it is important in ensuring that bowel function is normal and in preventing constipation. This is especially important in pregnancy when your bowel function often slows down due to the effect of pregnancy hormones on the intestine. Many women thus find constipation a problem during pregnancy, and eating a fibre-rich diet is very good at preventing this. You should eat foods with a high-fibre content, such as bran flakes, wholegrain cereals, and fruit and vegetables *(see table, overleaf)*. However, if you increase your fibre intake suddenly, you may find that you feel bloated and have excess wind,

Recommended amounts of food to eat in pregnancy

Food type	Servings per day
Carbohydrates (e.g. bread, potatoes, pasta, rice)	4–6
Fruit and vegetables (e.g. broccoli, tomatoes, carrots, courgettes, oranges, apples, bananas, apricots, avocados, pure fruit juice)	5–7
Protein-rich foods (e.g. fish, meat, chicken, eggs, nuts and pulses)	2
Calcium-rich foods (e.g. milk, yoghurt, cheese)	Half a litre (a pint) of milk per day or a quarter litre (half a pint) of milk and a yoghurt or portion of cheese

A diet that is high in fibre includes wholemeal bread, breakfast cereal, fresh fruit and vegetables and pasta.

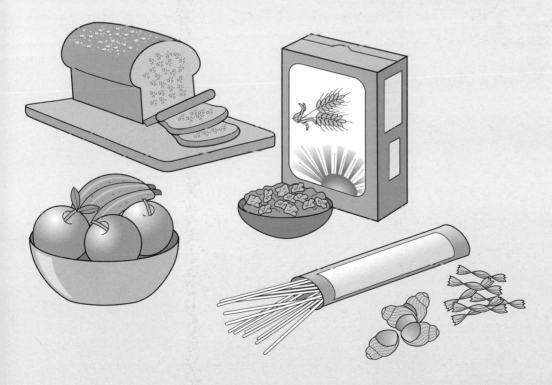

Typical fibre content of various foods

Bran flakes	3.4 g per 30 g (1 oz) serving
Wholemeal bread	3.3 g per thick slice
Pasta	3 g per 100 g ($3^1/2$ oz) serving
Apple	2.3 g per apple
Banana	1.3 g in an average-sized banana
White bread	1 g per medium slice
Cornflakes	0.9 g per 30 g (1 oz) serving

so it is better to increase your intake gradually. You should also 'match' the increase in fibre with an increase in fluid intake, preferably water. Ideally, you should have around 18 g ($^1/2$ oz) of fibre each day in your diet.

Is a vegetarian diet adequate during pregnancy?

There are not usually any problems with a well-balanced vegetarian diet during pregnancy; indeed, you will have some benefits, such as increased fibre in your diet from all the fruit and vegetables. Follow the advice given in *Preparing your body for pregnancy (p. 28)*.

Weight gain

How much weight should I gain during pregnancy?

Unless you are very underweight or overweight, doctors are not too concerned about weight gain in pregnancy. This is because the growth of the baby is not dependent on your weight gain, but rather upon the efficiency of transfer of vital nutrients across the placenta. However, on average, women gain around 12 kg (26 lb) during pregnancy. Some women gain less and some more, depending on several factors including how heavy you are to start with and how big your baby is. If you are worried about gaining too much or too little weight in pregnancy, you should discuss this with your doctor. If you are underweight or overweight, you may need specific advice from your doctor about diet and weight gain.

What makes up the weight gain in pregnancy?

Of the 12 kg (26 lb) weight gain in an 'average' pregnancy, most of this is made up by the womb, baby, placenta and amniotic fluid, which by full term

What the weight gain in pregnancy consists of

Baby	3.3 kg (7 lb 4 oz)
Placenta	0.5 kg (1 lb)
Amniotic fluid	0.8 kg (1 lb 12 oz)
Increase in weight of the womb	0.8 kg (1 lb 12 oz)
Breasts	0.4 kg (14 oz)
Blood volume	1.3 kg (2 lb 12 oz)
Fat	3.5 kg (7 lb 11 oz)
Fluid retention	1.4 kg (3 lb)

will weigh almost 6 kg (13 lb) in total. Extra fat and an increase in the weight of your breasts account for around 3.5–4 kg (7^1/$_2$–9 lb) of the weight gain, while the rest is made up of an increase in the volume of your blood and by retained fluid. These estimates vary enormously from woman to woman and the figures given are simply an illustration of how the weight gain is made up.

I have been on a diet to lose weight. Should I continue this in pregnancy?
Dieting to lose a lot of weight is not advisable or recommended during pregnancy. This is because you may disturb your nutritional balance at crucial stages of your baby's development. However, limiting weight gain in pregnancy is important for women who are overweight *(see p. 168)*. This can be achieved by carbohydrate restriction. It is usual to try to restrict weight gain to around 6 kg (13 lb), which is half of the usual weight gain in pregnancy. Most women who are overweight and who gain no or very little weight in pregnancy appear to have healthy babies. Limiting weight gain will reduce the risk of pregnancy complications such as high blood pressure and help prevent having a very large baby. It is important to discuss this with your doctor, who can give you specific advice about your weight and weight gain in pregnancy.

Exercise during pregnancy

Can I exercise in pregnancy?
In contrast to many years ago when women were advised to rest as much as possible and avoid strenuous exercise during pregnancy, doctors now know

that moderate exercise is beneficial. Athletes who continue training in pregnancy actually have an improved performance after the pregnancy as the pregnancy-induced changes in the cardiovascular system enhance the effect of training. Not only does regular exercise make you feel better and fitter, it also helps prepare you physically for labour and delivery. Walking, cycling, swimming and stretching are all good forms of exercise in pregnancy. However, you should avoid activities that are likely to lead to any falls or impacts on your abdomen such as contact sports. In later pregnancy, activities where balance is important, such as horse riding, can be hazardous due to the change in your centre of gravity. Swimming is a particularly good form of exercise when you are pregnant. This is because the water supports your body and you can exercise your arms, legs and back and also improve cardiovascular fitness without straining your body. Yoga is also a good form of exercise and an ideal preparation for labour because of the muscular stretching, control of breathing and posture, and emphasis on relaxation.

I haven't been taking regular exercise. Can I start in pregnancy?

If you are not used to regular exercise, you should start gradually with a low-intensity, low-impact activity like swimming or walking. A brisk 30 minutes of walking, ideally with part of it uphill, three times a week, will lead to improvements in fitness within two weeks. This will build up your stamina, which is one of the major objectives of exercising in pregnancy. Before you start each exercise session, it is worth spending 4–5 minutes on muscle warm-ups. A 'cool down' period of gradually declining exercise at the end of exercise is also advisable. It is usually best to limit your activity to 15-minute periods with five minutes' rest in between each session. However, if you have any medical or obstetric problems, you should consult your doctor before starting any exercise programme.

Can I have a sauna or hot tub after exercise?

The problem of saunas and hot tubs is the risk of getting overheated, which is more likely in pregnancy, especially after exercise, and can make you faint. They are best avoided. If you do have a sauna, however, you should limit the time to no longer than five minutes and also limit the temperature to less than 82°C (179.6°F). If you have a hot tub, limit the time to a maximum of 15 minutes at a temperature of less than 39°C (102.2°F). If you feel uncomfortable or faint, get out immediately. You should also make sure that you maintain your fluid intake as the heat can be very dehydrating.

Are there exercises or activities I should avoid?

You should avoid prolonged, high-intensity training. Do not get overheated or dehydrated; in particular, do not exercise if you have a high temperature. Ensure that you always have a good fluid intake after vigorous exercise. In terms of exercises, you should avoid sit-ups and straight leg raising while on your back. These can strain your abdominal muscles, which are already stretched by the growing pregnancy. The two large muscles that run longitudinally down the middle of your abdomen (known collectively as the rectus abdominus) normally separate in pregnancy to help accommodate the growing pregnancy. Exercises that stretch these muscles, such as sit-ups and straight leg raising, will stress these muscles further, which will slow down the speed at which they get back to normal after the pregnancy. In addition, when you get up from lying down, you should take care not to strain these abdominal muscles. Roll over on to your side, push yourself up with your arms, then get into a kneeling position and stand up, one leg at a time and keeping your back straight. Another reason not to exercise while lying on your back in pregnancy is to avoid feeling faint. When you are pregnant and lie on your back, the weight of the pregnancy can obstruct the large blood vessels in your abdomen, which are returning blood to the heart. The heart therefore has less blood to pump out and as a result you can feel faint.

If you feel any strain during exercise, you should stop at once to prevent damage to your ligaments. Your ligaments – very strong fibrous bands of tissue that hold bones together, including those of the pelvis – soften in pregnancy to allow more room in the pelvis to help ease the passage of the baby through the birth canal. However, this softening also makes them more likely to be strained if you stretch too far.

I usually jog several times a week. Can I continue this?
From 20 weeks onwards, it is thought best by some doctors to avoid exercises, such as jogging and jumping, that cause the womb and the baby to bounce up and down on your pelvic floor because this might lead to weakening of your pelvic floor. Other doctors believe that moderate amounts of jogging are not harmful, however. Jogging can stress your joints and your breasts, so if you do jog, wear a supportive sports bra and running shoes that will absorb some of the shock.

If you are a serious runner and jog frequently, it is probably best to reduce the number of kilometres you do after 28 weeks of pregnancy, and further reduce it after 36 weeks. This is because there is some concern that strenuous prolonged exercise at this stage of pregnancy could reduce the blood supply to the baby. You can, of course, replace jogging with less strenuous forms of exercise in later pregnancy.

Are there any medical conditions or pregnancy complications where exercise should be avoided?
You should avoid vigorous or strenuous exercise in certain situations and in other conditions more care and supervision may be required (see box overleaf). If you have one of these problems, you should talk to your doctor about exercise before you embark on it in pregnancy. It is sometimes best to restrict yourself to stretching-type exercises only.

Exercise in pregnancy

Conditions where strenuous exercise should usually be avoided

- Significant heart disease
- Recurrent miscarriage, particularly due to cervical incompetence
- Premature labour
- Ruptured membranes
- Vaginal bleeding in pregnancy
- A small-for-dates baby

Conditions where strenuous exercise in pregnancy needs more care and supervision

- Diabetes
- High blood pressure
- Anaemia

What are pelvic floor exercises?

The pelvic floor is a sheet of muscle and fibrous tissue lying across the bottom of the pelvis. It supports the pelvic organs, including the bladder, part of the bowel and the womb, while the vagina, bowel and urethra (the tube that takes the urine from the bladder to the outside) pass through it. The pelvic floor therefore helps you to keep control of your bladder and bowel function. When you want to stop passing urine mid-stream, it is the pelvic floor muscles that you will contract.

Unfortunately, these muscles can be stretched and damaged by the stress of pregnancy and delivery, which can lead to problems such as stress incontinence where increased pressure on the pelvic floor, such as with coughing, leads to a small leak of urine from the bladder. It thus makes sense to strengthen the pelvic floor during pregnancy to minimise the risk of problems later on. Pelvic floor exercises are designed to do this and should be performed both during and after pregnancy.

How do I do pelvic floor exercises?

First you pull up and tense the muscles round your urethra, vagina and rectum as if you are interrupting the flow of urine. Hold this for several seconds then release, relax and repeat several times. You should perform a series of pelvic floor exercises several times per day: 4–5 sets of 10 exercises is usually satisfactory. Many women try to fit these exercises into their daily routine, such as doing them each time they pass urine.

How can I avoid back strain?

The increased load on your body from the growing pregnancy often leads to backache. You need to think about your posture and avoid stooping or slumping forward as this will stress your back more. When you are sitting, it is a good idea to tuck a cushion behind the lower part of your back to help you sit up straight. You should avoid exercises and activities that might strain your back. Do not do any heavy lifting or load bearing as this can strain your back. If you have to lift something heavy, like a young child, you should bend your legs to get down, keep your back straight and lift by straightening your legs. Keep the child close to your body as lifting something at arms' length will add to the strain on your back.

Lifestyle in pregnancy

First trimester

0–13 Weeks

Your first trimester begins when your last period occurs and an egg starts to mature in your ovary. At the end of the second week your ovary releases a mature egg, which is 'picked up' by the finger-like ends of your fallopian tube. It is transported down the tube. Fertilisation of the egg by your partner's sperm occurs about one-third of the way down the tube. The fertilised egg is just a single cell, but not for long: it continues its journey down your fallopian tube to your womb, constantly dividing. At the end of the third week, only seven days after fertilisation, the ball of cells is implanted into the lining of your womb. Your developing baby is now an embryo.

4 WEEKS

Embryo size: The gestation sac is approximately 3 mm ($1/8$ in) in diameter and the embryo is just big enough to be seen by the naked eye.

Embryo development: Your embryo will develop within a bag of fluid in your womb, called the gestation sac. This sac is made up of membranes that contain the amniotic fluid that the baby grows in. The ball of cells making up the embryo grows into three distinct layers. The innermost layer, called the endoderm, will become the lungs, liver and intestines. The middle layer, called the mesoderm, will become the bones making up the skeleton, muscles and also the heart and blood vessels. The outermost layer, called the ectoderm, will form the brain and nervous system as well as the skin, hair and the lenses of the eyes.

The brain and eyes are already starting to develop by the end of week four.

6 WEEKS

Embryo size: The gestation sac is around 2 cm ($3/4$ in) in diameter. The embryo is 4–6 mm ($1/6$–$1/4$ in) long, cylindrical in form with a head and tail end present.

Embryo development: Amazingly a basic heart has already formed and an ultrasound scan will usually be able to visualise the heart beating. The limbs appear as tiny buds from the body. A rudimentary brain and spinal cord have formed and the lower jaw starts to form. The eyes start to develop as pigmented discs on either side of the head; as they develop further they will move round to the front of the head. The lungs, eyelids and ears also start to develop.

Changes to the mother: You will have missed your period and you may feel tired.

The umbilical cord linking the embryo to the afterbirth has formed.

8 WEEKS

Embryo size: The gestation sac is 3–5 cm ($1/8$–$1/5$ in) in diameter, and the embryo is approximately 15–18 mm ($3/5$–$3/4$ in) long.

Embryo development: The face is forming and tiny nostrils will be present. The upper and lower jaws have formed. The nervous system is developing. The heart is fully formed. The bladder, kidney and voicebox or larynx have developed. The elbows, eyelids, teeth and nipples start to appear. The tissues that will form the bones of the spine are developing.

The limbs are now well developed, with fingers and toes present; tiny movements are just discernible.

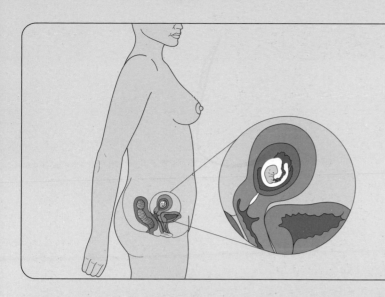

8 Weeks

- gestation sac is 3–5 cm (1$\frac{1}{4}$–2 in) in diameter

- embryo is around 15–18 mm ($\frac{3}{5}$–$\frac{3}{4}$ in) long

- the face is forming

- the heart has formed

Foetal size: The foetus is now over 3 cm (1$\frac{1}{4}$ in) long and weighs about 5 g.

Foetal development: From 9 weeks your developing baby is called a foetus rather than an embryo. The head is now a recognisably human shape. The trunk lengthens and becomes straighter and calcium starts to deposit in the bones of the skeleton. The internal organs have all formed and the limbs are becoming well defined. The arms and legs can move and the hands can move towards each other. The hard palate (the roof of the mouth) has developed. The ankles and wrists have formed. The brain is developing very rapidly.

Muscles are forming and both startle and general movements can be seen, although you will not be able to feel them for about 9 weeks.

10 WEEKS

Foetal size: The foetus is 5–6 cm (2–2$\frac{1}{4}$ in) long with a head circumference of over 6 cm (2$\frac{1}{4}$ in). The weight will have increased to about 18 g (just over $\frac{1}{2}$ oz).

Foetal development: By this stage the head containing the rapidly developing brain makes up around half the total body length, but the developing baby is recognisably human. If you were able to look at your baby at this stage, you could tell whether it is a boy or a girl. The baby will make breathing movements with its chest. When this happens the amniotic fluid around the baby flows in and out of the lungs, which is important for the lungs to develop normally. Finger and toenails are starting to develop. The foetus will start to pass 'urine' and can swallow the amniotic fluid.

Girl babies: The ovaries have started to form.

Boy babies: The testicles initially form in the abdomen. They descend into the scrotum later.

Your baby will be able to move around easily in the amniotic fluid, but you still won't feel these movements, as the baby is still small.

12 WEEKS

Some complications to look out for in the first trimester

Miscarriage and ectopic pregnancy: the key symptoms are lower abdominal pain and vaginal bleeding **See pp. 76–86** Morning sickness: if severe, seek the advice of your doctor to avoid problems such as dehydration **See p. 67**.

First trimester

Antenatal care & pregnancy complications

The vast majority of women remain healthy during pregnancy – pregnancy is a natural state, after all, and not an illness. But serious problems can arise both for you, the mother, and the baby. These problems might not only affect the pregnancy but can also affect you and your baby's future health and well-being. This is why regular checks by healthcare professionals during pregnancy are so particularly important. The aim of antenatal care is to prevent or identify and treat problems at an early stage so that both you and your baby remain healthy. It also provides an opportunity for health education, which can contribute to a healthy and safe pregnancy.

Antenatal visits

How is antenatal care provided?

Many healthcare professionals are involved in antenatal care. The main providers are family doctors, midwives and obstetricians, but physiotherapists, dieticians and other professions allied to medicine may be involved, depending on your needs. Antenatal care may be set in local community clinics or in hospital clinics or shared between community and hospital. The arrangement varies from place to place and from country to country, but care is organised to meet the particular needs of the mother. If you have a medical problem like

The aims of antenatal care are to:

- Treat minor problems you might encounter in pregnancy, e.g. heartburn
- Identify and treat any pre-existing medical conditions you may have, e.g. diabetes, epilepsy or heart disease
- Check whether you are at risk of complications arising in pregnancy, and if possible prevent these complications; e.g. if you are at risk of anaemia, this can be prevented with iron and vitamin supplements
- Identify and treat any new problems you may develop in your pregnancy, e.g. pre-eclampsia
- Make a plan for your labour and delivery
- Provide information on infant feeding and care
- Offer family planning advice, if required, for after delivery
- Provide advice, reassurance, education and support for you and your family regarding all aspects of pregnancy

diabetes, you will usually be seen at a specialist clinic. If you have no problems and have previously had one or more uncomplicated pregnancies and deliveries then you will be considered to be at low risk of developing complications and are therefore likely to receive most of your care in the community. Obviously, should a problem arise requiring more medical or 'high tech' input, this will be provided. The important issue is to ensure that you get the right level of care to meet your needs.

What happens on the first visit to the clinic?

The usual pattern in the UK is for you to have your pregnancy confirmed by your family doctor. You will then be referred to a hospital or community clinic. The first visit to the clinic is usually between 8–12 weeks after your last period. The earlier that you confirm your pregnancy and attend your doctor, the earlier you will be seen at the clinic. This first visit is often the longest as you will be asked detailed questions about your current and past health, your family history of medical problems and any previous pregnancies (see box overleaf). The answers to these questions help the doctor determine if you are at risk of any particular problems in pregnancy and help identify the right pattern of antenatal care for your particular needs. The outcome of any previous pregnancy is especially important in predicting problems in later pregnancies and deliveries. In addition, screening for foetal abnormality will be discussed at this visit – such as the nuchal ultrasound scan, the triple test and a detailed anomaly ultrasound scan (see pp. 120–4) – and organised as necessary. If there are specific problems to consider, amniocentesis or CVS may also be discussed (also see pp. 120–4).

Antenatal care & pregnancy complications

At the first visit, you will also be examined physically, taking into account any problems or medical conditions, such as high blood pressure or anaemia, and certain tests will be performed *(see box below)*.

Do I need to do anything to prepare for the first visit?

The main thing you should do before your first visit is to think about any questions or concerns that you and your partner have about your pregnancy and its management. It is easy to forget all the things you want to discuss when

What happens at the first visit to the antenatal clinic

The doctor or midwife will request:
- Details of your medical and family history
- Details of any medication that you are on
- A detailed pregnancy history for any previous pregnancies
- The date of your last menstrual period
- Details of any contraception used

Physical examination by the doctor:
- Blood pressure taken
- External examination of your abdomen – an internal (vaginal) examination is not usually required
- Measurement of your height and weight

Tests performed:
- Your urine will be checked for infection and also for the presence of sugar or protein
- An ultrasound scan to confirm the stage of your pregnancy and check for twins
- A cervical smear test can be carried out safely, if required

Blood tests to check for:
- Anaemia and your blood group
- Sickle-cell anaemia and thalassaemia, if required
- Syphilis, immunity to rubella (German measles), and hepatitis infection
- HIV testing may be performed after counselling

Future tests discussed:
- Screening for foetal abnormality, e.g. nuchal ultrasound scan, triple test, detailed anomaly ultrasound scan
- Amniocentesis and CVS, if required

you are at the clinic, and writing down a list of questions to ask can be very helpful. If you have particular preferences about the type of care you want or how you want to deliver then it is a good idea to raise these at your first visit and discuss them with the obstetrician or midwife. It is useful to check the date of your last period and also whether there are any family illnesses that may be relevant, before coming to the clinic. For many women, pregnancy – especially if it is their first or where a previous pregnancy has been complicated – can be a frightening experience, so it is essential that you and your partner raise all your anxieties and ask questions so you can discuss these issues fully with the obstetrician or midwife.

Why is urine taken?

A urine sample is needed to check for the presence of protein and glucose (sugar). Protein in the urine can indicate a kidney problem, bladder infection or pre-eclampsia *(see p. 136)*. Glucose can be found in your urine due to a diabetes problem, but it is not uncommon for small amounts of glucose to be present in the urine in a normal pregnancy, especially if you have eaten before providing the sample. The urine is usually checked specifically for infection at your first visit, as bladder and kidney infections are more common in pregnancy and may be more severe.

What blood tests will be performed?

Several blood tests are taken at the first visit. These check for anaemia, identify your blood group, and see if you are immune to German measles *(see p. 149)*. In the UK syphilis is screened for as this sexually transmitted disease can affect the baby. Although infection during pregnancy is rare in the UK, it can be easily and safely treated. Indeed, it is very important to cure the disease during pregnancy or the baby would otherwise get congenital syphilis. Other infections like hepatitis *(see p. 155)* are also screened for. If there is a risk of certain blood disorders (sickle-cell anaemia, or thalassaemia – *see p. 17*), your blood will be screened specifically for these. Some hospitals offer screening to determine if you and your partner are carriers of cystic fibrosis *(see p. 17)*. Additional blood tests will be required if you have a particular medical disorder, such as SLE, blood-clotting problems, diabetes or thryoid disease (all four conditions covered later in this chapter).

Will I need an internal (vaginal) examination?

Before the days of reliable ultrasound, it was usual for doctors to perform an internal examination at the first visit. The purpose of this was to check the size of the womb to determine if it was consistent with the menstrual dates as there was no other way of estimating the stage of the pregnancy. The pelvic examination would also identify any ovarian cysts *(see p. 86)* and check that the size of the pelvis was big enough for delivery. Ultrasound scans now provide much more information than a clinical examination with regard to dating a pregnancy, as well as identifying any ovarian cysts. The routine clinical

Antenatal care & pregnancy complications

estimation of pelvic size is no longer considered to be of value, as the best test of whether your pelvis is big enough for the baby to pass through is usually labour itself. An internal examination is therefore no longer part of routine examination at the first visit. However, if you have a specific problem, such as an abnormal vaginal discharge or bleeding after intercourse, then an internal examination might be required to diagnose and treat the problem.

I am due a smear test. Can I have one when I am pregnant?

If your cervical smear test is due, or overdue, you can have it checked in early pregnancy. This will not affect the pregnancy. A smear test involves the doctor gently scraping the surface of the neck of the womb (cervix) to obtain cells for testing for cervical abnormalities. It is not a painful procedure though it may be slightly uncomfortable.

Can I hear the baby's heartbeat?

Your doctor or midwife will be able to let you hear your baby's heartbeat using a small ultrasound device held against your abdomen.

Will I get an ultrasound scan?

An ultrasound scan will usually be performed at your first visit to confirm that the pregnancy is continuing and also establish your estimated date of delivery. It can provide additional information such as whether you are having twins and whether there is an ovarian cyst. A scan is often repeated at 11–16 weeks to confirm the stage of the pregnancy.

How often will I be seen after the first visit?

Traditionally in the UK pregnant women are seen at around every four weeks from diagnosis of pregnancy until week 28 of gestation, fortnightly until week 36 of gestation and then weekly until delivery. It is questionable whether low-risk woman with an uncomplicated pregnancy need so many assessments, but the correct frequency of assessment is not scientifically established and so this depends on the judgement of your doctor or midwife and should, of course, take into account your specific needs. An assessment of risk will determine the type of care you require. This risk assessment will be based on the medical information obtained at the first visit, the results of tests and any new complications or problems that develop. It is important to remember that your level of risk can change, up or down, as problems develop or resolve.

What sort of factors can indicate a higher level of risk for the pregnancy?

Examples of risk factors are shown in the table opposite. If you have no risk factors you will be designated 'low risk', but remember that risk factors, such as pre-eclampsia and breech presentation *(see p. 232)*, can be 'acquired' later in pregnancy and they will only be identified through good antenatal care and having regular checks.

Risk factors for pregnancy and delivery

General risk factors:
- Age under 16 or over 35
- The mother being very overweight or underweight (BMI more than 31 or less than 20)
- More than four previous pregnancies
- Pre-existing medical conditions, e.g. diabetes, blood clots or high blood pressure
- A history of alcohol or drug abuse
- A family history of foetal abnormality, genetic or chromosomal abnormality, or problems with thrombosis

Past pregnancy problems:
- Previous Caesarean section(s)
- Previous severe high blood pressure or pre-eclampsia
- Previous pregnancy complicated by premature labour
- Previous pregnancy complicated by an abnormality in the baby
- A small baby in a previous pregnancy (less than 2.5 kg/5 lb 8 oz at birth)
- A very big baby in a previous pregnancy (one that weighed more than 4.5 kg/10 lb at birth)
- Severe difficulty with delivery of the baby's shoulders in a previous pregnancy
- Previous stillbirth or neonatal death
- Recurrent miscarriages

Problems in the present pregnancy:
- Excess or reduced fluid round the baby
- Threatened premature labour
- Pre-eclampsia or high blood pressure
- Twins or triplets
- A very big baby
- A very small baby
- Breech presentation
- Bleeding in pregnancy

What happens at my subsequent antenatal checks?

At subsequent check-ups an enquiry will be made into any new problems. Your blood pressure will be checked and a urine specimen examined for protein and sugar. Your abdomen will be examined and the size of your womb assessed to ensure that your pregnancy is growing normally. Many doctors or midwives use a measuring tape. They measure from the pubic bone in the midline to the highest part of the womb, known as the fundus. The highest part is usually to one side of the midline, most commonly the right side as the womb often deviates to that side when it grows in pregnancy. In later pregnancy it is usual to check how the baby is lying in the womb and identify whether the baby's head or bottom (breech) is in your pelvis. You will be asked if you can feel your baby move as this is sign of well-being. Additional blood tests may be taken to check for anaemia and also for rhesus antibodies in those mothers who are rhesus negative (see p. 147).

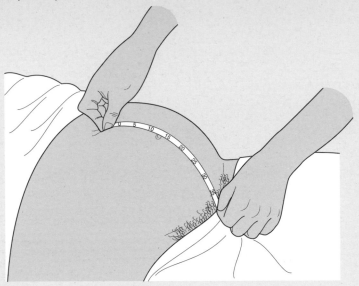

Measuring the size of the womb to check that growth is satisfactory. Doctors and midwives call this 'measuring the fundal height'. The fundus is the highest part of the womb. The measurement is taken from the pubic bone to the fundus.

Palpating the uterus. The midwife or doctor palpate your abdomen to assess what way the baby is lying and to determine where the baby's head is.

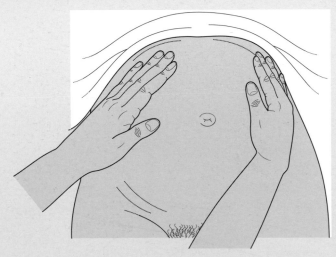

112

How big will my womb be at any stage in pregnancy?

Measuring the distance from the pubic bone to the top of the womb (fundus) gives doctors an approximate guide to the height of the womb in pregnancy. Between 16 and 36 weeks, the stage of the pregnancy in weeks should be roughly equal to the height of the womb in centimetres, give or take 1–2 cm (1/2–3/4 in). For example, the height of the womb will be around 24 cm (91/2 in) at 24 weeks and 32 cm (121/2 in) at 32 weeks of gestation. If you are concerned about the growth of your pregnancy, however, discuss this with your doctor, who will arrange an ultrasound scan, if necessary, as this can give a clearer indication of the baby's growth.

Will I have any more scans in pregnancy?

In later pregnancy you might require some more ultrasound scans if the doctor is concerned that a problem is developing or wants to check on the baby's growth. The doctor can also assess the site of the placenta and the lie and presentation of the baby if these are hard to determine by clinical examination. Ultrasound is routinely used to check the growth of twins as it is impossible to assess their size accurately by examination alone. A so-called 'detailed' or 'anomaly' scan is often offered at 18–20 weeks of pregnancy to check if the baby has any abnormality.

This illustration shows an ultrasound scan being performed. Warm jelly is placed on the skin so that the sound waves pass easily from the probe through to your body. The probe is then placed on the skin and the doctor, ultrasonographer or midwife will move the probe around to obtain a picture of the developing baby and the placenta. The image created is seen on a screen like a television set.

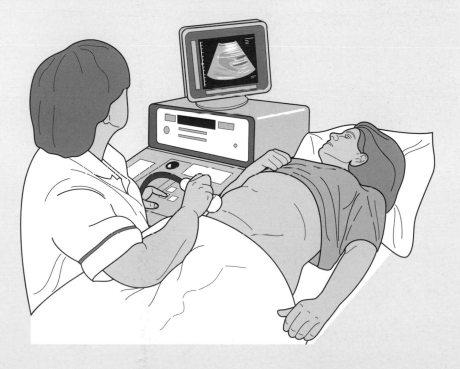

Ultrasound scans in the second and third trimesters

A detailed scan of the baby is performed in the mid-part of the second trimester at about 18–20 weeks of pregnancy. By now the face can be clearly seen, particularly when modern three-dimensional ultrasound techniques are used.

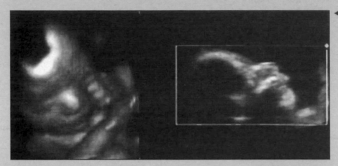

◄ A two-dimensional ultrasound scan of the baby's profile during a detailed scan in the second trimester (right). When this is imaged using three-dimensional ultrasound (left) a clear view of the face can be seen with the baby's left hand up at its eye and the right arm is visible crossing over the chest.

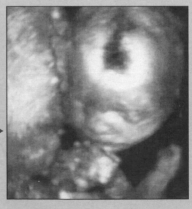

This is a cross-sectional scan through the bottom ▶ and thighs. The buttocks are to the left. The thighs are top and bottom and they are open wide; the male genitals can be seen between the open thighs.

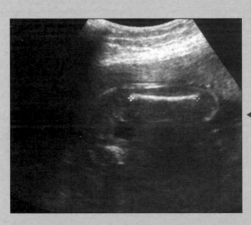

◄ The length of the femur or thigh bone can be measured as shown here. This can help estimate the age of the baby in the womb. The crosses mark each end of the thigh bone.

This three-dimensional ultrasound shows the baby's ▶ face with hand clenched in front of the face. The soft spot on the baby's head, called the fontanelle, can be seen as the dark area in the middle at the top of the forehead.

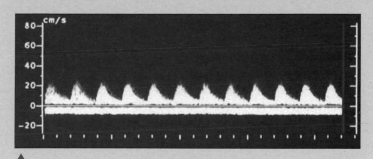

The blood flow from the baby to the afterbirth can be measured by ultrasound. The umbilical cord is identified on two-dimensional ultrasound. Then the blood flow pattern through the artery, which carries blood to the placenta, is measured. The peaks in the wave correspond to when the baby's heart contracts. This is a normal pattern.

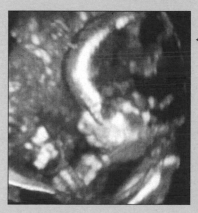

◄ This three-dimensional scan shows a baby in profile with its hand at its mouth. The other hand can also be seen in front of the face along with the two bones in the forearm and the bone of the upper arm.

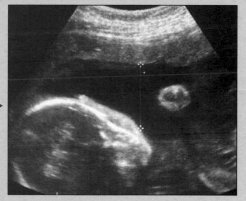

This ultrasound shows a measurement of how ► much fluid is around the baby. The depth of a pool of amniotic fluid is being measured.

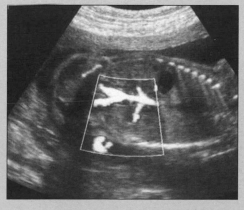

◄ This scan is using a type of ultrasound called power Doppler to 'light up' the major blood vessels. Here the aorta, the main blood vessel of the body, which runs down the trunk from the heart, is seen with its main branches going to the baby's kidneys and legs. The blood flow in the umbilical cord can also be seen at the bottom of the photograph. The shadowing of the baby's ribs is seen on the right.

Antenatal care & pregnancy complications

There are lots of abbreviations on my case record. What do they mean?

Doctors do tend to use lots of abbreviations and some medical 'jargon' to save them having to write out long words or statements time and time again. A list of some of the more common ones is shown below and overleaf. More and more women carry their own case records and it is interesting to look at what is being recorded at each stage in pregnancy. If you don't understand something, ask your doctor or midwife.

Common medical abbreviations and terms in maternity care

AFI	Amniotic fluid index: an ultrasound measure of how much fluid is round the baby in the womb
AFP	Alpha-fetoprotein: a substance found in the blood of pregnant women which can identify those at higher risk of certain foetal abnormalities, e.g. spina bifida
Alb	Albumen: a specific form of protein in the blood sometimes found in the urine when the kidneys are upset, such as with pre-eclampsia
Antenatal	The time before the baby is born
ARM	Artificial rupture of the membranes: where the doctor or midwife artificially breaks the waters during a vaginal examination, usually in labour or when labour is to be induced
APH	Antepartum haemorrhage: bleeding from the womb before the baby is born
BPP	Biophysical profile: an ultrasound test to look at the baby's movement pattern and the fluid around the baby to check that the baby is not stressed in any way
BP	Blood pressure
Br	Breech: the baby is bottom down in the womb
Ceph	Short for 'cephalic', meaning that the baby is head down in the womb

CS (or LUSCS or LSCS)	Caesarean section: LUSCS and LSCS stand for 'lower (uterine) segment Caesarean section', which is the most common type of Caesarean where the cut on the womb is across the lower part of the womb, which subsequently heals well with a strong scar
CTG	Cardiotocograph: a technique used to record the baby's heart rate in order to check that the baby is well
EDD	Expected date of delivery of the baby
Eng or E	Short for 'engaged', meaning that the biggest part of the baby's head has descended into your pelvis
Epis	Episiotomy
FD	Forceps delivery: sometimes expressed as MCFD or LCFD, meaning 'mid-cavity' or 'low-cavity forceps delivery' respectively, this indicates how high the baby's head was in the pelvis when the forceps were used
FH	Foetal heart
FHHR	Foetal heart heard and regular
FMF	Foetal movement felt
Fundus	The top of the womb
Fe	Iron, e.g. for iron tablets
GTT	Glucose tolerance test: a test for certain types of diabetes, in which the mother is given a glucose drink and the blood levels of glucose can subsequently be measured
Hb	Haemoglobin: an indication of your blood count for anaemia, which is normally above 10.5 g% in pregnancy
Hypertension	High blood pressure

Hypotension	Low blood pressure
IOL	Induction of labour
IUGR	Intrauterine growth restriction: in which a baby is smaller than it should be for the stage in pregnancy due to its growth being impaired
LFD	Large for dates
LMP	Last menstrual period
Lie	The way the baby is lying in the womb, e.g. 'longitudinal lie', where the baby is lying vertically in the mother's womb, or 'transverse lie', where the baby is lying horizontally across the womb
MSU or MSSU	Mid-stream specimen of urine
Multip	Multiparous: a woman who has had more than one pregnancy and delivery; a 'grand multip' is a woman with four or more previous pregnancies and deliveries
NAD	No abnormality detected
OA	Occipito-anterior: the back of your baby's head is pointing to the front of your pelvis
OP	Occipito-posterior: the back of your baby's head is pointing to the back of your pelvis
OT	Occipito-transverse: the back of your baby's head is pointing to one or other side of your pelvis – ROT would mean to the right and LOT to the left
Oedema or edema	Swelling of the soft tissues, such as round the ankles, due to fluid retention
Palpation	When the doctor or midwife examines your abdomen by moving their hands gently over it to determine the size, lie and presentation of the baby

Para 1, para 2, para 3	A women with one, two or three previous pregnancies and deliveries
PE or PET	Pre-eclampsia; 'PET' derives from the old term for pre-eclampsia, pre-eclamptic toxaemia
Perineum	The area of skin that is between your vagina and anus
Postnatal	The period after the birth of the baby
PPH	Post-partum haemorrhage: bleeding from the womb or vagina after delivery
Presentation or PP (presenting part)	The way your baby is pointing to the pelvis, e.g. cephalic, if its head is pointing to your pelvis, or breech, if its bottom is pointing into your pelvis
Primigravida (or prlm or para 0)	A woman in her first pregnancy
Premature or pre-term	Before 37 weeks of pregnancy
Puerperium	The first six weeks after the delivery
Quickening	The first movements of your baby, usually felt at about 18–20 weeks
Rh	Rhesus blood group
SFD	Small for dates
SROM	Spontaneous rupture of the membranes (breaking of the waters)
Term	Between 37 and 42 weeks of pregnancy, the normal stage at which delivery occurs.
U/S	Ultrasound
UTI	Urinary tract infection
VE	Vaginal examination
Vx	Vertex: the crown of the baby's head

Screening for abnormalities

How do doctors check for abnormalities in the baby before it is born?

Doctors use two approaches to try to identify babies that might have a serious abnormality: screening tests and diagnostic tests. Screening tests can be applied to large numbers of women. They don't give a definite answer as to whether your baby has an abnormality but provide an indication of your level of

Screening tests

Test	When is it done?	What does it tell you?
Nuchal (neck) ultrasound scan	10–14 weeks	Down's syndrome risk
AFP blood test (usually done as part of the double or triple test)	15–20 weeks (ideally 15–18 weeks)	Risk of neural tube defect
Double or triple blood test	15–20 weeks (ideally 15–18 weeks)	Down's syndrome risk (now often combined with the nuchal ultrasound scan)

Diagnostic tests

Test	When is it done?	What does it tell you?
Amniocentesis (sample of fluid taken from the womb)	15–18 weeks	Identifies genetic problems like Down's syndrome
CVS (sample of tissue taken from the placenta)	9–12 weeks	Identifies genetic problems like Down's syndrome
Cordocentesis (blood sample taken from the umbilical cord)	From 18 weeks	Identifies genetic abnormalities and also problems like viral infection and severe anaemia
Detailed ultrasound scan	18–20 weeks	Identifies structural abnormalities like spina bifida and cleft lip

risk for a particular abnormality. For example, a screening test for Down's syndrome might give you a risk of 1 in 1000 for the baby having Down's syndrome *(see p. 17)*. This would be a very low risk; while it does not guarantee absolutely that the baby will not be affected, it obviously would be extremely unlikely. Conversely, the screening test might give a result of 1 in 50, which would be a relatively high risk, but again does not mean that the baby is affected. Indeed, there are 49 chances out of 50 that it won't be! So screening tests help to show which mothers are more likely to have a problem, but don't provide a definite answer.

Where a definite answer is needed, a diagnostic test will be used. Here a sample of fluid, blood or tissue is taken from the womb, placenta or umbilical cord, as in amniocentesis where a sample of amniotic fluid is removed *(see overleaf)*. Because such tests are invasive, they carry a risk to the pregnancy, but a definite diagnosis can be obtained so that you will know for sure whether or not your baby is affected by a specific condition like Down's syndrome.

Do I have to have any these tests?

Whether or not you have any of these tests is entirely your own choice. Some women are happy to accept the outcome of the pregnancy no matter what, others want the reassurance of screening tests and some who might be at high risk want a diagnostic test. This is a very personal issue and your views should determine what tests, if any, are carried out. Your doctor or midwife can help advise you.

Can ultrasound tell if my baby is abnormal?

Ultrasound is one of the best ways to check that the unborn baby appears to be developing normally. By 18–20 weeks the baby is well developed and big enough to allow all the major parts of its anatomy to be seen on ultrasound scan. The sex of the baby can usually be determined, too. Many obstetricians now offer scans at this stage in order to check for any abnormality, referred to as detailed or anomaly scans. Ultrasound can be used for both screening and diagnosis.

What abnormalities can ultrasound diagnose?

The types of abnormality that can be diagnosed by ultrasound include neural tube defects like spina bifida and hydrocepahalus *(see p. 17)*, heart defects, abdominal wall defects, bladder problems, abnormalities of the limbs, and cleft lip and palate.

What is a nuchal scan?

Nuchal means 'neck', so a nuchal scan looks at the baby's neck. This is fairly new technique that has been introduced to help screen for Down's syndrome and can be performed at around 10–14 weeks. Babies with Down's syndrome have a thicker pad of fat at the back of their neck than babies without the condition. This test is by no means 100% accurate, however, as it is a screening

Antenatal care & pregnancy complications

test only. It simply aims to identify babies who are more likely to have a problem. So if your baby has a thickened nuchal pad of fat, you will usually be offered a diagnostic test such as an amniocentesis that can give you a more definite answer.

Do any blood tests help tell if the baby has an abnormality?

Yes, there are blood tests that are used to help screen for abnormalities in the baby. The most widely used screening tests on blood samples are for spina bifida (and other neural tube defects) and Down's syndrome. This blood test is usually offered between 15 and 20 weeks. Obviously it is best to get the test done as early as possible as further investigations might be required. The test measures three key substances in your blood. For this reason it is sometimes called the 'triple test', although some centres use only two of the three measurements, in which case it is called the 'double test'. The substances that are measured in the triple test are all produced by the placenta and consist of alpha-fetoprotein (AFP), oestriol and human chorionic gonadotrophin (hCG). In cases of spina bifida AFP is increased, whereas in cases of Down's syndrome there is a reduction of both AFP and oestriol while hCG is elevated. If you are found to have an increased risk of spina bifida, you will be offered a detailed ultrasound scan to look specifically at the baby's back and head. This will confirm whether or not the baby has a neural tube defect like spina bifida. If there is an increased risk of Down's syndrome, assessment of the risk may be modified via a nuchal scan. If the risk of Down's syndrome is considered high, you will be offered a test such as an amniocentesis, which will enable a definite diagnosis to be made.

What is an amniocentesis?

Amniocentesis is a procedure used to obtain a small amount of the amniotic fluid from around the unborn baby. A fine needle is inserted through the skin on your abdomen and into your womb. Ultrasound is used so that the doctor can see where the needle is going and avoid hitting the placenta or the baby. The needle is first inserted into a pool of fluid in the womb, then 10–15 ml (about three teaspoonfuls) of amniotic fluid is withdrawn by attaching a syringe to the end of the needle. This fluid contains some of the baby's cells, which are then grown in the laboratory.

From these cells doctors can determine the genetic make-up of the baby: its sex and whether it has Down's syndrome or suffers from a genetic disease like cystic fibrosis. It usually takes up to three weeks to get the final result, although sometimes a more rapid result can be obtained.

Why would I be offered an amniocentesis?

You would be offered an amniocentesis if you are over 35 years of age or if the blood test for Down's syndrome or a nuchal scan shows you are at increased risk. You might also be offered an amniocentesis if you have a family history of a genetic disease and you want to know if the baby is affected by it.

Is amniocentesis painful?

Amniocentesis can be uncomfortable for the mother so you will probably be offered a local anaesthetic to numb the skin.

When is an amniocentesis done?

This test is usually carried out at 15–18 weeks of the pregnancy.

What is CVS?

Amniocentesis is not the only procedure used to diagnose a genetic abnormality in the baby. CVS, or 'chorionic villous sampling', can also be used. The chorionic villi are the little fingers of tissue that form part of the placenta. As the placenta has the same genetic make-up as the foetus, this tissue can be used for the diagnosis of genetic and chromosomal problems in the same way as the cells cultured from amniotic fluid following an amniocentesis. The benefit of CVS is that it can be performed at 9–12 weeks and hence identify a problem earlier than can be done via amniocentesis. With CVS a needle is inserted through the abdomen and into the edge of the placenta. This is done under ultrasound control so that the doctor can guide the needle to the site of the placenta. A tiny sample of chorionic villous tissue is then sucked up the needle using a syringe. The tissue is then sent to the laboratory for the genetic make-up of the baby to be ascertained. Occasionally, CVS is performed through the vagina and cervix using a flexible plastic needle that is guided via ultrasound to the edge of the placenta and a sample of tissue is then obtained.

Is there any risk from amniocentesis or CVS?

Unfortunately, invasive tests like amniocentesis and CVS do carry a risk. The main worry is that the test disturbs the womb or placenta and triggers a miscarriage. The pregnancy loss rate associated with amniocentesis is about 1% and with CVS between 1 and 2%. This means that, with your doctor's help, you need to weigh up carefully the risks of the baby having a problem against the risk of having a miscarriage and losing the pregnancy. Many women wait for the result of screening tests like the triple test or nuchal scan before deciding on whether thay want an amniocentesis. If you are rhesus negative, you will need an injection of anti-D immunoglobin *(see p. 147)* after amniocentesis or CVS.

What is a cordocentesis?

A cordocentesis is a test to obtain a sample of the baby's blood while it is still in the womb. It is not often required to identify problems but is sometimes necessary in cases of suspected rhesus disease or serious viral infection in the baby. The procedure is rather like that for CVS, but instead of guiding the needle via ultrasound to the placenta, the doctor guides it through the placenta to the large vein that runs in the umbilical cord. The doctor can then take a sample of the baby's blood to test for particular problems like severe anaemia.

2

I am 40 years old. Am I more at risk of having a baby with Down's syndrome?

A couple of any age can have a baby with Down's syndrome, and it does not matter how many or how few children you have had before. However, the risk does increase with the age of the mother. At the age of 40 the chances of having a baby with Down's syndrome is around 1 in 100 compared to 1 in 400 at age 36 and 1 in 1000 at age 20.

What happens if the doctors diagnose an abnormality?

This very much depends on your wishes and the type and severity of the abnormality. Some abnormalities, like cleft lip, can be easily corrected by surgery after the baby is born. Other conditions, like severe spina bifida and hydrocephalus, might be very disabling or even fatal for the baby. If the baby has a severe or fatal abnormality, doctors will usually offer you a termination of the pregnancy. However, only you can decide the right course of action for you. You will probably need time to consider the options and get more information on the condition and what it would mean for you and your baby. The decision is yours and doctors and midwives are there to help give you accurate information and answer your questions.

The small baby

The World Health Organisation defines a small baby as being less than 2.5 kg (5 lb 8 oz) at birth. However, it is also important to consider how mature the baby is; thus the stage in pregnancy must also be taken into account. While 2.5 kg is an appropriate classification for a small baby at the end of pregnancy, the situation is different earlier in pregnancy. For example, a newborn baby weighing 2.5 kg at 32 weeks of pregnancy would be well grown for a premature baby; it is only 'small' because it was born early. If it had been allowed to continue to 40 weeks, it would obviously have been much bigger. If a baby weighed 1 kg (2 lb 3 oz) when it was born at 32 weeks, it would be considered small for dates as well as premature. It is important to be able to sort out what babies are considered small and what babies are deemed premature as their problems are very different. So when doctors are assessing the growth of your baby in the womb, they must take into account how far advanced your pregnancy is. When a baby is found to be small on examination or by ultrasound scan, doctors will try and work out why this is the case. Is it small because it is meant to be small, usually because its parents are small, or is it small because the placenta is struggling to supply it with all the nutrients it needs to grow normally? Doctors will carry out tests to check the well-being of the baby in the womb. If it is not coping then they will have to consider early delivery.

What influences my baby's growth?

Your baby's growth is influenced by many factors, including genetic make-up, race, sex, exposure to substances like alcohol and tobacco, infection while in the womb, maternal nutrition and the efficiency of the placenta.

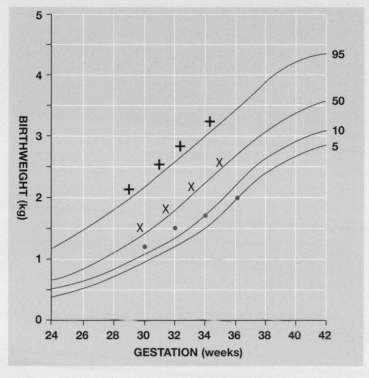

Graph showing the range of birth weights in kilograms for babies according to their stage in pregnancy (gestation). The numbers on the right refer to the so-called birth weight centile. The 50th centile is the average. Only 5% of babies will weigh more than the 95th centile and these babies are considered to be large for their dates. Small babies will weigh less than the 10th centile for their gestation. Some obstetricians prefer to use the 5th centile when trying to determine if a baby is small for dates. Here, the growth of a large-for-dates baby is plotted with the '+' signs; a baby growing slightly above the average weight is plotted with the 'x' signs; and the growth of a small-for-dates baby is plotted with the '.' signs.

How do doctors know if my baby is growing normally?

As previously noted, doctors can estimate the growth of your baby by examining your abdomen and measuring the size of your womb with a measuring tape. However, this is only an approximate measure. So where doctors are concerned that a baby might be small, ultrasound is used to assess its size. If it is confirmed that the baby is small for dates, doctors will usually monitor its growth by performing a series of ultrasound scans, usually carried out at two-week intervals.

What are the reasons for a baby being small?

When a baby is small it is important for doctors to try and work out whether it is a healthy baby that happens to be small, or a baby that is small because it has a problem. The most common cause of a baby not growing to its full potential is 'placental insufficiency', in which the placenta fails to provide the baby with sufficient nutrients for it to grow normally. In this condition the placenta can sometimes be damaged due to problems with the blood supply

Antenatal care & pregnancy complications

to and from the mother's womb. When the baby is unable to grow as much as it should because it is not getting enough nutrients, doctors term this intrauterine growth restriction, or 'IUGR' for short. Several techniques provide valuable information about whether the baby is getting enough nourishment.

How can doctors tell if the baby is getting enough nourishment?

By plotting the baby's growth on a chart, such as that shown below, doctors can look at its growth pattern, which will be seen to be slowing down where IUGR is present. Using ultrasound, a doctor will take various measurements of the baby in the womb, chiefly the size of the baby's abdomen and liver. In a well-nourished baby its abdomen will have laid down fat and its liver will be full of food stores. Thus both its liver and abdomen will be big. The food stores in the liver consist principally of a substance called glycogen that is broken down into sugar when the baby needs it. If the baby is not getting enough nutrients

Graph showing the size of a baby's head and abdomen as measured by ultrasound scans at different stages of pregnancy. Doctors can plot the growth of the baby on this chart. 'x' indicates normal growth and '.' indicates growth of a small-for-dates baby. The growth rate of the abdominal circumference declines as pregnancy advances.

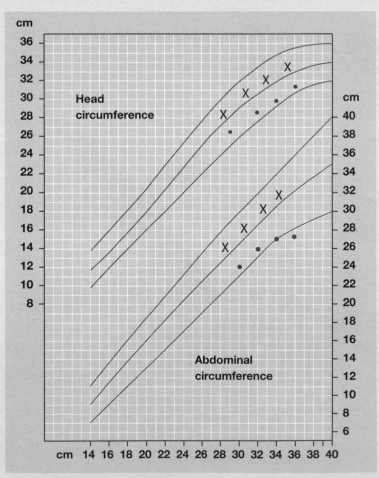

Problems linked to IUGR

Maternal factors:
- High blood pressure
- Medical conditions such as SLE
- Smoking
- Drug abuse
- Poor nutrition
- Low body weight (less than 50 kg/8 st before pregnancy)
- Age less than 16 or greater than 35 years

Pregnancy complications:
- Pre-eclampsia
- Bleeding from the placenta

Foetal and placental factors:
- Genetic abnormalities
- Malformations of the baby
- Infections of the baby like rubella (German measles)
- Twins

Placental problems:
- Placental insufficiency

from the placenta because of placental insufficiency, these stores will be used up. Thus the baby's liver and consequently its abdomen will be small. The insufficient nutrient supply will in time lead to the baby's growth being curtailed, and it will develop IUGR.

The size of the head and the size of the abdomen increase as the pregnancy advances. In the chart opposite, the three lines show the normal range of growth with the middle line being the average. Babies normally grow roughly in parallel to these lines. When a baby has IUGR its growth slows and stops running parallel to the lines and may cross over them. The dots show a baby that has IUGR and is not growing as well as it should. The abdomen growth is the first to fall off as the baby feeds its brain in preference to the rest of its body, which is nature's way of preserving brain function. Indeed, when doctors measure the size of the head in a baby with IUGR, it will often be normal as growth of the head is not affected until much later than the rest of the body. The growth of a baby without IUGR is shown on the chart opposite by the 'x' marks. When the head and body are differently affected, this is termed 'asymmetrical growth restriction'.

How is placental insufficiency measured?

The baby's heart pumps blood through the placenta, from which it draws nutrients and oxygen from the mother, and is then pumped back to the baby. In IUGR the blood vessels in the placenta are damaged, which makes it harder for the baby's heart to pump blood through the placenta. A special ultrasound technique known as Doppler ultrasound can measure the speed of blood flow in the umbilical artery in the cord going from the baby to the placenta. Normally blood will flow round the system all the time. Where there is serious damage to the placenta, however, blood flows through it only at the peak of the heartbeat when the pressure is highest but not between the heartbeats. When this occurs the baby is considered to be at high risk of developing problems.

Is there any test that can warn me if my baby is at risk of IUGR before it occurs?

Doctors have spent a great deal of time trying to devise a test that can detect which babies are at risk of IUGR. Currently, the best test is to use Doppler ultrasound to check on the blood flow to the mother's womb (as opposed to the flow of blood from the baby to the placenta, described above). This test, carried out at 18 and 22 weeks of pregnancy, measures how well the mother's blood vessels supplying the placenta have adapted. Normally, in the first half or

Doppler ultrasound scan to check on the blood flow to the mother's womb. This test, carried out at 18 and 22 weeks of pregnancy, measures how well the mother's blood vessels supplying the placenta have adapted. The upper part of the photograph shows an ultrasound scan that locates the mother's uterine arteries from which the blood flow pattern is measured, as seen in the lower part of the photograph. The large peaks show the blood flow when the mother's heart contracts and the blood surges forward. Between the peaks there is still some blood flow but a notch can be seen immediately after the large peak.

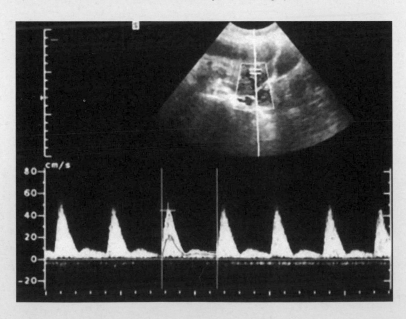

pregnancy, a so-called notch will be seen in the Doppler ultrasound waveform pattern. This usually disappears by 22 weeks, due to the placenta firmly embedding in the womb where it will obtain a good supply of blood from the mother. A notching pattern that persists after 22 weeks of gestation indicates an increased risk of placental problems that could lead to pre-eclampsia or IUGR. In IUGR the placenta does not embed deeply enough and so it can't get enough nutrients from the mother's blood. This does not cause a problem immediately – in the early part of pregnancy the placenta will still be able to deliver sufficient nutrients to the baby – but later, when the placenta can no longer meet the needs of the developing baby, the baby's growth will be reduced.

Can anything be done to prevent this problem?

There is no treatment that is known for certain to prevent IUGR. Recent research by a team in London has suggested that it can be prevented by high doses of vitamins C and E given to women whose scans show a continued notching pattern. However, larger trials are required to confirm this initially very encouraging finding before this treatment can be used widely in clinical practice. Low doses of aspirin (60–75 mg a day – no more than a quarter of a regular tablet) have been used to try and prevent IUGR. There is little evidence that it is of value in general, but it may benefit specific women at high risk as aspirin in low doses reduces the ability of the blood to clot. As some cases of IUGR are associated with an underlying tendency for the blood to clot, which in turn may damage the placenta, it may help prevent IUGR in certain instances. In any case, aspirin in these low doses has been shown in general to have no harmful effect on the mother or unborn baby.

What will doctors do if they think my baby is small?

If your baby is suspected to be small for dates, your doctor will probably perform an ultrasound scan at least every two weeks to check foetal growth. A Doppler ultrasound assessment of the blood flow from the baby to the placenta may be carried out. The doctor will also look for any risk factors associated with IUGR. These tests will help the doctor to decide if the baby is a normal small baby or is suffering from IUGR. If IUGR has been identified, the management will depend on the stage of the pregnancy at which the IUGR is identified. In early-onset IUGR, picked up before 32 weeks of pregnancy, the baby may be symmetrically small – it will have a small head and a small abdomen. Many of these babies are entirely normal, but simply small. But where the symmetrical growth restriction appears very severe, there is a possibility of underlying genetic problems or of an infection of the baby while in the womb. Where there is a high risk of a major genetic abnormality, then a cordocentesis might be considered to test for such an abnormality.

This situation is very uncommon, however. Late-onset IUGR, after 32–34 weeks of pregnancy, is far more common and is usually due to placental insufficiency. Once the problem is diagnosed, the baby must be carefully monitored. Simply because it is not growing well does not mean that your baby

Antenatal care & pregnancy complications

is at immediate risk or that it needs to be delivered. Indeed, it is important for the baby to be as mature as possible when it is delivered to prevent the additional problems of being premature as well as small. Monitoring tests will enable the doctor to determine if the baby is 'happy' in the womb, in which case the pregnancy can continue. By contrast, if the baby appears 'unhappy' or distressed then it is usually best to proceed to delivery.

Why are babies monitored in the womb?

Monitoring a baby in the womb is an important aspect of the care of women with complicated pregnancies, not just those with IUGR. The purpose of monitoring is to determine if the baby's condition is satisfactory and to look for evidence of it being distressed. Should there be evidence of distress then delivery, often by Caesarean section, is usually required. If the baby's condition is satisfactory and monitoring tests show that the baby is well, then the pregnancy can continue, with further monitoring. This is continued until the pregnancy is sufficiently advanced to allow the baby to be delivered without the risks of being severely premature. Where there is also a maternal problem like pre-eclampsia, delivery may be required to protect the mother, regardless of the baby's condition.

What tests are carried out to monitor the baby?

In addition to the measurement by Doppler ultrasound of blood flow from the baby to the placenta, outlined above, other ways to assess foetal well-being include cardiotocography, the most common test, as well as a biophysical profile *(see p. 133)* and 'kick charts' *(see also p.133)*.

What is cardiotocography?

Cardiotocography measures your baby's heart rate and any tightenings of the womb using a machine called a cardiotocograph, or CTG for short *(see opposite)*. Two small devices called transducers are strapped to your abdomen. The first of these is the heart rate (or cardiograph) transducer, an ultrasound device that measures your baby's heartbeat. The second transducer is a tocodynamometer, an instrument that measures contractions of the womb. You should bear in mind that even before labour the womb has irregular contractions, known as 'Braxton-Hicks' contractions, which are not usually painful, although their frequency increases as labour approaches. The heart rate and contractions are plotted on a long strip of graph paper by the cardiotocograph machine, examples of which are given overleaf. The upper part of the print-out on the graph paper shows the heart rate and the lower part the contractions of the womb.

What is a normal CTG?

A normal CTG taken before labour will show that the baby's heart rate lies between 110 and 150 beats per minute. The heart rate tends to be towards the lower end of this range as term approaches. The baseline heart rate is never absolutely steady, rather it fluctuates slightly from beat to beat. This is normal

Woman attached to a cardiotocograph (CTG) machine.

and doctors call it baseline variability or beat-to-beat variability. Indeed, when baseline variability is absent or markedly reduced, this can be a sign of distress. A normal CTG trace prior to labour will usually show at least 2–3 accelerations in a 40-minute period, usually associated with foetal movement or tightenings of the womb. (An acceleration can be defined as an increase in the foetal heart rate over the baseline heart rate by at least 15 beats per minute for at least 15 seconds.) Many CTG machines have a button for the mother to press when the baby moves. This puts a mark on the print-out so that doctors can see how many movements are occurring and if the heartbeat accelerates with them *(see the CTG print-out, centre right, overleaf)*. A normal CTG before labour will show a heart rate of 110–150 beats per minute, good baseline variability and several accelerations associated with foetal movement.

What are decelerations in the foetal heart rate?

Prior to labour, decelerations are unusual and can be of concern. There are different types that can occur. Variable decelerations are irregular in their shape, as traced on the print-out *(see the CTG print-out, bottom left, overleaf)*, and timing. They occur when the umbilical cord is compressed, which temporarily reduces the blood flow to the baby. A minor temporary reduction in blood flow on its own will not usually cause the baby any harm, but can be indicative of an underlying problem such as reduced amniotic fluid. Decelerations in the heart rate can occur with a contraction or tightening of the womb. When a deceleration occurs in synchrony with a uterine tightening – both the deceleration and the contraction starting and finishing at the same time – this is

CTG test print-outs

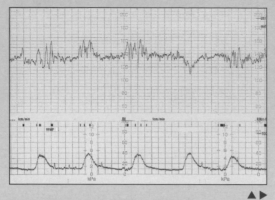

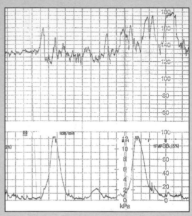

▲ ▶

These are normal CTG traces from women in labour. The regular contractions can be seen on the lower part of the trace and the baby's heart beat pattern on the upper part.

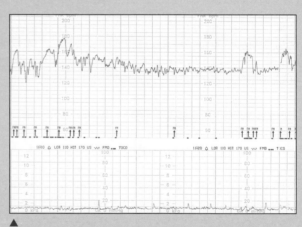

▲

A normal antenatal CTG shows the baby's heart rate to be between 110 and 150 beats per minute with accelerations, which often occur when the baby moves. The heart rate is the upper part of the trace while the lower part shows any contractions or tightenings of the womb. Whenever the mother feels the baby move she can press a button and a mark appears on the trace. This baby was active with lots of movements.

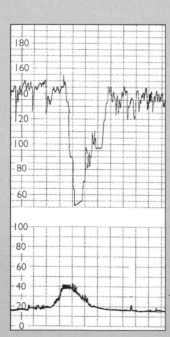

◀ This CTG shows a variable deceleration in the foetal heart rate (top part) occurring at the same time as a tightening of the womb (lower part).

called an early deceleration and is the type most commonly seen in labour. Early decelerations do not cause the baby harm and are simply due to the baby's head being gently squeezed by the womb tightening. When the deceleration occurs after a tightening or contraction of the womb – starting after the beginning of the contraction and finishing after the end of the contraction – this is known as a late deceleration. It can be a worrying sign and may indicate that the baby does not have enough oxygen. This type of deceleration is very unusual prior to labour. When combined abnormalities are present, such as a very fast heart rate (more than 160 beats per minute), with reduced baseline variability and late decelerations, this may indicate a serious problem. Thankfully, this situation is very rare prior to labour.

What is the difference between a non-stress CTG test and a contraction stress CTG test?

The use of cardiotocography on its own is sometimes termed by doctors as the non-stress test. A variety of techniques have been employed in an attempt to stimulate or 'stress' the foetus and look at the response. These include the contraction stress test where mild uterine activity is stimulated and the response of the foetal heart to this is observed.

Vibroacoustic stimulation of the foetus has also been used. With this technique a device that produces noise and vibration is held against the mother's abdomen and the response of the baby's heartbeat observed. However, none of these tests is widely used in the UK and the mainstay of foetal heart rate testing is cardiotocography without any stress being applied – the non-stress test.

What is a kick chart?

A kick chart is simply a record of how frequently you feel the baby move. Babies that are 'happy' in the womb tend to move a lot, so the chart is of value in assessing foetal well-being. A reduction in foetal movement, and particularly its absence, can indicate a problem. Sometimes, however, women are unable to feel the baby move even when movements are occurring. This might be because the fluid round the baby provides a cushioning effect so that the mother cannot feel them. During an ultrasound scan it is common to see many foetal movements that the mother does not actually feel. In any event, if you feel that there is a reduction in the baby's movements or kicks, you should seek advice from your doctor or midwife. Often a CTG or ultrasound scan will be performed to check that the baby is happy and to reassure you.

What is a biophysical profile?

This is a prolonged ultrasound scan, combined with CTG, to check that your baby is well. The doctor or ultrasonographer will observe the baby's movements with the ultrasound scan for up to 40 minutes. The test is usually conducted when a possible problem has been identified, such as the baby being small for dates. The whole 'profile' considers five factors:

- 'Foetal breathing' movements
- Gross foetal body movements
- Foetal tone
- Amniotic fluid volume
- Foetal heart rate, using the non-stress cardiotocograph or CTG

In practice, it is unusual to check all five of the variables. Often the CTG is omitted and only the other four factors are checked as these are very reliable indicators on their own. 'Foetal breathing' movements are not really the baby breathing, as gets its oxygen via the placenta, after all. But when a baby is happy in the womb, it moves its chest just as it would if it were breathing in air. This is easily seen on the scan. Gross body movements are where the baby moves its trunk. Foetal tone is flexion and extension movement of the limbs. Babies don't move a lot when they are stressed or ill – they lie still to conserve energy. Also, when babies are stressed because

The biophysical profile

		Score
Non-stress CTG test	Reactive: 2 or more foetal heart rate accelerations in a 20-minute period	2
	Fewer than 2 foetal heart rate accelerations	0
Foetal breathing movements	One episode of prolonged breathing (more than 60 seconds) within 30 minutes	2
	Foetal breathing movements absent	0
Gross foetal body movements	A minimum of three movements within a 30-minute period	2
	Foetal movements absent or reduced	0
Foetal tone	Normal: one episode of brisk limb flexion and extension (bending forward and back)	2
	Abnormal: no flexion movements	0
Amniotic fluid volume	Normal	2
	Reduced	0

the placenta is not supplying them with sufficient nutrients, they tend not to make much urine so the amount of amniotic fluid falls *(see p. 75).*

(see p. 75).

How is the biophysical profile score worked out?

Traditionally, doctors give a score out of 2 for each of the components *(see table opposite).* A normal score lies between 8 and 10 and an abnormal score is in the range of 0–4. A score of 6 would be equivocal and would usually lead to the test being repeated. Although a biophysical profile may in principle take 30–40 minutes to complete, in practice with a normal baby it is not unusual for full marks to have been obtained within five or 10 minutes, in which case the test can be stopped as the result is normal.

Why is my pregnancy large for dates?

There are several reasons that can explain the size of your womb being bigger than the doctors would have expected for your stage in pregnancy. Where the pregnancy is large for dates, doctors will check several possible causes.

- The dates might be inaccurate: your doctor will check back to the early ultrasound scan and make sure that your dates are accurate.
- The doctor will exclude twins if this has not already been done. This requires a simple scan.
- Your doctor will look for excess fluid round the baby, using ultrasound to measure the depth of the pools of fluid around the baby.
- On rare occasions, excess fluid can be associated with an abnormality of the baby and again the doctor will look for such a problem on ultrasound.
- The doctor will consider the possibility of your baby being much bigger than average, referred to as 'macrosomia'. Sometimes this is caused by pregnancy-induced diabetes *(see p. 178),* in which the baby gets too much sugar and grows very large.

Does too much fluid cause any problems?

When there is too much amniotic fluid round the baby, it is termed 'polyhydramnios' (excess amniotic fluid). As the excess fluid stretches the womb, it can sometimes lead to premature labour and a higher risk of bleeding from the uterus following delivery. Because there is more room for the baby to move about in the womb, the baby may be more likely to change position a lot. This means that the baby might be more likely to be in a breech presentation or have an unstable or constantly changing lie prior to labour. In view of these problems, pregnancies with excess fluid often require increased assessment and monitoring.

High blood pressure and pre-eclampsia

Why does high blood pressure or hypertension occur in pregnancy?

Hypertension is the medical term for high blood pressure. High blood pressure in pregnancy can be due to: pre-existing high blood pressure that you had before your pregnancy; a new medical condition arising coincidentally when you became pregnant; or, by far the most common situation, the development of pregnancy-induced hypertension or pre-eclampsia – disorders that occur only in pregnancy.

How is blood pressure measured?

Blood pressure is measured by wrapping an inflatable cuff around your upper arm. The cuff is then inflated by pumping in air. You will feel the cuff getting tight, which is slightly uncomfortable but not painful. Once the cuff is inflated, it will stop the blood flowing through the main artery in your arm. The doctor or midwife will then use a stethoscope to listen over the artery at the front of your arm above your elbow and release the pressure in the cuff. When the blood starts to flow through the artery again, pulses of sound are heard through the stethoscope. The level of pressure at which these sounds are first heard is called the systolic pressure – the highest point of your blood pressure. The pressure is highest when the heart contracts, pushing the blood round your blood vessels, and lowest between heart contractions. When the sounds heard through the stethoscope disappear, this level is called the diastolic pressure – the lowest point of the blood pressure.

In the past, blood pressure was measured by taking readings from a column of mercury. The higher the column of mercury when the sounds appeared or disappeared, the higher the pressure. So doctors would write the pressure as millimetres of mercury, or mmHg for short, Hg being the chemical symbol for mercury. Although mercury-based blood pressure machines (their technical name is sphygmomanometers) have now been phased out, doctors still refer to blood pressure as mmHg. When your blood pressure is recorded, the doctor will write, for example, 115/75. This means that your systolic pressure is 115 mmHg and your diastolic pressure 75 mmHg.

How do I know if I have high blood pressure before pregnancy?

A simple blood pressure check by your doctor is all that is needed. If you have used the pill for contraception, you will almost certainly have had your blood pressure checked. If not, it is usually easy to identify high blood pressure at the first antenatal visit, provided that you attend early in pregnancy. If you have pre-existing hypertension, this is usually picked up by a diastolic blood pressure of equal to or greater than 90 mmHg in the first 12 weeks of pregnancy. The most common type of pre-existing high blood pressure is known as essential hypertension *(see p. 188)*. However, sometimes high blood pressure can be caused by other medical conditions such as kidney problems. Pre-existing high blood pressure makes you more likely to suffer from pre-eclampsia and pregnancy-induced hypertension during pregnancy.

What are pre-eclampsia and pregnancy-induced hypertension?

Pre-eclampsia and pregnancy-induced hypertension are the most common blood pressure problems in pregnancy. They can only occur in pregnancy and will resolve within a few weeks or months of delivery. They in fact represent two forms of the same disorder. When the high blood pressure is combined with abnormally high levels of protein in the urine (known as proteinuria), this is called pre-eclampsia. The protein in the urine indicates that the kidneys are upset by the condition and that the condition is severe regardless of whether the blood pressure is moderately or severely elevated.

Where pregnancy hypertension occurs without proteinuria, then this is termed pregnancy-induced hypertension, or PIH for short. The level of high blood pressure is usually divided into mild–moderate hypertension (diastolic blood pressure 90–110 mmHg) or severe (diastolic blood pressure more than 110 mmHg). A systolic blood pressure of over 160 mmHg is also usually considered severe. It is not just the blood pressure and kidneys that are upset in these conditions; liver function can be impaired and occasionally the blood-clotting system will be disturbed.

How common are pre-eclampsia and pregnancy-induced hypertension?

Pre-eclampsia occurs in around 2% of pregnancies. Pregnancy-induced hypertension occurs in up to around 5–10% of pregnancies, although many of these cases are mild.

What are the features of pre-eclampsia?

The classic features of pre-eclampsia are high blood pressure, proteinuria and swelling of the legs, fingers and face (oedema). It usually occurs in the second half of pregnancy. Once it occurs, it progresses at a variable and unpredictable rate until delivery. Until it is very severe, it has no symptoms and you may feel entirely well. This is why regular antenatal check-ups are so important in order that this problem can be identified, as untreated it can be dangerous for both you, the mother, and the baby. In severe forms of the condition, you may have headache, blurred vision and see flashing lights, feel pain in your abdomen below your ribcage and sometimes vomit. In its most severe form, known as eclampsia, convulsions (fits) occur, due to the brain being upset by the condition (see overleaf).

What causes pre-eclampsia?

The cause of pre-eclampsia is unknown. It seems chiefly due to the abnormal implantation of the placenta into the mother's womb, although doctors don't really understand why this should occur. Pre-eclampsia can also occur when the placenta is very large, such as with twins. A signal (which doctors have not yet

Antenatal care & pregnancy complications

clearly identified) appears to be released from either abnormally implanted or very large placentas which triggers the condition. This causes a whole cascade of problems in the mother that upset the function of the blood vessels, resulting in high blood pressure. These changes also lead to leaky blood vessels, allowing fluid to collect in the tissues and causing the characteristic swelling (oedema). Abnormal clotting in tiny blood vessels can also occur, in addition to impairment of the function of organs such as the kidney and liver and occasionally the brain. Thus pre-eclampsia can affect every organ and system in the body, due to widespread disturbance in the function of the blood vessels.

Am I at risk of pre-eclampsia?

Any pregnant woman can get pre-eclampsia, though some women are more vulnerable than others. If you suffer from high blood pressure, migraine, diabetes or kidney disease, then pre-eclampsia is more likely. The risk also increases if you are over 35 or less than 20 years of age, have already had pre-eclampsia or if you are expecting twins. Pre-eclampsia is more likely in a first pregnancy or if there has been a long gap between pregnancies. If you have had a previous pregnancy and you did not get pre-eclampsia, you are unlikely to get pre-eclampsia in a future pregnancy. Equally, if you have had pre-eclampsia in your first pregnancy, the risk is usually similar in the next pregnancy. This risk is increased if you also had a baby that was small (less than 2.5 kg/5 lb 8 oz) as a result of the pre-eclampsia. Recurrence is more likely if you have an underlying medical condition, such as kidney disease or diabetes, which predisposes you to pre-eclampsia. In addition, there is a familial or genetic component to pre-eclampsia: if your mother or sister had pre-eclampsia then you will have a slightly higher risk of developing the condition.

Can my baby be affected by pre-eclampsia?

The baby can be affected because of the placenta not embedding properly into your womb. This can result in placental insufficiency which can impair the baby's growth, making it small for dates, or lead to premature delivery if the baby is distressed.

How do doctors diagnose pre-eclampsia?

At every antenatal check doctors look for high blood pressure and protein in the urine to identify pre-eclampsia and pregnancy-induced hypertension.

What level of blood pressure indicates that I have hypertension?

High blood pressure is usually diagnosed if your diastolic blood pressure is greater than 90 mmHg, provided that your blood pressure before pregnancy or in the first 12 weeks of pregnancy was less than this. Sometimes doctors will look at the increase in your blood pressure from early pregnancy to identify high blood pressure. This is useful if you normally have a very low blood pressure as you could have a very big increase in pressure, say from

50 to 85 mmHg, even if you not have reached the threshold of 90 mmHg. Thus high blood pressure can also be diagnosed when has been an increase of 20–25 mmHg over the diastolic blood pressure in early pregnancy. If your diastolic blood pressure exceeds 110 mmHg, this is severely high blood pressure, which will place you at high risk of problems if it is not treated. A systolic pressure of over 160 mmHg is also considered a severe form of hypertension if the blood pressure was previously normal.

How do doctors check for protein in my urine?

Proteinuria is easily diagnosed on 'dipstick' testing of your urine. This is why doctors always ask you to bring a urine specimen to every antenatal check. The dipsticks give a reading for protein in the urine of the following: none, trace, +, ++, +++, or ++++. You will probably see the doctor or midwife marking the result of the urine test onto your pregnancy record. Small amounts of protein can be found in the urine if you have a bladder infection or if a bit of vaginal discharge gets into the urine specimen. So a 'trace' of protein or '+' does not usually indicate a problem related to pre-eclampsia. However, if you develop high blood pressure and a '+' of protein is persistent over several checks, with no other cause of proteinuria, such as bladder infection, this would be significant. If the reading is '++' or more and your blood pressure is elevated, this usually indicates that you have pre-eclampsia. Sometimes the doctor will send a urine specimen to the laboratory to get an accurate measure of the amount of protein in your urine.

Does swelling of my ankles mean I have pre-eclampsia?

Swelling of the ankles, face and hands (oedema) occurs with pre-eclampsia and can be severe, but it is of no value in making a diagnosis of the condition. This is because oedema occurs in over 66% of normal pregnancies. So swelling of the ankles does not, on its own, indicate pre-eclampsia. Furthermore, severe pre-eclampsia and even eclampsia can occur without oedema.

Do blood tests help diagnose pre-eclampsia?

Blood tests can help with diagnosis. Doctors look for an increase in uric acid in the blood as this is a feature of the pre-eclampsia, occurring before protein is present in the urine. The more severe the pre-eclampsia, the higher the level of uric acid. So this is a useful test of how the pre-eclampsia is progressing. Blood tests can also check whether the liver is upset or if the clotting system is disturbed by severe pre-eclampsia.

What is HELLP syndrome?

HELLP syndrome is a form of pre-eclampsia and consists of *h*aemolysis, elevated *l*iver enzymes and *l*ow *p*latelets (hence the acronym HELLP). Haemolysis is the breakdown of the red blood cells that carry oxygen round the body. Elevated liver enzymes are substances that increase in the blood when the liver is damaged. Platelets are small cells that circulate in your blood and are important for making blood clot; their numbers are reduced in HELLP syndrome. The presence of all three indicates a very severe form of pre-eclampsia in which the liver and blood systems are upset by the disturbance in the blood vessels. Sometime the mother's skin will be jaundiced (yellow due to liver function being impaired).

How is pre-eclampsia monitored?

Once doctors have diagnosed pre-eclampsia, the severity of the problem and the rate of progression must be regularly assessed. This requires regular checks of blood pressure, protein in the urine and also blood tests. The baby's growth should be measured by ultrasound scan and tests like a CTG or a biophysical profile performed to check that the baby is well. In milder forms of the condition monitoring usually takes place by regular clinic visits, often to day assessment units. Where the problem is severe, admission to hospital will usually be required.

How is pre-eclampsia treated?

Pre-eclampsia will get better after the baby has been delivered. The aim of treatment is to protect the mother and the baby from the consequences of high blood pressure. Thus treatment with medication to control the blood pressure is often required. This will allow the pregnancy to continue for as long as possible to try to avoid premature delivery of the baby. The doctor will regularly weigh up the risk to the mother and baby of continuing with the pregnancy against the risks of delivery.

When is early delivery required in pre-eclampsia?

If severe problems are present at an advanced stage of pregnancy, after 34 weeks, then there is usually little to be gained by continuing the pregnancy. This is because the risk to the baby from premature delivery is usually small by this stage, while the risk to both the mother and baby from continuing with the pregnancy will usually be much greater. Where the baby is distressed or blood pressure cannot be controlled or if worrying symptoms occur, delivery is indicated no matter what stage of pregnancy. Such symptoms include abdominal pain, which can indicate liver impairment, headache and visual disturbances. These symptoms may be a prelude to the most severe form of the disorder, eclampsia, where seizures occur. When delivery is needed several weeks before term, a Caesarean section is usually required. Where delivery is needed before 36 weeks of pregnancy, high-dose steroid injections are usually given to the mother *(see p. 236)*. These steroids promote lung maturity in the baby and reduce the problems for the baby of being born before its lungs are fully mature.

Is there any treatment to prevent pre-eclampsia?

There is no proven treatment that can prevent pre-eclampsia. Low-dose aspirin (60–75 mg a day), which reduces the activity of certain parts of the clotting system, might be prescribed in some cases, especially women with a history of early-onset (before 30–32 weeks) pre-eclampsia and particularly when certain

Pre-eclampsia and heart disease

Pregnancy complications like pre-eclampsia may predict mothers at risk of heart disease later in life. Emerging evidence suggests that a link exists between pregnancy complications, such as pre-eclampsia, and later vascular disease, such as heart attacks. Studies suggest that women who have had pre-eclampsia and low-birthweight babies (less than 2.5 kg/5 lb 8oz) during pregnancy are more likely to develop heart disease in later life than women who do not develop this complication. If these associations are confirmed, then women who experience these pregnancy complications could benefit from screening after pregnancy for risk factors for heart disease and should seek preventive treatment, including lifestyle modifications such as better diet and increased exercise. Indeed, there is some evidence to suggest that exercise during early pregnancy or before pregnancy can also reduce the likelihood of pregnancy complications like pre-eclampsia.

additional medical problems are present. This will reduce the risk of pre-eclampsia by abut 15%. Some recent research (as yet unconfirmed) suggests that vitamin C and vitamin E supplements might help women at high risk. Doctors are currently researching the best ways to identify mothers at risk of pre-eclampsia and treatments that might prevent it or reduce the severity of the condition.

Does pre-eclampsia occur most often in the winter?

Recently it has been found that the likelihood of developing pre-eclampsia is highest in mothers delivering their babies in the winter months and lowest in the summer. Doctors don't yet know why this should be the case. It might be because cold weather affects the function of the blood vessels. Alternatively, it might be because something present during the early stages of pregnancy in the springtime, such as in the diet, influences the development of pre-eclampsia later in pregnancy during the winter.

Eclampsia

Eclampsia is convulsions or fits in pregnancy due to pre-eclampsia. It is caused by swelling of the brain and spasm of the blood vessels supplying the brain. It is thankfully rare in most countries of the developed world, typically 1 out of 2500 pregnancies, but it is considered a medical emergency once it occurs. Usually it is preceded by symptoms like upper abdominal pain, headache and visual blurring or flashing lights in a woman with pre-eclampsia. However, it can sometimes be the first sign that pre-eclampsia has been present as it can occur before the condition has been detected. Just over a third of cases occur during pregnancy, over 40% of cases occur after delivery and around 25% of cases occur in labour.

How is eclampsia treated?

The key features in treatment of eclampsia are stabilisation of the mother and immediate delivery of the baby. An intravenous infusion is set up to allow drugs to be given rapidly. Medication (usually magnesium sulphate) is given to stop fits and also to prevent further convulsions. Additional medication is given to control the blood pressure. Blood investigations are performed at once to check blood clotting and kidney and liver function. The baby is rapidly assessed: delivery is required as soon as possible, usually by Caesarean section. Treatment to control blood pressure and prevent fits is often required for several days after delivery.

Vaginal bleeding in pregnancy

In early pregnancy, vaginal bleeding can be caused by complications such as miscarriage *(see p. 76)*. This section will focus on bleeding in later pregnancy, after 24 weeks, referred to as 'antepartum haemorrhage' (that is, bleeding before delivery). The two main problems when bleeding occurs in late pregnancy are placenta praevia and placental abruption.

What is placental abruption?

Placental abruption is where the placenta separates from the wall of the womb, resulting in bleeding. It can occur at any time before the delivery of the baby and happens in around 1 in 80 pregnancies. Usually the degree of separation is relatively minor but the more severe forms are linked to a high risk of problems for the baby and sometimes the mother also. The risk to the baby depends not only on the severity of the abruption, but also the stage in pregnancy at which it occurs and the size of the baby.

Why does abruption occur?

Doctors don't know why most abruptions occur. They can be caused by severe trauma to the womb, such as in a road traffic accident, but usually there is no obvious cause. A few factors slightly increase the risk of having an abruption, however. These include deficiency in the vitamin folic acid and smoking. Women who give up smoking in pregnancy will reduce the risk of abruption by around a quarter and of losing the baby from an abruption by around a half compared to women who continue to smoke. There is also a risk of around 8% of abruption recurring in future pregnancies, but there are a few things you can do to help prevent a recurrence. You can make sure you have a good diet, take folic acid supplements before and during the pregnancy, and if you smoke, stop before becoming pregnant.

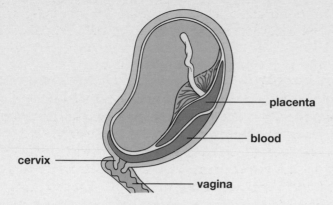

placenta

blood

cervix

vagina

Placental abruption is where the placenta separates from the wall of the womb, resulting in bleeding. In the diagram, partial separation of the placenta from the wall of the womb has occurred and vaginal bleeding will ensue as the blood will pass through the cervix and into the vagina.

What are the symptoms and signs of abruption?

The classic signs of severe abruption are vaginal bleeding, abdominal pain and tenderness over the womb. Because the bleeding irritates the womb, contractions can occur and may lead to premature labour. In severe cases the baby can be distressed and delivery might be required. Most cases are relatively minor, however, and do not harm the baby. If you have bleeding in pregnancy, you should contact your doctor or maternity unit immediately in case any treatment is required.

How is abruption treated?

In mild placental abruption, the bleeding and symptoms often settle down. It is important to check that the baby is well, however. This is usually carried out with an ultrasound scan along with tests like a biophysical profile or CTG. If everything settles, you will still need regular monitoring as occasionally a small abruption can recur and sometimes premature labour can be triggered some time after the abruption occurs. The management of moderate or severe placental abruption is first to correct any major blood loss. This usually requires fluids and sometimes blood to be transfused through an intravenous drip. The baby may need to be delivered. If the baby is distressed then delivery by Caesarean section is usually required. A rapid labour is sometimes triggered by abruption and if the baby is not distressed, vaginal delivery may be achieved, with the baby's condition being continuously monitored during the labour. After the baby is born, it is important to watch for further bleeding as an abruption increases the likelihood of bleeding from the womb after delivery. If you are rhesus negative, you will usually need an injection of anti-D immunoglobulin each time you bleed.

What is placenta praevia?

Placenta praevia is when the placenta lies wholly or partly in the lower part of the womb, close to or sometimes covering the cervix, or neck of the womb.

Because it is close to the cervix, bleeding will result when the cervix stretches open in labour, as this causes the placenta to be torn away from the wall of the womb where it is embedded. Placenta praevia occurs in less than 1% of pregnancies, but it is a significant cause of bleeding in pregnancy and can lead to premature delivery. There are varying degrees of severity of placenta praevia, which can be detected by ultrasound, as the position of the placenta or afterbirth is easily seen. There are four types of placenta praevia:

- Types I and II are considered by doctors to be minor degrees of placenta praevia
- Types III and IV represent major degrees of the condition

The severity or type is determined by how close the placenta is to the neck of the womb and whether or not it covers the cervix.

Why does placenta praevia occur?

Placenta praevia arises when the early pregnancy implants in the lower part of the womb. This can occur simply by chance, but a number of factors make it more likely to occur *(see p. 146)*. It is not known why some of these factors increase the risk, although in situations where the placenta is big, such as with a twin pregnancy, the size of the placenta alone makes it more likely.

What are the features of placenta praevia?

Episodes of minor, painless vaginal bleeding are often the first indication of placenta praevia. These small bleeds tend to occur when the lower part of the womb is stretching in late pregnancy, often between 28 and 36 weeks. However, very occasionally women with placenta praevia do not bleed until they go into labour. Because the placenta is in the lower part of the womb, it may stop the baby's head from settling into the pelvis. When you are examined, the baby's head will be 'high' in the abdomen rather than moving into your pelvis as normal in late pregnancy. This also makes problems such as breech presentation more common as the baby can't settle into a position with its head in the pelvis. Equally, when breech presentation occurs, the doctor will usually check whether the placenta is lying low in the womb.

Sometimes the only way you know that you have placenta praevia is from the ultrasound scan. A scan in early pregnancy can sometimes identify the condition. In this situation further scans are often carried out in later pregnancy to check if the placenta is still low. The vast majority of cases of placenta praevia picked up on an early pregnancy ultrasound scan do not persist, however, as the placenta will move away from the neck of the womb as the womb enlarges and stretches to accommodate the growing baby. Such cases tend not to cause any clinical problem.

How do doctors treat placenta praevia? Will I need a Caesarean section?

The treatment of placenta praevia depends on how severe the bleeding is and whether the type of placenta praevia is major or minor. If you have minimal

Types of placenta praevia seen with ultrasound

Type I	The placenta dips into the lower part of the womb and lies within 5 cm (2 in) of the opening of the cervix
Type II	The placenta reaches the cervix but does not cover it
Type III	The placenta covers the cervix but most of the placenta lies to one side of it
Type IV	The placenta is located centrally over the cervix

vaginal bleeding at around 32 weeks and a minor type of placenta praevia, then a 'wait and see' approach is usually adopted. The position of the placenta is carefully watched with regular ultrasound scans. In most cases the placenta will move well clear of the neck of the womb, due to the womb stretching as the pregnancy gets bigger, and a normal vaginal delivery can occur. If you have a major type of placenta praevia and one that persists, you will need to be delivered by Caesarean section. This is because when you go into labour the placenta will be torn as the neck of the womb stretches open. This will inevitably result in heavy bleeding. Hence if you have a placenta praevia, a Caesarean section is usually performed a week or two before your expected date of delivery to avoid this problem.

If at any time there is heavy bleeding from placenta praevia or if the baby is distressed, then delivery will be indicated and Caesarean section is virtually

There are four types of placenta praevia: types I and II are considered by doctors to be minor degrees of placenta praevia, while types III and IV represent major degrees of the condition. The severity or type is determined by how close the placenta is to the neck of the womb and whether or not it covers the cervix. This diagram shows two types of placenta praevia: a minor (type I) and a major (type III) type.

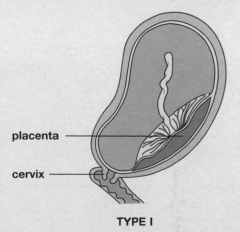

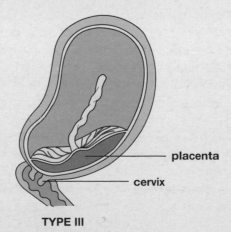

placenta

cervix

TYPE I

placenta

cervix

TYPE III

Factors that increase the likelihood of placenta praevia

- Women with several previous pregnancies
- Previous placenta praevia
- Previous surgical operations leaving scars on the womb
- Previous Caesarean section
- Being an older mother
- Smoking
- A large placenta such as with twins or triplets

always required. If you are rhesus negative, you will usually need an injection of anti-D immunoglobulin each time you bleed.

Are placenta praevia and placental abruption always the cause of bleeding in late pregnancy?

In at least half of cases where some bleeding occurs in late pregnancy, no obvious cause can be found. Some of these cases might be due to a very minor abruption that does not lead to any problem. Occasionally, the bleeding can come from the neck of the womb, such as from a harmless cervical polyp, a little outgrowth of skin that can bleed easily. However, until you are fully assessed by the doctor, it is impossible to determine the cause of bleeding in late pregnancy. As some of the causes of bleeding can lead to serious problems, however, it is important that you consult your doctor at once if you have any bleeding.

Rhesus disease

Everyone has a blood group. Blood group typing comprises two main categories: ABO, consisting of groups A, B, AB or O; and rhesus, consisting of rhesus positive and rhesus negative. You are likely to see your blood group written in your pregnancy record: for example, it might be 'A Rh+' meaning that you are blood group A and rhesus positive. Eighty-five per cent of people are rhesus positive and 15% rhesus negative. The problem may arise if you are rhesus negative and you are carrying a rhesus positive baby.

Some of the baby's blood cells can leak into your bloodstream during pregnancy. The risk of the baby's cells entering your bloodstream is high when bleeding occurs in pregnancy, such as with an abruption. Because you are rhesus negative your body recognises that these rhesus positive cells from your baby are not yours. It regards them as foreign cells and will respond by making antibodies (substances that attack and destroy foreign cells – in the case of infection, for example). The antibodies that you produce against rhesus positive cells can cross the placenta and enter your baby's bloodstream. If levels of these antibodies are high, they can cause the developing baby to become anaemic because they destroy the red blood cells in the baby's bloodstream, which will all be rhesus positive. This is called rhesus disease.

If I am rhesus negative, will the baby always be at risk of rhesus disease?

If you and your baby are both rhesus negative then this problem cannot occur. In addition, in the first pregnancy that you develop rhesus antibodies because your baby is rhesus positive, the baby is not usually significantly affected. Instead, it is the next pregnancy where you have a rhesus positive baby that it is more likely to be affected. This is because you will have a much greater antibody response when you subsequently encounter rhesus positive blood cells.

Can rhesus disease be prevented?

If you have an injection of anti-D immunoglobulin soon after any bleeding in pregnancy, this can help clear the baby's red blood cells from your bloodstream. This will prevent you from making these antibodies and so prevent rhesus disease. Indeed, where these injections are widely available, rhesus disease has become an uncommon problem. Injections of anti-D immunoglobulin are also given after any event where there is a risk of the baby's blood cells getting in to your bloodstream, such as amniocentesis and of course delivery itself.

Following delivery, it is usual to check your blood to determine how much of the baby's blood has entered your bloodstream. This is done with the Kliehauer test, which allows the doctor to ensure that you have had enough anti-D immunoglobulin to clear all of the baby's red cells from your bloodstream. This can prevent you getting a problem in your next pregnancy if the baby is rhesus positive again. Some doctors routinely give anti-D immunoglobulin in late pregnancy at 28 and 34 weeks to all pregnant women who are rhesus negative. This is useful in preventing rhesus disease.

If I have rhesus disease, how will it be managed in pregnancy?

If rhesus antibodies have been detected in your blood, your doctor will keep a careful check on the levels of these antibodies by carrying out regular blood tests to determine how mild or severe the problem is.

Your baby will also be scanned to look for any evidence of anaemia. If the baby should become anaemic, and thankfully nowadays this is a very uncommon occurrence, it may require a transfusion of blood while it is in the womb. This is a very specialised form of treatment. Sometimes you might find that early delivery is required and after delivery the baby may need further blood transfusions.

Infections in pregnancy

Am I more likely to get a urinary tract infection when I am pregnant?

You are more prone to urinary tract infection (UTI) when you are pregnant than outside pregnancy. This is because the flow of urine through the tubes that lead from your kidneys to your bladder is slower due to the effects of the pregnancy hormone progesterone.

What are the symptoms of UTI in pregnancy?

The symptoms are the same as when you are not pregnant. With bladder infection (cystitis), which is relatively common in pregnancy, you will feel the need to pass urine frequently, it will be painful when you pass urine – usually a burning feeling – and you will feel a sense of urgency when you need to go to the toilet. Sometimes these infections can even lead to blood appearing in your urine. If the infection spreads from your bladder to your kidneys, you will feel very unwell. This is called pyelonephritis but it is not a common problem in pregnancy. If it occurs you will have a fever, shiver, and usually have loin pain and tenderness. It is not uncommon to feel nauseated and vomit. Severe untreated infections can irritate the womb and lead to premature labour.

Can I take antibiotics for a UTI when I am pregnant?

An antibiotic is essential if you have a UTI. Prompt treatment is necessary to stop the infection worsening to a stage that it can upset the pregnancy. Treatment is usually by a broad-spectrum antibiotic (an antibiotic that kills all the usual bacteria that cause UTIs). Most antibiotics are safe in pregnancy. Some, like tetracycline, must be avoided as they cause staining of the unborn baby's teeth, but the antibiotics commonly used to treat UTIs, such as the penicillin or cephalosporin families of antibiotics, do not cause problems. If the infection has reached your kidneys, you will usually be quite unwell and require admission to hospital for intensive antibiotic and fluid therapy. If you get repeated UTIs when you are pregnant, long-term antibiotic treatment may be given, usually at night, when the antibiotic will stay in the bladder for several hours.

What else can I do to deal with a urinary infection?

Drink plenty of fluids to ensure a good flow of urine to help flush the infection out of your bladder. Cranberry juice is known to be helpful in fighting bladder infections. A medication called potassium citrate can neutralise the acidity of your urine, taking away some of the discomfort when you pass water, but it will not treat the infection.

Is thrush more common in pregnancy?

Thrush infection is very common, especially in pregnancy. Indeed, over 1 in 10 women will suffer from thrush at some point in their pregnancy. Thrush is caused by an overgrowth of a fungal organism called candida and causes a thick, white and curd-like vaginal discharge – sometimes described as looking like cottage cheese. It does not usually have any odour. A vulval itch is very common with thrush infection and it can be almost impossible to stop yourself from scratching. The skin often gets very red and inflamed and will be sore. Thrush is easily treated with a course of antifungal pessaries and creams that are safe to use in pregnancy. Your doctor or pharmacist can advise about the best treatment. It is not uncommon for infection to recur as candida is widely present – it is normally found in the bowel and is carried in small numbers in the vagina in over a third of healthy pregnant women. These small numbers of candida do not themselves cause a problem, but clearly can be a 'reservoir' for re-infection. To prevent re-infection, keep the vulva from being too warm and moist as this encourages the overgrowth of thrush. You should therefore avoid wearing tights, use cotton underwear and avoid douching (inadvisable in any case, especially in pregnancy).

What is listeria infection?

Infection with the bacterium *Listeria moncytogenes* usually occurs by mouth from contaminated food. Although such infections are uncommon, they can be severe when they occur. Symptoms are flu-like, accompanied by fever, and can initially mimic a severe urinary tract infection. Treatment is with intravenous antibiotics, which are unlikely to cause problems in pregnancy, although it is clearly best to avoid infection in the first place. Listeria is present in many foods, particularly soft cheeses made from unpasteurised milk. It can multiply readily at low temperature but is destroyed by cooking. Infection with listeria during pregnancy is significant as it may lead to miscarriage or loss of the pregnancy. It is also a cause of premature labour. The baby can be infected and the infection can be life-threatening. This is why pregnant women are advised to avoid soft cheeses, anything derived from unpasteurised milk, and pâté. Increased awareness and publicity about listeria has fortunately reduced the incidence of infection.

Viral infections in pregnancy

There are several viral infections that can potentially damage the baby. These include German measles (rubella), cytomegalovirus, 'slapped cheek' syndrome (parvovirus B19) and chickenpox.

What is German measles?

Rubella, probably better known as German measles, is a very common infection in children. It is usually a mild condition with a transient rash and swelling of the lymph glands behind the ears. It is caught from airborne droplets spread when infected people cough or sneeze. Infection in pregnancy, particularly in the first three months, is significant as it can cause malformations in your baby. These

> ## Foetal abnormalities caused by German measles infection
>
> - Small head
> - Inflammation of the brain
> - Deafness
> - Mental handicap
> - Eye problems
> - Anaemia
> - Enlargement of the baby's liver, jaundice
> - Heart abnormalities
> - Impaired growth of the baby in the womb

may include deafness, blindness and heart problems. However, it can only be caught if you are not immune to it.

Can these problems with German measles be prevented?

If you are immune to German measles, this will prevent your baby being affected. You will usually be immune if you have had German measles or have been immunised against it. If you are not immune, you should be immunised before you try to become pregnant as immunisation cannot be given during pregnancy (see p. 20).

What problems does parvovirus infection cause?

Infection with human parvovirus is relatively common in children. It causes a condition known as erythema infectiosum – sometimes called 'slapped cheek' syndrome, due to the characteristic rash on the face that looks as though one has been slapped. It is unusual for parvovirus to cause a problem in pregnancy, but infection in early pregnancy has been linked to miscarriage, and in late pregnancy infection can cause severe anaemia in about 3 out of every 100 babies infected. It does not appear to cause any congenital abnormality, however. If you come into contact with this condition or suspect you have it, you should consult your doctor.

Does chicken pox cause a problem in pregnancy?

Chicken pox is caused by a virus called varicella zoster. It usually occurs in children and produces fever and an itchy rash affecting the face and scalp that crusts over before healing. The incubation period is 10–20 days and the infectious period lasts from two days before the rash appears until it crusts over. This same virus is responsible for shingles, a painful, localised skin rash that can come and go. This is due to the virus lying dormant in some nerves in the body, after initial infection by the chicken pox virus, and then becoming active again at a later date. Shingles in an otherwise healthy mother will not cause any problem for the baby.

What happens if I am not immune to chicken pox?

Most adults in this country are immune to chicken pox, so although it is common to come into contact with chicken pox when you are pregnant, it is unusual to suffer from chicken pox in pregnancy. If infection does occur in a mother who is not immune, it can be severe, and a small number of infected mothers will develop a serious viral pneumonia (lung infection). Infection in the first half of pregnancy in a mother who is not immune only occasionally (in 1–2% of cases) affects the baby. If the baby is affected, however, eye problems such as cataracts, skin scarring, limb abnormalities and mental retardation can occur. Infection of the mother between 20 and 36 weeks will not cause any abnormality in the baby, although the baby may get shingles as a child. Infection of a non-immune mother after 36 weeks sometimes results in the baby getting chicken pox, usually after it is born.

If you are not immune, you should try and avoid contact with anyone with chicken pox. If you have a definite past history of chickenpox, you can assume that you will be immune. If you are uncertain whether you are immune, your immunity to chickenpox can be checked with a simple blood test. If you do come into contact with someone with chickenpox while you are pregnant and you are not immune, you can be treated with medication called zoster immunoglobulin that can prevent you being infected. If you are infected after 36 weeks, the baby will be given zoster immunoglobulin by injection to reduce the chance of it getting chickenpox. However, it is not yet known whether this will always prevent the baby from being infected, and a vaccine is not yet available for chickenpox. If you are worried about chickenpox in pregnancy or have come into contact with it recently, you should consult your doctor.

Does herpes virus infection cause problems in pregnancy?

A virus called herpes simplex is responsible for problems like cold sores and genital herpes. In genital herpes, painful blisters occur around the vagina and sometimes on the cervix. After the initial infection subsides, the virus lies dormant in the nerves and can become reactivated from time to time. This results in another crop of painful blisters. When the baby passes through the birth canal, it can sometimes become infected with the herpes virus if there is an active infection in the mother's cervix or vagina. Infection can be very severe in the newborn baby. So, when there is clinical evidence of active infection in the vagina or cervix, Caesarean section is often recommended to avoid the baby passing through the birth canal and becoming infected, especially if it is the first infection the mother has suffered. Where a recurrent infection is present, the risk of the baby being infected is much less. This is because the mother will have some immunity to herpes as she has had it before, and she will have passed this on to the baby while it is in the womb. Hence the baby will have some immunity, giving it some resistance to the infection. If you have had genital herpes in the past, you should let your doctor know. In particular, you should consult your doctor if you think that you have an active herpes infection while you are pregnant.

What is cytomegalovirus infection?

Most adults will be exposed to cytomegalovirus infection at some time in their lives, but will not usually have been aware of it as the infection is often symptomless, even during pregnancy. The major risk is for the woman who encounters this virus for the first time when she is pregnant. One or two mothers in every hundred will encounter cytomegalovirus for the first time in pregnancy. Transmission of the virus to the baby in the womb occurs in around 40% of mothers infected for the first time. Cytomegalovirus will lead to problems in only around 10–20% of these infected babies. This means that even if you do get this infection, the baby is unlikely to develop a problem. For those few babies who do develop a problem, the effects of infection depend on the stage of pregnancy. Infection in early pregnancy can lead to serious problems like miscarriage or abnormalities similar to those seen with German measles infection in early pregnancy. In late pregnancy it can cause severe anaemia in the unborn baby. Sometimes the baby will not develop a problem until later in childhood and cytomegalovirus infection in the womb can cause deafness. Infection in the mother can be diagnosed from blood tests and some of the potential effects on the baby can be checked with ultrasound scans. Amniocentesis or cordocentesis can confirm if the baby is infected. There is no effective treatment for cytomegalovirus infection and no vaccine is currently available to prevent it, although some progress is being made in the development of a vaccine.

What is toxoplasma infection?

Toxoplasma is not a strictly a virus but an organism that usually lives in cats and is found in soil, where it can remain viable for many months. It is excreted in cat faeces so litter trays are potentially a source of infection. Contaminated meat and soil-covered vegetables are also a source of infection. Recently, it has been found that cats are not the most common source of toxoplasma infection. This may be because cats excrete toxoplasma in their faeces only for the first two weeks after they have been infected for the first time. Most commonly implicated are raw, cured and undercooked meats, and, to a lesser extent, direct contact with contaminated soil as the organism can remain viable for long periods of time. For preventive measures, see box, opposite.

This infection, which can pass from the mother to the developing baby in the womb, has many features in common with congenital rubella and cytomegalovirus infection. Like cytomegalovirus infection, toxoplasma infection in adults is usually symptomless or mild. Infection should be considered in pregnant women with a mild viral illness and a blood test taken to check for toxoplasma, if this is a possibility. Infection of the baby is more likely to occur in later pregnancy, but the risk of damage at this stage is less than in early

How can I avoid toxoplasma infection?

- Avoid eating any meat that has not been thoroughly cooked
- Ideally, eat meat that has been previously frozen (and thoroughly cooked) as freezing kills the toxoplasma organism
- After handling raw meat, avoid touching your mouth or eyes
- Ensure that you wash your hands thoroughly after handling raw meats or vegetables covered with soil
- Thoroughly clean any surface that has come into contact with raw meat
- Wash all fruit and vegetables before you eat them as they might be contaminated with soil containing toxoplasma
- Avoid unpasteurised milk or milk products that are made from unpasteurised milk
- Wear rubber gloves when gardening or cleaning out the cat litter tray (avoid cleaning out the litter tray if someone else can do it)
- Take extra precautions when you are travelling outside Europe and North America

pregnancy, when it can be a cause of serious abnormalities or lead to miscarriage. However, it is uncommon for babies to be affected in the womb: only about 1–10 out of every 10,000 newborn babies in Europe will be found to be infected. Overall, about 70% of these infected babies have no problem, around 10% will have eye problems and the remainder will have similar problems to those seen with German measles infection. In some areas of the world where infection is common, maternal screening for toxoplasma is offered. If a toxoplasma infection is suspected in the baby, it will need regular ultrasound examinations and sometimes samples of the baby's blood or amniotic fluid are required to diagnose infection. The infection can be treated with an antibiotic called spiramycin.

I am HIV positive. Are there special considerations for pregnancy?

Being HIV positive is an important consideration in pregnancy because it is a condition that could not only affect you but also your baby. HIV (human immuno-deficiency virus), sometimes referred to as the AIDS virus, is a virus that attacks the body's immune system. It can be acquired sexually or through the blood such as when contaminated needles are shared between intra-venous drug abusers. The immune system protects us from infection. HIV progressively attacks the immune system until it is too weak to cope with infection. When infections or certain tumours occur because of the damage to the immune system, this is known as AIDS (acquired immune deficiency syndrome).

However, with modern anti-viral medication that can control the disease, HIV infection is regarded as more of a chronic infection or carrier state rather than necessarily progressing to full-blown AIDS.

HIV infection is not usually worsened by pregnancy and there is no evidence of pregnancy increasing the risk of progression to AIDS. Sometimes antibiotics will be given to you during pregnancy to help protect you from other infections that can cause problems, like pneumonia. Women with HIV infection do appear to have a higher risk of miscarriage, premature delivery and low-birthweight babies, although these complications may reflect more the mother's state of health and her level of nutrition, rather than the fact that either she or the baby is carrying the virus. Currently used anti-viral medication does not appear to be linked to any abnormalities in the baby, although there is insufficient information to be certain of this at present. As there are so many issues to consider that can have an impact on pregnancy, it is vital to obtain specialist advice from an HIV expert, preferably before you conceive. Because of the implications of HIV for the mother and baby and because treatment can reduce the risk to the baby, screening for HIV infection is now offered to pregnant women.

Will my baby be infected if I have HIV?

Your baby can be infected during pregnancy, but this is uncommon. Babies are most at risk of getting HIV at the time of delivery. This is thought to be due to the baby being exposed to your blood and body secretions as it passes through the birth canal. The risk of the baby being affected is about 1 in 5, but this can be reduced to less than 1 in 10 with the application of anti-viral drug therapy in pregnancy. The use of these anti-viral drugs is very specialised and it is important that you obtain the necessary specialist advice if you are HIV positive, especially as research in this area is moving so rapidly. Birth by Caesarean section can reduce the risk of the baby being infected and so you might want to consider this. As your baby can also be infected during breast-feeding, bottle-feeding is the best option (certainly in the developed world, where bottle-feeding is safe). After birth the baby should be examined by a paediatrician to check if there has been any transmission of the virus.

I carry the hepatitis virus. Will this affect my pregnancy?

The two main types of hepatitis virus that can be carried are hepatitis B and C. These viruses attack the liver but after the liver infection has subsided some people continue to carry the virus in their body. In the UK between 1 in 1000 and 1 in 200 women carry the hepatitis B virus and between 1 in 150 and 1 in 300 carry hepatitis C. If the baby is infected, both hepatitis B and C can cause hepatitis and the baby may become a carrier of either.

The hepatitis C virus was only identified about 15 years ago. It does not usually cause any particular problem in pregnancy and is not associated with any foetal abnormality. Pregnancy will not worsen any liver disease in the mother due to this virus. The risk of it being transmitted to the baby is around

10%, but this varies with the amount of virus in the mother's bloodstream. There is no vaccine available at present to prevent hepatitis C infection in either the mother or the baby. Transmission of hepatitis C to the baby by breast-feeding appears to be uncommon, however.

In contrast to hepatitis C, hepatitis B has a much higher risk of transmission to the baby. This transmission can occur at the time of delivery but about 1 in 20 babies are infected through the placenta before delivery. Because of this, babies are usually immunised against hepatitis B at birth if their mother is a carrier of hepatitis B. As with hepatitis C, the hepatitis B virus does not usually produce any other pregnancy complications. In addition, if the baby has been immunised, then there is no reason to avoid breast-feeding.

It is best to ask your doctor for information on the type of hepatitis you carry and the risk of transmission to the baby for your own particular case.

Twins

Twin pregnancy occurs in around 1 in 80 conceptions. There are two sorts of twins: non-identical or fraternal twins (referred to as dizygotic twins), and identical twins (referred to as monozygotic twins). Non-identical twins occur when the mother produces two eggs and both are fertilised and implant in the womb successfully. There is a marked variation throughout the world in the chance of having non-identical twins. Non-identical twins are less common in Japan and more common in Africa compared with Europe *(see table below)*. In addition, non-identical twins have a familial factor which can be passed from mother to daughter, making you more likely to have non-identical twins if your mother had twins. Recent studies have indicated that the likelihood of a mother having non-identical twins can be inherited from both her paternal and maternal sides. Other factors associated with a higher risk of non-identical twins include having had several previous pregnancies, being 35–39 years old, and increasing maternal height and body mass index *(see p. 168)*. On the other hand, a family history of twins in your partner's family does *not* lead to an increased risk of twins in your pregnancy.

The likelihood of non-identical twins and even triplets is increased in assisted conception techniques particularly with ovulation induction. With in vitro fertilisation *(see p. 57)*, where two embryos may be replaced, there is

Rates for non-identical twins worldwide	
Japan and China	2–7 per 1000 births
Nigeria and Jamaica	More than 20 per 1000 births
Europe, Australia and the United States	Between 8 and 20 per 1000 births

2

clearly an increased chance of twins. While a woman with a history of infertility may view twin pregnancy as a good outcome, there is a significant higher rate of complications with twin pregnancy that needs to be taken into account.

By contrast, identical twins occur following the splitting of a single fertilised egg. The egg effectively splits into two after fertilisation and two identical children will develop. Identical twins are less common than non-identical twins. They occur in around 1 in 250 pregnancies and this rate is fairly constant throughout the world.

What are Siamese twins?

As outlined above, if a single fertilised egg splits into two at a very early stage then identical twins result. Sometimes this process of splitting occurs after the point that the baby has begun to form. In this situation the split will be incomplete and the two babies will be joined at a part of their body. Most commonly, they will be joined at the chest or abdomen. The resultant twins are referred to as conjoined or, more commonly, 'Siamese' twins. The name derives from two brothers from Siam (now Thailand) born in 1811 called Chang and Eng, who lived into adulthood. They worked in Barnum's Circus, married English sisters and had children while still joined! They died in 1874. Thankfully, this condition is extremely rare, and when it does occur surgical separation is often possible.

What complications can occur in a twin pregnancy?

There is an increased risk of miscarriage. Furthermore, ultrasound scans in early pregnancy have identified the phenomenon of the 'vanishing twin'. This is where a twin pregnancy is identified on an initial scan early in pregnancy and a

Non-identical twins occur when the mother produces two eggs and both are fertilised and implant in the womb successfully. So each twin will have its own placenta and will grow in its own bag of waters – the amnion (left). Identical twins occur following the splitting of a single fertilised egg. The egg effectively splits into two after fertilisation and two identical children will develop. If the split occurs very early, within three days of fertilisation, they will each have their own placenta and bag of waters in which to grow. But if the split occurs at 4–8 days after fertilisation, they will have a single shared placenta with an umbilical cord going to each baby, but will each have their own bag of waters in which to grow (middle). If the split occurs 9–12 days after fertilisation, then the twins will share a single placenta with an umbilical cord going to each baby. They will also develop within the same bag of waters (right).

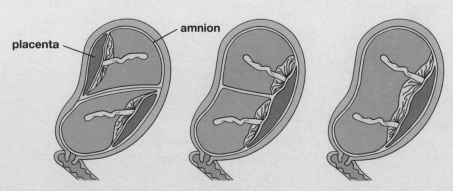

placenta   amnion

Length of pregnancy in singleton and multiple pregnancies

Singleton	40 weeks
Twins	37 weeks
Triplets	33 weeks
Quadruplets	29 weeks

subsequent scan shows only one baby. One of the twins may have been miscarried or even resorbed into the placenta, while the other twin continues to develop in the womb without any apparent problems.

Congenital abnormalities are also more common and most doctors recommend a detailed ultrasound scan of twins at around 18 weeks to look for any problems. If you are expecting twins, you will also be at risk of pre-eclampsia and premature labour. With regard to delivery, twin pregnancies tend to go into labour at around three weeks in advance of singleton pregnancies, with triplets a further 3–4 weeks earlier, and with quadruplets a further four weeks earlier. Thus, with increasing number of babies, the length of the pregnancy tends to shorten (see table above).

What is twin-to-twin transfusion syndrome?

A particular problem that can occur with a twin pregnancy is twin-to-twin transfusion syndrome. This can arise when the twins share the same placenta. In this situation the blood vessels from each twin merge together in the placenta in such a way that one twin loses blood from its circulation while the other gains it. The 'donor' twin will usually have impaired growth and anaemia as it is giving a lot of its blood to the other twin. By contrast, the 'recipient' twin may have problems from overloading of its circulation and high blood pressue. The recipient twin often has increased amniotic fluid production due to the circulation being overloaded, while the donor twin may have reduced amounts of amniotic fluid (referred to as oligohydramnios). Thus the womb often gets very much larger overall because of the increase in fluid in the recipient twin, which can lead to premature labour. Doctors have tried treating this condition by removing some of the excess fluid from the recipient twin, and laser treatment to the blood vessels that join the twins has also been tried. Clearly both twins are at increased risk of problems and specialised care is required.

How will having twins affect my pregnancy care?

The diagnosis of twins is usually made at an early stage of pregnancy due to the use of routine ultrasound scans. In view of the increased risk of problems in twin pregnancies, specialist care is usually required whereby the twins

Complications that arise more commonly in multiple pregnancies

- Exaggerated symptoms during early pregnancy, e.g. those of morning sickness
- Miscarriage
- Foetal abnormality
- Anaemia
- Placenta praevia (due to large placental site)
- Pre-eclampsia
- Premature labour
- Excess amniotic fluid (polyhydramnios)
- Twin-to-twin transfusion syndrome
- Bleeding in pregnancy and after delivery
- Small-for-dates babies

will be carefully monitored by ultrasound to check for problems such as disturbance in their growth or twin-to-twin transfusion syndrome. You should receive folic acid and iron supplements as maternal anaemia is more common in twin pregnancies because there are two babies to supply with nutrients. You will be advised of the risk of premature labour and you should seek medical advice if you suspect you might be in premature labour. You will be monitored carefully for the possible development of pre-eclampsia, your blood pressure and urinary protein being checked at every visit. You will therefore be seen much more frequently at the clinic than women with uncomplicated singleton pregancies.

Will I need a Caesarean section because I have twins?

There is a strong possibility that you will need delivery by Caesarean section if you have twins because of the increased risk of complications. If a twin pregnancy has any significant complication, such as breech presentation of the first twin or if there is pre-eclampsia, delivery is usually by Caesarean section. Where the first twin is coming into your pelvis head first, there are no other complications in your pregnancy and both twins are estimated to weigh more than 1.5 kg (3 lb 4 oz), it is usual to aim for spontaneous labour and vaginal delivery. During labour the heart rate of both twins must be monitored separately. If one of the twins becomes distressed, or if labour is not progressing well, Caesarean section will be required. Once vaginal delivery of the first twin occurs, you will be examined to determine if the second twin is coming head or bottom first. There is no point in trying to assess this prior to delivery as once the first twin is born there is a lot more space within womb for the second twin to move around and change its position. Sometimes the doctor will have to turn the second twin to make sure that it comes out head first. After delivery, because the womb has been so distended by the twins, there is a slightly higher risk of bleeding. Your doctors and midwives will watch carefully for this and give you medication to prevent bleeding after delivery.

Complications in a previous pregnancy

Most babies are born to mothers who have had no major complications during their pregnancy and delivery. Some women, however, do have problems, some of which are likely to recur while others may not. Most mothers want to know if a previous pregnancy complication is likely to recur and especially if there is anything they can do to prevent it happening again. Often there are measures you can take to reduce the risk or treatments that will improve the outcome in future pregnancies. It is therefore absolutely essential that you talk to your doctor about this before you try and get pregnant.

Can anything be done to prevent recurrent miscarriage?

The answer must depend on why you had a previous miscarriage. Early miscarriages are very common and investigations are unlikely to help unless you have had more than three in succession. Further investigations can help if you have a treatable condition. If, for example, you have recurrent miscarriage because the neck of your womb, the cervix, is weak this can be treated by inserting a special stitch to support the cervix and keep it closed. This stitch is inserted either before pregnancy or more commonly in early pregnancy. Women with blood-clotting problems that are associated with recurrent miscarriage can be treated in early pregnancy to correct the clotting problem. If corrected, the chance of a successful pregnancy is increased substantially. To be effective, treatment must start immediately you know you are pregnant and so it is best to organise this before you try to conceive. These examples stress the vital importance of pre-pregnancy advice. If you have any such problem, you should raise it with your doctor and seek specialist advice if required. *(See pp. 76–83 for full details on miscarriage.)*

Am I at risk of developing gestational diabetes again?

There is a form of diabetes that occurs only when you are pregnant. It is referred to as 'gestational' diabetes and is distinct from having diabetes before you get pregnant. If you have had gestational diabetes in a previous pregnancy, the recurrence rate is high. This condition is discussed in detail in *Your health in pregnancy (pp. 178–83)*.

Some risk factors for ectopic pregnancy

- Pelvic inflammatory disease
- Previous ectopic pregnancy
- Previous abdominal surgery
- Tubal sterilisation

I had a breech birth before. Is this likely to recur?

If you have had a previous breech presentation (in which the baby presents with its feet first) at term, the risk of it happening again is around 1 in 5. Sometimes the reason that a baby is breech is because the womb is abnormally shaped, thus preventing the baby from moving into the head-first position. There is nothing you can do to prevent recurrence. However, if a breech presentation is found at around 36–37 weeks, doctors can sometimes turn the baby round so that it is coming head first. This is referred to as external cephalic version, or ECV for short. *(See p. 233 for fuller details.)*

Am I likely to have another ectopic pregnancy?

This risk of ectopic pregnancy is high if you have already had one. A fallopian tube retained after surgery to remove the pregnancy from it, does, however, leave it more vulnerable to a future ectopic pregnancy. It should be borne in mind, though, that if you have had one tube removed, it is still possible to conceive using the other, undamaged tube to carry the fertilised egg to your womb. *(See pp. 83–6 for a fuller discussion on ectopic pregnancy.)*

Is premature delivery likely to recur?

Premature delivery is when labour and delivery occurs before 37 completed weeks of pregnancy. The complications of prematurity, or its associated conditions, are responsible for more than half of neonatal deaths in the Western world. Some premature babies die because they are born before they are mature enough to cope with life outside the womb, although advances in medical techniques mean that more and more premature babies are surviving. The baby's lungs are the last organ to mature before delivery at term. If your baby is born prematurely, the lungs may not be developed sufficiently to allow it to breathe properly. As a result, premature delivery can be associated with the baby having breathing problems, which in turn can lead to low levels of oxygen in the baby's blood and hence potential damage to other organs. However, steroid injections that are given to the mother 24–48 hours before the baby is born, substantially reduce the risk of breathing problems in the baby.

The precise cause of why mothers have premature babies is not properly known, though various risk factors have been identified *(see p. 235)*. If you have a past history of premature labour and delivery then there is a significant risk of it recurring, particularly if it has happened to you more than once. There is at present no proven treatment to prevent premature labour, although some of the factors that may precipitate it can be treated. If you have had a previous premature labour then it is worthwhile discussing this with your doctor and obtaining pre-pregnancy advice specific to your particular case.

2

Antenatal care & pregnancy complications

Second trimester

14–28 Weeks

Although your baby is fully formed by the end of the first trimester, there is still a lot of growing and development required to prepare the baby for life outside the womb. The second and third trimesters are designed to allow the baby sufficient time to grow and for its organs to mature so that they can support the baby after birth.

16 WEEKS

Foetal size: Average weight is 140 g (5 oz), head circumference is 12 cm (4½ in), abdomen circumference is 10 cm (4 in) and foot length is about 2 cm (¾ in).

Foetal development: Fine, downy hair develops on the skin, which is thin and almost translucent, allowing all the blood vessels beneath the skin to be seen. Eyebrows and eyelashes start to grow and eye movements can be seen for the first time, although the eyelids will not be able to open for another 12 weeks. Vigorous movements will be seen on the ultrasound scan. Generally, the baby will only lie still for about 6 minutes at a time at this stage.

Girl babies: The ovaries will have moved down from the abdomen to the pelvis. Already containing several million egg cells, they will allow her to have children when she, in turn, reaches adulthood.

By now your developing baby can hear sound and respond to light.

20 WEEKS

Baby size: Average weight is 325 g (11½ oz), head circumference is over 17 cm (6½ in), abdominal circumference or waist measurement is over 14 cm (5½ in) and foot length is around 3.2 cm (1¼ in).

Baby development: General growth of muscle enables the baby to move about in the womb much more vigorously; in particular, neck muscles strengthen, allowing the head to move. The beginnings of the permanent or second teeth are forming in the jaws. Hair develops on the head. The skin will now be covered with a white, waxy substance called vernix. This protects the skin from the amniotic fluid in which the baby is constantly immersed. There is still very little fat under the skin so the baby's body will appear thin on ultrasound scans.

Girl babies: The womb and vagina have formed by this stage.

Changes to the mother: Your waistline expands to accommodate the developing baby. You will be able to feel the top of your womb just below your navel or umbilicus. You will probably also have felt the first movements of your baby by this stage of pregnancy. In second and later pregnancies, movements are often felt a week or two earlier. The afterbirth or placenta is implanting deeper into your womb in order to be able to obtain sufficient supplies of nutrients and oxygen to meet the ever-increasing demands of the growing baby in the months ahead.

Most mothers-to-be will have felt the baby move by now as the increasing growth of muscle makes movement more vigorous.

Second trimester

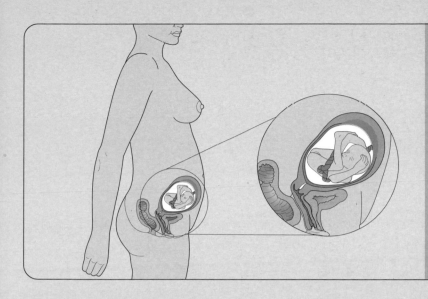

24 Weeks

- neck muscles strengthen allowing the head to move

- hair develops on the head

- skin covered with protective substance called vernix

- body appears thin as there is still little fat under skin

Baby size: Average weight is 650 g (1 lb 7 oz), height is 34 cm (13½ in), waist measurement is 19 cm (7½ in) and foot length is about 4.4 cm (1¾ in).
Baby development: Fingernails are fully grown by now. Development of the brain continues to advance. The digestive system can now absorb water and sugar. The baby's movements will be more vigorous and it will be able to reach out and touch the umbilical cord or rub its hands or body against the side of the womb.

Baby can swallow fluid and may get hiccups sometimes. When this happens you will be able to feel the regular jerks of each hiccup.

24
WEEKS

Baby size: Average weight is 1140 kg (2 lb 8 oz), height is 38 cm (15 in), waist is 23 cm (9 in), head circumference is 26 cm (10¼ in), foot length is 5 cm (2 in).
Baby development: The head, which until now will have been disproportionately large compared to the body, is coming into proportion with the body. The baby's eyelids can open at this stage. A cyclical pattern of activity develops, with the baby lying quietly or sleeping for about 20 minutes, then being active for 20 minutes, then lying quietly again for 20 minutes, and so on.
Changes to the mother: You will be able to feel the top of your womb about halfway between your navel and your breastbone by applying light pressure with your hands.

Fat builds up under the skin from now on, giving the baby its chubby looks at delivery.

28
WEEKS

Some complications to look out for in the second trimester

Thrush infections and urine infections **See p. 148** BEFORE 24 WEEKS: late miscarriage **See p. 76** AFTER 20–24 WEEKS: pre-eclampsia **See p. 136;** premature labour **See p. 235;** vaginal bleeding and abdominal pain **See p. 142.**

Second trimester

Your health in pregnancy

As we saw at the beginning of *Discovering you are pregnant (p. 64)*, your body will rapidly adapt to pregnancy in order to meet the demands of the growing baby. Some of these changes will be very apparent, but there are many changes that will not be so obvious to you. For a start, your heart will increase the amount of blood that that it pumps round your body every minute by about 40%. Before pregnancy your heart pumps just under 5 litres (8 pints) of blood every minute and this rises to about 7 litres (11 pints) per minute by 16 weeks of pregnancy. This is to ensure a good supply of blood to the placenta for it to deliver oxygen and nutrients to the baby.

This increased blood flow in your pelvis will lead to an increase in your normal vaginal secretions. The blood flow to your kidneys also increases in order to help them get rid of waste products in the urine, from both you and the baby, at a higher rate. To make it easier for blood to flow round the body, the blood vessels relax and open up. There is more blood flow to the skin and you will notice that blood vessels may be more prominent such as on your breasts. The amount of blood in your body also increases and you will be making more red blood cells to carry oxygen round the body.

The manufacture of red blood cells needs a good supply of iron and folic acid, so your body's demand for these important nutrients increases. Indeed, your body's ability to absorb iron from your food can increase by as much as

40% to meet these demands. To help ensure that there is enough oxygen for the baby, your breathing changes. Although you probably won't notice it, you will breathe more deeply and the amount of air passing in and out of your lungs may increase by as much as 40–50%.

The hormonal changes in your body also cause your bowel to slow down and this can lead to constipation. The ligaments that hold your bones together soften, in response to the hormonal changes of pregnancy, to prepare for labour. In particular, the pelvis is affected *(see p. 167)*, making you more prone to pain in your pelvis and lower back. Hence these adaptations in your body can sometimes lead to minor problems as well as having an impact on pre-existing medical disorders such as high blood pressure or heart problems. These changes can actually improve some medical conditions, however. For example, rheumatoid arthritis usually gets better in pregnancy. Other conditions may make you more prone to complications, such as high blood pressure, increasing the chance of your developing pre-eclampsia *(see p. 136)*.

So pregnancy can have an effect on your health, bringing with it a variety of symptoms such as the nausea of morning sickness *(see p. 67)*, backache and heartburn, which you might not have encountered before. You might also be prone to unwelcome changes such as acne, varicose veins and piles, although such changes are common in pregnancy.

Common minor physical ailments in pregnancy

I am getting a lot of heartburn. Is this normal in pregnancy?

Heartburn occurs when the acid secretions normally present in your stomach are pushed into the lower part of your gullet (or oesophagus). As the gullet is not designed to contain acid secretions, you will feel a burning sensation behind the lower part of your breastbone. Heartburn is more common in pregnancy. It is especially common in late pregnancy because of the pressure of the enlarging womb on your stomach, which forces the acid secretions up. It is often worse at night when you are lying down. To reduce heartburn, take small, frequent meals to avoid overloading your stomach and avoid fatty foods and strong tea and coffee. Often a glass of milk at bedtime will help. If you have trouble with heartburn, don't hesitate to consult your doctor, who will be able to recommend some treatment for it. Antacid medication can be helpful and is safe to take in pregnancy. If you get any pain in the upper abdomen, however, always consult your doctor immediately as this can occasionally be due to a problem associated with high blood pressure.

How common is constipation in pregnancy?

Constipation is very common in pregnancy as the pregnancy hormones tend to slow down the action of the bowel. Iron supplements can also lead to constipation. To prevent it you should drink a lot of water, and increase your fibre intake. Do not take any medications such as laxatives for constipation without first consulting your doctor or pharmacist.

Are varicose veins more common in pregnancy?

Varicose veins occur due to blood 'pooling' in your legs. The excess blood in your legs leads to stretching and bulging of the veins under the skin, causing them to become 'varicose'. Varicose veins are more common in pregnancy as the blood flow from the legs is much slower. This is due to the effect of pregnancy hormones and also the weight of the womb pressing on the blood vessels in your abdomen. If you have problems with varicose veins, you should avoid standing for long periods, keep your legs elevated when sitting and wear support stockings. Your doctor can advise you about this.

What are piles?

Piles are simply varicose veins around your anus. They tend to occur or worsen during pregnancy because of the pressure of the womb on the veins in your abdomen. This leads to sluggish blood flow in these veins, causing the blood to 'pool' in the veins around the anus. This 'stretches' the veins, leading to piles. You should avoid constipation as this will worsen piles; take plenty of foods rich in fibre. If your piles are very uncomfortable, consult your doctor, as there are some soothing medications that can be given.

I get 'pins and needles' in my hands especially at night. Why is this?

Pins and needles in your hands are quite common in pregnancy and are due to a nerve in your wrist getting trapped. This is caused by fluid retention – which is common in pregnancy – making the tissues swell. At the wrist, the nerves to the hand pass through a 'tunnel' of bone and ligaments. Swelling of the soft tissues in this 'tunnel' therefore leads to the nerve getting trapped and compressed, thereby causing the disturbed sensation that we feel as 'pins and needles'. Doctors refer to this as 'carpal tunnel syndrome'. This condition is very uncomfortable but does not lead to any serious problems and usually resolves soon after delivery. It can be eased if you sleep with your arm and hand on a pillow. If it is very troublesome, consult your doctor. A splint for the wrist worn at night will often help relieve the problem.

When I stand for a while or lie flat, I feel faint. Is this because I am pregnant?

During pregnancy you are more susceptible to feeling faint when you stand for long periods or lie flat. The blood flow from the legs slows down considerably in pregnancy and thus blood has a tendency to 'pool' in your legs. This results in less blood being available for your heart to pump round the body and in particular to your brain. Hence you will feel faint. When lying flat on your back in late pregnancy, you might also feel faint as your womb will press on the major blood vessels that carry blood from you lower body back to your heart. Again, this reduces the amount of blood for your heart to pump around the body.

Walking does not have the same effect, however. When you walk, the muscle activity in your legs pumps the blood back to your heart. Occasionally, you may feel faint if you stand up suddenly. This is because your body has not adjusted quickly enough to the change in position and reduced blood flow, so you should avoid getting up suddenly. If you feel faint, sit down or lie down on your side. Avoid getting too hot as this will lead to your blood pressure falling and make you more likely to feel faint.

What is pelvic diastasis?

When you are pregnant the ligaments in your body soften owing to the effects of the pregnancy hormones. In particular, the pelvis is affected. This is not a single bone but rather three large bones held together by ligaments. The softening of these ligaments allows a little more mobility of the pelvic bones, which is invaluable during labour as it helps the pelvis accommodate the baby's

This X-ray shows how widely separated the two pubic bones can become in pregnancy, marked with 'x'. This happens during pregnancy because the ligaments in your body soften owing to the effects of the pregnancy hormones. Pelvic diastasis occurs when the increased mobility of the pelvic bones is excessive, particularly at the joint at the front of the pelvis – the symphysis pubis.

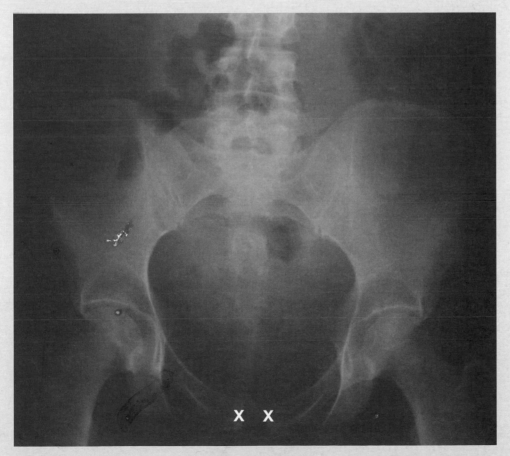

head as it passes through the birth canal. Sometimes, however, the softening of the ligaments and the increased mobility of the pelvic bones is excessive, particularly at the joint at the front of the pelvis – the symphysis pubis. This condition, known as pelvic diastasis, causes the symphysis pubis that is usually held rigid by the ligaments around it to slacken a great deal, leading to pain on movement. Pelvic diastasis can come on during pregnancy or delivery, or sometimes after delivery. If you develop this condition, you will feel pain in the pubic region and groin and often have low back pain. The pain is exacerbated by walking, climbing stairs or moving around in bed. You may even hear an audible click when you walk. You will usually be unable to stand on one leg and may find you have to walk with a waddling motion.

Pelvic diastasis occurs in about 1 in 800 pregancies. If it is very painful, medication for pain relief can help, but it is essential to take some of the stress off your pelvis. A pelvic support is often useful and sometimes elbow crutches are necessary. You should avoid any non-essential lifting or weight bearing, such as carrying shopping. If you swim, avoid the breaststroke as this stresses your pelvis. During delivery your birth attendants must be aware of the problem as separation of your legs must be kept to a minimum. This is especially important if you have an epidural anaesthetic as you will not be aware of pain and so will not naturally limit the separation of your legs. Even after delivery it is important to avoid excessive stress on your hips while the doctor or midwife is stitching an episiotomy, if one is required. After delivery you will need to have medication for pain relief and a pelvic support. In addition, you will need to rest and to mobilise gradually, so you will need a great deal of support with the baby. This condition usually resolves after delivery. If it persists, you should seek medical advice as specialised physiotherapy may be needed.

The overweight mother

Is there an ideal weight to achieve for pregnancy?

There is no 'ideal' weight for pregnancy. The way to work out if your weight is satisfactory is to calculate your body mass index, or BMI *(see p. 40; see also weight gain in pregnancy, p. 98)*.

Are many women overweight?

Yes, the proportion of people who are overweight in developed countries is increasing. In this country around 30% of women are overweight and as many as 15% have a body mass index of over 30 (obese).

Which BMI categories are associated with pregnancy problems?

The low (less than 20) and obese (31.0–40.9) BMI categories are associated with pregnancy problems. Although it is probably ideal to be in the normal range (20.0–25.9) before pregnancy, the overweight range (26.0–30.9) is not usually associated with major problems, provided there is no excessive weight gain in

Pregnancy complications that can arise in overweight mothers

- Miscarriage
- Increased risk of neural tube defects like spina bifida
- High blood pressure is four times more likely
- Pre-eclampsia
- Pregnancy-associated diabetes
- Thrombosis
- Slow progress in labour
- Increased frequency of Caesarean delivery
- Increased risk of wound infection following delivery
- Urinary tract infections
- A large-for-dates baby
- Difficulty with delivery because the shoulders are too big
- Foetal distress in labour

pregnancy. However, miscarriage rates do increase a little when the body mass index is in excess of 25.

Can I diet to lose weight in pregnancy?

Dieting to lose a lot of weight is not advisable during pregnancy *(see p. 95)*.

Is exercise important for weight loss?

Exercise is important for weight loss *(see p. 99)*. Try to find a form of exercise you enjoy and make it part of your routine. Your doctor can advise you on suitable forms of antenatal exercise.

What are the increased risks in pregnancy for the overweight mother?

Your pre-pregnancy weight has the strongest effect on the baby's birthweight and is a more important factor than weight gain in pregnancy. Women who are very overweight, particularly those with BMI over 30 when they embark on pregnancy, have an increased risk of problems – *see table above*.

How will being overweight affect my treatment in pregnancy?

Because of the increase in risk of neural tube defects, you should ideally start folic acid vitamin supplements prior to conception, and continue them for at least the first 12 weeks of pregnancy. As we saw in Preparing your body for pregnancy *(p. 28)*, folic acid supplements can reduce the risk of neural tube defects. Your doctor may offer you an ultrasound scan at around 18 weeks to check for foetal abnormality and you may be checked for pregnancy-induced diabetes. This requires a test in which you take a glucose drink after an overnight fast. Your blood sugar is checked before and after the glucose drink. Your doctors will also check regularly for the complications that are more common in overweight mothers, such as pre-eclampsia. Sometimes you will require treatment to prevent a thrombosis from occurring – your doctor will advise you about this. Your weight will be checked regularly throughout the pregnancy. There is no need for overweight women to gain the same amount of weight usually associated with pregnancy. Even if you put on no weight in pregnancy, this will not affect the baby provided you have a balanced diet *(see p. 36)*. The baby's growth is usually monitored by ultrasound scan as abdominal examination to estimate the size of the baby is difficult in the case of a very overweight mother.

Are there special considerations for labour and delivery if I am overweight?

Slow progress in labour is more common if you are very overweight, so you will have a higher chance of having a Caesarean delivery *(see p. 240)*. Emergency Caesarean carries a higher risk of complications than a planned one performed before labour, especially if you are very overweight. Sometimes a planned Caesarean section is considered the least hazardous mode of delivery. The plan for your delivery must be suited to your own particular situation and needs, however, and you should discuss this with your doctor, who will be able to give you the specific advice required. If you are having a normal vaginal delivery and the baby is large, the doctors and midwives will be watching for shoulder dystocia, in which the baby's shoulders cause difficulty in delivery because of their size.

After delivery will I need any special treatment if I am overweight?

You are likely to need treatment to prevent blood clots, often with injections of heparin under the skin, especially if you had a Caesarean section. You should be on the look-out for a urinary tract infection, which usually is associated with pain on passing urine. In addition, you should avoid dieting to lose weight while breast-feeding is being established. However, once feeding is established, you can lose up to 2 kg ($4^1/2$ lb) each month without influencing your milk production.

Common medical conditions in pregnancy

Many women entering pregnancy have an underlying medical condition, such as epilepsy, asthma, thyroid problems, high blood pressure, diabetes or migraine, and may be receiving medication for it. Others may have had a problem in the past, such as a venous thrombosis in the leg, which, although no longer present, can have particular implications for their pregnancy. Many medical conditions and the medication used to treat them can have an important effect on pregnancy. Conversely, pregnancy itself can also influence medical conditions and their medication. If you have a medical problem, and many women do, it is important to consider this before and during pregnancy. This will allow you to know whether your condition has any particular implications for your pregnancy, and also whether any alterations are required to your medication before or during pregnancy. There are a vast number of medical conditions that can be encountered in pregnancy and specific advice is often needed. The rest of this chapter will focus on some of the more common conditions. They are covered in alphabetical order:

- Anaemia *(see p. 171)*
- Asthma *(see p. 172)*
- Bowel problems *(see p. 173)*
- Connective tissue disease *(see p. 174)*
- Diabetes *(see p. 178)*
- Epilepsy *(see p. 183)*
- Hay fever *(see p. 186)*
- Heart disease *(see p. 186)*
- High blood pressure *(see p. 188)*
- Migraine *(see p. 189)*
- Thyroid problems *(see p. 190)*
- Venous thrombosis *(see p. 191)*

Anaemia

Can I become anaemic during pregnancy?

Anaemia is common in pregnancy due to the demands of the developing baby on your vitamin and iron stores. It is more likely if you have twins, which will make a heavy demand on your iron and vitamin stores, or if you have several pregnancies close together. The most common form of anaemia in pregnancy is iron deficiency anaemia. Deficiency of folic acid can also cause anaemia. Often iron deficiency and folic acid deficiency occur together. Vitamin B12 deficiency can cause anaemia but this is rare in pregnancy.

How will I know if I am anaemic?

You may feel tired but often you will have no symptoms. Your doctor will routinely check your blood count in pregnancy to look for anaemia. Usually anaemia in pregnancy is diagnosed when the haemoglobin level (the substance carrying oxygen in you blood) falls below 10.5–11 g% at any time during pregnancy. If you are anaemic, the doctor might check the levels of iron and folic acid in your body with a blood test.

How is anaemia treated in pregnancy?

Ideally, it is best to prevent anaemia with a good diet or with iron and folic acid supplements if you are at high risk of anaemia, such as with a twin pregnancy. The usual treatment of iron deficiency anaemia is with iron tablets. These should be combined with folic acid supplements. Vitamin C is sometimes prescribed along with the iron as this may enhance absorption, but taking a glass of fresh orange juice with the iron tablets is also effective. If you cannot take tablets then syrup forms of iron are available. Very occasionally, an iron injection can be given if you have a severe problem with anaemia and cannot take iron by mouth.

Asthma

Does pregnancy affect asthma?

Asthma commonly affects young women – around 5% are affected – so it is not unusual for doctors to encounter women with asthma in pregnancy. Pregnancy has a variable affect on asthma. In some women the asthma worsens and in others it stays the same, while there are others in whom it improves. Until you are pregnant it is generally impossible to predict what will happen, although it is unusual for a mother with well-controlled asthma and minimal symptoms to develop significant problems in pregnancy in the absence of some other complicating factor, such as a chest infection. However, women with severe asthma may find it gets worse in the later stages of pregnancy when the womb is very large and thus can affect breathing.

Will my asthma affect the pregnancy?

Well-controlled asthma is very unlikely to affect your pregnancy. However, uncontrolled severe asthma can be associated with low oxygen levels in your blood, which could potentially upset the baby. In modern medical practice in the UK, severe uncontrolled asthma is very uncommon. However, this emphasises the importance of maintaining your asthma medication while you are pregnant.

Will my asthma medication harm the baby?

Sometimes women stop their asthma therapy because they are worried about the effects of the medication on the unborn child. None of the medications commonly used to treat asthma, including the bronchodilators (medication that relieves wheeze), and inhaled and oral steroids and theophyllines (medication used to prevent wheeze) pose any significant risk to the baby. Indeed, the risks posed by uncontrolled asthma far outweigh the risks associated with any of these medications. Furthermore, all these medications are safe, take while breast-feeding. If you are on oral steroid medication, however, especially at high doses, there is an increased risk of developing gestational diabetes.

Will my asthma be treated differently when I am pregnant?

Treatment of asthma in pregnancy is virtually identical to treatment when you are not pregnant. You should avoid, if possible, anything that you know triggers your asthma. In some cases the doctor will recommend that you monitor your peak flow (measured when you breathe out as hard as possible into a special tube that gives a reading of how 'wheezy' you are). A 'dip' in your peak flow measurement, particularly in the evening, may precede worsening of your wheeze, and this can help you or your doctors adjust your therapy to prevent your symptoms getting worse.

Will asthma need special treatment in labour?

You should continue your usual asthma medication while in labour. If you have been on steroid tablets for a while, you may need some steroid injections in labour. Your doctor will advise you about this. All the usual forms of pain relief – epidurals, gas and air, and opiate painkillers like morphine – are safe. However, if you need a Caesarean delivery then epidural or spinal analgesia is better than a general anaesthetic if you have asthma.

If I have a severe attack of asthma, what should I do?

Severe asthma attacks can be dangerous in pregnancy, just as they are when you are not pregnant. You should seek medical help at once. You may require admission to hospital for treatment. If there is any evidence of a chest infection triggering the asthma attack, you will need treatment with antibiotics. The usual antibiotics prescribed for chest infections are safe in pregnancy, with the exception of tetracyclines, which should be avoided because they can cause staining of the baby's teeth.

Bowel problems

Can irritable bowel syndrome worsen in pregnancy?

Irritable bowel syndrome (IBS) is a relatively common condition in women. With IBS there is an alteration of the bowel's motility which leads to recurrent episodes of abdominal pain, due to bowel spasm, and altered bowel habit that can either be constipation or diarrhoea. Indeed, the constipation and diarrhoea may alternate. Doctors don't know the actual cause of IBS, but it is associated with a diet low in roughage and high in refined carbohydrates. Symptoms can be triggered or worsened by stress. Although uncomfortable, distressing and sometimes debilitating during attacks, the symptoms of IBS do not cause any long-term serious harm. Most women with irritable bowel syndrome will have had the diagnosis made by their doctor before their pregnancy. The diagnosis is usually made after investigation of recurrent bowel upsets or abdominal pain. Because pregnancy can reduce the bowel's motility, making you more prone to constipation, women who have constipation as a major symptom of their IBS can find that the condition may get worse. However, this will not harm the pregnancy. The best treatment is a high-fibre diet. Your doctor can also give you medication to make your stools more bulky and this will often help relieve the symptoms. Sometimes medication to relieve bowel spasm can help, but you should not take any medication for this during pregnancy except on your doctor's advice.

Does inflammatory bowel disease worsen in pregnancy or cause pregnancy complications?

There are two forms of inflammatory bowel disease: Crohn's disease and ulcerative colitis. These conditions together affect just over 1 in every 1000 young women. When uncontrolled they cause symptoms such as diarrhoea, abdominal pain and weight loss. They may even require surgery if complications arise. Pregnancy does not usually cause any worsening of inflammatory bowel disease. While a flare-up of ulcerative colitis can occur in pregnancy, this is no more likely to happen during pregnancy than when you are not pregnant. Indeed, the risk is lower if the problem is well controlled when you conceive. For Crohn's disease the majority of women do not experience any worsening of their condition during pregnancy. Nor is the risk of pregnancy complications significantly altered where inflammatory bowel disease is well controlled before conception and throughout pregnancy. So it is best to conceive when the problem is well controlled and inactive.

If you have had surgery for inflammatory bowel disease, this sometimes has to be taken into account when considering the best way for you to deliver. Your doctor will be able to advise you about this. The medications most commonly used to control inflammatory bowel disease, such as steroids, including steroid enemas, and mesalazine, are considered safe for pregnancy and breast-feeding, but you should review your medication with your doctor when you are planning to conceive. In addition, it is usual to recommend that you take folic acid vitamin supplements before and during pregnancy.

Connective tissue disease

Connective tissue diseases are a group of conditions where inflammation attacks various parts of the body. Two examples of connective tissue disease are SLE (systemic lupus erythematosis) and rheumatoid arthritis. In rheumatoid arthritis it is the joints that are affected, while in SLE the joints, skin, kidneys and many other organs can be affected.

I have rheumatoid arthritis. Will it get worse in pregnancy?

People with rheumatoid arthritis suffer from painful, stiff and sometimes swollen joints. The hands and wrists are often affected. It is more common in women than in men and is found in only 1–2 pregnancies in every 1000. Rheumatoid arthritis rarely causes significant problems in pregnancy, however, and in fact improves markedly during the course of the pregnancy in around three-quarters of women. Doctors think that this improvement may be due to increased production of anti-inflammatory steroid hormones by your body during pregnancy. Thus it is often possible during pregnancy to reduce the medication used to control the symptoms of rheumatoid arthritis. However, especially in women in whom the condition has improved during pregnancy, there is a risk of the rheumatoid arthritis worsening after the pregnancy is over.

Does rheumatoid arthritis cause complications in pregnancy?

Unlike SLE, rheumatoid arthritis does not itself cause any significant complications in pregnancy.

Is my medication for rheumatoid arthritis safe to use in pregnancy?

Three of the most commonly used medications for rheumatoid arthritis are paracetamol, non-steroidal anti-inflammatory drugs (NSAIDs) and steroids. Paracetamol is safe in pregnancy and is useful as a simple first-line painkiller for rheumatoid arthritis. NSAIDs are commonly used to control rheumatoid arthritis outside pregnancy. However, long-term use of this medication in pregnancy can sometimes result in low levels of amniotic fluid round the baby, due to the baby's kidneys producing less urine. Hence doctors generally try to avoid using NSAIDs in the last 2–3 months of pregnancy. Sometimes this medication has to be used. If treatment with NSAIDs is required for more than a short time in late pregnancy, it is often useful to check the amount of amniotic fluid round the baby with an ultrasound scan.

Steroid therapy is safe for the baby in pregnancy as there is no evidence of this medication causing any abnormality. However, steroid therapy puts the mother at greater risk of developing gestational diabetes. If you are on steroids for more than a couple of weeks during pregnancy, you will usually need steroid injections when you are in labour. This will allow your body to cope with the stress of labour. Several other medications may be used to control rheumatoid arthritis, some of which appear safe to use in pregnancy, while others need to be avoided. You should discuss your medication with your doctor, ideally before you try to become pregnant and particularly if you have any doubts or concerns about your health or medications.

What is SLE and how can it affect pregnancy?

SLE affects roughly 1 in every 1000 women, but as it often occurs at around 25–35 years of age, it is therefore not unusual for women with SLE to be pregnant. Men are only very rarely affected. SLE is an inflammatory condition that most often affects the joints and skin, and a rash over the cheeks is common, such as when you are exposed to sunlight. The kidneys can be involved and this can cause kidney damage and high blood pressure. Other organs like the lungs can sometimes be affected, too. It can also upset the blood, leading to problems like anaemia. The condition tends to come and go, with relapses and remissions.

SLE can be associated with particular problems in pregnancy, including miscarriage, premature delivery, a small-for-dates baby, pre-eclampsia and thrombosis (see box overleaf). However, you are less likely to encounter these problems if you conceive when your SLE is not active and where medication is minimal. SLE is very variable in its severity and in the problems it can cause. The condition can be mild and not cause serious problems in pregnancy; where it is more severe, however, it can be associated with serious complications both for the mother and the baby. The particular problems you

SLE and possible problems in pregnancy

- Miscarriage
- Small-for-dates baby (due to intrauterine growth restriction)
- Premature delivery
- Temporary lupus-like condition in the baby
- Flare-up of SLE, particularly in early pregnancy and after delivery
- Pre-eclampsia
- Deterioration in kidney function
- Thrombosis

will be at risk of in pregnancy because of SLE will be determined by the severity of your condition, the particular organs involved, and by the level of key factors in your blood.

What happened in any previous pregnancies will also be important. In general terms, the likelihood of pregnancy complications is much less if you conceive while the SLE is in remission, and do not have high blood pressure, kidney involvement, or substances known as antiphospholipid antibodies *(see opposite)* in your blood. This is a very specialised area and ideally you should obtain advice from a physician or obstetrician with specific expertise in this area of medicine.

Can I continue with my medication for SLE during pregnancy?

Your medication may have to be modified before and during pregnancy as some drugs used in SLE are best avoided when you are pregnant. Steroids, which are commonly used, are not associated with major pregnancy problems in the usual doses for controlling SLE. In particular, steroids are not associated with any abnormality in the baby. The overriding concern regarding SLE when you are trying to get pregnant and also in pregnancy is to keep the disease from flaring up. There is generally no need to avoid steroid medication. You should obtain advice from a physician or obstetrician with specific expertise in SLE about drug therapy for your condition, ideally before you become pregnant.

Will pregnancy make my SLE worse?

It is somewhat controversial as to whether SLE tends to worsen or not in pregnancy, but some experts consider that a flare-up of lupus is slightly more likely when you are pregnant. There may also be a risk of a flare-up after delivery. When SLE does worsen during pregnancy, the blood and kidneys tend to be more affected than the joints. For women with significant kidney involvement in SLE, this can worsen in pregnancy but will be no worse in the longer term.

What problems can the baby have?

The baby's growth can be affected in the womb if SLE damages the placenta, which can lead to premature delivery. After it is born, there is a small chance that the baby will develop a temporary form of SLE that will resolve over a few weeks or months. Sometimes this takes the form of a characteristic rash and sometimes the baby's blood will be upset by problems such as anaemia. However, most babies will not be affected. One very rare problem is where the electrical system that controls the baby's heart rate is damaged. This leads to a problem called 'heart block' where the heart beats at a slow, steady pace and cannot go faster in response to stress. This occurs only if the mother has a certain antibody in her blood known as 'anti-Ro', and even if this antibody is present, the chance of the baby getting heart block is around only 2%. Doctors can watch for this developing while the baby is in the womb using ultrasound and can sometimes treat it before the baby is born. Your doctor can also check if you have anti-Ro antibodies in your blood and give you advice for your situation. Most women with SLE do not have this antibody. Even if you do have it, remember that the baby has only a very small chance of being affected.

What is antiphospholipid antibody syndrome?

Antibodies are substances normally made by the body to fight infection. In conditions such as connective tissue disease, the body directs antibodies against itself. These antibodies can therefore damage various parts of the body. Antiphospholipid antibodies are present in between 5 and 20% of women with SLE. However, they can be present in women without underlying SLE. Indeed, around only half the women with antiphospholipid antibodies have SLE. These antibodies can upset the blood-clotting system and lead to an increased risk of blood clots (thrombosis), which in turn can affect the placenta, leading to problems such as miscarriage, which can be recurrent, pre-eclampsia, venous thrombosis and a small-for-dates baby. Where recurrent miscarriage occurs because of this problem, treatment with low doses of aspirin and heparin injections will substantially reduce the risk of miscarriage. Your doctor can find out if you have antiphospholipid antibodies by taking a simple blood test. It is important to remember that many women with these antibodies do not have problems. If a woman has a problem such as a thrombosis or recurrent miscarriage associated with these antibodies, then she will be said to have antiphospholipid antibody syndrome.

How will SLE influence my pregnancy care?

The treatment of SLE in pregnancy ideally requires collaboration between specialist physicians, obstetricians and paediatricians. It is best to discuss the problems of SLE in pregnancy with your doctors before you try to become pregnant. The aim is for you to conceive when the SLE is in remission and with a level of medication suitable for pregnancy. If you have antiphospholipid antibodies, for instance, you may require low-dose aspirin and heparin to prevent problems with recurrent miscarriage and thrombosis. Even where antiphospholipid antibodies are not present, many doctors will sometimes prescribe low-dose aspirin to try to reduce the risk of complications in SLE. Careful, regular monitoring of both you and the baby is required to check for problems like pre-eclampsia and impaired foetal growth. This means that you will usually be seen more frequently for antenatal checks and will have more frequent ultrasound scans to determine that the baby is growing well. Your doctor will also be watching for any evidence of a flare-up of your SLE. If one occurs, it will probably be managed with steroid medication. If you have high blood pressure, this should be controlled with suitable medication.

Diabetes

I have diabetes. What risk is there to my baby in pregnancy?

If you have insulin-dependent diabetes, you are at an increased risk of pregnancy complications, which can affect both you and your baby. There is a small increase in the risk of congenital abnormalities in the baby, such as cleft palate, heart and kidney abnormalities, and neural tube defects like spina bifida. This risk is about three times higher than that of a non-diabetic mother and appears to be related to high levels of glucose (sugar) in the blood in early pregnancy, at the time that the baby's organs are forming. Hence good blood-glucose control before and in the early stages of pregnancy reduces this risk of abnormality, and illustrates the critical importance of really good diabetic control in the early weeks of pregnancy. To be certain of this, it is best to make sure that your diabetes is well controlled before you try to conceive.

Miscarriage is also more common in women with poorly controlled diabetes. In addition, the baby is at risk of being large, due in part to the excess sugar it may receive, which can lead to problems in labour and delivery. It is not unusual for the baby to have excess fluid around it in the womb, making your womb large for dates. Often the doctor will monitor the baby's growth with ultrasound scans throughout the pregnancy. If there is a disturbance of the baby's growth, then monitoring tests like the CTG or biophysical profile are employed to confirm the baby's well-being *(see pp. 124–35)*.

Am I at risk of any pregnancy complications because of my diabetes?

Diabetes puts you at increased risk of problems like pre-eclampsia. You will also be a little more prone to bladder infections and thrush.

How does pregnancy affect my diabetes?

During pregnancy you will find your insulin dose will increase, rising by the end of your pregnancy to 2–3 times that of your pre-pregnancy requirements. This is because of changes in the hormones that influence your blood-glucose control, due, in particular, to a hormone called human placental lactogen (produced by the placenta) which antagonises the effects of insulin. After delivery of the afterbirth, your insulin requirements generally return to those of pre-pregnancy.

If you suffer from morning sickness, it is critically important to maintain a reasonable intake of glucose (glucose-rich drinks can be helpful) and maintain your insulin treatment. The dose of insulin may need to be adjusted in such instances. In addition, you should try the usual remedies for morning sickness, such as small, frequent meals, and eating dry toast or biscuits before getting out of bed in the morning. Where you are having difficulty with morning sickness and diabetic control is difficult, you should not hesitate to get medical advice.

If you have eye or kidney problems because of your diabetes, these can sometimes worsen in pregnancy. Your doctor will check your eyes and kidney function when you become pregnant. It is well proven that good blood-glucose control during the pregnancy reduces the likelihood of diabetic complications like eye problems developing. You should discuss the effect of pregnancy on your diabetes with your diabetic physician. It is best to have this discussion before becoming pregnant so that you have all the information you need before you conceive.

How will diabetes influence my pregnancy care?

There are special clinics for pregnant women with diabetes, with an obstetrician and a diabetic physician in attendance. There may also be specialist support from other professions, such as dieticians or midwives with an interest in diabetes. These clinics have been shown to be highly effective in managing diabetes in pregnancy. You should, for instance, receive advice about the importance of good blood-glucose control during the early weeks of pregnancy to minimise the risk of foetal abnormality. Many doctors will check that your thyroid gland is working normally, as it is not unusual for women with diabetes to have thyroid problems, which can be easily treated in pregnancy. You will also be advised to take folic acid supplements to reduce the risk of foetal abnormality. You may be offered a blood test at around 16 weeks and a detailed ultrasound scan at around 18 weeks to check for any abnormality in the baby. Your doctor will check regularly for complications like urinary tract infection and pre-eclampsia and also carefully assess the baby's growth. You will therefore usually be seen more frequently than a mother without diabetes.

How will pregnancy influence my diabetic management?

You will need to keep a careful record of your blood-glucose levels and insulin dose so that your insulin dose can be adjusted to maintain good control. A home glucose meter can be useful in providing accurate measurements of your blood glucose. Diet is important – a high-fibre, low-sugar, low-fat diet is usually recommended – and your doctor will set targets for your blood sugar. A typical target range would be a blood glucose concentration of 4–6 mmol/L before meals and less than 7.5–8 mmol/L one hour after meals. However, the targets need to be realistic and achievable ones for your particular situation and this requires individual advice from your diabetes physician.

Your insulin therapy will often need to be adjusted. Switching from twice-daily insulin injections to four times daily injections can help provide optimal

Your health in pregnancy

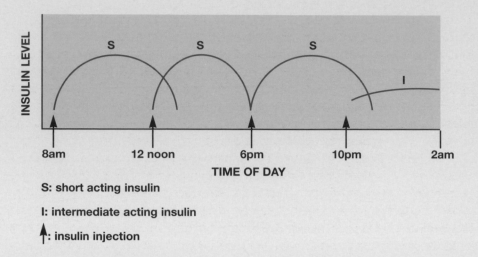

Typical insulin regimen in pregnancy.

blood-glucose control. Short-acting insulin may be used before breakfast, lunch and dinner, with an intermediate-acting insulin at night. Low blood glucose (hypoglycaemia) is relatively common when you are trying for such good diabetic control, and snacks taken mid-morning and afternoon can help to prevent this happening. It is essential that both you and your partner are able to recognise the symptoms of low blood glucose *(see box below)* and how to correct it. In addition, you should carry a source of glucose with you at all times. Check your blood glucose before driving or operating machinery, in case of a hypoglycaemia. Your doctor will discuss all this with you.

Will my diabetes influence labour and delivery?

Because there may be risks for the baby from going beyond the due date, most doctors try and deliver women with diabetes by their due date and often a little earlier. Diabetic mothers have a higher rate of Caesarean delivery; indeed, more than half of women with diabetes may require a Caesarean

Symptoms of low blood glucose (hypoglycaemia)

- Lack of coordination
- Slurred speech
- Sweating
- Tremors
- Nausea
- Dizziness
- Hunger
- Confusion
- Abnormal behaviour
- Headache
- Visual disturbance
- Inability to move

section. This may be because the baby is very big, or because of complications that require an earlier delivery like pre-eclampsia or excess fluid round the baby. If your labour is progressing very slowly or if the baby is found to be too big to deliver safely through your pelvis, then Caesarean delivery will be performed. If a Caesarean section is performed, you will usually be treated with antibiotics to prevent infection. This is because of the slightly higher risk of infection with diabetes, particularly bladder and kidney infection and wound infection. In a vaginal delivery one of the main considerations with a larger baby is shoulder dystocia, where there is difficulty in delivering the baby's shoulders. The doctor and midwife will be watching for this and will take prompt action to remedy the situation if it occurs. During labour your diabetes is usually controlled by an intravenous infusion of glucose and insulin. Your blood-glucose level will be measured regularly and the insulin dose adjusted to keep the blood glucose at a satisfactory level, usually between 4 and 7–8 mmol/L. Following the delivery, your insulin dose should be reduced, usually to the pre-pregnancy level.

How will my baby be affected?

The baby will have a slightly higher risk of jaundice *(see p. 251)*, which is common in newborn babies, but a little more prevalent where the mother is diabetic. In addition, the baby will be at risk of having low blood glucose (sugar) and may need to have its glucose levels checked for the first few days. When a baby is born prematurely (before 37 weeks), the baby of a diabetic mother is more likely to have breathing difficulties, as the lungs tend to be a little more immature. The paediatricians can usually treat this, however. If the doctor anticipates a premature delivery then injections of steroid given to you 24 hours or so before delivery can substantially reduce this problem by enhancing the maturity of the baby's lungs *(see p. 236)*. However, as these steroids can upset your diabetic control, extra care is required to make sure that good blood-glucose control is maintained.

There is no evidence that diabetes in pregnancy has any harmful effects in the long term on your child's intelligence or development. If your partner does not suffer from diabetes, there is about a 2 in 100 chance of your child developing insulin-dependent diabetes before the age of 20. Interestingly, in pregnancies where only the father and not the mother has insulin-dependent diabetes, the baby has around a 1 in 20 chance of developing diabetes in later life – higher than if only the mother is affected!

What is pregnancy-induced diabetes?

Pregnancy-induced or gestational diabetes is the situation where you develop high blood-glucose levels and therefore become temporarily 'diabetic' while you are pregnant. This is because the pregnancy changes in your body antagonise the effects of insulin, the hormone that controls your blood sugar. If your body cannot compensate sufficiently for this by making more insulin, you will develop abnormally high levels of blood glucose (sugar). The high level of glucose in

Reasons doctors look for gestational diabetes

- If you have high levels of glucose in your urine on two occasions (this is one reason your urine is examined at each antenatal check)
- If you have a strong family history of diabetes
- If you have previously had a very large baby
- If you have a history of gestational diabetes
- If you have previously had an unexplained stillbirth
- If you develop too much amniotic fluid (polyhydramnios)
- If you are very overweight

your blood will pass through the placenta to the baby and will therefore affect the baby's growth.

How do doctors check for gestational diabetes?

Some doctors check all pregnant women for gestational diabetes. Others only check if there are specific indications. This is mainly because gestational diabetes varies considerably in different populations. In some parts of the world it is much more common than in others. For example, there is a higher incidence in women from southern Asia and in Afro-Caribbean women. Doctors check for gestational diabetes using a glucose tolerance test (as described above). Your blood sugar is checked before and after the glucose drink. High levels of blood glucose indicate gestational diabetes.

What happens if my glucose tolerance test is abnormal?

If you have an elevated blood-glucose level, you will usually be given dietary advice by your doctor or a dietician. As for pregnant women with pre-existing diabetes, your diet should be low in sugar and fat and high in fibre. If possible, increase your dietary fibre up to 35 g (1 oz) per day *(see p. 97 for good sources of fibre)*. Your carbohydrate intake, the main source of energy, should be from sources like bread, pasta and potatoes.

If you are overweight, you will be advised to limit your weight gain in pregnancy and you will need special advice on diet and weight from your doctor or dietician. In addition, you will need careful and regular assessments of your blood glucose. Sometimes, if diet alone does not correct the problem, insulin injections will be needed.

Why is gestational diabetes a cause for concern?

Gestational diabetes can lead to the baby being large due to the extra glucose it has been receiving from you. Just as in insulin-dependent diabetes, the condition can lead to problems in pregnancy, labour and delivery, as outlined above. If you develop gestational diabetes there is an increased likelihood of your baby being overweight in later childhood. You may also be at increased risk of developing non-insulin dependent (diet- and tablet-controlled) diabetes in later life. However, the risk can be reduced if you adjust your diet and lifestyle to correct or avoid obesity after pregnancy, as the risk of developing this form of diabetes in later life is related directly to how heavy you are. As each case is different, you should discuss your own condition with your doctor, who can advise you about the implications of gestational diabetes in your own particular situation.

Epilepsy

What effects do epilepsy and anti-epileptic medication have on pregnancy?
Epilepsy occurs in about 1 in 100–200 women, so it is not unusual for doctors to encounter women with epilepsy who are pregnant. The problem that worries women with epilepsy most is the higher rate of foetal abnormalities related to anti-epileptic medication, possibly due to folic acid metabolism being upset by the treatment, although genetic factors might also play a part. This is why it is especially important for women on anti-epileptic medication to take folic acid when planning a pregnancy and to continue this in early pregnancy.

There is also an increased risk of pregnancy complications like severe morning sickness, anaemia, vaginal bleeding and of having a baby that is small for dates. The anaemia may be due to folic acid metabolism being upset by anti-epileptic therapy, but doctors don't really know why these other complications arise. In addition, some anti-epileptic medications antagonise vitamin K, important for the production of clotting factors that stop us bleeding. As vitamin K levels may be upset by your anti-epileptic medication, your doctor may prescribe vitamin K tablets from around 36 weeks of your pregnancy. These will boost not only your own but also your baby's vitamin K level before it is born.

Can an epileptic fit harm my baby?
There is no evidence that a single fit will cause the baby any problem. However, when you have a prolonged series of fits, this can be dangerous for both you and the baby. Fortunately, this complication in pregnancy is uncommon, but it indicates the importance of continuing to take your anti-epileptic medication during pregnancy.

What sort of abnormalities can occur in the baby?
The abnormalities most commonly seen in the babies of women suffering from epilepsy and on anti-epileptic therapy are cleft lip and palate, heart defects and neural tube defects, such as spina bifida. These abnormalities can be screened for in pregnancy. Minor abnormalities like club foot can also occur. But it must be borne in mind that the majority of babies born to mothers with epilepsy *do not* have any abnormality.

Can all drugs used for anti-epileptic therapy cause foetal abnormalities?

No anti-epileptic medication is known to be totally free of risk, but the risks are known to increase when multiple anti-epileptic drugs are used. The risk of foetal abnormality ranges from around 6% of women on one anti-epileptic drug to over 20% in women on four drugs. Remember that the rate of abnormality is usually about 2–3% in women without epilepsy. The risk of abnormality is not yet fully established with some of the newer anti-epileptic drugs, although initial reports suggest that they are certainly no worse in this respect than older medications. Wherever possible, it is best if your epilepsy is controlled with one drug alone. You should see your doctor, who can advise you if your therapy needs to be changed. Do not stop or alter your treatment without first consulting your doctor, or you may place yourself at increased risk of seizures, which can be harmful both to you and your developing baby.

Will my baby suffer from epilepsy?

If you suffer from epilepsy, the chance of your baby being affected in is in general terms about 4–5 in 100, so overall the likelihood of the baby having epilepsy is small. If both you and your partner have epilepsy then the chance of the baby developing epilepsy increases to about 2 in 10. The risk can vary according to the type of epilepsy that you have. Your own doctor can advise you about this.

What effect will pregnancy have on my epilepsy?

In most women there is no change in the frequency of fits when they are pregnant. But around 25% do find that the number of fits they have increases, which is more likely if their epilepsy is not well controlled prior to pregnancy. Overall, the change in frequency is unpredictable and will not necessarily follow the pattern set in a previous pregnancy. Some of these increases in the frequency of fits may be due to women deliberately not taking their anti-epileptic medication as they worry that the drug will cause an abnormality in the baby. In any case, they usually stop their therapy too late to make a difference. A major concern among such women is a neural tube defect like spina bifida, but as the neural tube closes at seven weeks of gestation, stopping therapy after that time cannot prevent this abnormality and will increase the risk of fits, which in itself can cause problems. You should not discontinue your therapy without discussing this with your doctor, preferably before you get pregnant, as the risk of major defects applies very early in pregnancy.

Other reasons that fits may increase are if you have morning sickness and because of this can't keep the tablets down. Towards the end of pregnancy, when you become more uncomfortable because of the size of the womb, it is often difficult to get a good night's sleep and tiredness can often result in increased frequency of fits.

Epilepsy and care in pregnancy

- You should discuss the problems of epilepsy in pregnancy with your doctor before you try to conceive
- Prior to pregnancy, your anti-epileptic therapy should be reviewed by your doctor
- You should take folic acid supplements (5 mg per day), three months before you try to conceive, if possible, and for at least the first 12 weeks of the pregnancy, and ideally throughout pregnancy
- At 15–16 weeks you will usually be offered the AFP blood test to screen for neural tube defects spina bifida
- At 18–20 weeks you will usually be offered a detailed ultrasound scan to check for any foetal abnormality
- Sometimes your doctor will check the blood levels of anti-epileptic medication but this is not always necessary
- Do not alter the dose of your medication without medical advice
- When taking certain types of anti-epileptic medication, you will receive vitamin K supplements in the weeks leading up to delivery
- Anti-epileptic medication should be continued through labour
- If your dose of anti-epileptic therapy was changed in pregnancy, this will need to be reviewed after delivery

Does pregnancy affect my anti-epileptic medication?

Pregnancy can affect the levels of anti-epileptic medication in your blood, which can sometimes be another explanation for an increase in the frequency of fits. However, you should not adjust the dose of your medication without consulting your doctor. If there is an increase in the number of fits then an increase in dose might be advised, provided that you have been reliably taking the medication.

Can I breast-feed if I have epilepsy?

Generally speaking, you will be able to breast-feed your baby. There will be a small amount of anti-epileptic medication in the breast milk but will be very small and less than the baby would have been exposed to while in the womb. Your doctor can give you specific advice.

Are there any precautions I should take when looking after the baby?

There are some precautions that are worth taking, especially if you tend to lose consciousness during your fits. You should take a shower rather than a bath, and ideally have someone else close by while you are showering. When you feed the baby you should sit on the floor with cushions around you, you should not bathe the baby without someone else being around, and you should ensure that that fires and cookers are guarded and take care when making up bottles with boiling water.

Can I take the oral contraceptive pill?

The effectiveness of the commonly prescribed forms of the combined (oestrogen-containing) contraceptive pill is reduced by certain anti-epileptic medications – such as carbemazepine, phenytoin, primidone and phenobarbitone – which increase the ability of the liver to break down the oestrogen contained in the pill. This means that you will not have high enough levels of oestrogen in your blood to provide reliable contraception. To get round this problem, women on such medication need a contraceptive pill that contains a higher dose of oestrogen. The effectiveness of the progesterone-only pill, or mini-pill, is similarly reduced by such medication, and higher doses of progesterone are thus required.

Other anti-epileptic medications, such as valproate, and the newer types, such as gabapentin and lamotrigine, do not cause this problem. Alternatively, you can use other methods of contraception, like the coil (IUCD). This is an important area of consideration, and you doctor will be able to provide you with advice on contraception.

Hay fever

My hay fever is troublesome. Can I take my regular medication during pregnancy?

Hay fever is a common problem, affecting many women. In pregnancy, nasal congestion is more common and this can sometimes make the hay fever seem worse. Hay fever is usually well controlled by antihistamine tablets and steroid nasal sprays, which are generally suitable for use in pregnancy. There is no evidence that these forms of medication cause any problem for the developing baby, but you should check with your pharmacist or doctor that the particular preparation you use is suitable to take in pregnancy.

Heart disease

Most women with heart disease will know before they get pregnant that they have a problem. The condition will usually have been treated and controlled long before they think about pregnancy. It is important to determine how severe the problem is, however. Heart disease is often graded on the basis of the New York Heart Association classification of severity, which ranges from grade I, where there is no significant compromise to health, through to grade IV, where health is severely compromised (see table opposite). Regardless of the cause of heart problems, women with grades I or II levels of symptoms are unlikely to have major problems during a pregnancy. None the less, it is important if you

Severity of heart problems (based on the New York Heart Association classification)

Grade I	No breathlessness and no problem with ordinary physical exercise
Grade II	No problem at rest but slight limitation of activities, such as walking, due to breathlessness
Grade III	Marked limitation of physical activity although no cardiac symptoms at rest
Grade IV	Breathlessness at rest

have a heart problem and are considering pregnancy, to obtain specific advice about your own situation. Your doctor should be able to advise you.

I have a mechanical heart valve and am on anticoagulant medication. What does this mean for pregnancy?

The majority of women with significant valvular heart disease will have had a valve replacement operation. The replacement valve is usually mechanical (metal) as tissue valves deteriorate more rapidly and are not commonly used in young women. People with mechanical valves are usually treated with the anticoagulant warfarin, which prevents any blood clots forming round the valve as these can cause serious problems. However, continued warfarin treatment is not ideal as it freely crosses the placenta and can occasionally cause problems in the baby. If taken between six and 10 weeks of pregnancy, it can cause abnormalities in the baby's development, which has been shown to occur in about 1 in 20 pregancies where the woman has continued to take warfarin in early pregnancy. In late pregnancy warfarin can cause bleeding problems for both the mother and the baby if it is not stopped before labour starts.

Heparin can be used as an alternative anticoagulant during early pregnancy and prior to labour. It does not cross the placenta and so can cause no problem with abnormality or bleeding in the baby. However, heparin must be given by twice-daily injections or infused through a vein as it cannot be taken by mouth. In order to avoid the small risk of abnormality in the baby due to warfarin, it is possible switch to heparin, but the switch has to be completed by six weeks of pregnancy to be certain of preventing a problem, which is often difficult or impractical unless it has been planned and organised before conception. After 10–12 weeks of pregnancy, the risk of abnormality has passed and warfarin can be restarted. It is advisable to switch back to heparin a few weeks before labour and delivery are expected because of the high risk of bleeding associated with continued treatment with warfarin at that time.

However, some experts believe that heparin is not as effective as warfarin in preventing thrombosis round the valve in early pregnancy and prefer to leave the mother on warfarin in the first part of pregnancy. This means that the small risk of abnormality in the baby must be balanced against the serious problem of valve thrombosis. Other experts prefer to keep women on high doses of heparin throughout the pregnancy to avoid any problem for the baby. This is obviously an important and controversial area, and if you have a mechanical valve, you should speak to your doctor and get advice on these issues, ideally before becoming pregnant.

High blood pressure

Why do some women have chronic high blood pressure?

Many women, probably between 2 and 5 in every 100, have chronic high blood pressure before they become pregnant. High blood pressure is known as 'hypertension' and, in 90% of cases, is due to so-called 'essential hypertension'. Doctors do not know the cause of essential hypertension, but it does tend to run in families. This is one of the reasons why doctors ask if you have a family history of high blood pressure. Other medical conditions such as kidney disorders can also cause high blood pressure, but this is much less common than essential hypertension.

Can high blood pressure affect my pregnancy?

Essential hypertension, indeed chronic high blood pressure of any type, will increase the risk of pre-eclampsia and of having a small-for-dates baby *(see p. 124)*. In addition, it will be important to review any medication that you are on for high blood pressure as some medications are best avoided in pregnancy – although many are safe. You should consult your doctor, ideally before pregnancy, or, if you are pregnant, as soon as possible. Normally, blood pressure falls in the first half of pregnancy. This same reduction occurs in most women with essential hypertension, in which case your doctor may be able to stop your blood pressure medication for part of the pregnancy.

Will my high blood pressure get worse because of pregnancy?

It is very unusual for pregnancy itself to change the outlook for women with essential hypertension, although superimposed problems like pre-eclampsia can worsen high blood pressure together with the risk of complications while you are pregnant.

How will chronic high blood pressure affect my pregnancy care?

There will need to be careful assessment of your blood pressure and urine at each antenatal check to look for problems like pre-eclampsia, which are more common if you have essential hypertension. The baby's growth will also be monitored. Sometimes the doctor will recommend a test that checks if you have an increased chance of getting pre-eclampsia or a small-for-dates baby. Currently, the best test is Doppler ultrasound to check on the blood flow to your womb. In mothers at high risk, low doses of aspirin are sometimes used to try and prevent pre-eclampsia occurring.

Migraine

I suffer from migraine. Will it improve when I am pregnant?

Many women, and more women than men, suffer from migraine so this is a question frequently asked. Migraine should be distinguished from more common tension headaches. Migraine causes a throbbing, one-sided headache. Indeed, the name migraine is derived from the Greek words *hemi* and *kranion* meaning 'half the skull', reflecting that the headache is on one side of the head only. The headache is often accompanied by sweating, nausea and vomiting and light tends to make it worse, so your natural instinct is to stay in a darkened room. Many women get warning of impending migraine as they get a visual disturbance with flashing lights or wavy lines. Sometimes strange sensations or ringing in the ear or a feeling of dizziness herald an attack. The true mechanism of migraine is unknown, but doctors have found that it is related to changes in the blood vessels that are supplying the brain. These seem to open up more during a migraine attack. In some cases the tendency for migraine seems to run in families. Interestingly, women who suffer from migraine have a higher chance of developing pre-eclampsia in pregnancy, although doctors do not fully understand why this should be the case. However, in over half of women who suffer from migraine the condition actually improves during pregnancy.

You should bear in mind that some of the medication used to treat and to prevent migraine attacks is not advised when you are pregnant, so it is important to consult your doctor or pharmacist before taking any of these. Paracetamol is not associated with any problems for the baby in pregnancy and so is safe to use for treatment although again you may wish to discuss this with your doctor. Some anti-nausea medications are also safe. For prevention of attacks, low doses of aspirin (60–75 mg) can be effective and there is good evidence from large trials that this has no harmful effect on the unborn child. Other medications that can be used in pregnancy are available to prevent attacks, but these need to be prescribed by a doctor. If you are a migraine sufferer, consult your doctor about your medication before you get pregnant. This will allow your therapy to be adjusted, if required, and will also allow you to have a supply of suitable medication to treat an attack if you have one while pregnant. One final point is that women with migraine should not take the combined (oestrogen-containing) contraceptive pill.

Thyroid problems

I have an overactive thyroid gland. Will this cause problems in pregnancy?

The thyroid gland helps control the body's metabolism. Hyperthyroidism is the medical term for an overactive thyroid gland. The features of an overactive thyroid include weight loss, palpitations, tremor, increased appetite, goitre (swelling of the thyroid gland in the neck), intolerance of heat and increased bowel function. This is a relatively common condition that is found in around 1 in 500 pregnancies. It will not usually pose any special problems in pregnancy provided that the condition is kept under control. If it is uncontrolled there is a risk of problems like miscarriage, a small-for-dates baby and premature labour. This condition may in fact get better in pregnancy but possibly worsen slightly after delivery. You will need to have your thyroid function tested during pregnancy by a simple blood test, to make sure that your overactive thyroid is under control. Sometimes the doctor will check on the baby's growth with ultrasound in the last 10–12 weeks of the pregnancy. The antibodies that overstimulate the thyroid gland and cause hyperthyroidism can cross the placenta and lead to temporary overactivity of the baby's thyroid gland, usually after the baby is born. However, this condition usually lasts for only a few weeks following delivery.

Can I continue to take my medication while pregnant?

Hyperthyroidism is usually controlled during pregnancy with medication, in particular carbimazole, methimazole and propylthiouracil. Such medications do not cause any serious abnormalities in the baby, but you should follow your doctor's advice about your own treatment in pregnancy. These medications are safe for breast-feeding as only very small amounts are found in breast milk and do not appear to cause the baby any problem. On rare occasions these drugs can cause side-effects in the mother, however, such as a rash or reduction of the amount of cells in the blood that fight infection. If you have a problem like a skin rash or sore throat while on medication for an overactive thyroid, you should consult your doctor.

I have an underactive thyroid gland. Will this affect my pregnancy?

The medical term for an underactive thyroid gland is hypothyroidism and it affects around 1 in 100 women. The symptoms of hypothyroidism include tiredness, weight gain, constipation, hair loss, dry skin and very infrequent menstrual periods. It is usually identified and treated before pregnancy. This is because, without treatment, you will be unlikely to conceive because of the effect on your periods. It is unusual for hypothyroidism to cause any significant problems in pregnancy. Treatment is with supplements of thyroid hormone in the form of thyroxine tablets taken daily. They are safe to take in pregnancy and during breast-feeding – thyroid hormone occurs naturally in your body, after all. Your thyroid hormone levels will usually be tested during pregnancy and the dosage of thyroxine adjusted if necessary to prevent hypothyroidism. Should dosage adjustment be required during your pregnancy, this should be reviewed after delivery in case your hormone levels have changed.

Venous thrombosis

What is a venous thrombosis?

A venous thrombosis is simply a blood clot in the vein. The vast majority occur in the leg veins. In pregnant women most of these clots arise in the left leg, usually at the top of the leg or in the pelvis, whereas in non-pregnant women they most often arise in the veins in the calf muscles of either leg. It is a clot in the veins lying deep within the leg muscles, not the veins under the skin, that cause most problems. This type of clot is known as a deep venous (or deep vein) thrombosis, or DVT for short. Such DVTs are troublesome, particularly when part of this clot breaks off and travels to the lung where it can block part of the circulation. This is known as a pulmonary thromboembolism and can be life-threatening. Although death in such cases is rare, it is the most frequent cause of mothers dying in pregnancy. It is therefore important to try to prevent DVT before it occurs or to treat it before it becomes life-threatening.

Does pregnancy make a blood clot in the leg veins more likely?

Clots are caused by sluggish blood flow, increased clotting tendency of the blood and damage to the veins, although all three of these factors do not need to be present for a clot to occur. In pregnancy there is a marked reduction in the speed of the blood flow through the leg veins. This reduced rate of blood flow is present from 16 weeks and is maximal at term. It takes around six weeks to

Some common risk factors for deep vein thrombosis in pregnancy

- Being over the age of 35
- Being overweight
- Immobility (which leads to sluggish blood flow)
- Delivery by Caesarean section
- Severe varicose veins
- Pre-eclampsia
- Previous DVT
- An inborn tendency for the blood to clot (thrombophilia)
- Paraplegia
- Sickle-cell disease
- Infection
- Dehydration
- Long-distance travel

Your health in pregnancy

return to normal after you have the baby. The blood-clotting system changes in pregnancy, with increased levels of clotting factors in the blood – doctors believe that this is how your body prepares for any blood loss at delivery. However, this also leads to an increased tendency of the blood to clot when you are pregnant. Minor damage to the veins in the pelvis can easily occur at the time of delivery as the baby presses on these veins. Because of these changes, the risk of having a clot increases when you are pregnant and also after delivery. However, overall only about 1 in 1000 women will get a deep vein thrombosis in pregnancy.

What is thrombophilia?

The body has natural systems to stop excessive clotting. Some people are born with a tendency for these systems not to work properly, which gives them an increased risk of blood clots. This condition is called thrombophilia and it comes in many forms. Many cases of DVT in young women during pregnancy are the first sign of an underlying thrombophilia. Often there is a family history of thrombosis, with the mother, father, an uncle or aunt having been affected. This is because thrombophilia can be a genetic problem that is passed down through the generations. If you have had a venous thrombosis or there is a family history of clotting, you will often be offered a blood test to determine if you have a thrombophilia.

What are the signs of a deep vein thrombosis?

Leg pain and marked swelling, especially in a woman with risk factors for thrombosis, is the usual way that a blood clot in the leg first comes to light. However, many pregnant women have swollen legs in pregnancy and some discomfort is not uncommon also. If the doctor is concerned that you might have a clot in your leg, a specific test, usually an ultrasound scan, will be carried out to determine if there is a blood clot in the large vein at the top of the leg.

How is a DVT in pregnancy treated?

The treatment of DVT in pregnancy is similar to the treatment you would receive when you are not pregnant. A medication called heparin is given. Heparin is an anticoagulant that 'thins' the blood. It does not break down a clot but simply prevents it getting bigger. This allows your body time to gradually dissolve the clot naturally. Heparin can either be injected under the skin or given through the veins by a small pump that carefully controls the rate of the infusion. Blood tests may be required to check that you are getting the correct dose, which often has to be adjusted to ensure that the treatment is optimal. In non-pregnant women with a thrombosis, several days of heparin treatment are followed by warfarin, another anticoagulant, this time in tablet form. However, warfarin freely crosses the placenta and can cause problems in the baby. Wherever possible, doctors will avoid prescribing warfarin in pregnancy and continue with heparin injections as heparin does not cross the placenta and so the baby will not be exposed to it. It is safe to switch to warfarin following delivery, however, as almost none of this medication gets into breast milk and so is safe to take while breast-feeding. *(See p. 187 for further details about the administering of warfarin and heparin during pregancy.)*

Does heparin have any adverse side-effects on the mother?

There are some potential side-effects on the mother during pregnancy, although as it does not cross the placenta there is no direct risk to the developing baby. With use over several months there is a small risk of heparin-induced osteoporosis or thinning of the bones. Occasionally, an allergic reaction to heparin can occur. Recently, a new form of heparin, known as low-molecular-weight heparin, has been used to treat DVT in pregnancy, which has fewer side-effects and a much lower risk of osteoporosis. Because of this, this form of heparin is now preferred to be prescribed by most doctors for use in pregnancy. If you have had a DVT, you should discuss treatment with your doctor if you wish to find out more.

I had a DVT before I became pregnant. How should I be treated?

If you have had a previous DVT, your risk of another will be increased during pregnancy, especially if no cause was found. Many doctors believe that women with a previous clot should be tested for thrombophilia. This requires a simple blood test and ideally should be done before you get pregnant. If you have had more than one DVT, doctors will usually recommend treatment with conventional heparin or low-molecular-weight heparin to prevent any clots recurring. If you have had a previous clot and also suffer from a thrombophilia then usually either type of heparin is recommended. If you have had only one previous DVT with no underlying thrombophilia then it is essential to weigh up all the risk factors for your particular case to determine if you need heparin treatment. This is a highly specialised area and specific advice about your particular situation must be obtained. Most doctors now prefer low molecular weight heparin in this situation as it has fewer side effects than conventional heparin and often can be given just once per day. With conventional heparin, twice daily injections are required.

Does heparin have to be given by injection?

Heparin is not effective if given by mouth so it has to be injected. It is injected under the skin of the leg or the abdomen, and most women can be taught to inject themselves without difficulty.

Can I take the oral contraceptive pill if I have had a DVT?

If you have had a DVT, you should not usually take the combined (oestrogen-containing) oral contraceptive pill because of the association with venous thrombosis. You should use alternative forms of contraception. The progesterone-only pill, sometimes called the 'mini-pill', does not appear to be linked to any extra risk of thrombosis, and so can be used if you have had a previous DVT. You should, however, get specialist advice about contraception if you have had a DVT.

Your health in pregnancy

Third trimester
28–40 Weeks

The last trimester of the pregnancy is now well under way. The baby is starting to make the final preparations for delivery – maturing the key organs and building up fat stores beneath the skin.

32 WEEKS

Baby size: Average weight is 1800 g (nearly 4 lb), head circumference is 29–30 cm ($11\frac{1}{2}$–$11\frac{3}{4}$ in), abdomen circumference is 27 cm ($10\frac{1}{2}$ in) and foot length is about 6.5 cm ($2\frac{1}{2}$ in).

Baby development: Skin creases have formed on the front third of the sole of the foot. The baby can respond to sound and can recognise certain sounds such as pieces of music that it may hear a lot, or your voice. It can also respond to bright lights. Its cyclical pattern of waking and sleeping is lengthening from 20 minutes, which it was at 28 weeks, to about 30 minutes of alternate waking and sleeping. Its head will usually be down, ready to enter the pelvis as labour approaches. Some babies are breech at this stage but there is still time for the baby to change how it is lying, and most will turn round to be to be head down before labour.

Boy babies: The testes are descending towards the scrotum.

You will often feel kicks below your ribs.

36 WEEKS

Baby size: Average weight is 2550 g (just over $5\frac{1}{2}$ lb), height is 46 cm (18 in) (over the last weeks the baby has been growing at a rate of 1 cm [$\frac{1}{2}$ in] in height per week); head circumference is over 32 cm ($12\frac{1}{2}$ in), abdominal or waist measurement is over 30 cm (12 in) and foot length is around 7 cm ($2\frac{3}{4}$ in).

Baby development: The last organs to mature are the lungs. These will mature fully in the next 1–3 weeks when they make enough of a substance called surfactant, which makes the lungs easy to inflate. Without enough surfactant the lungs are stiff, making it hard to breath. A lack of surfactant is why some premature babies have breathing difficulties. The fingernails have reached the end of the fingers and the baby may have scratched itself in the womb. The cyclical pattern of waking and sleeping is lengthening from 30 minutes, which it was at 32 weeks, to about 40 minutes of alternate waking and sleeping.

Boy babies: The testes will now usually have fully descended and will be found in the scrotum.

Changes to the mother: At 36 weeks the top of your womb reaches its highest point, usually just below the breastbone. You may feel quite uncomfortable now because of the size of the womb and the baby kicking against your ribs. The head may engage around this time, especially in a first pregnancy. When the head is said to be engaged, this means that the biggest diameter of the baby's head has entered the pelvis and only two-fifths of the baby's head will be felt in the abdomen. This is sometimes called 'lightening' as the amount of baby in your abdomen will have decreased as the head moves into the pelvis. As this happen you may feel an urge to pass urine more frequently due to the pressure of the head on your bladder. In some women the head may not engage until later, especially if it is a second or subsequent pregnancy. Occasionally the head may not engage until labour starts and the contractions push the head down.

More fat is being deposited under the skin and the baby will look chubby.

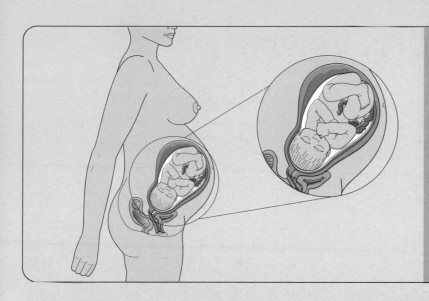

36 Weeks

- the baby is now almost fully mature

- fingernails reach ends of fingers

- head is ready to engage

- hair is growing

Baby size: Average weight is 3300 g (7 lb 8 oz), waist measurement is 34 cm (13 in) and foot length is around 8 cm (3$^{1}/_{4}$ in).

Baby development: The hair on the baby's head will be 2–4 cm ($^{3}/_{4}$–1$^{1}/_{2}$ in) long. There are skin creases all over the soles of the feet in a criss-cross pattern. Because the baby will be more cramped in the womb, movements may not feel so vigorous, but they should be just as frequent. The cyclical pattern of waking and sleeping is lengthening from 40 minutes to about 60 minutes of alternate waking and sleeping. It is now 280 days from the start of your last period or 266 days from the time of conception. Although this is your expected date of delivery most babies are not born on the day they are due. This is because babies reach their final maturity at slightly different times. Only when the baby is sufficiently mature will it send the signal to start labour. Sometimes this is before the due date and sometimes after it. Because of this full term is considered to occur after 37 and before 42 completed weeks of pregnancy.

Changes to the mother: Your womb will have been preparing itself for labour for three weeks or so before the contractions of labour start. During this time, the neck of the womb, the cervix, softens and thins out. This allows the contractions of labour to more easily open the neck of the womb to allow delivery of the baby. Once the womb is fully prepared, regular painful contractions start. These painful contractions will often come on quite suddenly, although you may have been aware of a progressive increase in the number of so-called Braxton-Hicks contractions you have been having over the past few weeks.

It is the baby who 'decides' when labour should start and sends a chemical signal to the tissues of your womb.

40
WEEKS

Some complications to look out for in the third trimester

Premature labour (before 37 weeks) **See p. 235** rupture of the membranes before labour **See p. 199** vaginal bleeding **See p. 142** pre-eclampsia **See p. 136** a large-for-dates baby **See p. 135** excess fluid around the baby **See p. 135** a small-for-dates baby **See p. 124** reduced foetal movements **See p. 133** Breech presentation **See p. 232.**

Third trimester

Labour & delivery

Labour and delivery are an intense emotional and physical event. The day that you have anticipated with excitement for so long suddenly arrives. It is a day that will change your life for ever, with the miracle of the birth of your baby. At the same time it can be a worrying and an unpredictable experience for both you and your partner. An understanding of the processes involved, some of the problems that might arise and options for care, such as the different techniques that are used to relieve pain, can help you make the right choices for your labour and delivery.

Traditionally, labour is divided into three stages:

- The first stage starts when regular, painful contractions develop which stretch and pull open the cervix (neck of the womb).
- The second stage starts when the cervix is fully dilated. At this stage it is open wide enough to allow the baby to pass out of the womb. You will usually feel an urge to bear down and push. A combination of the contractions of the womb and your efforts will push the baby through the birth canal until the baby is delivered.
- The third stage starts when the baby is delivered and ends when the afterbirth (placenta) is expelled after it separates from the wall of your womb.

The first stage of labour

How does labour start?

Labour is not a sudden event, rather it starts slowly. Your womb will actually have been preparing itself for labour for three weeks or so before the womb starts to contract in proper labour. You will probably not be aware of this happening. Doctors sometimes call this phase 'pre-labour' *(see table overleaf)*. During this time, the neck of the womb, the cervix, softens and thins out (known as effacement). This allows the contractions of labour to open the cervix more easily to allow delivery of the baby. The womb also prepares itself to contract strongly. Once the womb is fully prepared, regular painful contractions start. These painful contractions will often come on quite suddenly, although you may have been aware of a progressive increase in the number of so-called Braxton-Hicks contractions you have been having (Braxton-Hicks was an English physician who described these contractions in the 19th century). Braxton-Hicks contractions are irregular tightenings of the womb sometimes referred to as 'practice' contractions. They are not usually painful but can be uncomfortable, especially near term, and tend to last for 30 seconds or so. They are different from the contractions of 'proper' labour, which are painful and powerful, increase in frequency, become regular and don't go away once established. It is these contractions that will pull open the cervix and push the baby through the birth canal. It is the baby who controls when labour starts. When it is mature, hormones in the foetus and placenta signal to the womb to stimulate production

The cervix softens prior to labour establishing itself. It also becomes thinner and more stretchy so that the inside opening of the cervix, called the internal os, will be pulled past the baby's head as labour approaches and contractions start. This is called effacement. Once the cervix has thinned out then its external opening (the external os), which faces into the vagina, will start to open up, or dilate, in response to contractions.

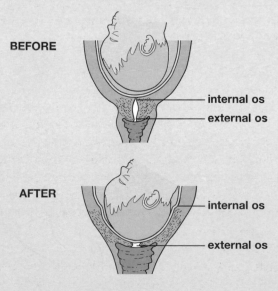

BEFORE — internal os / external os

AFTER — internal os / external os

The stages of labour

Pre-labour	Softening of the cervix and preparation of the womb for labour
First stage	Regular contractions that will stretch and pull open the cervix (neck of the womb) until it is fully dilated
Second stage	The time from full dilatation of the cervix until delivery of the baby
Third stage	The time from delivery of the baby until delivery of the placenta is completed

of substances called prostaglandins that soften the neck of the womb and also stimulate contractions.

How do I tell the difference between a Braxton-Hicks contraction and a labour contraction?

Braxton-Hicks contractions are irregular, with no pattern. They are not usually painful, although they can sometimes be strong enough to make you stop what you are doing. You will feel your womb getting hard then relaxing after 30 seconds or so.

By contrast, labour contractions get progressively stronger and closer together. For example, they could progress from every 30 minutes to every 15 minutes, then every 10 minutes. They then progress further and come every 2–3 minutes when you are in established labour. They are also different in nature from Braxton-Hicks contractions. Labour contractions build up to a peak of intensity then die away. A low backache and pain in the inside of your thighs often accompany such contractions.

How will I know when I am in labour?

It can sometimes be very difficult to know for certain that you are in labour during the early stages. Doctors and midwives look for several features to tell if you are in labour. Regular, painful contractions, usually coming at least once every five minutes, and dilatation of the cervix occurring together indicate that labour has definitely started. Obviously an internal (vaginal) examination by a doctor or midwife is required to determine if the cervix is opening. Other signs can suggest that labour has started or is imminent. These are a 'show' and ruptured membranes, often referred to as 'breaking of waters'.

What is a 'show'?

During pregnancy, the neck of the womb is 'sealed' with a plug of thick mucus, like jelly, in the centre. When the cervix thins out and starts to dilate as labour approaches, the plug falls out. The release of this plug of mucus, which is usually bloodstained, into your vagina is called a 'show'. Sometimes it comes out as a single large blob of mucus and sometimes in several smaller blobs. It may be pink in colour due to the bloodstaining and sometimes a dark red-brown colour if the bloodstaining is older. When a show occurs, it is a sign that the neck of the womb is changing and that labour is approaching. The show can appear just a few hours before labour or even several days before. If a show occurs several days before labour, this will not cause you or the baby any problems. The presence of a show without contractions does not mean that you are in labour. However, if you are in doubt or feel worried, you should contact your doctor or midwife.

What are ruptured membranes?

The membranes form the bag of amniotic fluid in which the baby grows and develops. They tend to break or rupture when the neck of the womb opens. This is due to weakening of the membranes after the cervix opens, coupled with the force of the contractions which cause the membranes to burst and the amniotic fluid to be released. Sometimes the membranes rupture before labour starts and sometimes the labour may be quite advanced before the membranes rupture (see p. 236 for a fuller discussion). Rupture of the membranes sounds like a painful experience, but it is not. All you will feel is wet! However, if you are in labour, contractions often become much stronger and more painful after your membranes rupture.

How do I know if my membranes have ruptured?

If there is a big gush of fluid then there is usually no doubt that your membranes have ruptured. However, sometimes there is only a slight trickle of fluid, which can be confused with a small leak of urine. Small leaks of urine are quite common in late pregnancy, as the baby's head will be pressing on your bladder. If you are uncertain then wear a sanitary towel and look at the fluid that collects in it. Amniotic fluid is usually clear or slightly straw-coloured – possibly bloodstained initially from the 'show' – and does not smell at all like urine. You won't be able to control the trickle of fluid if your membranes have ruptured. Once your membranes have ruptured, the best thing to do is to contact your maternity hospital, doctor or midwife for advice. They will usually want to assess the situation.

My contractions are coming every 10 minutes, and are painful and regular. What should I do?

Contractions usually create a very tight sensation across your abdomen and are often felt in your back or at the tops of your legs. They build up to a peak of intensity then die away, rather like period pains but much more painful. As you go into labour they will become more painful and more frequent. When you experience frequent regular painful contractions that are increasing in frequency to one in every 10–15 minutes, you should contact your doctor or midwife or

Labour & delivery

delivery unit for advice. Generally, this is the stage when you should go to hospital if you are intending to have a hospital delivery.

How long will the first stage of labour last?

The first stage of labour lasts from the onset of labour until the cervix is 10 cm (4 in), or fully, dilated. The duration will depend on many factors, but what influences the duration most is usually whether it is your first labour, which is generally slower than subsequent labours. Once a first labour is properly established, at which point the cervix will be about 3 cm (1$^{1}/4$ in) dilated, it usually takes somewhere between seven and 11 hours for the cervix to reach full dilatation. The length of time tends to be much shorter than this in subsequent pregnancies.

How often will my contractions come?

The frequency of your contractions will build up in labour until they are coming every 2–3 minutes.

What happens to me in the first stage of labour?

The first stage of labour, when the neck of the womb gradually opens up, can take several hours. During this time it is important to check that both you and the baby are coping well and that your labour is progressing normally. Your pulse, temperature and blood pressure will be measured regularly and the baby's heart rate will be checked at regular intervals. The midwife or doctor will time your contractions, noting how long they last and how frequently they come. They will discuss pain relief with you *(see 203)* and make sure that you are as comfortable as possible. In order to assess progress in labour, your abdomen will be examined to check that the head is engaged.

When two-fifths or less of the head can be felt in your abdomen, the biggest part of the head has entered your pelvis and the head is said to be engaged. The only way to be certain that progress is occurring is to find out how fast the cervix is dilating. In order to determine this you will need regular vaginal examinations. The doctor or midwife who examines you will be assessing how effaced (thinned out) the cervix is, how dilated it is, how deep the head is in your pelvis (referred to as the 'station' of the head) and which way the baby's head is facing.

I have prepared a birth plan. When is a good time to discuss this with the doctor or midwife?

It is best to go over your birth plan *(see also p. 227)* at one of the antenatal checks, but when you are admitted in labour you should discuss your preferences for labour with your doctor or midwife. You should do this while in the early stages of labour when you will be more able to discuss this. If you find it difficult, your partner can indicate your preferences for you. It is best not to be too rigid in your plans and preferences, especially when it is your first baby. This is simply because until you get into labour you do not know what is going to happen. For example, you might decide that you want to avoid having an epidural before you go into labour, but when you are in labour you might change your mind if you find that opiates like morphine don't suit you or because your labour is longer than anticipated.

How often will I have an internal examination?

During the first stage of labour, the number of vaginal examinations is very variable. The number will depend on how quickly you progress in labour and whether you have any complications. In general your progress will be assessed at least every four hours.

How quickly should my cervix open up?

Progress in the first stage of labour is determined by how quickly your cervix opens. This will depend on how strong your contractions are, how big your baby is and also the position of its head, and finally how easily the baby can pass through your pelvis. In a first pregnancy and labour, doctors are generally looking for an average rate of cervical dilatation of about 1 cm (1/2 in) per hour. If you were 4 cm (1 1/2 in) dilated at your first examination and 8 cm (3 in) dilated by the time of your next examination four hours later, then you would have made good progress. Everyone is different and progress may sometimes be slower than this. It can also be more rapid, especially if you have had a baby before. Progress is often recorded in a graph on your case record. This graph is called the partogram.

Will the doctor or midwife break my waters?

If your waters do not break themselves, then sometimes the doctor or midwife will break them for you. This is done during a vaginal examination with a small plastic instrument that looks a bit like a crochet hook. Breaking your waters is usually no more uncomfortable than any other vaginal examination, but as contractions often get stronger after the membranes rupture, your contractions may feel more painful. There may be several reasons for breaking your waters. For instance, if you are progressing slowly, it can help speed up your labour. Doctors think this happens because when the waters break there is an increase in the production of prostaglandins – substances made by your womb to stimulate contractions. Alternatively, your waters may need to be broken in order to put a clip on the baby's head to monitor its heartbeat more accurately. If you baby appears to be in distress, your waters may be broken so that the doctor or midwife can check for meconium staining of the amniotic fluid.

Sometimes, if the baby is distressed its bowels may move while in the womb. The baby has never eaten so its bowels don't contain digested food. Instead, they contain a substance called meconium, which will stain the amniotic fluid brown/green in colour. If there is meconium staining, it does not always mean that the baby is distressed, however; with more mature babies there is often meconium staining of the amniotic fluid, even when the baby has not been distressed.

Do I have to have my waters broken?

If you are making good progress in labour and if the baby shows no evidence of distress and is not at high risk, then breaking your waters does not usually offer any great advantages to you. You can discuss this with your midwife or doctor and if you have a preference you can make this clear on your birth plan.

Preparing to go into hospital

What do I need to do before going in to hospital?

You will not know exactly when you will go into labour. It is therefore best to be prepared in case things happen faster than you had anticipated. Keep your pregnancy record somewhere easily accessible, and keep a note of the hospital, your midwife or your doctor's phone numbers by the telephone. Make sure you know how to get in touch with your birth partner quickly. The last thing you want to do when contractions start is to be rummaging about for phone numbers. You should plan how you will get to hospital and who will help look after any other children, especially if you need to go to hospital quickly or in the middle of the night.

What do I need to take with me to hospital?

Have a bag packed with all the essentials you will need and any special items you want. If you pack in a hurry while in labour, you will probably forget something. You will need something to wear in labour, a nightdress or large T-shirt. You might want to take several changes so that you can freshen up during labour and also have a clean nightdress or T-shirt after delivery. Bear in mind that things you wear during labour may become soiled. A bathrobe is also useful for after delivery. You might want to bring socks and slippers, too, especially if you plan to walk around while in labour. Take your own toiletries, sponge, face flannel and towels. Some women like a water spray to cool their face in labour. If you want to see your baby's head as it crowns, you can take a hand mirror. If you would like particular music or massage oils to help you relax, you should pack these also. If you are using TENS for pain relief *(see p. 207)* don't forget to take your machine with you. After delivery you will need sanitary towels, underpants (some disposable pants are ideal for the first day or so), maternity or nursing bras and breast pads. You might want to bring some drinks and snacks. Many women want to capture their baby's first moments on camera, so don't forget your camera or video camera. There will be lots of people to phone with your news. Take a phone card or plenty of coins for the payphone. Remember that you cannot usually use mobile phones in hospitals as they can sometimes affect vital electronic equipment. Don't forget your medical notes if you usually keep them.

What do I need for the baby?

You will need some baby clothes: at least two or three vests and sleepsuits are ideal. For taking the baby home you will need extra outdoor clothes, a hat and a

Labour & delivery

shawl or baby blanket. You will need your own supply of nappies and cream to protect the baby's bottom, and cottonwool balls. Baby wipes are not usually recommended for a newborn baby's bottom as they are often perfumed and might cause a minor skin rash. It is best to use cottonwool balls dipped in warm water instead. Scratch mittens can often come in useful to prevent the baby scratching its face with its fingernails. If you are taking the baby home by car then a babyseat will be needed. It is not safe to travel with the baby on your lap. If you have a passenger airbag fitted, then make sure the baby travels in the back seat.

Pain relief in labour

Will I be in pain during labour?

Pain will occur with each contraction during labour, getting more severe towards the end of the first stage. Each woman feels and copes with pain differently as everyone has a different tolerance of pain. One of the major objectives of your care in labour is to help you cope with the pain. Some women would like to be able to get through labour with no pain relief other than perhaps some gas and air. The vast majority want and need some pain relief. Very few women will get through labour without some help with pain. It is important to find the right choice of pain relief for you. You will probably have some idea of the type of pain relief you would prefer. If so, put this in your birth plan. However, it is important to be open-minded about pain relief, especially in your first pregnancy. Until you experience the pain of labour, you cannot tell how you will cope. In addition, there may be factors you could not anticipate, such as making slower progress than you had hoped or the baby being in a position that can cause more pain. This in turn might lead you to be more exhausted and less able to cope with the pain. So your needs for pain relief might change.

There are some interesting clinical studies that back up the need to be open-minded about pain relief in labour. One such study conducted in London in the late 1980s found that the number of first-time mothers who requested an epidural during labour was four times greater than the number of mothers who had intended to use an epidural for pain relief prior to labour. However, it is important to remember that pain relief in labour is a very personal matter; only you can judge how much pain you have and how much help you need.

How do I cope with the pain of labour?

The first thing that can help you cope is removing as much as possible the fear of the unknown. Labour can be scary: arriving while in labour at a delivery unit with unfamiliar surroundings, not knowing what will happen, or how your pain can be controlled, can make you more anxious and therefore less able to cope with pain. Learning about labour, the choices in pain relief and the way the delivery unit looks and works can be very useful in helping you cope with the pain. If you know what to expect during labour, and are aware of the different

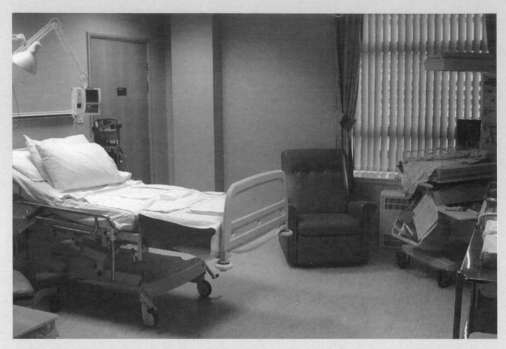

A delivery room in a modern maternity hospital labour suite.

methods of pain relief available to you, you will be more likely to cope well during labour itself. Delivery units usually provide tours to let you see the place and familiarise yourself with it. There are usually antenatal groups or classes that can provide information and discussion on different techniques to help you cope with pain and control it.

One of the most important factors in how you cope, however, is having a supportive birth partner with your throughout labour. The benefits of having a birth partner are enormous. In addition, the support, encouragement and reassurance of a midwife letting you know what is happening and why at all times is also a major factor in how well you cope. Research has found that having someone with you all the time you are in labour can make it less likely that you will need painkillers, or have a forceps or ventouse delivery (see p. 237) or Caesarean section (see p. 240) and more likely that your labour will be shorter. In addition, it can reduce the risk of depression after the delivery and help breast-feeding get off to a good start.

What does my birth partner do?

You will usually want your birth partner to be with you all the time to encourage and reassure you, as well as helping to keep you comfortable by getting you drinks, mopping your brow, and helping you move around and get into comfortable positions. You might want this person to hold you or massage your back or feet or head. Your birth partner can also help you tell your midwife or doctor what you want or what your preferences are in labour. Everyone is different and you should consider what you would like and talk about it first with your birth partner.

What should I do to cope with painful contractions?

When a contraction comes, try and be as relaxed as possible: don't tense up your body. Try not to resist the contraction: don't grit your teeth, tighten your shoulders or clench your fists. Concentrate on your breathing, slowly in and out. Focusing on your breathing is a good way of distracting yourself from the pain and helps relieve tension in your muscles, which heightens the pain. Try rocking your pelvis and, if you want to make a noise, you should do so if it helps. As the contraction disappears, try to relax. Move about and try different positions as this often helps you cope better. Walk about the room; lean forwards while standing up and hold on to the back of a chair or your partner's shoulders; sit in your partner's lap while he sits on a beanbag with his back propped against a wall; sit astride a chair, leaning over its back with a pillow to cushion it; kneel on all fours – anything goes, so long as it helps you. Studies have shown that if a woman is not restricted in her position or movements in labour, she will usually favour an upright position rather than lying down and she will also cope better with labour. Think positive: each contraction you get through is one fewer on the road to delivery of the baby you have been waiting for.

What are the options for pain relief in labour?

The main options for pain relief in labour are: gas and air, opiate medication like morphine, a TENS machine and an epidural *(see table below)*. There are also a number of alternative therapies for pain relief, such as aromatherapy, water buoyancy, massage and acupuncture.

What is gas and air?

The trade name for gas and air is Entonox. This is a mixture of 50% nitrous oxide, a pain-relieving medicinal gas, and 50% oxygen. It is widely used in the UK for pain relief in labour and has no harmful effects on the baby.

How do I use gas and air?

You administer gas and air to yourself through a mask or a mouthpiece attached to a gas cylinder. In hospital it is often piped to the bedside. It is fast-acting with

Choices for pain relief in labour

- Gas and air (Entonox)
- TENS
- Opiates: pethidine, morphine, diamorphine
- Epidural: 'top-up' epidural, continous epidural, patient-controlled epidural analgesia

a short duration of effect. When you feel the contraction coming, inhale through the mask or mouthpiece slowly and deeply. It will be effective by the time the contraction reaches its peak. Gas and air should not be inhaled between contractions.

How effective is gas and air?

Gas and air rarely provides complete pain relief, but is highly effective in reducing pain. This is often enough to deal with the contractions of early labour or while you are waiting for an epidural or opiate injection to take effect. As it is fast-acting, it is useful if you are having a very rapid delivery. Many women describe its effect as taking the edge off the pain, which can be enough to allow them to cope. Gas and air can be used on its own or combined with other techniques like opiates. This makes it useful as an adjunct to other painkillers in late labour when your contractions may be at their most powerful. Another time to use it is during internal examinations. Internal examinations should not be painful provided you can relax, but if you feel that they are too uncomfortable for you, gas and air can sometimes help relieve the discomfort and make you relax more.

What are opiate painkillers?

Opiates are medications of the morphine family. They are very potent painkillers that have been used for pain relief in labour from the time of the ancient Egyptians, when extracts of opium were used. The best-known and most widely used forms are morphine itself, diamorphine and pethidine (also called meperidine or Demerol). There is good evidence to suggest that diamorphine is more effective than pethidine.

How are opiate painkillers given?

They are given by injection into the muscle of your thigh or your buttocks. Injections are usually repeated every 3–4 hours in labour, as required. They can be given by injection into your veins (usually those of your arm or the back of your hand); although this takes effect faster, the pain relief also subsides more quickly. A newer technique is patient-controlled analgesia, used most commonly after surgical operations like Caesarean section. Here the mother, by pressing a button, controls how much opiate she gets by way of a computer-driven pump. The computer prevents any possibility of overdose but leaves you in control of how much pain relief you receive. This technique may not provide better pain relief in labour but does tend to reduce the amount of medication that you use, which in turn reduces any side-effects.

How effective are opiates in labour?

Some women find opiates very effective while others find them inadequate for the control of their labour pains. Indeed, opiates are not as good as epidurals in relieving labour pain. As opiates cause a degree of sedation, this can sometimes be enough to make you drop off to sleep in early labour, and an hour or two of sleep may be no bad thing at that point, helping give you some rest before the later stages of labour. The sedative effect can make you relax more easily and this will help you cope with pain. Opiates can cause a sense of euphoria, and many women describe a 'high' or a sensation of floating. Some women do not like these sensations, however, and so prefer to avoid opiates.

What are the side-effects of opiates?

A major side-effect of all opiates is a feeling of nausea and vomiting. Because of this, opiates are usually combined with an anti-sickness medication. All opiates cross the placenta and so the baby also receives a dose. This can cause respiratory depression in the baby, possibly reducing its drive to breathe after it is born. However, this effect can be quickly reversed by the administration of an opiate antidote to the baby when it is born and so is not usually a major problem. The baby may also be sleepy because of the opiates crossing the placenta and consequently it may be slower to establish feeding.

What is TENS?

TENS is the abbreviation for transcutaneous electrical nerve stimulation. The TENS machine is a battery-operated device about the size of a cigarette packet, connected to two pairs of pads (electrodes) that are taped to your back. The first pair is placed about halfway up your back on either side of the spine and the second pair is taped on either side of the base of your back, just above the buttocks. The device sends electrical impulses through the skin of your back to the nerves. This blocks the perception of pain from the womb by your brain. In essence, the electrical signals from the TENS device are transmitted through high-speed nerve fibres and reach the brain faster than the pain impulses from your womb, conducted by slower-speed nerve fibres. As the electrical impulses arrive at your brain before the pain impulses, they help block the feeling of pain. In addition, the TENS machine appears to release endorphins, which are substances that occur naturally in the body and are many times stronger than opiates for killing pain.

How do I use TENS?

It is best to acquire a TENS machine some time before your labour is due as you will need a few practice runs to familiarise yourself with it. Many maternity units have these devices and can supply you with one but numbers may be limited. It is also possible to rent or buy them. First you need to find out the correct postion on your back to stick the electrodes, most of which are self-adhesive now. If you are uncertain where to place the pads, ask your midwife, physiotherapist or doctor. They will show you. You and/or your partner should practise putting them on. In addition, you need to practise using the handset to control the level of electrical impulses. Try this for a day or so before labour, using the device whenever you feel a Braxton Hicks contraction. You will feel a slight tingling sensation when you use it, which will become more marked as you turn up the level. When it comes to labour, the best results with TENS occur

Labour & delivery

when you start to use it early in labour. This might be because of a build-up in endorphins. In general it is easier to deal with pain before it becomes severe. So leave the device switched on throughout labour, turn up the level when a contraction occurs and back down again after the contraction subsides.

How effective is TENS in relieving labour pain?

Results for TENS are variable. It has been suggested that TENS is no more effective than the traditional remedy of back rubbing. Some trials have not found it to be of benefit, especially during the second stage of labour and pushing, while others report that TENS relieved back pain and contraction pain in the abdomen. However, there is no doubt that some women do benefit from using TENS. The only way to find out if it would help you, is to try one of the devices yourself. If it does not give you enough help with pain then you can always switch to another form of pain relief.

Are there any problems with TENS?

Other than the tingling you feel when using it, there are no significant side-effects or problems with TENS. Neither does it affect the baby. There are some situations where it cannot be used. If you have a heart pacemaker, for instance, then you should avoid TENS. When the baby's heartbeat is being monitored electronically with a small clip attached to its head, TENS will interfere with this. In addition, you cannot use the TENS machine in water (such as in a bath or a birthing pool – *see p. 212*).

What is epidural analgesia?

Epidural analgesia numbs the nerves from your abdomen and lower limbs at the point where these nerves join the spinal cord. As these nerves carry the pain signals to your brain, numbing them will stop you feeling pain. This is undoubtedly the most effective method of pain relief available for labour, but it is also the most invasive as it involves local anaesthetic being injected into your spine.

How is an epidural given?

First of all, a drip will be set up so that you can be given fluids through your veins. This is because your blood pressure can fall when you have an epidural, possibly making you feel sick or dizzy. Any fall in blood pressure can be treated or prevented by intravenous fluids and medication. Anaesthetists rather than obstetricians or midwives provide epidural analgesia. You will be asked to sit or lie on your left side, depending on the preference of the anaesthetist. A fine, hollow needle is inserted into your back just above the level of your waist. It is inserted through a gap in the bones making up the spinal column. A thin, plastic catheter (tube) is fed through the hollow needle so that it lies in the 'epidural' space lying between the bony walls of the spinal canal and the protective membrane that covers the spinal cord. The catheter is taped to your back so that it cannot move. Local anaesthetic is injected into the catheter, a test dose usually being given first to ensure that the catheter is in the correct position.

This is followed by a larger dose to provide relief of pain from the abdomen by numbing or blocking the nerves from the abdomen and legs as they cross the epidural space. (All nerve fibres have to cross the epidural space to get to the spinal cord.) The local anaesthetic is sometimes combined with a small dose of a powerful opiate as this can give better relief of pain. As the catheter remains in place, the epidural can be 'topped up' with further doses of local anaesthetic so that no matter how long your labour, you can continue to have pain relief from the epidural. Sometimes the medication in the epidural can be given by a continuous infusion where a small amount of medication is pumped down the epidural catheter continuously, so there is no need for intermittent top-ups. After delivery, the catheter can be gently removed.

How effective is an epidural?

An epidural is usually highly effective in dealing with labour pain, but it takes up to about 30 minutes to set up and work. It will usually last for several hours between top-ups, but the duration obviously depends on the dose of local anaesthetic given and whether it is given by a continuous infusion. Over 90% of women who have an epidural think that it is very effective and about 80% of them say that they would like to have an epidural in their next labour. Some women feel absolutely no pain after the epidural takes effect, which considerably reduces the stress of labour. In addition, there are none of the effects that opiates produce on you mood. A relatively new development is patient-controlled epidural analgesia where you control the infusion of local anaesthetic through a special pump. You can thus give yourself a top-up whenever you feel that you need it. The specially programmed pump controls how much is given and prevents overdose by blocking any further top-up for a pre-set minimal time. This technique actually results in less local anaesthetic being required than when a doctor or midwife tops up the epidural.

Will the epidural stop me completely from moving my legs?

When epidurals were first brought into practice for relieving labour pain in the 1970s, the strength of local anaesthetic used was quite high. It blocked not only the perception of pain but also the nerves that control the legs, making if very difficult for the woman to move her legs at all.

However, anaesthetists realised that adequate pain relief could be obtained with lower strengths of local anaesthetic. While not affecting the pain-relieving abilities of an epidural, this has dramatically reduced the effects on the legs from virtually complete loss of movement to a little weakness at the hips. This means that you will usually be able to move about the bed with minimal assistance. Your anaesthetist can advise you about the types of epidural in use at the hospital.

Will I have to stay in bed if I have an epidural?

If an epidural makes it very difficult to move your legs or makes them feel numb, you will need to stay in bed as it would not be safe for you to try and walk. Your

Labour & delivery

doctor or midwife can advise you about this. Some epidurals can also prevent you from feeling if your bladder is full and you may therefore need to be catheterised to empty your bladder. However, some anaesthetists are now providing 'mobile' epidurals. These usually involve a lower dose of local anaesthetic coupled with an opiate medication being injected into the epidural space. This results in effective pain relief without preventing your legs from moving. So you can change position and walk around while in labour and also have the ability to empty your bladder. Although you can move around, it is none the less best to confine walking to a level surface, to avoid falling, with your partner or midwife close by. In addition, some women find that the morphine-like medication causes an itchy feeling in their body.

Will an epidural make my labour longer?

An epidural can make the first stage a little longer. The second stage can also be prolonged. This is because it is more difficult for you to push, as a fully effective epidural stops you feeling the urge to push that occurs when the baby's head is deep in the pelvis. You will still be able to push, but will have to rely on your doctor or midwife telling you when to push. Sometimes it is useful to allow the epidural to wear off a little so that you feel the urge to push, but obviously this may result in you feeling pain.

Will I need a forceps or vacuum delivery if I have an epidural?

Because it is more difficult for you to push effectively, there is a slightly higher chance of needing a forceps or vacuum delivery, especially if it is your first delivery. However, a large number of women will have a normal delivery through their own efforts while benefiting from the pain relief provided by an epidural. If pushing can be delayed until the doctor or midwife can see the baby's head before asking you to push, then there may be less chance that you will need a forceps or ventouse delivery.

Will I develop backache because I had an epidural?

A study published in 1990 suggested that women with backache after delivery were twice as likely to have had an epidural in labour. At the time of this study, however, relatively high concentrations of local anaesthetic were being used, which would markedly reduce the ability of the mother to move and control her posture. As posture is so critical to the development of backache, this might explain the finding. More recent studies have found that when a mother has backache before delivery she is more likely to suffer from it afterwards and that this was a more important factor than whether she had an epidural. The cause of backache is usually poor posture and strain of the joints at the bottom of the back and pelvis during pregnancy. Posture in labour is therefore important in minimising future backache. There are benefits from good back support in labour and regular changes in position.

In a recent study of over 300 women in England, the researchers randomly allocated the women to have an epidural or another form of pain relief in labour.

The women were followed up for more than two years, on average, after their delivery. Over two-thirds of all the women experienced backache after delivery and in over 10% of them it was severe. However, there was no difference in the number of women who reported backache after an epidural compared with those who had other forms of pain relief. Indeed, the women who did not have an epidural were more likely to have persistent and recent back pain compared with the women who had had an epidural. Furthermore, physiotherapists found that there was no difference in the mobility of women's backs between the groups. Hence while backache is common after having a baby, it would appear that modern epidurals for pain relief in labour are not the cause.

Do epidurals cause headache?

About 1% of women get a bad headache because of an epidural. This is usually due to a small leakage of the fluid that surrounds the brain and spinal cord into the epidural space. Most of these leaks will stop within a few days and, in rare cases, last for more than a week or so. The headache is usually relieved by lying flat, taking painkillers and plenty of fluids. Caffeine can sometimes help, too. If the headache is very severe and not responding to these measures, then the anaesthetist can treat you with an injection into the epidural space that will slow down or seal the leak.

Do epidurals always work?

Occasionally the epidural will not be fully effective. Sometimes only one side of the body is numbed or a patch of the abdomen still feels pain. This is usually because the local anaesthetic has not spread evenly throughout the epidural space and so has not numbed all the necessary nerves. This can often be dealt with by changing position to help the local anaesthetic move around the epidural space. Occasionally, the epidural insertion has to be repeated.

If a woman is very overweight, an epidural may be more difficult to set up as it will be harder for the anaesthetist to feel the correct place to put the needle into her back.

Are there any specific situations where the doctor or midwife might recommend an epidural?

There are a few situations when doctors often prefer you to have an epidural, such as if you are expecting twins or if you have high blood pressure or a heart condition. It is also useful if you need a forceps or ventouse delivery. Your doctor can advise you about this.

Does an epidural have any effect on the baby?

There is no evidence that epidurals have any long-term effects on the baby.

What other techniques are available for pain relief in labour?

Some women try out other techniques to assist them in dealing with the pain of labour. These include moving about and frequent changes of position, massage

Labour & delivery

Acupuncture for pain relief in labour

Acupuncture, which has been used in China for thousands of years, involves the insertion of special needles at strategic points on the body. This appears to relieve pain. While it has been used by some women for the relief of labour pain, doctors are uncertain how effective it is and also how it compares with other forms of pain relief, such as opiate medication and epidurals.

A Swedish group of researchers have recently studied the effectiveness of acupuncture during labour. The researchers randomly allocated 100 women in labour to receive either acupuncture or no acupuncture for pain relief. The acupuncture could be used on its own or combined with conventional forms of pain relief. Thus all the women were able to use any of the conventional methods of pain relief such as TENS, opiate medication, epidural or 'gas and air'. In the group who had acupuncture the number of women using epidurals was 12% compared to 22% in the group who did not receive acupuncture. The women receiving acupuncture also tended to feel more relaxed during labour and fewer of them used TENS. There was no difference in problems during labour or delivery between the two groups. These findings suggest that acupuncture could be valuable in the management of labour pain, in particular reducing the need for epidurals. However, further trials with greater numbers of patients are necessary before the value of acupuncture can be confirmed and also to establish whether it works by relieving pain or by improving relaxation in labour.

and aromatherapy combined with massage. There is no doubt that these techniques significantly reduce tension, enhance relaxation and thereby have a significant pain-reducing effect. Some women successfully use acupuncture, reflexology and hypnosis, but these techniques need expert assistance from skilled practitioners. If you plan to use any of these techniques, you should discuss them with your doctor or midwife to make the necessary arrangements for your labour.

Is water a useful option for pain relief in the first stage of labour?

Some may think that the use of water for easing the pain of labour is relatively new, but it isn't. Taking a bath in labour has been encouraged for hundreds of years. In the first stage of labour a warm bath has several benefits. It encourages relaxation, supports your body and assists your movement and posture. The warm water may also encourage the release of endorphins, the natural, opiate-like substances that help counter pain. Thus a warm bath in labour may be of significant value in helping you cope with labour. If you use this technique, make sure that the water temperature is no higher than 37°C

(98.6°F) – body temperature. Many women prefer it to be a bit cooler than this as labour can be hot work and this helps them keep cool. A change of environment also helps you cope in labour and getting into a warm bath or birthing pool can be a great psychological boost. Water can be used at any point in the first stage of labour, but you should always have someone near you while in a bath or a pool when in labour. While you are in water you can still have regular checks of blood pressure and temperature and the baby's heartbeat can be monitored intermittently. If you want to use water in labour, discuss this with your doctor or midwife.

Are there any times when I can't use water?

Water cannot be used in the first stage of labour if the baby needs to be monitored continuously such as when foetal distress is suspected or the baby is more at risk of becoming distressed – for example, if it is very small for dates *(see p. 124)*. It is also inadvisable to use water if you have complications such as pre-eclampsia *(see p. 136)*. If you have had opiate painkillers you should also be very cautious as these can make you drowsy and this can be dangerous in a bath or pool. So if you have recently had an injection of a painkiller like morphine, you should avoid water. As previously stated, you cannot use TENS while in water. Your doctor or midwife can advise you about these issues.

Monitoring the baby during labour

Why should my baby be monitored in labour?

Labour is a time of potential danger for the baby. The blood flow to the placenta decreases during the contractions of your womb, which can lead to a slightly reduced supply of oxygen and nutrients to the baby during contractions. However, this rarely causes a problem if the placenta is functioning normally and the baby is healthy. Indeed, the placenta usually has 'spare' capacity to cope with this. When there is a problem, such as your contractions being too frequent, or where the placenta is damaged or you have pre-eclampsia, which can upset placental functioning, then the baby may not cope with the stress of labour. Monitoring is thus used to detect early signs of the baby being distressed because of lack of oxygen supply.

How is the baby monitored?

There are various ways in which the baby can be monitored during labour. These include intermittent measurement of the baby's heart rate, assessment of the amniotic fluid for meconium staining, electronic foetal monitoring and foetal blood sampling.

How are intermittent checks of the baby's heart rate obtained?

The midwife or doctor will listen to the baby's heart rate at regular intervals using a Pinard stethoscope, which looks like a small plastic trumpet, or a hand-held ultrasound device. The Pinard stethoscope is pressed against your abdomen over the location of the baby's back. The midwife or doctor will place their ear on the other end of the stethoscope and listen to the heartbeat. During labour the baby's heartbeats are then counted: it is usually checked for one minute after every 15 minutes or so of contractions in the first stage of labour, and after every contraction in the second stage. The normal foetal heart rate at term is between 110 and 160 beats per minute. An advantage of this technique is that it is non-invasive, so it won't restrict your mobility in labour. However, as the checks are intermittent, abnormalities in the baby's heart rate pattern may go unnoticed if the heart rate is normal at the time of the check. It is best to assess the baby's heart rate during and immediately after you have a contraction, but this is difficult to do when you are having a contraction. Thus these checks are generally performed as soon as possible after a contraction.

What does meconium staining mean?

Meconium is the content of the baby's bowel. When a baby is distressed its bowels can move while in the womb and cause meconium staining of the amniotic fluid. The premature baby rarely passes meconium, however, as the nervous system controlling the bowel is not usually sufficiently mature. Sometimes the staining will be termed 'old meconium' . This indicates that the fluid is slightly discoloured and often simply reflects a more mature baby, rather than one in distress. If the meconium in the fluid can be described as thick, fresh or 'pea-soup', this indicates that it has recently been passed. As it is so thick, this suggests that there is not a great deal of fluid round the baby to dilute it. Reduced levels of fluid can be a sign of the baby being at risk, so thick meconium can be of greater concern than 'old' meconium staining.

How is the baby's heart rate monitored?

The baby's heart rate is monitored continuously. Your contractions will also be recorded, as this is important for the interpretation of changes in heart rate. The machine that does the monitoring is known as a cardiotocograph, or CTG for short *(see p. 130)*. Two small devices are strapped to your abdomen. One of these picks up the baby's heart rate using ultrasound and the other picks up the contractions. Alternatively, the heart rate can be picked up more accurately with a small clip (a foetal scalp electrode) attached to the baby's head, which is connected to the CTG machine by means of a thin wire. The clip is applied to the baby's head during a vaginal examination. The heart rate and contractions are printed out on a long strip of graph paper. The upper part of the print-out on the graph paper always shows the heart rate and the lower part the contractions of the womb. The midwife or doctor can interpret the tracing of the baby's heart rate pattern to look for any signs that might indicate that the baby is not coping with labour. If you wish, feel free to ask the midwife or doctor to explain the trace to you. When you are attached to the CTG machine, you will not be able to walk around freely or go for a bath.

Do all pregnancies need continuous monitoring of the baby's heart rate in labour?

If you have a high-risk pregnancy where the baby is at great risk of becoming distressed in labour, then it makes sense to monitor the baby continuously once you are in labour. *(See table below for specific factors.)* However, for the majority of women the baby will be at low risk of such problems. With a low-risk pregnancy in uncomplicated labour, continuous electronic foetal heart rate monitoring in labour is controversial. This is because it has not been shown to have any advantages for the baby compared to intermittent checks of the baby's heart rate, whereas it has been associated with a higher risk of Caesarean section. So intermittent monitoring, being safer, is the method

Reasons why continuous monitoring of the baby's heart rate might be recommended

Problems with the mother's health	Pre-eclampsia
	Diabetes
	Infection
	Heart disease
	Connective tissue disease
	Kidney disease
Factors relating to the current pregnancy or labour	Pregnancy has advanced to 42 weeks or more
	Bleeding from the womb during the pregnancy
	Twin (or triplet) pregnancies
	The baby is small
	Labour is premature
	Labour is induced
	Slow labour is accelerated using medication
Factors relating to a past pregnancy	Previous Caesarean section
	Previous loss in late pregnancy
The mother's choice	If you want to have continuous CTG monitoring then you should be able to have it if it is available

Labour & delivery

recommended for low-risk pregnancies. It also has the advantage of allowing you to be as mobile as you wish between checks.

Electronic monitoring is recommended, however, where contractions are weak or infrequent and need to be enhanced medically. In addition, some mothers like the reassurance of the continuous monitoring while others prefer to avoid this if possible. Many doctors recommend a CTG for 20 minutes or so when you are admitted in labour. If the foetal heart rate is normal and you are at low risk of problems and have an uncomplicated labour, monitoring can be continued using intermittent checks on the baby's heart rate. If abnormalities are picked up on the admission CTG or following intermittent checks, or a complication arises in labour, then continuous electronic foetal heart rate monitoring would usually be recommended. Your doctor or midwife can advise you on the best form of monitoring for your particular situation.

What is the significance of accelerations and decelerations in the baby's heart rate?

As we discussed on p. 130, accelerations are when the baby's heart beat speeds up by more than 15 beats per minute for more than 15 seconds. They usually come on with contractions or when the baby moves. This is perfectly normal – just as our heart beats faster when we exercise. Accelerations are very reassuring of the baby's well-being. Decelerations are when the baby's heart rate slows down temporarily for at least 15 seconds. Decelerations do not necessarily suggest that there is any problem with the baby. For example, so-called early decelerations are normal responses of the baby to your womb contracting. An early deceleration coincides with the contraction and are believed to be caused by the baby's head being slightly squeezed during the contraction. Other deceleration patterns such as 'late' decelerations, which come on after a contraction, can indicate a possible problem for the baby due to a shortage of oxygen. There are also variable decelerations that usually indicate that the cord is being squeezed by contractions. If these are persistent, they can sometimes cause problems for the baby.

It is not just the deceleration patterns that are significant, however. Other aspects of the baby's heart rate pattern, such as if it is beating too fast, more than 150 beats per minute, or too slow, less than 110 beats per minute, can also help the doctor or midwife work out if the baby might be having problems. In addition, the baseline heart rate normally varies by more than 5–10 beats per minute. Reduced levels of this baseline variability can occur when the baby is distressed but can also occur for other reasons such as after the mother has been given opiates for pain relief, as the medication can make the baby 'sleepy', thus affecting the heart rate. Your doctor or midwife will watch the CTG for any abnormal pattern and advise you about any treatment that may be necessary. If you wish, feel free to ask the midwife or doctor to explain the CTG trace to you.

Why would a foetal blood sample be taken?

Where there is concern that the baby may be distressed, a tiny blood sample can be taken from the baby's head to measure the degree of acidity of the baby's blood. The blood becomes more acidic when the baby is deprived of oxygen. The sample is taken using a tube-like instrument (inserted into your vagina) that lets the doctor see the baby's scalp. However, sometimes, especially in early labour, it is impossible to obtain a blood sample this way. Foetal blood sampling should be avoided if the baby has any problem that might cause it to bleeding excessively. It should also be avoided if the mother has certain infections that might be passed on to the baby because of the small cut on its head. If a blood sample cannot be obtained, the doctor or midwife will rely on the CTG to assess the baby's condition.

Eating and drinking in labour

Can I eat in labour?

Traditionally, women were advised not to eat or drink in labour except take sips of water. This was in case an emergency arose and a general anaesthetic was required. Many maternity units have moved away from this policy unless you are considered to be at high risk of needing an emergency Caesarean delivery. Labour itself leads to a reduction in the speed at which your stomach will empty. Opiate painkillers like morphine also reduce the rate of emptying. Obviously, it is best not to have a full stomach when in labour, just as during any strenuous form of exercise. While you are unlikely to be hungry when you are in established labour, there is no doubt that you need to keep your energy levels up. Labour is hard work, after all. So a snack of high-energy carbohydrate food in early labour can be useful, such as a couple of digestive biscuits, a simple sandwich or a banana. You should avoid fatty foods, as these will further reduce the rate of stomach emptying.

Can I drink in labour?

Even if you don't feel like eating, it is best to take some fluids during labour – plain water is ideal. You tend to lose a lot of fluid when in labour and it is easy to become dehydrated. You may sweat a lot and even if you are not aware of sweating you will still lose a lot of fluid through your skin and in your breath. You should check with your doctor or midwife with regard to their policy on eating and drinking in labour.

The second stage of labour

What is the second stage of labour?

The second stage of labour lasts from full dilatation of your cervix until delivery of the baby. It is divided into two phases: a passive phase, during which the baby's head descends deep into the pelvis; and an active phase when you will feel an intense urge to push the baby out. The passive phase is really an extension of the first stage of labour and is sometimes called 'transition'. Some women may feel sick or vomit at this point.

How long will the second stage of labour last?

The passive phase may be very short or may last for 1–2 hours. This transitional phase often lasts longer if you have an epidural, as you will not feel the urge to push while the epidural is fully effective. The duration of the second stage will depend on many factors, including the strength of your contractions, the position of the baby's head and the size and shape of your pelvis. However, most women, especially those who have had a baby before, will deliver within one hour of starting to push.

How will I know when to push?

You may get a strong and irresistible urge to push. However, sometimes you will feel this sensation slightly before full dilatation, so your doctor or midwife will usually check that you are fully dilated by examining you before you start to push. If you are not fully dilated, you should try to resist the urge to push the baby out as pushing can make the cervix swell up and delay the delivery. Taking short, shallow breaths when your contraction comes helps you to avoid pushing, as good pushing requires a deep breath in. If you have an epidural, you may not be aware of the 'urge to push' sensation, so your midwife or doctor will examine you and tell you when to push.

How do I push?

Often you will push instinctively in response to the urge to push. When you feel the contraction starting, take a deep breath in. This fills your chest and helps put pressure on the womb as you bear down. If you are in a sitting position, it usually helps if you put your chin on your chest. If you are squatting, then a deeper squatting position will help you to put more pressure on your womb. During a long contraction you will be able to let your breath out and then take a deep breath and start again. If you want to make a noise when you are pushing, do so if it helps you to push effectively, but don't let it distract you from effective pushing.

Will my contractions be the same in the second stage as in the first?

In the second stage of labour your contractions may slow down in frequency but increase in duration. This increase in duration gives you more time in which to push effectively.

What positions can I use for the second stage of labour?

There are many positions that women deliver in; you should choose the position that suits you best. As upright positions allow gravity to help the baby come through the birth canal, you should avoid lying flat, however. You can squat, stand, kneel, deliver on all fours, sit upright, or lie on one side. You need to find the position that you find most helpful. You can stay in the same position or change position – whatever helps best. Being upright during the second stage could mean kneeling, squatting, sitting fairly straight, or using a birthing stool.

Does being upright help?
Being upright for the second stage can make it more comfortable and less painful. Pushing is easier and, when you squat or kneel, your pelvis may open wider thus making more room for the baby to come through. The second stage may therefore be shorter if you use an upright position. In addition, there may be less chance of tearing your vagina or perineum (the skin between your vagina and anus) when you are upright, although there may be more chance of tears occurring to the labia (the lips of tissue around your vagina).

What should my partner do?
Your partner can help by just being there to support you emotionally and encourage you when pushing. If you are squatting or standing, you should get your partner to sit or stand behind you to help support your weight. Your partner can support your leg if you are lying on your side. If you need to change position, your partner can help you move. A back rub from your partner can help to ease backache and pain. Your partner can use a cool flannel to wipe your brow between contractions and can help with delivery and cutting the cord.

Can I deliver in water?
As we have seen, water is useful for helping relieve labour pain. Some women choose to stay in water for the birth itself. While it is not fully clear how safe or effective water births are, a recent study, assessing the outcomes for water births in the period 1994–6 in England and Wales, showed no difference in the numbers of neonatal deaths or admissions to special care baby units as compared with low-risk pregnancies undergoing conventional deliveries. If you have a pregnancy complication such as severe pre-eclampsia, a water birth is perhaps best avoided. However, with an uncomplicated pregnancy, a water birth can be beneficial. As during the first stage of labour, the water will support your weight and enhance posture and mobility. There may also be a reduced need for painkillers.

There are potential hazards and dangers to be taken into account, however. If a serious complication arises, how do your carers get you out of the pool quickly? In addition, it is more difficult to examine you and monitor the baby. There is a theoretical risk of infection, too, as most women move their bowels, even if only slightly, at some point during labour and delivery. This is difficult to avoid as the baby presses so hard on the lower bowel during delivery. So there will be faeces in the water with you. These can be 'fished out' with a kitchen sieve kept beside the pool for this purpose. There have also been concerns expressed regarding the safety of the baby being born underwater. One problem

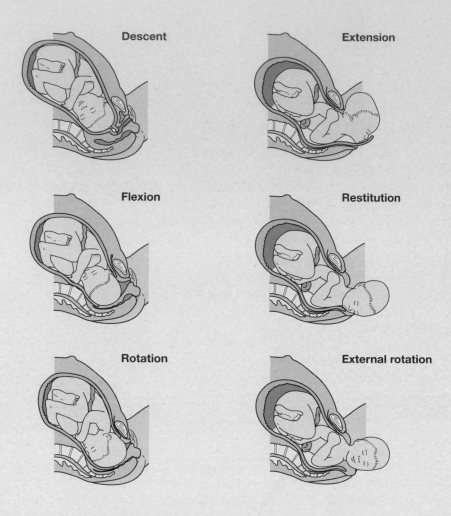

Descent

Extension

Flexion

Restitution

Rotation

External rotation

The baby's passage through the birth canal (*see box opposite*).

that has arisen is the baby's umbilical cord snapping, which can lead to the baby losing blood. This may happen if the baby has a short cord and is brought to the surface of the water too quickly. Reducing the depth of water for the second stage and bringing the baby to the surface gently may reduce the risk. Overall, however, there is no indication at present to suggest that water births should not continue or that they pose any clear risk for the baby. If you are interested in having a water birth, you will need to find a midwife or doctor with experience of this technique and a hospital with a birthing pool. It is also possible to rent a birthing pool for use either in hospital or for a home birth.

How does delivery occur?

As you push, the baby's head will progressively move down through the pelvis, slipping back a little between each contraction, giving the tissues of the vagina

The baby's passage through the birth canal

The baby's head usually enters your pelvis looking towards your right or left side (referred to as the occipito-transverse position of the head). During labour, certain parts of the baby's head are too big to pass through the pelvis, requiring the head and trunk to go through a series of manoeuvres.

Descent: The baby's head descends into the pelvis, either before or during labour. It will now be resting on the pelvic floor muscles.

Flexion: The flexion of the baby's neck occurs during descent, so that the baby's chin will be on its chest. This results in the smallest section of the baby's head passing through the pelvis.

Rotation: The pelvic floor consists of a shelf of muscle that slopes to the front. The first part of the baby's head to reach the pelvic floor will rotate towards the front. If the baby's neck is well flexed and the crown of the head is leading, this will rotate the head to the occipito-anterior position (back of the head towards the abdomen). But if the head is not well flexed, the top part of the head near the forehead will reach the pelvic floor first. When this part rotates towards the front, the back of the baby's head will be towards your back. This is referred to as the occipito-posterior position.

Crowning: The baby will be pushed further down the birth canal by the contractions. When the top of the head is seen emerging from the vagina, this is called crowning.

Extension: This is followed by straightening up of the baby's neck (referred to as extension), releasing the face and chin from the vagina.

Restitution: The head emerging from the vagina will turn so that it faces towards the front of the baby's body. This is called restitution.

External rotation and delivery: The shoulders will rotate into the anterior-posterior position (one shoulder pointing towards the mother's abdomen and the other towards her back). This is followed by rotation of the baby's head so that its face looks at the inside of one of the mother's thighs. Bending the body to either side allows the shoulders to be delivered – the shoulder nearest the mother's abdomen usually appears first. After the shoulders are delivered, the rest of the body then follows quickly and easily.

time to stretch to accommodate the baby's head. When the top of the baby's head no longer slips back into the vagina between contractions, this is called crowning and indicates that delivery is imminent. If you put your hand down, you will be able to feel the top of your baby's head. Some women take a small mirror with them in labour so that they can see the baby's head at this point. This will show you just how close delivery is. Your midwife or doctor will control the delivery of the head with gentle pressure to avoid or minimise damage to the perineum. Once the head crowns, you usually need to stop pushing and start to pant, with short, shallow breaths, to allow a slow, controlled delivery of the head. This allows a little time for the tissues at the vaginal entrance to stretch and can prevent tearing. If the midwife or doctor thinks that you will tear, then an episiotomy can be performed (see below). Once the head is delivered, the midwife or doctor will check if the baby's cord is round the neck. If it is, it will be released often by simply slipping the cord over the baby's head. Any mucus around the baby's mouth nose and eyes will be wiped away. The rest of the baby's body usually follows easily. The baby can be delivered on to your abdomen, allowing you to touch and hold your new baby immediately.

Will I tear when my baby is delivered?

It is impossible to predict until delivery is occurring whether or not you will tear. Small tears are quite common, especially in your first delivery. It will depend on many factors, such as the size of the baby, how well the tissues stretch and the position of the baby's head. If a bad tear seems likely then you will probably be offered an episiotomy.

Why should I avoid having a bad tear?

Tears are uncontrolled and can therefore extend in any direction, occurring at the point where the resistance of the tissues is least – usually towards the back. Tears towards the front can be particularly painful; they are not common but are more likely if you deliver on all fours. Most often the tear will not be large. Tears can involve just the skin (a first-degree tear) or the skin and muscle of the vaginal wall (a second-degree tear). Most worrying is where the tear is large and extends through the anus, tearing the muscles that control your anal continence. This is called a third-degree tear. When this occurs, it usually needs to be repaired by an experienced senior doctor.

What is an episiotomy?

An episiotomy is a cut made with scissors at the entrance to your vagina to enlarge the vaginal opening. This can make it easier for you to push the baby out without the tissues tearing.

How is an episiotomy made?

You will be given an injection of local anaesthetic into the tissues behind the vagina in order to numb them. At the height of a contraction a small cut will then be made with scissors to enlarge the vaginal opening. This can either be a midline or a medio-lateral episiotomy. A midline episiotomy is made in a straight line from the back of the vagina towards the anus, but stopping well short of the anus itself. This is more common in North America. A medio-

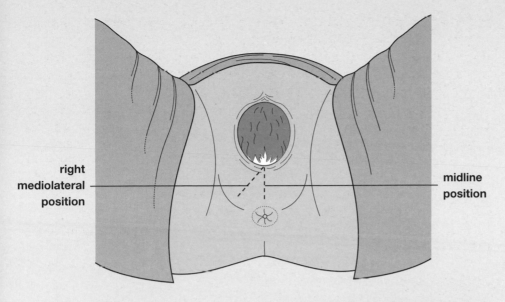

right
mediolateral
position

midline
position

The positions of an episiotomy. The right mediolateral position is the most common type of episiotomy in the UK.

lateral episiotomy starts at the back of the vagina in the midline and is directed diagonally to one side of the anus, usually the mother's right-hand side. This is more common in the UK.

Do I have to have an episiotomy?

Episiotomy should *not* be carried out routinely. Whether or not an episiotomy would be useful to you can only be assessed by the midwife or doctor conducting the delivery. If it seems likely that you will tear badly, then an episiotomy will usually be offered. It should only be carried out with your permission, however. Some women would prefer to tear than have an episiotomy. If you would prefer this then you should let your doctor or midwife know. This can be set out in your birth plan. There are some situations where an episiotomy is usually considered necessary, such as when the baby is being delivered by forceps or ventouse, is in the breech position (see p. 232), or if the baby is very large and the delivery is difficult.

Is an episiotomy better than a tear?

Damage to the pelvic floor is more common with large babies, long labours and forceps deliveries. A tear can sometimes occur even if you have an episiotomy. Episiotomies have generally not been shown to prevent tears into the anus and rectum, although one recent study did find that episiotomies helped reduce the likelihood of such a tear. Tears involving the skin can often heal well without the need for stitches, while an episiotomy will need to be repaired with stitches. Larger tears involving muscle also need to be repaired with stitches. It is usually easier to repair a clean-cut episiotomy than a ragged complex tear involving the skin and the muscle.

Labour & delivery

Massaging the perineum to help prevent tearing

The perineum is the area of skin between the vagina and anus. Until recently it was not clear whether massaging and stretching the skin of the perineum during labour would reduce the risk of a tear occurring or an episiotomy being required. Researchers in Australia have recently conducted a study to determine if perineal massage in labour is useful in preventing tears. Over 1340 women were studied. They were randomly allocated to receive either perineal massage with every contraction during the second stage of labour or routine midwifery care for delivery. The number of women requiring an episiotomy or who had a tear was similar in both groups, although there was a tendency for fewer severe tears involving the anus to occur in the women who had had perineal massage. There was no difference in pain or other problems after delivery between the groups. So massaging the perineum does not appear to prevent episiotomies or tears or reduce pain after delivery.

How is the cord cut?

Once the baby is born, it is usually placed on your abdomen so you can hold, stroke and see your baby straight after delivery. The cord will then be clamped and cut. If the labour and delivery are uncomplicated, there is no reason why you or your partner cannot help cut the cord.

Sometimes it is better to delay cutting the cord to allow as much blood as possible to return from the placenta to the baby. In this situation a few minutes can elapse before the cord is cut. Once the cord stops pulsating, there is no benefit from further delay in cutting the cord. If you have a preference about cutting the cord, let your doctor or midwife know and put this in your birth plan.

The third stage of labour

The third stage of labour starts immediately after delivery of your baby and ends with the delivery of the afterbirth (placenta). The muscle of the womb contracts strongly after the delivery of the baby. This does two things: first, it helps detach the afterbirth from the wall of the womb and push it out; and second, the tight contraction of the muscles constricts the large blood vessels that supplied the placenta, so preventing bleeding from the site of the placenta in the womb.

What will happen to me in the third stage?

Just as the baby is being born, your doctor or midwife will give you an injection into your thigh or bottom. Most women do not even notice it as they are focusing on the delivery. This injection contains oxytocin or a combination of oxytocin and ergometrine – medications that stimulate the womb to contract tightly. Oxytocin is actually a natural substance – a hormone made by your body to help the womb contract. You may be aware of your womb contracting down in the third stage. When the womb has contracted to the size of a small football, your midwife or doctor will ask you to push a little to help deliver the afterbirth. At the same time they will be putting some traction on the cord. They will also place a hand on your abdomen to keep the womb in position. This will lead to delivery of the afterbirth, which is usually collected in a special bowl. After it is delivered, the afterbirth is examined to check that it is complete and that there is no placental tissue remaining in the womb. Retained tissue can lead to infection and bleeding.

What is the benefit of these medications for delivery of the afterbirth?

Prompt delivery of the afterbirth with the help of medication like oxytocin has been shown to reduce the risk of heavy bleeding immediately after the delivery by over 50% even in women at low risk of such a complication. The combination of ergometrine and oxytocin produces more side-effects than oxytocin alone, however. This is because ergometrine can make you feel nauseated and sometimes cause vomiting. It can also increase your blood pressure and therefore should not be used if you have high blood pressure or pre-eclampsia. Because of this, many doctors and midwives use oxytocin alone as this has virtually no side-effects and there is very little difference in the effectiveness of these two medications. Thus oxytocin is the medication usually recommended to prevent bleeding from the womb after delivery.

Must I have an injection to help delivery of the afterbirth?

Whether or not you have an injection to help the third stage of labour is up to you. Your midwife or doctor will talk to you about it in early labour. You will only receive this medication if you give your permission. If you do not have this medication then the third stage will usually last longer and you will have an increased risk of heavy bleeding that can sometimes lead to problems. One study assessed over 1500 women where half received such medication for the third stage and half did not: 16% of those who did not receive the medication had a haemorrhage after delivery, compared to fewer than 7% of those who received the medication.

Can I help the delivery of the afterbirth without medication?

When the baby suckles at your breast, the nipple stimulation will cause your body to release oxytocin, which encourages your womb to contract and can thus help in delivery of the afterbirth.

How long does the third stage of labour last?

It usually lasts about 10–20 minutes if medication is given and up to an hour if delivery of the afterbirth occurs without this assistance.

Medical terms used to describe labour in your pregnancy record

Cervical effacement   Before labour the cervix is thick and long. Prior to labour proper, it shortens and thins out. This process is called effacement.

Cervical dilatation   Cervical dilatation is the opening of the cervix (neck of the womb). When the cervix is 10 cm (4 in) dilated, it is fully dilated (open) – wide enough to let the baby's head pass through.

Engaged   When the head is engaged, the widest part of the baby's head has entered your pelvis. This is gauged from examination of your abdomen. Sometimes doctors and midwives write it as the number of fifths of the baby's head that they can feel in your abdomen. When two-fifths or less of the head is in your abdomen, the head will be engaged.

Lie   The 'lie' is the relationship of the long axis of the baby to the long axis of the womb. The normal lie is longitudinal, which is when the baby is lying vertically in the womb.

Presentation   The presentation is the part of the foetus that is leading into the mother's pelvis. The most common presentation is cephalic, where the baby enters the mother's pelvis head first. Sometimes this is called a vertex presentation, which indicates that the neck is bent forward and the top of the baby's head, the so-called vertex, is leading. When the baby is coming bottom first this is a breech presentation.

Position   Position describes the way that the baby's head is facing. Doctors always indicate where the back of the baby's head is relative to the mother's back. The hindmost part of the baby's skull is called the occiput. So if the back of the baby's head points to your abdomen, this is referred to as the occipito-anterior position. This is the normal position of the head for delivery. If the back of the baby's head is towards your back this is the occipito-posterior position. This can be associated with a slower labour and with more backache in labour.

Station of the head   The 'station' tells the doctor or midwife how far into the pelvis the baby's head has descended. It is assessed during a vaginal examination. The level of the head is gauged relative to bony prominences on either side of the pelvis called the ischial spines. These are easily felt during examination.

What happens if the afterbirth is retained?

Sometimes the afterbirth is retained in the womb, which can occur even if medication is given. If this happens there is a high risk of bleeding if the afterbirth is not removed. Sometimes a full bladder will prevent delivery of the afterbirth, so it is important to make sure that your bladder is empty. A catheter may need to be inserted to be certain that the bladder is empty. If the afterbirth is retained, you will need an operation known as a manual removal of the afterbirth. Under a general anaesthetic or an epidural, the doctor will insert his or her hand into the womb through the vagina and remove the afterbirth.

Birth plans

Your choices in childbirth are important. If you have specific preferences for your management in labour and delivery, then you should think about setting them out in a birth plan. A birth plan is simply a way of communicating your preferences in writing to those looking after you in labour. It can be placed in your pregnancy record. Labour is a stressful time and you may not be able to think about and express all your preferences when you are having regular painful contractions, so it is helpful for both you and your carers to have a written record to refer to. It can also help you feel that you are in control of what is happening to you.

Is there a set format for a birth plan?

There is no set format. You should include all the choices that are important for you. It is often useful to discuss such items with your midwife, doctor or local pregnancy support group. However, there are several issues that tend to feature commonly in birth plans and these are discussed below.

Who do you want to be with you in labour?

You may wish to specify who you want to have with you in labour, such as your partner or a friend or relative. In addition, you might want to indicate anyone you specifically do not want to be present. You can consider whether you want your birthing partner to be with you all the time or to be absent at certain points, such as while you are being stitched after birth, for instance. If you are planning to have a Cesarean section, you can also specify who you want to be with you while it is being performed.

What pain relief would you prefer?

It is common to indicate your preference for pain relief in a birth plan. You will probably have some idea of the type of pain relief you would prefer. However, while it is important to set out your preferences in a birth plan, be prepared to be flexible so that you get the right pain relief for your particular needs in labour when the time arrives.

What position would you prefer for labour and delivery?

Would you prefer to move around the room in early labour? Is there a particular position you would like to be in for delivery, such as standing up or sitting? Would you rather be examined while lying on your back or on your side, or even while standing? If so, you can indicate your preference in your birth plan. Again, remember to be flexible in your approach. Until you are in labour you will not know how you feel in any given position and sometimes you will want to try several to find the right one for you. Your preferences here can also influence other aspects of your care. For example, if you want to move around but be as pain-free as possible, you could consider a mobile epidural; or, if you want a water birth, you cannot use TENS for pain relief.

What are your views on electronic monitoring of the baby's heart beat?

If you have an uncomplicated pregnancy and delivery and are at low risk of complications then you may not need continuous monitoring of the baby. If this is the case then you can set out the method you would prefer to check on the baby's condition (usually intermittent checks).

What else should I consider for the first stage of labour?

You can set out your views on having labour induced or accelerated. This will include whether or not you would like your waters broken. What sort of surroundings would you prefer? Would you like music playing. If so, what sort of music would you like to bring with you? Would you prefer dimmed lighting or for the room to be brightly lit?

What else should I consider for the second stage of labour?

Would you prefer to be allowed to tear or have an episiotomy? Do you want to feel or see the baby's head being delivered? Do you want the baby to be delivered onto your abdomen? Who do you want to cut the cord? Do you want to see the afterbirth?

What choices should I consider after the baby is born?

Are you happy to have an injection of oxytocin to lower the risk of bleeding from the womb after delivery? How do you want to feed your baby? Do you want to put your baby to the breast immediately? Do you want to be left alone with your baby and your partner after delivery? How long do you want to stay in hospital if your delivery is uncomplicated – would you like a rapid, six-hour discharge, rather than staying for a day or two?

If I have a Caesarean section, are there any choices to be made?

Even if you have a Caesarean delivery, there are still choices to be made. Do you want to be awake, with an epidural or spinal anaesthetic, or be asleep with a general anaesthetic? Do you and your partner want to see the baby as the surgeon delivers it?

Home deliveries

Is a home birth safe?

There is no evidence that well-planned home births with an experienced midwife or doctor in attendance are less safe than hospital births for women with an uncomplicated pregnancy and no risk factors for labour. Indeed, there is a lower rate of medical intervention than in hospital, but this is at least partly due to the fact that only women with a low risk of complications tend to deliver at home. The facilities for supporting home births vary from place to place and you will need to check with your doctor or midwife whether a home birth is possible and whether it would be suitable for you. About 15 out of 100 women who plan a home birth are advised to switch to a hospital delivery because of pregnancy complications.

What are the advantages of home births?

Home births let you stay in your own surroundings. This familiarity can help you feel more relaxed and in control. You can control the ambience through your own choice of room, furnishings, music and light. A home birth can be as private as you wish, rather than a 'public' event, surrounded by hospital staff. Your other children can see the baby as soon as it is born.

What are the disadvantages of a home birth?

Giving birth can be messy so you will need to identify a suitable room, ideally near the bathroom, and cover the birthing area and your mattress with protective plastic sheeting. If you are planning a water birth, you will need sufficient space for the birthing pool, a strong floor (the weight of the pool filled with water can be quite considerable) and easy access to a tap. The same range of pain relief will not be available. Epidurals are not possible at home, for instance. However, you can still have TENS, opiates and gas and air, as well as using techniques such as massage. If problems arise during the labour or after delivery, full medical back-up will not be immediately available and you may need to be transferred to hospital as an emergency. The usual reasons for a transfer being necessary are either a very prolonged labour or concern for the baby's well-being. In first pregnancies about 30% of women having their labour at home will need to be transferred to hospital during their labour, but this is much less common if you have already had a straightforward vaginal delivery. Occasionally after delivery either you or the baby may need to be transferred to hospital for treatment of complications.

Is boiling water really needed for home births?

Boiling water was used in the past to sterilise instruments. Nowadays instruments come in sterile packs, so there is no need to boil instruments to sterilise them. However, warm water is needed to clean you and the baby after the birth.

Induction of labour and slow progress in labour

What is induction of labour and why is it carried out?

When your labour is started medically, before your body goes into labour spontaneously, this is called induction of labour. There are many reasons for induction. It might be carried out because of medical problems such as high blood pressure or diabetes. Sometimes it is carried out because of personal or family reasons or because you request it at term. It may be carried out because there is considered to be a risk to the baby in allowing the pregnancy to continue. An example would be where the baby's growth has slowed down or stopped due to a problem with the placenta supplying the baby with nutrients. Another example is in pregnancies that are overdue. There is an increased risk to the baby when pregnancies go beyond 42 weeks; so most doctors will organise an induction if you have not gone into labour by 41 weeks. If you do not want to be induced by 42 weeks then it is important to monitor the baby regularly (usually around twice-weekly) to be certain that the baby is not getting into difficulties. Monitoring is usually carried out by checking the baby's heart rate pattern on a CTG (heart rate monitor) strapped to your abdomen, or by looking at its movement patterns on an ultrasound scan. Often the amount of fluid round the baby is also measured by ultrasound scan.

How do doctors know if an induction will be successful?

The induction technique used will depend on how close your own body is to labour. As we have seen, your womb prepares for labour when the neck of the womb, the cervix, softens, shortens and starts to open slightly. Your doctor or midwife can perform an internal examination to determine the state of your cervix. When the cervix has changed in preparation for labour, it is said to be 'ripe'. If it is ripe then induction is usually straightforward. If the cervix is not ripe then induction may be unsuccessful and so should be delayed or the cervix should be ripened with medication. Ripening is more commonly required in a first pregnancy and your doctor will advise you about the need for this in your particular situation.

What is a membrane sweep?

A membrane sweep is a technique to help labour start. It has been shown to increase the chances of your labour starting naturally within the 48 hours after the sweep is performed and to reduce the need for other methods of induction of labour. Membrane sweeping can be performed when your doctor or midwife carries out the internal examination to determine the state of your cervix prior to planning an induction. They will place a finger just inside your cervix and make a circular, sweeping movement to separate the membranes from the cervix in front of the baby's head. Sweeping may cause you some discomfort and release of the 'show', but will not cause any harm to your baby. Neither will it increase the chance of you or your baby getting an infection.

How is the cervix ripened?

Your doctor can advise you on the best technique for cervical ripening in your own case, but cervical ripening is often carried out with prostaglandin tablets or gels placed in the vagina or the neck of the womb. Prostaglandins are natural substances produced by the cervix and the womb that lead to softening of the cervix and also stimulate contractions of the womb. Sometimes several doses of prostaglandins are required, several hours apart, to ripen the cervix. The ripening process itself sometimes triggers the onset of labour. There is good evidence to show that ripening will make your subsequent labour shorter and less painful, reduce complications for both you and the baby and also reduce the likelihood of Caesarean section. It is usual to monitor the baby with a CTG for 30 minutes or so after you receive prostaglandins to ripen the cervix.

How is induction of labour carried out?

Once the cervix is ripe then induction can be carried out. There are several methods of induction. Your doctor will advise you on the best method for your particular situation. Induction can be carried out by putting prostaglandin tablets or gels into the vagina. These will stimulate the womb to contract, although the contractions may not start for a few hours after you receive the medication. A labour induced with prostaglandins is no more painful than a natural labour. Sometimes induction is carried out by breaking your waters artificially. After your waters are broken, the womb will naturally produce more prostaglandins which in turn should stimulate contractions. If your womb does not contract well after your waters are broken then oxytocin, administered through a drip in your arm, can be given to stimulate your womb to contract. The amount given is carefully controlled by a special pump, to avoid over-stimulation of the womb. Women who have an induction with oxytocin are more likely to have an epidural for pain relief in labour. Overall, prostaglandins are generally superior to oxytocin in terms of the likelihood of a successful vaginal birth. This might be because with prostaglandins you can remain mobile, or because the prostaglandins also soften the neck of the womb, making it easier for the contractions to work. However, when deciding on the best method of induction, the doctor must take into account a great deal of information about your overall situation before deciding which technique is best for you.

Does the baby need to be monitored when I am being induced?

It is usual to monitor the baby during induction, as occasionally the contractions can become too strong or too frequent and this can lead to the baby becoming distressed. Your doctor or midwife will advise you about the need for monitoring if you are being induced.

Labour & delivery

Why do some labours make slow progress?

Slow progress in labour is more common in a first than a subsequent labour. The most common cause is relatively weak or infrequent contractions (referred to as inefficient uterine activity). This affects around a quarter of women in their first labour compared to less than 10% in subsequent pregnancies. Sometimes slow progress is associated with the baby's head not being in the best position for delivery. However, this in turn is often due to the contractions not being strong enough to turn the baby's head into the best position for delivery. The other major cause is when the baby is too big to come through the pelvis (referred to as cephalo-pelvic disproportion), which usually leads to progress being slow or stopping in the later stages of labour.

How is slow progress in labour treated?

First of all, it is important to try to determine the cause of the problem. The doctor will then be able to advise you about the best way to correct the situation. If progress is slow because contractions are weak then this is often treated by rupturing your membranes or, if this has been done already, giving an oxytocin drip to help the womb contract more strongly. This will successfully correct slow progress in about 80% of women. If the delay in progress is due to the baby being too big for your pelvis, then a Caesarean section will be required. When oxytocin is used to speed up the labour, it is important to monitor the baby's heartbeat continuously with CTG.

The different types of presentation

What is a breech presentation?

Breech presentation is where the baby's bottom or feet are leading the way down the birth canal. Many babies are breech in early pregnancy. This is because there is plenty of space within the womb for them to move around. So they will frequently change position and sometimes they will be breech. At around 32 weeks of pregnancy, babies usually take up the head down position. At this stage there is less space in the womb to move around in, so they usually stay in this position until delivery. However, around 3% of babies stay in the breech position at term (37–42 weeks). In a breech presentation your baby presents with its legs first, buttocks first or legs crossed, sitting over the birth canal. Breech presentation is more common in premature labour. Some breech babies can be delivered vaginally, but there can be an increased risk of problems for the baby. Because of this, Caesarean section is usually the preferred way to deliver breech babies.

What problems can occur with a vaginal breech delivery?

The largest part of the baby is its head. In a breech delivery the body is delivered before the head, so there is a possibility that there could be difficulty delivering the head. This is especially true if the feet are coming first as they can

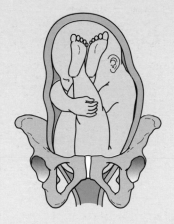

With a breech presentation your baby presents with its legs first, buttocks first or legs crossed, sitting over the birth canal. In the illustration this baby is presenting with its bottom first, known as a 'frank' breech.

slip through the neck of the womb (the cervix) before it opens wide enough to let the head through. There can also be a greater risk of the baby becoming distressed during labour due to a shortage of oxygen supply. Sometimes this can be because the cord gets tangled in the legs and comes down into the vagina before the baby is ready to be born. If serious problems arise during a breech labour, a Caesarean section can be performed.

Can anything be done to turn a breech baby to a head-first presentation?

Sometimes the doctor can turn the baby round in your womb by gently pressing on your abdomen to change the way the baby is lying. This can manoeuvre the baby so that it is head down in your womb instead of bottom down. Doctors call this procedure external cephalic version, or ECV for short. The best time for this to be done is at 37 weeks. It is usually performed in the ultrasound room, so that the doctor can check on the baby's condition at any time. This procedure is successful in more than half of breech presentations, who will subsequently remain head first at term, but sometimes the baby will turn back to a breech position. If your baby is very big, or does not have a lot of fluid round about it in the womb, then it may not be possible to turn it round. Your own doctor will advise you about whether an external cephalic version would be useful for your own situation.

What is a face presentation?

A face presentation occurs when a baby, coming head first, has its neck arched back so that its face is leading the way down the birth canal. As a result, the baby's face can become quite swollen and bruised due to being pushed against the tissues of your pelvis with each contraction, although the swelling and bruising of the face will usually resolve over several days. This type of presentation is uncommon, however, and occurs in only around 1 in 500

Delivering a breech baby by Caesarean section

Researchers in the Term Breech Trial Collaborative Group recently reported their study involving 2088 women with a breech presentation at term in 26 countries. Women with large babies or with other contraindications for a vaginal breech delivery were not included. The 2088 women were randomly assigned to have either a Caesarean section or a planned vaginal breech delivery. They found that around 43% of the women with a planned vaginal breech delivery were delivered by Caesarean section, mostly because of complications in labour. There were a lower number of baby deaths and serious problems in those delivered by Caesarean section, with 5% of babies born vaginally having such problems compared to only 1.6% delivered by Caesarean section. The authors calculated that, for every additional 14 Caesareans carried out, one baby death or serious problem would be avoided. Between the two groups there was no overall difference in complications for the mother in the first six weeks after delivery, but three months after delivery, the women delivered by Caesarean section were shown to have a lower risk of incontinence. According to this report, therefore, Caesarean section appears to be the best way to deliver a breech baby.

deliveries. Face presentations can sometimes be delivered naturally if the chin is pointing towards your abdomen; but sometimes the delivery needs to be assisted with forceps.

What is a brow presentation?

A brow presentation is where the baby's neck is tilted back so that its forehead is leading the way down the birth canal. It is very uncommon, only occurring in about 1 in 4000–5000 deliveries at term. A brow presentation may correct itself so that the crown of the baby's head is leading the way. If a brow presentation persists, however, then a Caesarean section is often required. This is because the head of a normal-sized term baby in the brow position is usually too big to pass through the pelvis.

What is a transverse lie?

When the baby is in a transverse lie, it is lying across the birth canal so that its feet are on one side of your abdomen and its head on the other. This means that the shoulder is often leading the way into the birth canal. It is impossible for the baby to be delivered vaginally when lying this way. A transverse lie is usually detected very easily by the doctor or midwife when they examine you. It sometimes happens when there is still a lot of fluid aound the baby at term, allowing it too much space to move around and preventing it from settling head down in the womb. Sometimes the baby can be manoeuvred into a head down position, but if a transverse lie persists, a Caesarean section is usually required. Your own doctor will advise you about the best course of action if your baby is lying transversely.

What is an unstable lie?

An unstable lie is where the baby does not settle head or bottom down, but keeps changing. It might be transverse one day, head down the next and breech the next. This can cause problems if labour starts, especially if the baby is lying transversely at the time. Vaginal delivery is impossible in this situation, and the baby can also become distressed. Just as in a transverse lie, an unstable lie often occurs when there is a lot of fluid round the baby, allowing it too much space to move around in. Sometimes induction of labour when the baby is head down can allow labour and vaginal delivery to occur, but often a Caesarean section is needed. If you have an unstable lie, you should discuss the management with your doctor, who can advise you about the best management for your particular situation.

Premature labour

A premature labour is one that starts before 37 completed weeks of pregnancy. It occurs in about 5–7 of every 100 pregnancies. In the majority of cases doctors do not know why it occurs, although it can sometimes be triggered by bleeding from the placenta or infection in the womb. There are a number of risk factors, however *(see table overleaf)*. A history of premature labour and delivery in a previous labour means that you are at risk of it happening again, and if you are expecting twins (or more babies) then the likelihood of premature labour is high. If you are concerned about the risk of premature labour, you should discuss this with your doctor. The risks to the baby depend on how early the delivery occurs. Problems are usually greatest if the baby is born before 28 weeks of pregnancy when it will usually require intensive care and help with breathing. By contrast, babies born between 34 and 37 weeks do not usually have severe breathing problems.

What are the signs of premature labour?

Premature labour can start just like normal labour with painful contractions, your waters breaking and a 'show'. Sometimes it can be triggered by infection or bleeding. If you feel that premature labour has started, contact your doctor, midwife or hospital immediately.

Can doctors stop premature labour?

Doctors can give you medication to suppress the contractions, but often this has only a short-term effect, lasting just a few days. Sometimes, such as when premature labour is triggered by bleeding, it may be dangerous to try to stop the labour. Antibiotics may be given if infection is a possible cause. One of the

Risk factors for premature labour

- Poor maternal nutrition and low pre-pregnancy weight
- Smoking
- Recreational drug abuse
- Maternal age below 20
- Muliple pregnancies (twins, triplets)
- Infections during pregnancy, including severe urinary tract infections and infection of the womb
- Abnormality of the womb or excess amniotic fluid
- Previous premature labour
- Weakness of the cervix
- Bleeding from the placenta (abruption)

benefits of stopping the contractions, even if this delays the delivery by only a few days, is that it gives your doctor time to adminster steroid medication (betamethasone or dexamethasone) to accelerate the maturing of the baby's lungs. This, in turn, reduces the likelihood of breathing problems at birth, which can lead to other complications for the baby, due to lack of oxygen. In particular, administering this medication will reduce the risk of necrotising enterocolitis (see p. 284).

What is premature rupture of the membranes?

Sometimes your waters can break before 37 weeks of pregnancy and before the onset of labour. This is referred to as premature (pre-labour) rupture of the membranes (or PPROM) and it can frequently trigger contractions shortly afterwards, leading to premature labour. However, in some cases labour may not occur for several days or even weeks.

One of the risks after your waters break is that infection can get into the womb. This is because the membranes, which form a protective barrier for the baby, have been broken. Such an infection may itself trigger premature labour, but obviously may also affect the baby.

If you develop this problem, your doctor will carefully monitor you for any evidence of an infection in the womb and advise you about treatment. It is usual to give a course of antibiotics when premature rupture of the membranes occurs as this results in a lower risk of infection and associated problems, for both the mother and the baby. Significant infection in the womb usually requires immediate delivery of the baby.

What happens if my waters break before I go into labour at term?

Pre-labour rupture of the membranes (PROM) occurs in more than 5% of pregnancies. When it happens, around 70% of women will go into labour naturally and deliver within 24 hours. By 48 hours after the membranes rupture,

90% of women will have given birth. However, for the small number of women who have a delay in labour starting, there is a risk of infection getting to the baby because the membranes have been broken. The longer the time between your waters breaking and the birth of the baby, the higher the risk of infection.

There are two ways this can be managed. Labour can either be induced after 24 hours or so, or you can wait for labour to start naturally. If labour is not to be induced then it is important to check regularly for any signs of infection such as an increased temperature. If there are any signs suggestive of infection developing, or any other problem, then it is usually best to proceed to delivery. If you have not gone into labour after around four days, induction is usually recommended. In this situation induction via an oxytocin drip is the preferred option as there is less risk of infection for you and the baby, compared with vaginal administration of prostaglandins.

What is a cord prolapse?

A cord prolapse is where the umbilical cord that carries oxygen to the baby drops into the vagina before the baby is born, which can lead to the baby being deprived of oxygen. It is more common where the baby is breech, or where the lie is unstable or where there is an excessive amount of fluid round the baby (see p. 135). It is an emergency situation, however, and the baby must be delivered quickly as a prolonged lack of oxygen could cause damage. If cord prolapse occurs in the first stage of labour, before the cervix is fully dilated, then an emergency Caesarean section is required. If it occurs in the second stage of labour when the baby is ready to be delivered, then a forceps or ventouse delivery can be carried out. While you are being prepared for delivery, a midwife or doctor will hold the cord up in the vagina or womb in order to take any pressure off the cord and prevent the oxygen supply to the baby being upset.

Assisted vaginal delivery

What is an assisted vaginal delivery?

An assisted vaginal delivery is where instruments, either forceps or a ventouse, are used to help deliver the baby in the second stage of labour. While the ventouse has only been used in the last 50 years or so, forceps have been used in Western medical practice since the 16th century. Assisted vaginal deliveries are carried out by doctors who are trained in the use of forceps or the ventouse.

Why would I need an assisted vaginal delivery?

There are many reasons why an assisted vaginal delivery could be necessary. The most common reasons are: maternal exhaustion, when you become less able to push strongly; a prolonged second stage of labour; or if there is concern that your baby is distressed. There can also be medical reasons for an

Labour & delivery

assisted vaginal delivery, such as some types of heart disease or severe high blood pressure, where the effort of excessive pushing by the mother might be harmful to her.

How common is an assisted vaginal delivery?

The rate of assisted vaginal delivery varies between different places and different maternity hospitals. However, around 15–20% of births in the UK are assisted vaginal deliveries.

What happens if I need an assisted vaginal delivery?

Prior to conducting the delivery, the doctor will examine you to ensure that there are no contraindications to assisted vaginal delivery. It is also important to make sure that you have adequate pain relief before an assisted delivery starts. If there is sufficient time, an epidural or a spinal anaesthetic can be set up to numb the lower part of the body. Alternatively, injections of local anaesthetic can be given to numb the tissues around the lower vagina. If you already have an epidural, this can be 'topped up' to provide good pain relief for an assisted delivery. In addition, you will probably need to be catheterised to ensure that your bladder is empty before the delivery proceeds.

What is a forceps delivery?

Forceps are metal instruments that look like large tongs or spoons. They are curved to fit snugly around the baby's head. The two sides or blades of the forceps come apart. Each blade is inserted separately into the vagina and then joined together when they are in place round the baby's head. The doctor will pull gently on the forceps while you are pushing with contractions to assist the delivery of your baby.

You will usually have an episiotomy to further assist the delivery and prevent tearing. If the baby's head is facing the wrong way for delivery, special forceps, known as Kielland's forceps, can be used to rotate the head into the best position for a vaginal delivery.

A forceps delivery.

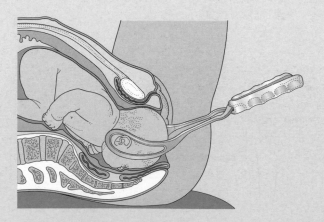

What is a ventouse delivery?

A ventouse is an instrument that uses suction to assist delivery of the baby. The doctor will examine you to make sure that you are a suitable case for ventouse delivery. A suction cup will be inserted into your vagina and placed over the crown of the baby's head. This is usually a soft plastic cup but occasionally a rigid or metal cup is used. The cup is attached by tubing to a vacuum machine. The machine is switched on and the suction cup becomes firmly applied to the baby's head by the vacuum. The doctor will then gently pull on the suction cup while you push with the contractions. The combined efforts of your womb contracting, you pushing and the doctor pulling will lead to delivery of the baby.

The relative merits of forceps and ventouse deliveries

There are advantages and disadvantages to both types of assisted delivery. Forceps and ventouse both carry a slightly higher rate of bruising and tears to tissues around the vagina compared with a spontaneous delivery, and these problems are a little more common with forceps than with the ventouse. Apart from tears or an episiotomy requiring stitches, no further treatment is usually required, however. The tissues will generally heal well without any difficulty.

A ventouse delivery may require less pain relief than a forceps delivery. However, it is more common for a ventouse delivery not to succeed, usually because the suction cup comes off, than it is for a forceps delivery to fail. Indeed, in situations where the ventouse cup does not form a good seal on the baby's head and keeps coming off, the doctor will often switch to forceps. Where the baby's head is in the wrong position and needs to be rotated round for delivery, forceps are often more reliable, too. If the baby is distressed, forceps may be a faster method than a ventouse delivery. A ventouse delivery can sometimes cause bruising to the baby's scalp and a 'lump' where the suction cup was applied. The 'lump' will usually disappear within a few days while bruising will take a week or so to disappear. However, as bruising might be more of a problem in babies that are premature, some doctors feel that the ventouse should be avoided in premature births. A forceps delivery may produce some slight bruise marks on the side of the head, where the head was grasped by the forceps. This will usually settle in a matter of days.

The majority of babies will have no complications from either type of assisted vaginal delivery. Studies have found no difference between babies born using the ventouse and those born using forceps when followed up over a five-year period. In the end, the technique used will depend on the particular circumstances. Your doctor will assess the situation and select the most appropriate method for you.

How long does a forceps or ventouse delivery take?

It may take half an hour or so to organise and prepare you for an assisted vaginal delivery, but the actual delivery tends to take only 10–15 minutes.

What happens if a forceps or ventouse delivery fails?

The doctor will not proceed with an assisted vaginal delivery unless it is fairly certain that it will succeed. If the doctor is not certain that an assisted delivery will succeed, a 'trial' of forceps or ventouse will be performed. This is carried out in an operating theatre set up for performing a Caesarean section. If there is any difficulty in performing an assisted delivery, perhaps because the baby is too big, the doctor will stop and proceed immediately to a Caesarean section.

Caesarean section

What is a Caesarean section?

A Caesarean section or birth is a surgical operation where your baby is delivered through an incision in your abdomen and womb instead of through the vagina. It is carried out when a vaginal delivery is considered to carry a high risk of complications for you or the baby or where vaginal delivery is impossible. Caesarean sections can be carried out as an emergency either before or during

Usually the incision for the Caesarean section is across the lower part of the abdomen along the 'bikini line'.

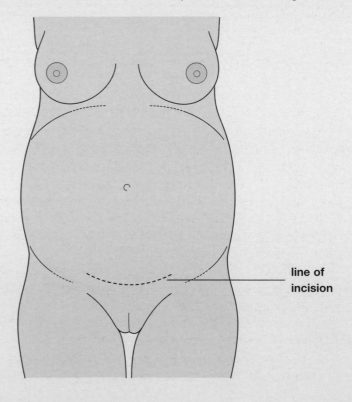

line of
incision

labour, or on a planned basis before labour. A planned Caesarean is referred to as an elective Caesarean section. The most common procedure is known as a lower (uterine) segment Caesarean section, often abbreviated to LUCS or LSCS *(see below)*.

How common is Caesarean section?

Caesarean section rates vary between countries and between hospitals. In many Western countries about 20% of all births are Caesareans. In some countries the rate is less and in others it is more.

Why might I need an emergency Caesarean section?

There are many indications for an emergency Caesarean section. Before labour it might be carried out as an emergency for a serious maternal complication such as severe pre-eclampsia or haemorrhage. Alternatively, if the baby is distressed before labour, a Caesarean delivery may be required. In labour an emergency Caesarean will be performed if the baby is distressed because of a shortage of oxygen, or if your labour is not progressing, such as when the baby is too large to get through your pelvis.

Why might I need an elective Caesarean section?

An elective Caesarean section prior to the onset of labour might be recommended for several reasons. If you have had a previous Caesarean section, perhaps because the baby has been too big to pass through your pelvis and you again have a big baby, then a Caesarean delivery is likely to be recommended. Other reasons for elective Caesarean section include: a breech presentation; placenta praevia *(see p. 142)*; certain twin pregnancies; and some medical conditions where labour might be best avoided. Your own doctor will advise you about the need for Caesarean section in your particular case.

What sort of anaesthetic can I have for a Caesarean section?

Most Caesarean sections are now carried out under epidural or spinal anaesthesia rather than general anaethesia. (If you already have an epidural, this can be topped up for a Caesarean section.) So you will be awake when the baby is born and you will usually be able to see your baby immediately. In an emergency you may need to have a general anaesthetic if there is insufficient time for an epidural or spinal anaesthetic to be carried out. In addition, a general anaesthetic is used when you would prefer to be asleep for the procedure, or if you have a condition where an epidural or a spinal anaesthetic might be contraindicated. With an epidural or spinal anaesthetic, you will not feel any pain but you might be aware of sensations in your abdomen. Your doctors can advise you on the best type of anaesthesia for your own situation.

What happens if I need a Caesarean section?

First of all, it will be important to prepare you for the procedure. A drip will be set up in your arm so that fluids and medication can be given intravenously.

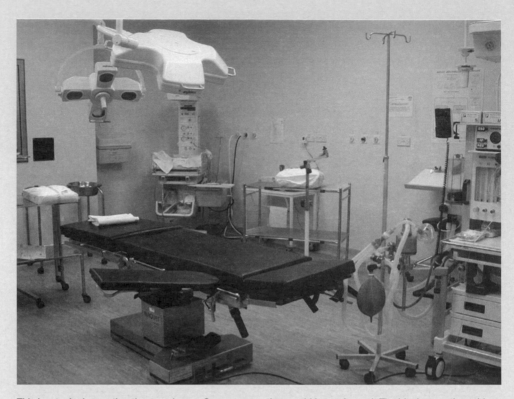

This is a typical operating theatre where a Caesarean section would be performed. The black operating table that the mother lies on is in the centre of the photograph, with two large operating lights overhead. The anaesthetic machine is on the right of the photograph. The resuscitaire that the baby is placed on after delivery (see also page 248) is in the corner.

Then you will be given an anaesthetic, as outlined above. The top of your pubic hairline usually needs to be shaved in preparation. A catheter will be inserted into the bladder to make sure that it is empty. This is because the surgeon will be operating close to the bladder. Once the anaesthetic is effective, your abdomen is washed with antiseptic to reduce the risk of infection. Your abdomen will then be draped in sterile towels so that only the part of your abdomen where the surgeon will operate can be seen. The surgeon will then make a cut in your abdomen and womb and deliver the baby. If you are awake you will often be aware of some pulling and pushing as the baby is being delivered. Sometimes the surgeon will use forceps to help gently lift the baby's head out. Once the baby is delivered, the surgeon will remove the placenta and then close up the womb and abdomen.

Can my partner be with me during a Caesarean?
If you have a spinal or epidural anaesthetic and are therefore awake for the procedure, your partner will usually be able to be with you in the operating theatre. Often there is a screen set up across your chest so that you and your partner will not be able to see the operation. However, you will both

be able to see the baby as soon as it is born. Some surgeons will drop the screen so that you can see the actual delivery. If this is something you would like, you or your partner can ask the surgeon if this would be appropriate in your case.

How long does a Caesarean take?

Once the surgeon starts to operate, it usually takes about 5–10 minutes to deliver the baby. After delivery it usually takes around 20–30 minutes to close up the womb and abdomen. The procedure can take a little longer if you have had previous operations on your abdomen.

If I have a Caesarean, will I be able to have a vaginal delivery in a subsequent pregnancy?

If your Caesarean was for a cause that can recur – for example, because you had a baby that was too big to deliver through the birth canal and you are expecting another big baby – then a repeat Caesarean would often be recommended. However, in the majority of women a vaginal delivery is possible after a Caesarean section. A Caesarean section obviously leaves a scar on your womb. If this scar is across the lower part of your womb, as is almost always the case, then the scar is usually very strong. The risk of the scar rupturing is extremely small, but your doctors and midwives will take care that your womb does not over-contract as this could stress the scar. Your own doctor can advise you about the advisability of vaginal birth after a Caesarean section.

What is a 'classical' Caesarean section?

The classical type of Caesarean section was the way in which this operation was originally carried out many, many years ago. The key difference between the classical Caesarean section and the lower segment operation (LSCS) is the place where the cut is made on the womb. In a classical Caesarean the cut on the womb runs up and down (vertically) in the midline. By contrast, in the case of a LSCS the cut on the womb runs across the lower part of the womb, usually parallel to the bikini line. The upper part of the womb is made of muscle and the lower part is more fibrous or 'gristle-like'. Gristle forms a stronger scar than muscle when it is healing. Because of this, scars on the lower part of the womb heal more strongly than scars on the muscular part. So women who have had a classical Caesarean section should not be allowed to go through a labour in any subsequent pregnancy because the risk of the scar rupturing is high, which would be very dangerous for both the mother and the baby.

Classical Caesarean sections are very rare in modern medical practice, however. Very occasionally, they will be used in conditions such as very premature deliveries or where the baby is stuck horizontally across the womb, instead of being head first, with no fluid around it, making it difficult or actually impossible to deliver through a cut in the lower part of the womb.

3 Part

Post-pregnancy

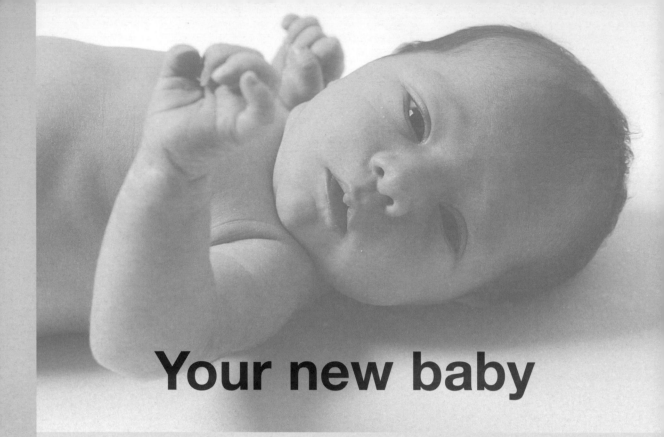

Your new baby

Embarking on a new life with your baby is a wonderful and exciting experience. While it should be a special and rewarding time for you, it is also a time of immense change for you and all your family. As a first-time mother, you will be faced with enormous physical and emotional adjustments, and you will have lots of questions to ask about your miraculous new baby.

How your baby looks, feels and sounds

What will my baby look like when it is born?

Newborn babies often look quite blue in colour, particularly the skin of their arms and legs. This will disappear in a few minutes after they take a few breaths and gradually turn pink. Your baby's skin may also have some blood on it. This is usually your blood from a tear or episiotomy. The skin may also be wrinkly and coated with the white, greasy vernix that protected it while the baby was in the womb, surrounded by fluid.

My baby's head seems to have a strange shape. Is this normal?

When your baby was making its way down the birth canal, the head had to squeeze through your pelvic bones. The skull of a baby is not rigid like an adult's skull; instead it is made up of plates of bones that can move slightly to

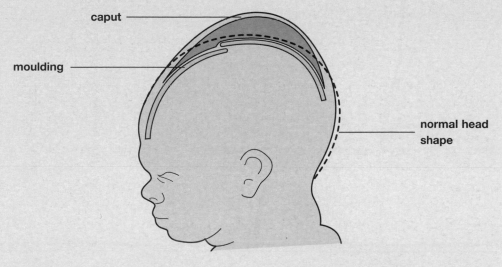

caput

moulding

normal head shape

The baby's head moulds to help it pass through the pelvis. The baby's skull is not rigid like an adult's skull. Instead it is made up of plates of bone that can move slightly to allow the shape of the baby's head to change, making it narrower and therefore easier to pass through the pelvis. As well as moulding there can be some swelling over the skin at the top of the baby's head. This is called caput.

allow the shape of the baby's head to change, so that it can squeeze its head through your pelvis more easily. This change in shape is called moulding and may take several days after delivery to resolve. As well as moulding there can often be some swelling of the skin over the top of the baby's head. This is where the head has been forced against the neck of your womb and the tissues of your pelvis as your contractions pushed your baby through the birth canal. This swelling is called caput and will resolve over a day or so. Occasionally, there can be some bruising on the baby's head, which will also fade after several days.

Do all babies cry when they are born?

Not all babies cry when they are born, although many certainly do. Sometimes it will be a brief cry and some babies may cry for a few minutes, then settle. If you have had an opiate painkiller like morphine then this may make the baby more sleepy and less likely to cry at birth.

How will the doctor or midwife check the baby at birth?

The first check that is carried out is usually the Apgar score *(see overleaf)*. This helps to identify those babies that needed help because of problems like breathing difficulties after they were born. The score, named after an American anaesthetist, Virginia Apgar, measures five features of the baby's condition – heart rate, breathing, colour, movements and response to stimulation – allocating a score of 1–2, a score of 2 being normal for each feature. The Apgar scores are often assigned at one and five minutes after birth. A total score of 7 or more is considered normal. A score of 3 or less

Your new baby

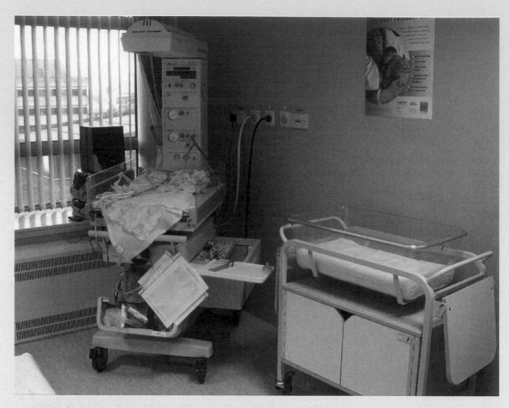

After delivery the baby may be placed on a machine called a resuscitaire, seen on the left of the photograph. There is a heat lamp overhead to keep the newborn baby warm and the towels that it will be dried and wrapped in will have been warmed. There is a suction tube to remove any mucus and fluid from the baby's nose and mouth. There is also a supply of oxygen in case the baby needs a little help with her breathing at first. All the equipment that the nurses and doctors who look after the newborn baby might need is kept on the bottom part of the resuscitaire. The baby will often get her injection of vitamin K while on the resuscitaire. She will also have a name tag attached. On the right is a typical cot used in maternity hospitals.

The Apgar scoring system

Score	0	1	2
Colour	Blue or pale	Blue extremities	Pink
Breathing	Absent	Weak	Regular
Muscle tone	Absent	Some flexion	Active movement
Heart rate	Absent	Less than 100 beats per minute	More than 100 beats per minute
Response to stimulation	Absent	Weak movements	Cries

suggests that the baby is distressed and having difficulty adjusting to life outside the womb, especially if the score remains low at five minutes. If the baby has a low Apgar score, expert paediatric doctors (neonatologists – specialists in the care of newborn babies) will usually be called at once to help resuscitate the baby.

Why is vitamin K given to the baby following delivery?

Clotting factors that help us stop bleeding when we are injured are made in the liver and their production requires vitamin K. A baby's liver is still slightly immature at the time of birth, even at term. This can mean that the production of clotting factors is reduced and could put the baby at risk of bleeding problems, although these problems are now very uncommon. Making sure that the baby has enough vitamin K can help prevent this problem. This is why many doctors recommend that vitamin K is given soon after birth.

How soon can I feed my baby?

If you plan to breast-feed your baby then the ideal time to start is soon after delivery – within the first hour *(see p. 256)*. After the first hour or so after delivery, your baby may become sleepy as, like you, he will be exhausted after the efforts of labour.

When is the baby examined to check that everything is normal?

The midwife or doctor will make a quick check for abnormalities immediately after birth. The baby will also be weighed and measured. A more comprehensive check will usually be carried out 1–2 days later.

What happens at this baby check?

A doctor will examine your baby from head to toe to make sure there are no problems. Her head will be checked and its size measured with a measuring

Measuring the baby's head.

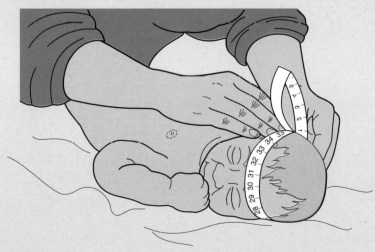

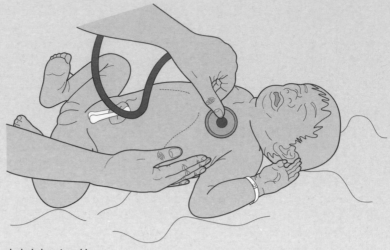

Examining the baby's heart and lungs.

tape. The baby's length may also be measured. Her eyes, ears and mouth will be checked. Your baby's heart and lungs will be listened to with a stethoscope. A healthy baby at term will have a heart rate of 110–140 beats per minute and will breathe between 30 and 40 times per minute. Your baby's abdomen and back will be examined. Her legs and arms will be checked and fingers and toes counted. Her hips will be specifically checked for any problem with the hip joint. This is because some babies are born with a hip out of position or dislocated. The doctor will want to know if your baby's bowels have opened and whether she has passed any urine. Her genitals will be checked. In a male baby, the doctor will ascertain that both testicles are in the scrotum.

To assess the nervous system, your baby's reflex responses will be checked. One of these is the so-called Moro or 'startle' reflex. When the baby is startled or if her head is allowed to drop backwards slightly, she will throw both her arms and legs up and out, then bring them back in again. Both left and right sides should show the same response. Another reflex is the grasp reflex. When

Checking the baby's hips.

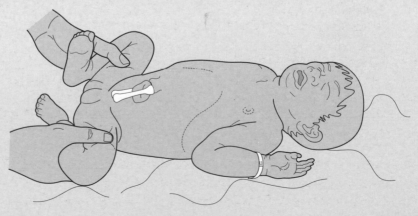

the palms of her hands are gently stroked with a finger, your baby will grasp the finger. The soles of the feet show a similar response when stroked. The rooting reflex occurs when the baby's cheek is stroked and she then turns her head to that same side to try and find a nipple to suck on. There is also a walking reflex. If your baby is held upright with her feet on a flat surface, she will make stepping movements.

What is the Guthrie test?

This is a simple blood test, taken from the newborn baby, that checks for a rare condition called phenylketonuria, where the baby is born with an abnormality in his metabolic system (which maintains all the body's functions, including energy production and growth). Phenylketonuria affects only about 1 in 16,000 babies. If the baby is born with this condition, he will not be able to metabolise a substance called phenylalanine properly. This can result in an accumulation of phenylalanine in the bloodstream, which in turn can lead to brain damage and mental retardation. However, any damage can be prevented with a special diet that can allow affected babies to develop normally. So it is obviously important to identify the condition. To do the test, some blood will be taken from the baby with a pinprick, usually to the heel. The blood is then spotted onto a card for testing. In the UK thyroid deficiency is also routinely checked using the same blood sample.

Is jaundice common in newborn babies?

Slight jaundice (yellow discoloration of the skin and the whites of the eyes) is commonly seen in newborn babies. It is usually noticed on the second or third day and will gradually fade within 1–2 weeks. Jaundice occurs because the liver is still slightly immature even in a term baby and has some difficulty in excreting the yellow pigment (bilirubin – produced when the red blood cells that carry oxygen get old and are broken down) that causes jaundice. The bilirubin will therefore build up in the skin. Mild degrees of jaundice are not usually a problem, although the baby may need a test to check the level. If the doctor considers that the level of jaundice is high then it is usual to give the baby phototherapy – exposing the skin to ultraviolet light under a sun lamp for a few hours each day – to help break up the yellow pigment. Occasionally, medication will be prescribed to help the liver break down the bilirubin. If you are concerned about jaundice in your baby, you should discuss this with your doctor or midwife.

My baby's breasts and genitals seem swollen. Is this normal?

The breasts and genitals of a newborn baby can appear swollen after birth. This is because of the very high levels of oestrogen in your body during the pregnancy which cross the placenta and have a temporary effect on the baby. Both boys and girls can be affected. This will settle over a few days, however.

There is a slight orange or pink staining on my baby's nappy. What is this?

The presence of chemicals called urates in the urine of a newborn baby can cause a slight pink or orange discoloration of the urine. This is harmless and will resolve without any treatment. However, blood in a nappy or in the urine is always abnormal. If you have any concerns, you should raise them with your midwife or doctor.

My baby has lost a little weight since she was born. Is this a problem?

It is usual for newborn babies to lose a little weight in the first few days, before they start to regain weight, recovering what was lost and continuing to grow. Around a tenth of their birthweight can be lost in the first few days, but by the time your baby is 10–14 days old, she will be around the same weight as at birth. If you are concerned about your baby's weight gain, you should discuss this with your doctor or midwife.

How soon will it be before my baby has a bowel movement?

A bowel movement usually occurs in the first 24 hours. The first few bowel movements consist of meconium, the dark, sticky, green-black material that was inside the baby's bowels while he was in your womb. But as milk works it way through the baby's bowel, the meconium will be replaced with bright yellow stools.

Is it important to clean the stump of the baby's cord?

The stump of the baby's cord, which has the cord clamp on it, will dry up and drop off spontaneously in about 5–6 days. It is best to keep the cord dry, only cleaning round the base of the cord at the baby's navel. Many doctors or midwives even recommend cleaning the base of the cord with surgical spirit to kill germs, help prevent infection and help the cord tissue out. However, saline solution or just clean water can be equally effective. It is also important not to enclose the cord in the nappy where it may get moist or contaminated with the baby's bowel movements. If the base of the cord gets inflamed, swollen or has a discharge, you should consult your doctor or midwife.

What is nappy rash?

Nappy rash is usually caused by the baby's skin becoming irritated by urine. Fresh urine does not harm the skin, but when urine becomes stale ammonia can form in the urine and this will irritate the skin. The skin in the nappy area will become red and sore if nappy rash develops. Sometimes the irritated skin can also become infected, such as with thrush, which will damage the skin further and may need medication to help it heal. If you have concerns about a rash on your baby's bottom, you should consult your doctor or midwife. The baby's skin is very sensitive and easily irritated, not just by urine. Sometimes baby wipes or perfumed soaps can irritate the skin.

To prevent nappy rash, change your baby's nappy regularly, keep his bottom clean using warm water and non-perfumed soaps, gently dab it dry and apply a barrier cream like zinc and castor oil to prevent irritation of the skin. It is also good to allow your baby to lie for a while without a nappy in a warm environment so that his skin can dry properly.

Gently wash your baby's hair with the bath water before drying the hair and putting the baby in the bath.

How do I bath my baby?

Prepare your bath and check the temperature of the water. It is best to bath your baby in a warm room so she does not get too cold when you are undressing, drying and dressing her. Undress her down to nappy and vest. Clean her eyes and face with cotton wool moistened with warm water without any soap. Then take off her vest and nappy and wrap her in a dry, warm towel. Hold her so she lies along your forearm, supporting her head with your hand. Using your other hand, wash her hair with the bath water. Then dry her hair with a towel. Unwrap her from the towel. Supporting her shoulders securely with one arm and using the other to cradle her bottom, gently place her in the bath. Keeping her shoulders supported with one arm so that her shoulders and head are out of the water, use your free arm to gently wash her in the warm water. Let her enjoy the feeling of the water and talk to her as you bath her. When you are finished, take her out by cradling her bottom with your free hand. Wrap her in a warm, dry towel and gently pat her dry, then dress her again.

How long should new babies sleep for?

New babies tend to sleep for only 3–4 hours at a time, although overall they may sleep for around 14–18 hours a day. Their sleeping pattern may be quite variable. During the day they will nap for a few hours between feeds. They don't usually sleep right through the night and will usually wake to be fed, or to have their nappy changed. Sometimes they will wake during the night, even if they are not hungry or needing a nappy change. As this can be exhausting for you,

you should try to get back to sleep as soon as your baby has finished feeding. Many mothers like to have the baby beside the bed in a cot or a crib to make it easier to get to him to feed and comfort the baby when he wakes. Over the first few months your baby should get into a routine, with longer sleeps at night and shorter naps during the day. To help establish the pattern, many mothers have a bedtime routine, such as a bath for the baby at a regular time, changing the baby into a sleepsuit, dimming the lights or singing. The baby will soon associate these activities with 'bedtime'.

How can I reduce the risk of cot death?

Cot death is the sudden and unexplained death of an infant. Thankfully, it is very rare. Boys are more often affected than girls and most deaths occur in the first six months, especially between two and four months of age. Doctors do not yet know why cot death occurs, but they have established some ways to reduce the chance of it happening:

- Check on your baby regularly if he is not sleeping in the same room as you. It is often easier to keep the baby in the same room as you for the first six months, after which time the risk of cot death falls sharply.
- When you check on your baby, make sure that he is not too warm. If you think that your baby feels too warm or is sweating, take off some of the bed covers.
- Put your baby on his back when sleeping rather than allowing him to lie on his front.
- Position your baby's feet at the bottom of the cot or crib and do not put the blankets any higher than the baby's shoulders, in order to prevent him sliding

Baby immunisations and cot deaths: no link

Sudden unexplained death in infancy, or cot death, is a devastating experience for any parent. Parents often seek an explanation for the death and wonder if there was anything that might have prevented it. In the UK childhood immunisations against diptheria, tetanus, whooping cough and polio are given at two, three and four months of age. This represents an accelerated immunisation programme as, until 1990, these immunisations had been given at three, five and nine months. The timing of these baby immunisations corresponds with the peak time of cot death and has raised fears of a connection between the two. However, research has shown that, even after taking account of sleeping position and other risk factors for cot death, there is no link between the UK accelerated immunisation programme and cot death. Indeed, there has been a trend towards a reduction in the risk of cot death in those babies who have been immunised. Although the cause of cot death remains unexplained, it appears that infant immunisation can be removed from the list of suspects.

down under the blankets and getting too hot. Do not let your baby's head get covered by the bedding.

- Avoid overheating the room that your baby sleeps in and do not wrap him too warmly in clothes or blankets.
- Do not smoke near the baby, especially where he sleeps. Ideally, no one should smoke in the house and you should avoid going into smoky environments with your baby.
- Do not let the baby share your bed with you if you or your partner smoke or if either of you take any medication or alcohol that might make you sleep heavily.
- If you think the baby has a high temperature or is unwell, seek the advice of your doctor without delay.

When should a baby have a BCG vaccination?

The BCG is a vaccination against tuberculosis (or TB for short), an infection that usually affects the lungs but can also attack other parts of the body. The TB germs are coughed out by people with the infection and this is how it spreads from person to person. It can have severe effects if not treated. Babies can be at risk of infection from TB if someone in their close family has it. They can also be at risk if their family comes from an area where there is a high incidence of TB, such as parts of Africa and southern Asia, or if they live in an area where TB is common. If your baby is considered to be at risk, a BCG can be given in the first few days after birth and is not painful. Indeed, it is a very effective and safe vaccination. After about two weeks, a spot will appear on her arm where the vaccination was given. This will last for a few weeks and sometimes will ooze some clear fluid. It will heal without treatment, however, and should simply be covered with a clean, dry dressing, if required. Your baby should not have any injections in the same arm for three months after the BCG. If you think your baby might need a BCG, or if you have questions about the BCG vaccination, you should discuss this with your doctor.

Feeding your baby

Feeding your baby: breast or bottle?

Feeding your baby well is critically important. Babies approximately triple their weight in the first year of life and two-thirds of their total postnatal brain growth occurs in this first year also. Breast milk provides the best nutrition for babies as it is specially formulated by nature to give them all the nourishment they need for the first 4–6 months of their life. Breast milk has many advantages: it is free, more digestible for the baby than formula feeds, protects the baby against some infections like gastro-enteritis, reduces the risk of some allergic condition developing in later life, and helps promote bonding between mother and baby. The benefits apply not only to the baby's health but also to that of the mother, as it will reduce her risk of developing cancer of the breast and ovary, as well as fracture of the hip caused by osteoporosis in later life.

The main disadvantage of breast-feeding is that it is usually more restrictive for the mother than bottle-feeding. Breast milk can be expressed and given by bottle, so that other people can feed the baby on occasion, but this can be difficult to organise. Some mothers might decide that they do not wish to breast-feed their baby, as it does not suit their particular circumstances. Sometimes the mother or the baby might have difficulties with breast-feeding, or the mother may not get enough support to start or continue breast-feeding, and because of this may lack confidence. Very occasionally, there are medical reasons to avoid breast-feeding. In these situations bottle-feeding may be best. Sometimes, such as where the baby is premature or small for dates, supplements to breast-feeding may be required. You can discuss your plans for feeding with your doctor or midwife, who will be able to answer any questions and help you make the right choice for your own situation.

What is formula milk?

Formula milk is usually modified cow's milk. For babies who cannot take formula milk derived from cow's milk, soya-based formula milk is available. The modification of these milks makes them similar in composition to breast milk. They can provide the baby with all the nourishment he needs for about the first six months of life. Formula milk usually comes as a powder or in granules to be mixed with water. Ready-mixed or ready-to-feed formula is also available in cartons, but is usually more expensive than the powders or granules. The type of formula can vary with the age of the baby. There are two different proteins in milk: casein and whey. The whey-based formula milk tends to be used for younger babies and can be given from birth, while casein-based formula tends to be used for older or hungrier babies, although it too can be given from birth.

Can a baby be given ordinary cow's milk?

Newborn babies should not be given ordinary cow's milk. Indeed, most experts recommend that babies should not receive cow's milk until they are a year old as it has the wrong composition for the immature digestive system and could cause problems. However, cow's milk products like yoghurt can be given from around four months of age. Your doctor or health visitor can advise you.

How do my breasts produce milk?

The increased levels of pregnancy hormones leads to an increase in the breast tissue that makes milk and also enhances the development of the ducts that carry milk to the nipple. Fat is deposited in the breasts during pregnancy and the blood supply increases. These changes prepare your breasts for milk production. Although there is often a slight leakage from your breasts in pregnancy, milk production is inhibited because of the high levels of the female hormone oestrogen normally found in pregnancy. The oestrogen levels fall rapidly in the first two days after delivery, which allows another hormone, prolactin, which increases in pregnancy, to stimulate milk production in your breasts. Prolactin is produced by the pituitary gland at the base of your brain. When the baby sucks at your breast, this sensation stimulates your pituitary gland to release prolactin, which in turn stimulates more milk production.

The more your baby feeds, the more milk you will make. In addition, suckling at the breast also stimulates release of another hormone, oxytocin, released from a different part of the pituitary gland. Oxytocin stimulates the ducts in your breast to contract and so bring the milk down to the nipple. Incidentally, oxytocin also causes the muscle of your womb to contract and women who are breast-feeding frequently experience cramps, like period pains, in their abdomen when the baby is suckling.

Is the milk produced by my breasts the same at the beginning of a feed as it is at the end?

Interestingly, the milk produced at the beginning of the feed is different in from the milk produced at the end. The foremilk, produced first, is more watery and rich in the milk sugar called lactose. This gradually changes as the feed progresses to hindmilk, which contains more fats and is therefore rich in energy and fat-soluble vitamins. So even if there does not seem to be much milk at the end of the feed, the baby may still be getting substantial nourishment from the smaller quantities of fat-rich hindmilk. It is important to allow the baby to decide when she has had enough so that you do not stop feeding before she has drunk sufficient hindmilk.

Does breast milk contain anything that formula milk does not have?

Formula milk contains similar amounts of carbohydrates, fats and protein as breast milk. However, the composition of the fats is quite different. Breast milk contains a much higher proportion of unsaturated fats as well as more essential fatty acids. Special fats known as long-chain polyunsaturated fatty acids are essential for the formation of brain cells. Our livers can manufacture these polyunsaturated fats from the essential fatty acids that we get from our diet. However, a baby's liver cannot usually make all the polyunsaturated fats for its own needs until about four months of age. Therefore the baby will depend on the supply of such fats from milk.

When should I start to breast-feed?

You can start to breast-feed as soon as you want to after delivery. Ideally, this should be within the first hour, as the baby will usually be alert in the first hour or so after delivery and will instinctively want to feed, with strong rooting and sucking reflexes. Indeed, if you are both well, you can put the baby to the breast straight away. Even if your baby does not wish to feed immediately, it is still good to hold him close with skin-to-skin contact as this helps to encourage breast-feeding.

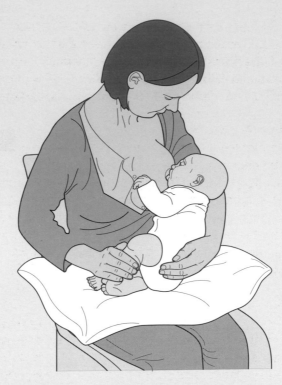

When breast-feeding it is best to be sitting comfortably, as you are likely to be feeding for half an hour or so. Sometimes a pillow or cushion on your knee is useful to help support the baby.

What position should I be in to feed?

Make sure that you are sitting comfortably – remember, you are likely to be feeding for half an hour or so. Sometimes a pillow or cushion on your knee is useful to help support the baby. When you are trying to feed, hold your baby with her chest turned towards yours, her head opposite your breast and her nose close to your nipple. This makes it easier for her to latch onto your breast. Allow her mouth or cheek to brush against your nipple. This will stimulate her mouth to open. When her mouth is open wide, gently bring the baby to your breast and allow her to take your nipple into his mouth. You can help by placing the nipple into your baby's mouth, but avoid pushing her onto the breast or pushing your nipple into her mouth. The baby needs to get a mouthful of your whole nipple. This should include a good part of the darker skin around your nipple, the areola, and not just the tip of the nipple itself. If the baby takes just the tip of the nipple, this will make it difficult for her to feed and also cause your nipples to become sore and cracked. Once latched on properly, the baby should suck on your nipple.

How long should I allow my baby to suck at the breast?

Ideally, your baby should be allowed to feed for as long as he wants. A baby may pause when feeding and this should not be misinterpreted as the end of the feed. Let him come off the breast when he wants. Offer the breast again a few minutes later. If your baby does not want to reattach then he will usually be satisfied. If he is taken off the breast before having had enough milk, this can lead to him being hungry. It can also reduce milk production. Frequent feeding, where the breast is emptied, is a strong stimulus to further milk production.

Should I use both breasts at each feed?

You should find the pattern of feeding that best suits you and your baby. Your baby may take one or two breasts at every feed. You should let your baby stay on the first breast for as long as she wants, then offer her the other breast. At the next feed, start with the breast that wasn't used or was offered second. Remember that the milk at the beginning of the feed, the foremilk, is different from the milk at the end of the feed, the hindmilk. Hindmilk contains a lot of high-energy fat. So it is important that your baby gets a good feed of hindmilk before switching breasts.

How often should I feed my baby?

Most experts believe that the frequency and duration of feeds should, ideally, be led by the baby. Remember that your baby will often have to feed frequently as his stomach is relatively small. In the first day or two there may be around six hours between feeds. After the first couple of days, babies usually feed around six times in every 24 hours, although feeding as often as 8–10 times in 24 hours is not unusual in the early stages. However, every mother and baby will develop their own pattern that suits them specifically.

Do I need a special diet when I am breast-feeding?

There is no need for a special diet. However, it is important to have a healthy, balanced diet with plenty of fruit and vegetables and a good fluid intake *(see Preparing your body for pregnancy, p. 28)*. Some women find that they need to drink more when they are breast-feeding. Sometimes you will find that certain foods you eat can cause a reaction in your baby and you may wish to avoid them. If there is a family history of allergic conditions like hay fever, asthma or eczema, then peanuts are best avoided.

What is colostrum?

Colostrum is the highly concentrated yellow fluid produced by your breasts for the first two days or so after delivery, before your milk comes in. It contains all the nourishment your baby needs for the first few days. It is also particularly rich in antibodies, which help protect your baby from infections in the first few weeks of her life *(see overleaf)*. After about 2–5 days, the colostrum is replaced by milk.

Why do my breasts feel so hard and painful after feeding for only 3–4 days?

It is common for your breasts to feel hard and painful after 3–4 days. This is known as engorgement of the breasts and is very common during the period when the colostrum is being replaced by your proper milk 2–4 days after delivery. The engorgement usually passes in a day or two, but cool or warm compresses or a warm shower can ease the discomfort. It is important to allow your baby to empty the breast when feeding, as this helps relieve engorgement.

How does breast-feeding prevent my baby getting infections?

There are two key substances in breast milk that help prevent infection: antibodies and lactoferrin. Antibodies will line your baby's stomach and the bowel and will protect him from infection from viruses and harmful bacteria. Colostrum is particularly rich in antibodies, which are not found in formula milk. Lactoferrin is a substance that binds iron into food while in the bowel. As certain bacteria need iron, lactoferrin thus acts as a natural antibacterial agent. Breast-feeding also prevents infections arising from contaminated milk or food, causing vomiting and diarrhoea. In addition, breast-fed babies suffer from fewer ear and chest infections, with a lower incidence of infection generally. Interestingly, this protection against infection persists long after breast-feeding ceases and there appears to be a positive benefit to the baby's own immune system, helping him to fight infection.

Does breast-feeding have any other health benefits for my baby?

Some studies have found that breast-fed babies appear to have a lower risk of cot death, of obesity in childhood, and of developing certain allergic disorders.

Can I mix breast- and bottle-feeding?

This is possible but you need to bear in mind that if bottle-feeding is used in the first few weeks while breast-feeding is being established, it can sometimes hinder the success of your breast-feeding. If you want to mix feeding methods, it is therefore best to delay mixing breast- and bottle-feeding until breast-feeding is well established.

How do I know if my baby is getting enough nourishment?

Weight gain is an important factor in assessing how well your baby is doing. However, it is only one factor. As well as gaining weight, a well-nourished baby will be alert when awake, will be able to latch onto your breast without too much difficulty, and will usually be content after feeds. She will usually have about 5–6 wet nappies each day and will pass yellow, soft stools, although stools can be green. The frequency of bowel movements varies from baby to baby. Some babies who are breast-fed will have more than one bowel movement per day and others may not have a movement every day. If you have any concerns about your baby's development, you should consult your doctor.

When I go back to work, can I continue to breast-feed?

You can continue to breast-feed after you return to work. While you are away, your baby can be fed by bottle with either expressed breast milk or formula milk. If you want your baby to have nothing but breast milk, this may mean that you need to express breast milk while you are at work and keep the milk cool so you can take it home for the baby. You should continue to breast-feed your baby when you have the opportunity, such as in the mornings and evenings and at weekends. Your breast-feeding counsellor or doctor can advise you about mixed feeding and continuing to breast-feed when you go back to work.

How do I express breast milk?

Milk can be expressed from your breasts either manually or with a breast pump. Expressing by hand is much slower than using a pump but requires no special equipment. Before expressing by hand, first wash your hands, support your breast in one hand and with the other hand massage round the whole breast several times, stroking towards the nipple. You can then gently squeeze the milk out of your nipple. This is best done by feeling for the ducts just behind the nipple where the milk is held prior to being released from the breast. You can

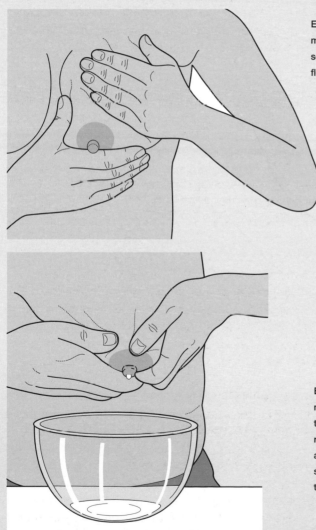

Expressing your milk (1). First massage around the entire breast several times. This encourages the flow of milk through the milk ducts.

Expressing your milk (2). Feel for the milk ducts behind the nipple, where the milk is held before being released. With your thumb above the areola and a finger below, gently squeeze. Take care not to squeeze the actual nipple.

usually feel these ducts – which midwives often describe as being like a pod of peas – quite easily. With your thumb above the areola and a finger below it, gently squeeze. This will squeeze the ducts holding the milk and release the milk from your breast. Do not squeeze your actual nipple. You should collect the milk in a sterilised container. Express each breast in turn for about 4–5 minutes, switching to the other breast when the flow stops or slows. It generally takes up to 30 minutes to express breast milk. There are several other techniques for expressing by hand and your midwife or breast-feeding counsellor can advise you about them. The amount of expressed breast milk you will need for a feed varies with the age and size of your baby. Your doctor, midwife or breast-feeding counsellor can also advise you about this.

How do I express breast milk with a pump?

Breast pumps can be bought from most baby stores and pharmacies. If you use a pump to express, the equipment for collecting the milk must be sterilised. A funnel is fitted over your nipple and this forms a seal. Suction is then used to 'suck' the milk out of your breast into a sterilised bottle attached to the pump. Some pumps work by hand and others are battery- or electrically operated.

How do I store expressed breast milk?

You can store expressed breast milk in the refrigerator, where it can usually be kept for up to three days. Breast milk can also be frozen and stored for 3–6 months, depending on the rating of your freezer. It is best to store it in small batches, such as in ice-cube trays. You should not add to or top up any milk previously stored, and you should discard any milk not used during a feed. When you need to use frozen breast milk, it can be thawed out by standing the milk container in warm water.

When should I express my milk?

The best time for you to express milk is usually in between your baby's feeds. If you try and express breast milk after a feed, there may not be any milk left to express. Equally, if you try to express just before a feed then there may not be enough milk left for the baby to have a satisfying feed. However, if you have enough milk in one breast to satisfy your baby at a feed, then the other breast could be used to express from after a feed.

Can I prevent cracked and sore nipples?

It is very common for nipples to be tender during the first few days or weeks of breast-feeding. This will pass as the nipples get tougher. However, if your baby is not latching on to the whole nipple and just sucking or chewing on the tip, this will make your nipples sore and can cause cracking of the skin. When this occurs, it is not unusual for small blisters to appear on the nipple, or the nipple may look inflamed. One of the best preventive measures is to ensure that your baby latches on fully. At the end of a feed, if the baby is gripping tightly onto your breast do not pull him off the breast as this can injure your nipple. Instead, slip a finger into the side of his mouth and gently press on the gums in the lower jaw, which will cause him to release the breast. In addition, try and keep your nipples from being constantly wet. Wet skin becomes swollen and sore and cracks as it dries. Use frequent changes of breast pads and avoid those with plastic backings, as while these stop milk leaking through to your clothes, they also keep moisture in. Some experts advise rubbing some of your hindmilk into the nipple at the end of a feed, because of the antibacterial properties of breast milk. Clean your nipples and breasts regularly, but avoid using soap; warm water is usually satisfactory. There are also some soothing creams you can obtain from your pharmacist or breast-feeding support group. If you are having problems with sore or cracked nipples, consult your doctor, midwife or breast-feeding counsellor, who will be able to give you specific advice.

Can thrush affect my nipples?

Thrush infection can sometimes affect your nipples when you are breast-feeding, making them red, sore and itchy. Thrush is often carried in the body, such as in the bowel *(see p. 149)*, but only causes problems when it grows in an uncontrolled way. This can happen when the tissues have been damaged. The baby may also develop thrush in her mouth, where it takes the form of white patches on the inside of the cheeks. If you think you have thrush, you should consult your doctor as specific medication is needed for your nipples and often for your baby's mouth.

What is mastitis?

Mastitis is inflammation of the breast. It can be caused by a blocked milk duct, which leads to a build-up of milk behind it. The affected breast will often develop firm, tender and inflamed patches. It will get more painful with feeding and sometimes can cause you to feel feverish. Because the milk is stagnant, bacteria settles in the milk and infection can occur. If you think you have mastitis, you should consult your doctor, midwife or breast-feeding counsellor. It is best not to delay getting help. Specific treatment such as antibiotics are needed when infection is present and painkilling medication may also be required. It is important that the breast is emptied regularly and that you continue breast-feeding, if at all possible. However, your doctor will advise you about this. Breast massage may help encourage the breasts to empty or help relieve blocked ducts.

What equipment do I need for bottle-feeding?

You will need 4–6 bottles and teats, a sterilising unit, a bottle brush, formula milk, a scoop for the milk powder (though this usually comes with the formula milk) and something like a plastic knife to level off the scoopfuls of milk powder.

How do I sterilise the bottles and teats?

Sterilising is very important in order to prevent your baby from getting any infections, especially those causing vomiting and diarrhoea. First the bottles, teats and bottle caps must be thoroughly washed with detergent in warm water. You will need the bottle brush to get any remaining milk from the inside of the bottles. Turning the teats inside out can help ensure that the inside of the teat is clean. Rinse the equipment thoroughly to make sure that no detergent is left on the bottles or teats. You should then place the equipment in a sterilising unit. There are a variety of sterilising units: steam sterilisers, sterilising tanks that immerse the equipment in sterilising fluid, and sterilising units that can be placed in microwave ovens. If you use a sterilising tank, make sure that all the equipment is below the surface when sterilising, and that there are no air bubbles, rinse the equipment in cooled boiled water before use, and change the sterilising fluid each day. If you use a steam steriliser, make sure that the equipment has cooled down before use.

How do I make up a feed?

It is important to follow the instructions on the formula feed that you are using very carefully. The amount your baby needs will depend on his age. Wash your hands thoroughly before starting. Boil some water and leave it to cool, then put the correct amount of water into each bottle and add the correct number of levelled scoops of formula milk. If you lose count of the number of scoops of milk you have used for a bottle, discard the milk and start again. The wrong number of scoops, either too many or too few, could upset your baby. Put the teat and cap on the bottle and mix by tipping the bottle several times. Make sure the milk is cool enough. You can test this by dripping a few drops of the milk onto the back of your hand. Do not reuse or reheat unfinished milk.

Can I make up bottles in advance?

You can make up feeds and store then in the refrigerator for up to 24 hours, with the teats covered by the bottle caps. Warm up a bottle by placing it in warm water or a special bottle warmer, which can be bought from most baby stores, before each feed.

How do I give my baby a bottle?

Most experts consider that the bottle-fed baby, just like the breast-fed baby, should be fed on demand. When you start to give you baby a bottle, you should first of all check that the milk is not too warm (as above). Cradle your baby in your arms with her head tilted slightly backwards. As you feed her, keep the bottle well tipped up so that there is no air in the teat, otherwise she will suck in and swallow air, which can lead to her having a lot of wind. Indeed, bottle-fed babies have a tendency to have more wind than breast-fed babies. After the feed, wind your baby by holding her over your shoulder or sitting her upright and gently patting her back. If you plan to bottle-feed, you should ask your midwife to go over the feeding routine with you.

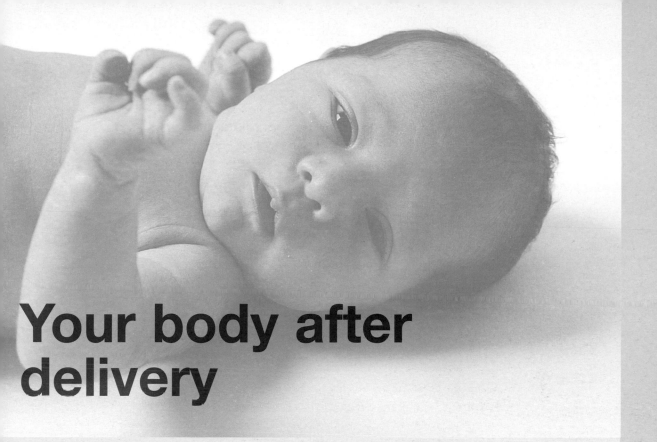

Your body after delivery

After delivery you may experience a wide range of physical symptoms and emotions, brought about by the changes in your body following pregnancy and delivery. Over the previous nine months, your whole body, not just the womb and breasts, has been adapting to pregnancy, reaching a peak at the time of labour and delivery. Then, suddenly, the baby is here and dramatic changes rapidly occur to your body. While many of these changes occur quickly, it will be several months before your body returns to its normal, pre-pregnant state and inevitably some changes, such as stretch marks and varicose veins, will never disappear. Your abdomen will be soft and saggy, your pelvic floor will be weak, causing you to leak sometimes when you cough or sneeze, and your breasts will feel fuller and more tender when your milk 'comes in'. There are emotional changes too. The fears and anxieties you may have had through the pregnancy may be relieved by a safe arrival, but you will still experience emotional changes that last several months due to the enormous adjustments that you must make in your own life following the arrival of your new baby.

Getting back to normal

What are afterpains?

Afterpains are contractions of your womb that continue after delivery. They are often relatively mild but in some women they can be severe enough to require painkilling medication. Some women feel that afterpains are similar to the cramps that occur with their menstrual periods; others find these pains to be as bad as labour pains. Afterpains seem to be more common in women who have had a baby before. In addition, women who breast-feed tend to notice or be troubled by afterpains more often than those who bottle-feed their baby, due to the release of oxytocin *(see p. 256)*. Afterpains tend to settle by the end of the first week following delivery.

How long will it take my womb to go back to its pre-pregnant size?

By the end of the third stage of labour, after delivery of the afterbirth, your womb will usually have contracted down to the level of your navel. At this stage it will weigh about 1 kg (2 lb 3 oz). Gradually, the muscle fibres in the womb will shrink down. By the end of the first week after delivery, your womb will weigh about 500 g (1 lb 2 oz) and will be felt above the pubic bone. However, 10–12 days after delivery, your womb will not usually be detectable on feeling your abdomen. By 6 weeks after delivery, it will weigh about 60 g (2 oz) and will essentially be back to its normal, pre-pregnant size.

What should my vaginal discharge be like after having my baby?

The vaginal discharge after having a baby is called lochia. Initially, following the birth of the baby, the lochia will be bloodstained and sometimes contain small clots. The blood comes from the part of the womb where the placenta was implanted. This is a fairly large, 'raw' surface that will heal over several days. The discharge tends to be a little lighter in women who breast-feed as this stimulates the womb to contract and so reduces the amount of blood lost from the site of the placenta. After a few days, the discharge will become a brown-red colour, fading to pink as the amount of blood in it declines. After about two weeks, the pink-coloured lochia will be replaced by a white or cream-coloured discharge that will last for a further 2–4 weeks.

It is best to use sanitary towels to absorb the lochia rather than tampons. This is because you will often be too uncomfortable after delivery to use a tampon and also because inserting a tampon may increase the risk of infection. Persistently heavy, bloodstained or offensive discharge, or the passage of large clots or heavy bleeding, can sometimes be caused by infection in the womb or by retained fragments of the afterbirth or membranes. In these situations, it is common for the discharge to be accompanied by pain in the lower part of your abdomen. If you are at all concerned, you should seek advice from your doctor or midwife.

Why does heavy bleeding sometimes occur after delivery?

When heavy bleeding occurs after delivery, it is referred to as a post-partum haemorrhage and occurs after 1 or 2 in every 100 deliveries. The most common cause of heavy bleeding in the first day after delivery is the womb not contracting down well. This allows bleeding to occur from the site where the placenta was implanted. If the womb has been over-distended, such as by a twin pregnancy or excess fluid around the baby(see p. 135), then this problem is a little more common. It is also more likely to occur after a prolonged labour. Sometimes a very full bladder can stop the womb contracting down well. Another cause of heavy bleeding in the first day after delivery is retention of all or part of the placenta in the womb. This prevents the womb from contracting down properly and so leads to bleeding arising from the site of the placenta. Heavy bleeding can sometimes occur with a tear or even from an episiotomy wound.

How is heavy bleeding after delivery treated?

This is treated by stopping the bleeding and by restoring the blood and fluid lost because of the bleeding. A drip might be set up in the arm to give fluids intravenously. Your blood count will be checked to determine how much blood has been lost and whether a blood transfusion is necessary. If the womb has not contracted down well, medication can be given to promote contraction of the womb. If part of the afterbirth has been retained, the doctor will have to remove this (see p. 225). If bleeding is from the episiotomy or a tear, this will have to be repaired with stitches. If bleeding occurs after the first 24 hours, it is most commonly due to retained fragments of the afterbirth or membranes and/or infection. Any significant fragments of afterbirth or membranes will usually have to be removed and any infection treated with antibiotics.

Will it be difficult to open my bowels after delivery?

Having your first bowel movement after a vaginal delivery is something new mothers often worry about. They worry about how painful it might be when their bottom is bruised or has stitches. It is not unusual to be constipated at this time, which can add to the concern. Constipation is common in the first few days after delivery. This is because you can often become slightly dehydrated and will not have eaten much around the time of labour and delivery. To ease the situation, it is important to try to avoid constipation by keeping your fluid intake high and eating plenty of fruit and vegetables. Sometimes you may need some medication, like a suppository or mild laxative, to help your bowels move. Your doctor or midwife can advise you about this. When you do have a bowel movement, it is important when cleaning yourself to wipe from front to back rather than from back to front. This will help reduce the risk of infection getting into your womb.

Will I have difficulty passing urine after delivery?

Sometimes there can be difficulty in passing urine after delivery, but most women will pass urine within 12 hours without any problem. Indeed, it is common to pass quite large volumes of urine after delivery. Difficulty urinating can sometimes be caused by bruising or swelling of the tissues around the bladder. This is a little more common after forceps deliveries or a long labour. Hot baths, painkilling medication and ice packs can often help relieve the discomfort and make it easier to urinate. Very occasionally, a bladder catheter may be required to empty the bladder if you can pass no urine. The catheter may be needed once only, or it may be needed for 24–48 hours. Even if you are fearful about urinating, you should not cut down on your fluid intake as you will need the fluid to replace that which you have lost through sweating during labour.

If you have grazes or wounds around the area where urine comes out, the urine may cause the tissues to sting. Sitting in a shallow bath to pass urine will help relieve the stinging as the urine will immediately be diluted so that it will not irritate the tissues so much. The concept of passing urine in the bath may not appeal to you, but it often solves the problem. You can always have a fresh bath afterwards! Alternatively, some women find it helpful to stand in the shower and use the showerhead to spray water over their vulva to sooth the tissues and help make urinating easier. The same effect can be achieved using the bidet.

Bladder infection (cystitis) occurs in about 10–15% of women after delivery. If you develop a bladder infection, you will usually need to pass urine frequently and have pain and a burning sensation on urination. Bladder infections usually need treatment with antibiotics. If you have problems passing urine, you should consult your midwife or doctor.

Will my abdomen still look large after delivery?

It is usual for your abdomen to look large even after delivery of the baby. This is because of the skin being stretched and slack, the muscles being stretched and having less tone, and also because of some extra fat that your body will have laid down during pregnancy to prepare for breast-feeding. Use the exercises given opposite to help your muscles regain their tone. The shape of your abdomen will soon return to its pre-pregnancy shape, although it may never look quite the same as it did before pregnancy.

I get small leaks of urine when I cough or laugh. What can I do to stop this?

The pelvic floor muscles can be stretched and damaged by the stress of pregnancy and delivery *(see p. 102)*, which can lead to problems such as stress incontinence, in which increased pressure on the pelvic floor, as occurs with coughing or laughing, leads to a small leak of urine from the bladder. This is especially common after delivery. It thus makes sense to strengthen the pelvic floor during pregnancy to minimise the risk of problems after you have the baby. Following delivery, you may feel that you have no control over your pelvic floor for the first couple of days. Pelvic floor exercises *(described on p. 102)* will strengthen these muscles and help you regain control of them.

How can I relieve the pain of stitches?

The stitches from an episiotomy or tear are the most usual cause of discomfort in the days following delivery and it is common to need painkilling medication. Sitting on a cushion or rubber ring can also help. You should keep the episiotomy wound clean and dry by having regular baths or showers, or by using a bidet. Many women find that a warm bath in particular helps to soothe the discomfort. Try to avoid rubbing a towel over the area to dry it; instead, dab it dry with your towel or, if necessary, use a hairdryer. The stitches used nowadays are usually 'dissolving' and will often be placed below the skin. This

Exercises to improve the abdominal muscles

If you have had a Caesarean birth, check with your physiotherapist, mid-wife or doctor before exercising.

Pelvic tilt. Lie on your back with your knees bent. Gently pull in your tummy. Then tighten your buttocks, tilting your bottom upwards. You will feel the small of your back pressing into the floor. Slowly release. Perform several of these and repeat frequently.

This is a good exercise for the abdominal muscles and you can do it in the first week after delivery. As you get stronger you can make your muscles work harder, holding the tilt position and curling forward a little to lift your head off the pillow.

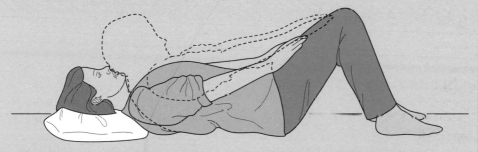

Curl up. You should start doing curl-ups 2–3 weeks after delivery. Lie on the floor with your knees bent and your head on a pillow. Breathe in and then slowly lift your head and shoulders, reaching towards your knees with your hands. Breathe out during the exercise, then uncurl slowly. Begin with 5 repetitions only and build up as your abdominal muscles get stronger. Do not attempt sit-ups or double straight leg raising as these should not be done after having a baby.

Diagonal reach. Tighten your tummy muscles, then lift your head and left shoulder and reach with your left arm across your body towards your right ankle. Lie back for a few moments, then repeat on the other side. Begin with 5 repetitions only and build up as your abdominal muscles get stronger.

means that you will not be able to see any stitches and also that there will be no need to remove them. When you have a bowel movement this may sometimes cause pain at the wound, but this can be helped by gently pressing on the wound with a sanitary towel to support the stitches while moving your bowels. Some women worry that when they move their bowels the stitches might give way. However, the stitches are strong enough to cope with this. Most episiotomies heal in about 10 days; in only a few cases will the discomfort last for up to several weeks. If you have problems with your episiotomy stitches, you should not hesitate to consult your doctor or midwife.

How can I avoid back strain?

Pregnancy places an increased load on your back. Softening of the ligaments that hold your bones together is a normal feature of pregnancy. When this is combined with the stress placed on your back during labour and after delivery, it is not surprising that backache is common in the days and weeks after delivery. The most common site of backache is at the junction of the spine and pelvis. You therefore need to think about your posture and avoid stooping or slumping forward, such as when changing the baby's nappy, as this will stress your back more. It is especially important to sit comfortably, with your back well supported, when feeding your baby. *(See pp. 103 and 258 for further advice.)*

How soon after having the baby can we have sex?

There is no physical reason to avoid having sex once any tears or episiotomy stitches have healed, and bruising and discharge have settled down, or you have recovered from a Caesarean section. At least 30% of couples have sex within four weeks of having their baby. However, many couples feel simply too tired for sex in the first few weeks after having a baby. Every couple varies in how soon they want to resume having sex. Even if you don't feel up to making love, you can still be physically close and affectionate and you should try and make some time for yourselves.

It is not uncommon to have some difficulty in resuming sex. This can be caused by problems such as persistent discomfort from an episiotomy wound or tear. Sometimes the vagina can be dry, in which case this can be treated with lubricants. If you have a problem with resuming sex, you should discuss this with your doctor or midwife, or with the staff at a family-planning clinic, who will often be able to help with practical advice or treatment.

When will I need to use contraception?

Experts recommend that you start using contraception within four weeks of delivery. If you normally use the combined (oestrogen-containing) oral contraceptive pill, you may be advised to avoid taking it in the first few weeks after delivery. If you are breast-feeding, this type of pill can theoretically reduce your ability to produce milk, although this has not yet been proven to be a problem in clinical practice. The combined pill is associated with a small increase in the risk of developing a blood clot (thrombosis – *see p. 191*). There is also a slightly increased risk of developing a blood clot after delivery, due to the effects of pregnancy and delivery on your body. Thus it is possible that the combined effects of the oestrogen-containing pill and the effects of pregnancy might produce a higher risk of clotting problems. The progesterone-only contraceptive pill is usually suitable for contraception while breast-feeding. It contains a very low dose of progesterone and it does not appear to influence breast-milk production.

If you use a diaphragm or cap for barrier contraception, you should make sure that it still fits well as the shape and size of the neck of the womb may change after having a baby. The coil, or intrauterine contraceptive device, can also be used for contraception after having a baby. Natural family planning (avoiding intercourse at around the time of ovulation – *see p. 24*) is more difficult to use in the first few months after delivery until your normal menstrual cycle re-establishes itself. Condoms are best used for contraception in the first few weeks after delivery until you decide on the method of contraception you want to use long term. It is important that you get specific contraceptive advice for your own particular situation. Your doctor or family-planning clinic can provide this.

If I breast-feed, will I need contraception?

If you are breast-feeding, this can suppress ovulation and thus your regular menstrual cycle. Breast-feeding can therefore act as a form of contraception and has been shown to be nearly 99% effective as a form of contraception, but only in the first six months in women who breast-feed, giving mimimal amounts of formula milk or food supplements to the baby, and who have not had a period from the time of delivery. However, it should be remembered that breast-feeding is *not* reliable as a contraceptive after you have a period, or if you supplement the baby's diet with formula milk or other food, or if more than six months have passed since delivery. Hence many women who breast-feed do not rely solely on breast-feeding for contraception. If avoiding pregnancy is important to you, then you should consider using an alternative or additional form of contraception, rather than relying on breast-feeding alone. Your doctor or family-planning clinic can advise you about this.

When will I have my first period?

This will depend on many factors, in particular whether you are breast-feeding. If you are bottle-feeding or have only breast-fed for a short time, your period may resume within about six weeks and usually within 2–3 months. If you are concerned that your menstrual period has not returned, consult your doctor.

Postnatal depression

Is it normal to feel depressed after having a baby?

Between 50 and 80% of women experience the so-called 'baby blues' in the first week after delivery, probably most often on the third or fourth day. So it is really a normal feature of childbirth and may be due to changes in hormone levels that occur rapidly after delivery. It may also reflect the enormous adjustment in your own life that inevitably occurs after having a baby, especially if it is your first. The symptoms women experience with the baby blues will include feelings of depression, weepiness, exhaustion, isolation and a lack of self-confidence. Insomnia and anxiety can also occur. In addition, you may feel disappointed in yourself for not feeling happy after having had the baby.

Usually the baby blues settles within a week with reassurance and support and without specific medical treatment. You can help matters by getting as much rest as possible in the first week after the baby is born. This is easier said than done, but it is important to try and get a least one proper rest in bed every day in the first week. Share your feelings with your partner, making it is easier for him to support you, both emotionally and practically. It is also good to let yourself be emotional and cry when you want to. Sometimes these feelings of depression don't fade, however. They can progress to a more severe or persistent form of depression – postnatal depression, or PND for short. If you are concerned about a problem with depression, you should consult your doctor or midwife.

How common is postnatal depression?

As many as 10–15% of new mothers suffer from a degree of postnatal depression. Although many women are aware of PND, few know that it is also common to feel depressed during pregnancy. Indeed, in about a third of cases of postnatal depression the problem starts during pregnancy. It is important to identify the problem as, unchecked, it can persist for months, while early recognition and treatment can help it get better and reduce the stress on you and your family.

What causes postnatal depression?

Doctors don't really know why postnatal depression occurs. It may be linked to the huge hormonal changes that occur so abruptly in your body after delivery or a combination of these hormonal changes, emotional stresses and changes in your lifestyle. However, doctors have identified some women who might be at increased risk of this problem. Women who have previously experienced a problem with a depressive illness have an increased risk of developing postnatal depression. Depression, excessive anxiety and stressful life events during pregnancy, such as bereavement or unemployment, are also associated with an increased chance of developing PND. Women who lost their own mothers in childhood are at greater risk, as are those who lack the support of their partner. Complications during and after the pregnancy, such as delivery of a premature baby, might also contribute.

However, PND can happen to any mother. It can occur even if the whole pregnancy and delivery go smoothly and you have a healthy baby. You may have been looking forward to having a baby for months or years, and be well supported by your partner, yet still feel miserable. This does not mean that you are not a good mother or are not thankful that everything went well and that you have a healthy baby; it simply means that you may be suffering from one of the commonest medical conditions to affect new mothers.

When does PND occur?

It usually starts about 1–2 weeks and generally within a month after you have had the baby, and therefore it often occurs after you have returned from hospital. It can, however, occur up to six months after delivery.

What treatment is there for postnatal depression?

There are a number of treatments that can improve postnatal depression, so it is important to acknowledge the problem in the first place and seek help. Do not let yourself suffer in silence: you should not feel embarrassed or ashamed at confiding in your doctor or midwife that you feel depressed. Indeed, in the weeks after delivery all healthcare professionals should be looking out for signs of postnatal depression. Some even use a special questionnaire (the Edinburgh scale), consisting of 10 questions, to help identify those women with a depressive problem. It is often helpful to know that yours is a specific medical problem, a common problem that any mother can encounter, and one that can be treated and will get better.

The symptoms of postnatal depression

Postnatal depression is not usually diagnosed until several of the characteristic symptoms have been present for at least two weeks. Although depression, feeling low, unhappy and wretched, is probably the most common symptom of PND, there are a number of other symptoms:

- Feeling tearful and crying for no obvious reason, or for a reason you would usually consider trivial
- Feeling irritable with your other children and particularly with your partner
- Lacking self-confidence
- Feelings of unfounded guilt and worthlessness
- Feeling rejected
- Difficulty in concentrating or organising your day, or feeling that minor things you need to do require considerable effort
- Difficulty in laughing or even smiling
- Loss of enjoyment of things that would normally give you pleasure
- Lack of interest in sex
- Insomnia or excessive sleeping, and waking up feeling exhausted
- Marked disturbance in weight and appetite, including loss of appetite and comfort eating
- Feeling excessively anxious or having panic attacks
- Recurrent thoughts of death
- Sitting for long periods without noticing the passage of time

In addition, it is important for your partner to be involved so that he understands the difficulties you face, although sometimes he too will need or benefit from a little support. You will need patience and understanding – not just practical help with the baby, but also sympathetic emotional support, affection and encouragement. It is useful to have someone you are close to, other than your partner, that you can confide in. It can also help to talk through your feelings with a sympathetic and non-critical counsellor. 'Offloading' your feelings can make a big difference. Getting a proper rest every day will help your state of mind and it is important to eat well. Sometimes more specific psychological treatment is helpful and sometimes anti-depressant medication is what is needed. This medication is not a tranquilliser and is not addictive, but it takes at least two weeks to work and should usually be continued for six months after symptoms of depression have disappeared. Medical treatment will usually depend on your specific needs and preferences and will not prevent you from breast-feeding. If you experience the symptoms of postnatal depression, you should consult your doctor or midwife. They will be able to give you advice about treatment.

What to expect after a Caesarean section

You should not underestimate the fact that a Caesarean section is a major operation. It can take some time to recover from one, especially if it is carried out after a long exhausting labour. Remember that you will also have to cope with a new baby. Most women can become mobile reasonably quickly after a Caesarean section, but you might feel sore and sometimes a little dizzy when you start to move around. After a Caesarean you may want to stay in hospital a little longer to give yourself more time to recover. The scar may be quite painful and you may need painkilling medication for several days. If you need to cough, it is useful to have a pillow at hand to support the wound.

In the first day or so, the wound might leak a little bloodstained fluid, but this is normal. If there is heavy or prolonged leakage from the scar, or the wound becomes red, swollen and inflamed, you should consult your doctor or midwife as this might mean that you have an infection. Wound infections are usually treated with antibiotics. The most common techniques for wound closure are 'dissolving' (absorbable) sutures and metal staples. Dissolving sutures tend to be used (as with episiotomies), placed beneath the skin, so there is no need for the stitches to be removed – they simply disappear over a number of weeks. Staples and stitches that need to be removed are taken out usually after about five days. Removing them should not be painful, although it can be uncomfortable.

Will I have a vaginal discharge after a Caesarean?
The vaginal discharge, or lochia, that occurs after a Caesarean section is similar to that seen after a vaginal delivery and will last about the same length of time. Just as in vaginal deliveries, persistent, heavy, bloodstained or offensive

discharge, or the passage of large clots or heavy bleeding, can sometimes be caused by infection in the womb. In this situation it is common for the discharge to be accompanied by pain in the lower part of your abdomen. If you are concerned about your vaginal discharge after a Caesarean, you should seek advice from your doctor or midwife.

Why can't I feel anything around the Caesarean section scar?

The tiny nerves that run in the skin are inevitably cut at the skin incision for a Caesarean section. This causes the area round the wound to feel numb when you touch it. These tiny nerves will grow back over a period of months, however, and you will usually find that the sensation has returned.

Why do some women need heparin injections after their delivery?

Heparin injections are given after a delivery, especially a Caesarean section, if it is considered that the woman is at increased risk of venous thrombosis. Heparin, usually given in relatively low doses by injections under the skin, does not appear in breast milk and so appears safe for breast-feeding. Treatment is usually required for a only a few days, but where the woman is considered at ongoing high risk, treatment may be needed for longer.

Is there any treatment apart from heparin that can prevent a thrombosis after delivery?

There are also special stockings that can be worn to help improve blood flow and reduce swelling of the legs *(see p. 93)*. These can sometimes be used instead of heparin, or they can be used in conjunction with heparin, especially where the risk of thrombosis is considered high. Early mobilisation – getting up and about as soon as possible after a Caesarean section – can also reduce the risk of thrombosis.

What are the risk factors for a thrombosis after delivery?

The risk factors for thrombosis can include immobility for several days prior to labour, Caesarean section (especially if carried out during labour) and infection, in addition to the factors outlined in the box on p. 191. Your doctor can advise you about the need for heparin injections in your individual case.

Why does my midwife or doctor take my temperature each time they check me after delivery?

A high temperature can sometimes indicate a problem after delivery and can alert your doctor or midwife to this. Infections in the wound following Caesarean section can be a common cause of raised temperature, as can bladder infections, infections in the womb, thrombosis or clot in the leg, and mastitis *(see p. 263)*. If you have a persistently high temperature after delivery, your doctor or midwife should identify the cause and treat the particular problem. For example, if the cause is a bladder infection, a specimen of urine will usually be taken for analysis and antibiotics will be prescribed.

The postnatal check

It is useful to have a check by your doctor about six weeks after delivery. The purpose of this is to see that everything is returning to normal and to deal with any problems. Any tears or an episiotomy will usually be well healed by that time. If you had a Caesarean section, the scar should be well healed. Your breasts, if you are not breast-feeding, should have returned to normal. If you are breast-feeding, your breasts and nipples will have adapted to feeding.

Your doctor will usually examine you and perform any necessary tests. For example, if you appear anaemic, blood will be taken to check for this. If you are due a cervical smear test then this can be carried out. If you are not immune to rubella (German measles – *see p. 149*), you can be vaccinated at this time. The postnatal check is also an ideal time to review the pregnancy and delivery. If you had any problems or concerns, you should raise them with your doctor. For example, if you had a Caesarean section, you may wish to go over why you needed it and what it means for any future pregnancy, or if you developed pre-eclampsia *(see p. 136)*, you will probably want to know the risk of it happening again. Contraception is usually discussed at this time, too.

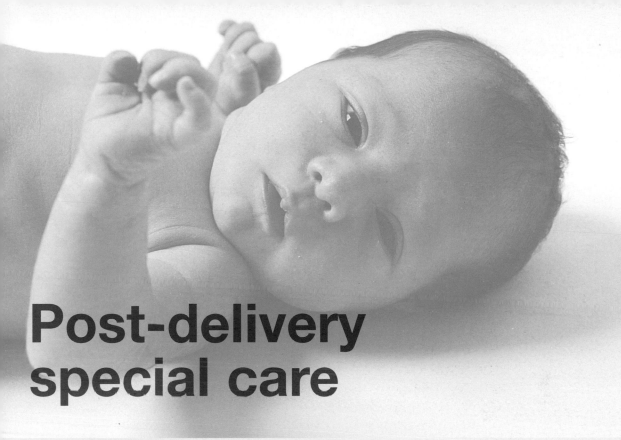

Post-delivery special care

Sometimes newborn babies have particular problems that require special care. Special care baby units offer a range of care for the baby, from observation for minor problems through to intensive care of the small number of babies who are seriously ill. These units are run by specialist nurses and doctors with particular expertise in the treatment of newborn babies. Babies can be admitted to the special care baby unit for just a few hours of observation or for weeks of essential medical and nursing care.

Some of the most common reasons for admission are breathing difficulties and premature delivery, which often occur together as breathing problems are more common in premature babies due to their lungs not being fully developed and mature. Babies who are small for their stage in pregnancy, even if not premature, sometimes need to be admitted for observation. Other reasons for admission include: a low temperature, infection or suspected infection, vomiting, serious feeding problems, severe jaundice, fits and sometimes where the mother has a medical condition that might have an effect on the baby after delivery. For example, babies of mothers with diabetes are frequently admitted because of low levels of sugar in their blood or breathing difficulties. So babies can be admitted to special care baby units for quite minor reasons or to treat serious problems.

The special care baby unit

There is a lot of equipment in the special care baby unit. What does it all do?

The baby in special care may be in an incubator – a special cot that allows the baby to be kept at a constant temperature. This is because newborn babies, especially premature babies, are vulnerable to cold as they lose heat easily. The baby may also be attached to monitors that provide the nurses and doctors with continuous information on his condition. A heart and breathing monitor is commonly used to give information on the rate and rhythm of the heart and breathing, for instance. This type of monitor is attached by wires to the baby's skin using adhesive pads. Another monitor that can be attached to the skin with an adhesive pad is a temperature monitor. Oxygen levels in the baby's blood are measured using a device called a pulse oximeter, usually attached to a finger or a toe, which works by shining a small beam of light through the tissues to determine how much oxygen the baby has in his blood.

Some babies will need to receive fluids and medication through an intravenous drip. When this is required, a small plastic needle is inserted into a vein and attached to a bag of fluid. The plastic needle can be put into the veins of the scalp, arm or leg. Sometimes fine plastic tubing is inserted into an artery or vein in the umbilical cord. The drip can be used to give the baby fluid,

Left: The baby in special care may be in an incubator like this one. An incubator is simply a special cot that allows the baby to be kept at a constant temperature. Newborn babies, especially if they are premature, are vulnerable to cold as they lose heat easily. While in the incubator the baby may also be attached to monitors that constantly provide the nurses and doctors with checks on the baby's condition.

Right: When a very premature baby is delivered and needs to be transferred from the delivery room or operating theatre to the special care baby unit, the baby may be placed in a portable incubator. This will keep her warm and also has equipment to help the baby with her breathing, if this is required. The two 'port holes' on the front are used to allow the nurse, doctor or parent to handle the baby without taking her out of the incubator.

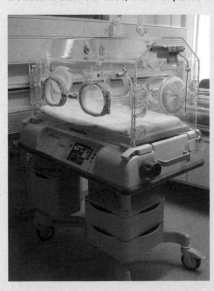 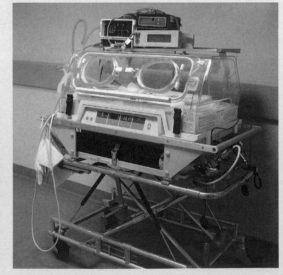

nutrients or medicine and can also be used to take small blood samples for tests. It is a painless way of getting blood from the baby.

If you want to know what a piece of equipment does, you should ask the nurse or doctor caring for your baby to explain it.

How are babies given help with their breathing?

The type of help given to your baby will depend on the particular problem that she has. The main techniques are CPAP (continuous positive airway pressure) and mechanical ventilation. With CPAP, a mixture of oxygen and air is given through tubes attached to the baby's nostrils or through a face mask that fits over her nose and mouth. Sometimes the air is given through a tube that is inserted into the baby's windpipe through the mouth or nose. This is more commonly used when the baby is being 'weaned off' a mechanical ventilator. The air is given at a level of pressure that helps keep the lungs open, thus making it easier for the baby to breathe and get enough oxygen.

With mechanical ventilation, a tube is inserted into the baby's windpipe through the mouth or nose and held safely in place with tape. This tube attaches to a ventilator, a machine that helps the baby to breathe. If the baby needs a ventilator, medication to sedate him and make him more comfortable may be given. High-frequency ventilators are sometimes used to help the baby breathe by keeping the lungs open with constant pressure and using very, very rapid (between 600 and 900 cycles per minute) and very small puffs of air.

Premature babies

Apart from breathing difficulties, what problems can a premature baby face?

The problems that a premature baby will face depends on how premature she is, but common complications include problems with feeding, bowel problems, hypothermia, low blood sugar, jaundice, infection, anaemia and a bleeding tendency (most worrying if there is a bleed into the brain – *see overleaf*).

How is a premature baby fed?

The way a premature baby is fed depends on how premature he is and how sick. Premature babies usually cannot coordinate their sucking and breathing to take a breast- or bottle-feed safely until about 34 weeks of pregnancy, although this varies a great deal from baby to baby. Some might be ready a week or two earlier and others a week or two later. A very premature baby may be fed all the nourishment he needs by intravenous drip (a procedure known as total parenteral nutrition, or TPN for short). However, wherever possible doctors prefer the baby to be fed milk through a tube into his stomach, although there are circumstances such as when the baby has bowel problems, where tube feeding has to be avoided. So the very premature baby may progress gradually from drip feeding to tube-feeding to breast- or bottle-feeding.

Just as with term babies, the premature baby will lose weight in the first few days after delivery and will not regain his birthweight until about two weeks of age. To encourage sucking, the baby may be given a 'dummy' to suck on while being tube fed. Alternatively, the baby could suck on an empty breast. This can help maintain milk production and prepare both mother and baby for later breast-feeding. Your baby's doctors and specialist nurses will advise you about the best way to feed him.

Can a premature baby be given breast milk?

Yes. Breast milk is ideal for premature babies. All the advantages a term baby would have from breast milk apply to premature babies also. In either case, breast milk will reduce the risk of infections, bowel problems and allergy. If your baby is not ready to be breast- or bottle-fed, your milk can be given by tube feeding. If she is not ready for tube feeding, your milk can be frozen and stored. This means that you will have to express your milk (see p. 261). Even if you can only do this for a few weeks, it is still very worthwhile for your baby. A premature baby may need also extra vitamins and iron. There are very few situations, such as in the case of a mother with HIV infection, where it would not be advisable to breast-feed the baby. Your doctor can advise you if you have a medical problem or are on a type of medication where breast-feeding should be avoided.

Can premature babies have problems that affect their brain?

In premature babies there can sometimes be bleeding into or around spaces (ventricles) in the brain that are normally filled with fluid. Hence this condition is known as intraventricular haemorrhage (or IVH for short). It arises because the blood vessels in the developing brain are fragile and can bleed easily, especially in very premature babies. Doctors will regularly check the brain of a premature baby using an ultrasound scan to look for this problem. There is no way at present to treat this once it arises other than good all-round medical and nursing care of the premature baby to minimise the extent of the problem and allow healing to occur naturally. There are various levels of severity of this problem.

Are premature babies more likely to get jaundice?

Slight jaundice is commonly seen in newborn babies and is a little more common in breast-fed babies. As has been noted (p. 251), it occurs because the liver is still slightly immature even in a term baby. In premature babies the liver is even more immature and so jaundice is more common. It is also found in babies with certain forms of anaemia and with infections. Mild degrees of jaundice are not usually a problem, although the baby may need a test to check the level. It is uncommon for premature babies to need any treatment other than phototherapy for jaundice, but if levels do become very high then an 'exchange' blood transfusion might be performed, in which the baby's blood, which has high levels of bilirubin, is replaced with donor blood. Occasionally, medication will be prescribed to help the liver break down the bilirubin. If you are concerned about jaundice in your baby, you should discuss this with your doctor or midwife.

Post-delivery special care

The chances of survival for a premature baby

There are many factors that will influence the chances of survival for a premature baby. The most important factors are:

- How far advanced the pregnancy was when the baby was born as this determines how mature the vital organs are (the greatest risk is in babies born at less than 26 weeks of pregnancy)
- The baby's weight
- Whether the baby has any serious birth defects or abnormalities that affect her development
- Whether the baby develops severe breathing problems
- Whether any additional problems arise, such as a serious infection

Clearly each case must be assessed individually and only the baby's doctor can make an assessment of this. In general terms, babies born after 30 weeks of pregnancy have a greater than 95% likelihood of survival in modern special care baby units, while those born at 25 weeks may have around a 60% chance of survival, rising to about 90% or more by 27–28 weeks.

What is the risk of my premature baby developing a handicap?

There is a risk of the premature baby developing a disability or handicap. This is most likely in very premature babies born at 24 or 25 weeks with complications such as intraventricular haemorrhage or infection. In general terms, the risk of serious long-term problems drops sharply in babies born between 24 and 28 weeks of pregnancy, with a rate usually of less than 10% by 27 weeks. Disabilities can range from cerebral palsy or visual and hearing problems to learning difficulties or poor coordination. As the risk of problems varies greatly from case to case, only the doctors looking after the baby can judge the likelihood of problems developing and this is often difficult to predict.

How do the parents of a premature baby feel?

Most parents find it a very stressful experience to have their baby in an intensive care baby unit. Emotions can be in turmoil. The situation can be made more difficult when there is also concern for the mother, such as when she is recovering from a Caesarean or has been ill with a problem like pre-eclampsia. Parents may feel guilty or inadequate that their baby has been born prematurely, but in truth there is very little, if anything, anyone can do to prevent premature birth. It can happen in even the best-cared-for pregnancy, where the parents have taken excellent care of their diet and health. The majority of premature labours are unexplained *(see p. 235)*. Parents may also experience a sense of grief for the pregnancy they had hoped for when complications like premature delivery arise. They may be worried about the baby or the effects of the problems on other members of the family. Feelings of sadness and depression are common, and relationships can be put under stress. The doctors and nurses can offer support, however, and there are parent-support groups that can also help. Parents should not be afraid to ask the doctors and nurses questions about their baby and the care they are giving. Information and understanding of the baby's condition often makes it easier to cope.

Other reasons for special care

Why might my baby have breathing difficulties?

Babies can have breathing difficulties because of many problems. The most common ones are perhaps prematurity (respiratory distress syndrome), transient tachypneoa (temporary rapid breathing) of the newborn, and meconium aspiration.

What is respiratory distress syndrome?

Respiratory distress syndrome (RDS) usually occurs in premature babies as their lungs have not developed fully through to maturity. The more premature the baby, the greater the likelihood of respiratory distress syndrome developing. With RDS the baby's lungs do not make enough of a substance called surfactant, contained in the fluid forming a very thin layer over the inside surface of each lung and important for keeping the lungs open, allowing easy entry of air into them. A baby with RDS will have difficulty breathing, taking rapid breaths – usually more than 60 breaths a minute – and grunting as he breathes, accompanied by flaring of the nostrils. RDS can get worse for around 3–4 days before improving. Milder cases of RDS, where no ventilator is required, can get better within a week. Severe cases are more common in very premature babies and can take much longer to resolve. RDS is treated with extra oxygen that can be given through tubes that are inserted into the nostrils or via a ventilator. Surfactant can be given to the baby through a tube that goes from the nose or mouth to the lungs. The baby will usually be in an incubator and will be monitored to check on heart rate, breathing and oxygen levels.

Are there any longer-term implications if a baby has RDS?

RDS can sometimes lead to a lung condition called bronchopulmonary dysplasia, or BPD for short, which develops in babies who have had severe RDS or are very premature. BPD can arise as a reaction of the baby's lungs to being on a ventilator for a prolonged time. It is usually identified when a premature baby still needs extra oxygen and has breathing difficulties when she has reached the stage equivalent to 36 weeks of pregnancy. BPD can sometimes occur in babies who have had other lung problems such as severe pneumonia. If a baby has BPD, then extra oxygen may be required for several months, along with medication to reduce any wheezing and help the lungs recover. However, the baby may still be well enough to go home and oxygen therapy can be continued there. Babies with BPD are more vulnerable to viral chest infections. The lungs will heal as they grow and most infants have no symptoms by the age of two.

What is transient tachypneoa of the newborn?

Transient tachypneoa (rapid breathing) of the newborn is, by definition, a temporary condition and arises where there is slightly too much fluid on the lungs after the baby is born. While the baby is in the womb, the lungs are normally full of fluid, which is important for lung development. During labour, contractions and the passage of the baby through the birth canal squeeze this fluid out of the lungs. The lungs will absorb the small amount of the fluid remaining. With transient tachypneoa of the newborn, this absorption will take between several hours to a few days because of the extra fluid on the lungs. This condition is more common where the baby is delivered by Caesarean section before labour and is thought to occur because there was no labour to squeeze the fluid out of the lungs. However, transient tachypneoa of the newborn occurs in only a very small number of babies delivered by Caesarean section. It is also a little more common in boys than girls and also in babies at 34–36 weeks and therefore a little premature. It is usually easily diagnosed by the clinical features and can be confirmed with a chest X-ray. Treatment is by giving extra oxygen – sometimes by CPAP – which speeds up the absorption of fluid in the lungs. Transient tachypneoa of the newborn usually resolves within 48 hours and is unlikely to lead to breathing difficulties in the future.

What is meconium aspiration?

When a baby is distressed before birth, leading to shortage of oxygen, it can sometimes pass a lot of meconium. If the meconium is thick and fresh and there is not a lot of fluid round the baby to dilute it down, then this can sometimes get into the baby's lungs. The baby may also gasp when it is distressed and this can make it easier for the meconium to get into the lungs. Once in the lungs, meconium can block some of the small tubes taking air in and this can lead to breathing difficulties. It can also irritate the lung tissues. If a baby is born with this problem, the mouth and nose are usually 'sucked out' at once to remove the meconium. If some has passed into the lungs, this may need to be sucked out by passing a tube into the baby's windpipe. Meconium aspiration may cause very mild or sometimes quite severe breathing problems and the baby may need some help with its breathing, just as with respiratory distress syndrome, because of this. Occasionally, a chest infection may also occur, which can be treated by antibiotics.

What problems can a small-for-dates baby face?

Only around 1 in 10 babies who are small for dates at term need to be admitted to the special care baby unit, and this is more common if the baby is both premature (before 37 completed weeks of pregnancy) and small for dates (because he has not being getting enough nutrients due to the placenta being damaged – *see p. 124*). The types of problem from which small-for-dates babies might suffer are low blood sugar and low body temperature (hypothermia). These problems arise simply because the baby has fewer fat and sugar stores to provide energy and insulation. Small-for-dates babies are also more vulnerable to damage from a shortage of oxygen during labour and delivery. This is why doctors continuously monitor the baby that is considered to be small during labour to watch for these problems. If there is any sign of the baby becoming distressed and not coping with the labour, then a Caesarean section or a forceps or ventouse delivery would be performed, depending on the stage in the labour.

What is necrotising enterocolitis (NEC)?

Necrotising enterocolitis (NEC) is a bowel problem that premature or very low birthweight babies are more vulnerable to as their bowel is immature. The name of the condition indicates that some of the tissue of the small (entero) and large (colon) bowel is inflamed (itis) and dying (necrotising). It is less common in premature deliveries where the mother has been given steroid medication before delivery to enhance the maturity of the baby's lungs. NEC is associated with an upset in the blood supply to the bowel and consequent infection. It is usually localised to certain parts of the bowel: sometimes it only involves the inner lining of part of the bowel, but in more severe cases the full thickness of some parts of the bowel can be affected. When a baby is fed with breast milk, the risk of this condition is reduced because of the infection-resisting properties of the milk. However, in babies at high risk of this condition, delaying milk feeding for a few days can be helpful in preventing NEC as the baby's bowel will not tolerate feeding and must be 'rested'. This means that the nutrition must be given through a drip in a vein (TPN, see above). The bowel is kept empty by aspirating any fluid from the stomach using a small tube. Antibiotics will be used to deal with infection and the baby's condition will be regularly checked. If complications arise or the baby is not responding to medical therapy, then sometimes surgery is needed to deal with the problem.

What happens if my baby has low blood sugar?

Babies whose mothers have diabetes are more prone to low levels of blood sugar, that are babies who are small for dates or premature. Babies at risk will be watched carefully for signs of low blood sugar and blood-sugar levels will be checked by taking a pinprick sample of blood from the baby's heel. A baby with low blood sugar may be jittery and irritable and his temperature can be unstable. There may be breathing problems, too. Low blood sugar is treated by giving the baby more sugar by increasing the frequency of feeds and giving glucose-rich fluid, or if he is on a drip, more sugar can be given through the drip. Once feeding is well established, low levels of blood sugar are uncommon.

Can intraventricular haemorrhage lead to long-term problems?

The less severe forms of intraventricular haemorrhage may not cause any long-term problem. However, the more severe forms of this condition can lead to problems such as brain injury around the areas where the bleeding occurred and hydrocephalus *(see p. 32)*. Hydrocephalus, if untreated, leads to excess fluid accumulating in the brain. This in turn puts pressure on the brain tissue and can make the skull grow too quickly. Hydrocephalus develops because the channels that normally allow the fluid to circulate in the brain get blocked by the bleeding, so leading to high pressure. This condition may need surgery to take the pressure off the brain by diverting the fluid through a so-called shunt. However, this may take some time – usually a few weeks – to become apparent. This is why doctors carefully follow up babies who develop these complications. The types of problem they are looking for vary in severity. They include disturbed movement patterns or difficulty in crawling or walking, delayed development, problems with eyesight and hearing, and poor coordination and learning difficulties.

What if the baby has an abnormality?

Birth defects are abnormalities that are present in a baby at birth, whether premature or not. Some will be obvious at birth or soon after the baby is born. Others will not be easily detected and so may take weeks or even months to be identified. Around 2–3% of babies will have an abnormality of some sort. Most will be minor like a 'stork mark' – a birthmark on the skin that can resolve spontaneously over months – but some will be more serious, such as a cleft lip or palate, or a heart abnormality that may require surgery. Some abnormalities can be corrected and others can have long-term consequences for the baby and the family. Each abnormality is different in terms of its implications for the baby and the treatment required.

It is important to get the correct information about the baby's abnormality from the doctors looking after the baby. Sometimes this information will not be available until the doctor has carried out some tests to determine the extent of the problem. The parents of a baby with a serious abnormality will usually be shocked at first and often just cannot believe that their baby has a problem. Some will feel angry, even though no one is to blame for the problem and everything possible is being done for the baby. It is important to be able to talk about these feelings with partners, friends and relatives, the family doctor or a counsellor. After the initial shock, parents will usually reach a stage where they can cope with the problem and learn to live with any difficulties that it poses.

The death of a baby

How often do babies die?

Many women fear for the loss of their pregnancy. A stillbirth is the delivery of a baby after 24 weeks of pregnancy where the baby has not shown any sign of life after delivery. However, in modern maternity practice in the developed world, few babies are stillborn. Indeed, there has been a dramatic improvement in the numbers of stillbirths over the last 40 years. In the 1960s, for example, around 17 in 1000 babies were stillborn. Today this has fallen to less than 6 in 1000.

Babies can also die after delivery and, again, there has been a marked reduction in the numbers of babies dying in the first four weeks following delivery. This has fallen from around 14 in 1000 births in the early 1960s to less than 5 in 1000 in the late 1990s.

Why do babies die?

The main reasons that babies are lost are serious congenital abnormalities, very premature labour or delivery and a depleted oxygen supply from the placenta. Often the reason a baby dies cannot be explained, but doctors can perform some tests to try and identify the cause of death. These can include blood tests on the mother to look for any underlying medical condition, checks for infections in the mother and baby and examination of the baby and afterbirth.

What if a baby dies?

Losing a baby, whether stillborn or after birth, is an extremely difficult time for any parent. It is a time of tremendous pain and loss – a tragedy that may change the lives of the parents. Not only have they lost their baby, but their hopes and dreams for the future have also been dashed. The parents may feel that the pain will never disappear and the grieving process can take a very long time. Many bereaved parents find that it helps to have mementoes of their baby. Photographs, foot and hand prints, the name band, a lock of hair, can all be kept. Emotions following the loss of a baby go through many different stages – shock, panic, anger, anxiety, guilt – before reaching a stage of acceptance. Good support can make a great deal of difference. It helps the parents if their loss is acknowledged, as it can be hurtful if other people act as though the baby never existed. Phone calls, sympathy cards, visits from friends and relatives can all help. It is important for them to be able to talk about their feelings and feel that somebody cares. But sometimes it can be difficult to talk, even to friends and family, and a great deal of stress can be placed on relationships. Family doctors and professional counsellors can help in such instances. There are also specialist organisations that can offer consolation and advice to parents who have lost a baby (see p. 298).

Glossary

abruption: Where the afterbirth separates from the wall of the womb before the baby is born, resulting in bleeding. It can occur at any time before the delivery of the baby. It happens in around 1 in 80 pregnancies.

afterpains: Contractions of the womb that continue after delivery of the baby.

albumen: A specific form of protein in the blood sometimes found in the urine when the kidneys are upset, such as with pre-eclampsia.

alpha-fetoprotein (AFP): A substance found in the blood of pregnant women used to identify women at higher risk of some abnormalities.

amniocentesis: A sample of fluid taken from the womb using a needle guided by an ultrasound scan. This is usually performed between 15 and 18 weeks to assess the baby for genetic problems.

amniotic fluid: The fluid within the womb in which the baby develops. Amniotic fluid is usually clear or slightly straw coloured. In early pregnancy the amniotic fluid comes from the membranes encasing the foetus and placenta. In later pregnancy the fluid is produced by the developing baby's kidneys and excreted as urine. This fluid helps cushion the baby from any injury and allows it to move within the womb.

amniotic fluid index (AFI): An ultrasound measure of how much fluid is surrounding the baby in the womb.

amniotic sac: The sac of membranes within the womb containing the developing baby and amniotic fluid.

anaemia: An insufficient amount of red blood cells, which carry oxygen round the body.

anomaly scan: An ultrasound scan to screen the baby for an anatomical abnormality.

antacid medication: Medication that neutralises the acid in the stomach or that prevents the formation of acid.

antenatal: The time before the baby is born.

antepartum haemorrhage (APH): Bleeding from the womb before the baby is born.

anti-D immunoglobulin (anti-D): A medication given soon after any bleeding in pregnancy or after delivery to rhesus negative mothers who may have a rhesus positive baby. This can help clear the baby's red blood cells from the mother's bloodstream to prevent rhesus disease.

Apgar score: A scoring system that helps identify babies that might have some difficulty adjusting to life outside the womb. Five features of the baby's condition: heart rate, breathing, colour, movements, and response to stimulation, receive a score from 0 to 2. A score of 2 is normal for each feature. The Apgar scores are often assigned at 1 and 5 minutes after birth. A total score of 7 or more is normal. A score of 3 or less suggests that the baby is distressed and having difficulty adjusting to life outside the womb.

assisted conception: The use of techniques to bring sperm and egg together and so facilitate pregnancy.

assisted vaginal delivery: Delivery assisted by forceps or the ventouse.

BCG vaccination: A vaccination against tuberculosis.

bilirubin: See jaundice.

biophysical profile: An ultrasound scan to check that the baby is well. The doctor or ultrasonographer will watch the baby's movements with the ultrasound scan for up to 40 minutes. The whole profile looks at five factors. These are called 'foetal breathing' movements, gross foetal body movements, foetal tone, amniotic fluid volume and the non-stress cardiotocograph, or CTG. In practice it is unusual to check all five of the variables. Often the CTG is omitted and only the other four factors are checked as these are very reliable on their own.

birth plan: A way to communicate your preferences in writing to those looking after you in labour. It can be placed in your medical records.

birthing stool: A seat designed specifically to allow a woman to give birth in the sitting position.

blighted ovum: Where placental tissue develops in the womb but no embryo or foetus is ever found. Without an embryo or foetus a pregnancy cannot continue. Therefore a blighted ovum will eventually progress to an inevitable miscarriage with bleeding and pain, and in turn to an incomplete or complete miscarriage if untreated.

body mass index (BMI): A guide to relative body weight which gives a better indication of body fat content than weight alone. The BMI is calculated by taking your body weight in kilograms and dividing it by your height squared (height multiplied by height).

Braxton-Hicks contractions: Irregular contractions of the womb. They are not usually painful. You feel your womb getting hard then relaxing after 30 seconds or so. They are sometimes called 'practice contractions'.

breaking of waters: See ruptured membranes.

breech presentation: Where the baby's bottom or feet are leading the way down the birth canal.

bronchopulmonary dysplasia (BPD): A lung condition that develops in babies who have had severe respiratory distress syndrome (RDS) or are very premature. It occurs because their lungs react to being on a ventilator for a prolonged time with extra oxygen supplements.

brow presentation: Where the baby's neck is tilted back so that its forehead is leading the way down the birth canal. It is very uncommon, only occurring in about 1 in every 4000 or 5000 deliveries at term.

Caesarean section: Sometimes abbreviated to LUSCS and LSCS. This stands for lower [uterine] segment Caesarean section and is the most common type of Caesarean where the cut on the womb is across the lower part of the womb, which heals well with a strong scar.

cardiotocograph (CTG): Cardiotocography measures the baby's heart rate and any tightenings of the womb. The machine that does this is called a cardiotocograph, or CTG for short. Two small devices called transducers are strapped to your abdomen. The first of these is the heart rate (or cardiograph) transducer, which is an ultrasound device that measures your baby's heart rate. The second transducer is called a tocodynamometer, which measures contractions of the womb. In labour the baby's heart rate can be more accurately picked up by attaching a clip to the baby's head.

cephalic presentation: When the baby is head down in the womb.

cephalo-pelvic disproportion: When the baby is too big to come through the pelvis. This leads to progress being slow or stopping in the latter stages of labour.

cervical dilation: The width of the open cervix (neck of the womb). When the cervix is 10 cm dilated it is fully dilated (open), wide enough to let the baby's head pass through.

cervical effacement: Before labour the cervix is thick and long. Prior to labour proper starting it shortens and thins out. This is called effacement.

cervical incompetence: Weakness of the cervix that can lead to recurrent miscarriages.

cervix: The neck of the womb. The outer part of which opens into the vagina and the inner part opens into the cavity of the womb.

chloasma: Patchy pigmentation on the face around the chin, forehead and nose and mouth associated with pregnancy.

chorionic villous sampling (CVS): The chorionic villi are like little fingers of tissue that form part of the afterbirth. As the afterbirth has the same genetic make up as the foetus, this tissue can be used for the diagnosis of genetic and chromosomal problems. A CVS can be performed at 9–12 weeks, a needle is inserted through the abdomen and into of the afterbirth. This is done under ultrasound control so that the doctor can guide the needle to the afterbirth site. A tiny sample of chorionic villous tissue is then sucked up the needle using a syringe. The tissue is then sent to the laboratory for the genetic make-up of the baby to be studied.

chromosomal condition: A condition that arises when there is a defect in the number of the chromosomes making up each cell. An example of a chromosomal condition is Down's syndrome where an extra chromosome number 21 is present.

chromosomes: The genetic code made from DNA is made up of thousands of genes that are carried on structures called 'chromosomes'. Each of us has 23 pairs of chromosomes in every cell in our body – a total of 46 chromosomes per cell. Of the 23 pairs of chromosomes in every cell, 22 pairs are 'general' chromosomes and one is a pair of 'sex' chromosomes.

cleft lip: A congenital condition where the upper lip has a split in the middle that runs up towards the nose. This can be repaired surgically. It is sometimes associated with cleft palate where there is a cleft or defect in the middle of the hard palate in the mouth.

colostrum: The highly concentrated yellow fluid produced by the breasts for the first two days or so after delivery, before the breast milk 'comes in'.

connective tissue diseases: A group of conditions where inflammation attacks various parts of the body.

continuous positive airway pressure (CPAP): A technique to assist a baby's breathing after birth.

contractions: Regular, strong and painful tightenings of the muscle of the womb.

cord prolapse: The situation where the umbilical cord that carries oxygen to the baby falls down into the vagina before the baby is born. This can lead to the baby being deprived of oxygen. It is more common where the baby is breech, or where the lie is unstable or where there is an excessive amount of fluid round the baby. It is an emergency situation as a prolonged lack of oxygen could damage the baby. The baby has to be delivered quickly if a cord prolapse occurs.

cordocentesis: A test to obtain a sample of the baby's blood while it is still in the womb. The procedure is rather like a CVS. Instead of guiding the needle to the afterbirth the doctor guides the needle with ultrasound through the afterbirth to the large vein that runs in the umbilical cord. The doctor can then take a sample of the baby's blood to test for particular problems like severe anaemia.

corpus luteum cyst: A small cyst on the ovary filled with yellow material. It produces hormones important for the continuation of the pregnancy. A corpus luteum cyst is normal and will shrink as the pregnancy advances and the afterbirth takes over the production of essential hormones.

cot death: The sudden and unexplained death of an infant.

crowning: When the baby's head appears at the vulva just prior to delivery.

CVS: See chorionic villous sampling

cytomegalovirus: Infection with cytomegalovirus is often symptomless in adults, even during pregnancy. The major risk is for the small number of mothers who encounter this virus for the first time when pregnant. Transmission of this virus to the baby can sometimes occur and a small number of these pregnancies can develop a problem like miscarriage or abnormalities similar to those seen with German measles.

dermoid cyst: Cysts on the ovary that can contain a whole variety of tissues such as skin, sweat glands, teeth, and thyroid tissue. These form because the tissue of the ovary gets 'confused' and makes the wrong type of tissue.

diamorphine: See opiates.

diastolic pressure: See systolic pressure.

DNA: Deoxyribonucleic acid, the chemical substance that makes up your genetic code.

donor insemination (DI): A technique where donated semen is placed at the cervix or inside the womb at the time of ovulation. It can be used where the male partner has no sperm production or severe sperm problems.

Doppler ultrasound: A type of ultrasound that can measure the speed of blood flow.

double test: See 'triple test'.

Down's syndrome: A chromosomal condition where an extra chromosome number 21 is present.

eclampsia: Eclampsia is convulsions or fits in pregnancy due to pre-eclampsia. It is caused by swelling of the brain and spasm of the blood vessels supplying the brain. It is rare in most First World countries (1 in 2500 pregnancies in the UK). Usually it is preceded by symptoms like upper abdominal pain, headache and visual blurring or flashing lights in a woman with pre-eclampsia.

ectopic pregnancy: Ectopic pregnancy occurs when the fertilised egg implants in a location other than the womb. This happens in around 1 in every 300 pregnancies. The most common site for ectopic pregnancy is the fallopian tube as over 95% occur there.

embryo: The developing baby is called an embryo until the 8th week of pregnancy. By the 8th week the outward appearance of the foetus is recognisably human and from this stage until delivery, it is called a foetus.

endometrium: The lining of the womb.

endometriosis: A condition where tissue similar to the tissue found in the lining of the womb (endometrium) occurs in small patches in sites outside the womb. It can sometimes be found in the muscle of the womb when it is termed adenomyosis. Where it is found at other locations in the body, it is termed endometriosis. The most common sites are on the ovaries, fallopian tubes and the ligaments in the pelvis that support the womb.

engaged: When the head is engaged the widest part of the baby's head has entered your pelvis. This is gauged from examination of your abdomen. Sometimes doctors and midwives write it as the number of fifths of the baby's head that they can feel in your abdomen. When 2/5 or less of the head is in your abdomen the head will be engaged.

Entonox: This is a mixture of 50% nitrous oxide, a pain relieving medicinal gas, and 50% oxygen. It is widely used in the UK for pain relief in labour. It has no harmful effects on the baby. It is sometimes called 'gas and air'. Entonox is its trade name.

epidural analgesia: Epidural analgesia numbs the nerves from your abdomen and lower limbs just before these nerves join the spinal cord. As these nerves carry the pain signals to your brain, numbing these nerves will stop you feeling pain. It involves local anaesthetic being injected into your back, just about waist level.

episiotomy: A cut made at the entrance to the vagina to ease the delivery of the baby's head.

ergometrine: A medication given to cause intense contraction of the womb after delivery to prevent or control bleeding from the womb.

estimated date of delivery (EDD): The EDD is 40 weeks after the first day of the last menstrual period in women with a regular 28-day cycle, or 38 weeks from the date of conception.

external cephalic version (ECV): When a breech baby is turned round in the womb by the doctor gently pressing on the abdomen to change the way the baby is lying. This can manoeuvre the baby so that it is head down instead of bottom down.

face presentation: When a baby, coming head first, has its neck arched back so that its face is leading the way down the birth canal. It is uncommon and only occurs in around 1 in every 500 deliveries. Face presentations can sometimes deliver naturally if the chin is pointing towards your abdomen.

fallopian tube: A tube running from each corner of the womb to the ovaries, which picks up the egg released by the ovary and transports it to the womb. Fertilisation of the egg occurs in the fallopian tube.

fibroid: A benign lump of muscle in your womb. It can sometimes cause your periods to be heavy simply because it makes the womb bigger so that there is more endometrium to shed at each period

foetal alcohol syndrome: A characteristic syndrome in the baby due to extremely high consumption of alcohol on a regular basis in pregnancy by the mother. Foetal alcohol syndrome has several features: the baby will be small; there may be abnormalities in the brain and nervous system, affecting development and intellectual ability; there may also be physical abnormalities such as a short, up-turned nose, receding forehead and chin, and asymmetrical ears, causing a characteristic facial deformity.

foetus: See embryo.

folic acid: An important member of the B vitamin family (vitamin B9). It is soluble in water and is stored mainly in the liver. Folic acid is essential for the production of healthy red blood cells, which carry oxygen round the body. An adequate folic acid intake is also essential for the formation of the developing baby as a deficiency can result in neural tube defects.

forceps delivery: Forceps are metal instruments that look like large tongs or spoons. They are curved to fit snugly around the baby's head. The two sides or blades of the forceps come apart. Each blade is inserted separately into the vagina and then joined together when they are in place round the baby's head. The doctor will pull gently on the forceps while you are pushing with contractions to assist the delivery of your baby. Sometimes abbreviated to MCFD or LCFD, meaning mid or low cavity forceps delivery respectively. This indicates how high the baby's head was in the pelvis when the forceps were used.

formula milk: Artificial milk for bottle-feeding babies that contains similar total amounts of carbohydrates, fats and protein as breast milk. However, the composition of the fats is different.

fundal height: A measurement of the size of the womb. The distance from the top of the pubic bone to the top of the uterine fundus, the higest part of the womb, is measured in centimetres.

fundus: The top of the womb.

gas and air: see Entonox.

genetic condition: A condition due to a mistake or mutation in the genetic code on a chromosome. The gene can be passed from parent to child. An example of a genetic condition is sickle-cell anaemia, in which there is an abnormality in the gene controlling the formation of the red blood cells that carry oxygen around the body.

genetic counselling: Counselling aimed at determining the risk you run of passing on an inherited disease to your child.

German measles: See rubella.

gestational diabetes: A form of diabetes that occurs only in pregnancy when the body is not able to make enough insulin to cope with the extra demands of pregnancy. Gestational diabetes usually improves when the pregnancy ends, although some women who develop gestational diabetes will become overtly diabetic in later life.

glucose tolerance test: A test where the mother is given a glucose drink and the blood levels of glucose measured after it. This screens for types of diabetes.

heartburn: A symptom that occurs when the acid secretions normally present in the stomach are pushed into the lower part of the gullet (or oesophagus). As the gullet is not designed to contain acid secretions a burning sensation is felt behind the lower part of the breastbone.

heel prick: A skin prick on the baby's heel to obtain a small blood sample.

HELLP syndrome: A very severe form of pre-eclampsia where the liver and blood systems are upset by the disturbance in the blood vessels. This syndrome consists of *h*aemolysis, *e*levated *l*iver enzymes and *l*ow *p*latelets. These features make up the acronym HELLP. Haemolysis is the breakdown of the red blood cells that carry oxygen round the body. Elevated liver enzymes are substances that increase in the blood when the liver is damaged. Platelets are small cells that circulate in the blood, which are important for making blood clot. Platelets are reduced in HELLP syndrome.

heparin: A specific medication that reduces the ability of the blood to clot and which is used to prevent or treat venous thrombosis.

hepatitis: Viral infection of the liver. The two main types of viral hepatitis are hepatitis C and hepatitis B. After the liver infection has subsided some people continue to carry the virus in their body and this can sometimes be passed to the baby during pregnancy and delivery.

herpes virus: The herpes simplex virus is responsible for problems like cold sores and genital herpes.

high blood pressure: See hypertension.

HIV infection: HIV (human immuno-deficiency virus), sometimes referred to as the AIDS virus, is a virus that attacks the body's immune system. It can be acquired sexually or through the blood such as when contaminated needles are shared between intravenous drug abusers. HIV progressively attacks the immune system until it is too weak to cope with infection. When infections or certain tumours occur because of the damage to the immune system this is called AIDS (acquired immune deficiency syndrome).

human chorionic gonadotrophin (hCG): A specific pregnancy hormone, made only by the afterbirth (placenta). It passes from the afterbirth into your circulation. It then passes through your kidneys and is found in your urine in early pregnancy. Pregnancy tests measure hCG in urine or blood.

hydrocephalus: A condition that, if untreated, leads to excess fluid accumulating in the brain.

hyperemesis gravidarum: A very severe form of morning sickness.

hypertension: High blood pressure, where the pressure of the blood flowing through the arteries is higher than normal.

hypotension: Low blood pressure, where the pressure of the blood flowing through the arteries is lower than normal.

hypoglycaemia: Low levels of blood sugar.

hypothermia: Low body temperature.

incubator: A special cot that allows the baby to be kept at a constant temperature because newborn and especially premature babies are vulnerable to cold as they lose heat easily. The baby may also be attached to monitors that constantly provide the nurses and doctors with a check on the baby's condition.

induction of labour: Where labour is started medically before it starts spontaneously.

inherited disorder: A disorder passed from parent to child due to an abnormality or mistake in a gene on a chromosome or an extra or missing chromosome.

intracytoplasmic sperm injection (ICSI): An assisted conception technique using direct injection of a single sperm into the egg. As with IVF, eggs are obtained by stimulation of the ovaries with hormones called gonadotrophins to bring about multiple egg production and the eggs are collected in the same way. ICSI is the best treatment in cases where the sperm count is very low or where the sperm fail to move properly. Where there is an obstruction to sperm getting to the penis, sperm can be taken surgically from the testicles and used in ICSI.

intravenous drip: Fluid administered through a plastic needle inserted into a vein.

intraventricular haemorrhage (IVH): Bleeding into or around spaces in the brain that are normally filled with fluid.

iron: A mineral essential for the formation of red blood cells that carry oxygen round the body.

IVF: In vitro fertilisation, an assisted conception technique that was developed to treat tubal blockage but it is now also used for couples with unexplained infertility and in some couples where there are problems with the sperm count. IVF involves stimulation of the ovaries with hormones to stimulate multiple egg production. The response of the ovaries to stimulation is checked by ultrasound and sometimes also by measuring hormone levels in the blood. When the eggs have reached maturity, they are retrieved. This is done by passing a needle through the vagina into the ovary, while the woman is under sedation. The needle is guided into position using an ultrasound scan, then the eggs are sucked down the needle and collected. The eggs are incubated with sperm from the woman's partner. Fertilised eggs are transferred to the womb through the cervix two days later.

intrauterine growth restriction (IUGR): Where a baby is smaller than it should be for the stage in pregnancy. Due to its growth being impaired as a consequence of an insufficient supply of nutrients for the baby's needs because of the placenta being damaged.

jaundice: Yellow discoloration of the skin and the whites of the eyes. This is caused by the liver having difficulty in excreting a yellow pigment called bilirubin. The bilirubin will therefore build up in the skin. Bilirubin is produced when the red blood cells that carry oxygen get old and are broken down.

kick chart: A record of how frequently the mother feels the baby move.

Kliehauer test: A test to measure the amount of foetal blood in the mother's system.

lactoferrin: A substance found in breast milk that binds iron in food while in the bowel. The iron is then not available for bacteria in the bowel. As certain bacteria need iron, lactoferrin acts as a natural antibacterial agent.

laparoscopy: A surgical procedure, which usually requires general anaesthesia. A laparoscope (a telescope-like instrument) is inserted below the navel (umbilicus) so that the surgeon can view the womb, fallopian tubes and ovaries.

large for dates: The size of the womb is bigger than would be expected for your stage in pregnancy.

lie: The lie is the relationship of the long axis of the baby to the long axis of the womb. The normal lie is longitudinal when the baby is lying vertically in the womb.

linea nigra: A thin pigmented line running from the pubic area to the navel (umbilicus) that develops during pregnancy.

listeria: A bacteria called *Listeria moncytogenes* can occasionally cause infection in pregnancy. Infection usually occurs by mouth from contaminated food. This type of bacteria is present in many foods particularly soft cheeses made from unpasteurised milk. It can multiply readily at low temperature but is destroyed by cooking. Infection with listeria during pregnancy is important as it may lead to miscarriage or loss of the pregnancy. It is also a cause of premature labour. The baby can be infected and the infection can be a life-threatening problem. Women with listeria infection have a fever and feel flu-like. It can mimic a severe urinary tract infection when it first presents. Treatment is with intravenous antibiotics.

lochia: The vaginal discharge that occurs after having a baby. Initially the vaginal discharge or lochia will be bloodstained and will sometimes have some small clots. After a few days the discharge will become a brown-red colour then will be more pink in colour as the amount of blood in it declines. After about two weeks the pink coloured discharge will be replaced by a white or cream coloured discharge, which will last for a further two to four weeks.

macrosomia: The baby is very much bigger than average.

mastitis: Inflammation of the breast. This can be caused by a blocked milk duct, which leads to a build up of milk behind it. The breast will often develop firm, tender and inflamed patches. Because the milk is stagnant, infection can occur when bacteria settle in the stagnant milk.

meconium: The content of the baby's bowel.

meconium aspiration: The situation where meconium is inhaled into the baby's lungs. Once in the lungs, meconium can block some of the small tubes taking air in and this can lead to breathing difficulties. It can also irritate the lung tissues.

membrane sweep: A technique to help labour start. Membrane sweeping can be performed during an internal examination to determine the state of the cervix prior to planning an induction of labour. A finger is placed just inside the cervix and a circular, sweeping movement made to separate the membranes in front of the baby's head from the cervix.

miscarriage: The spontaneous loss of a pregnancy before the 24th week of pregnancy.

Montgomery's tubercles: Small raised glands that develop in the pigmented skin round the nipple, the areola, in pregnancy. These little glands produce an oily secretion that lubricates and protects the skin of the nipples during breast-feeding.

morning sickness: Nausea and vomiting associated with pregnancy. This is usually limited to the first 14 weeks of pregnancy. Morning sickness is a misleading name as it can occur at any time of day. It may be worse when the stomach is empty, hence the association with morning.

morphine: See opiates.

multiparous: A women who has had more than one pregnancy and delivery. A 'grand multipara' is a woman with four or more previous pregnancies and deliveries.

necrotising enterocolitis (NEC): A bowel problem that premature or very low birthweight babies are more vulnerable to as their bowel is immature.

neonatal death: The death of a baby occurring in the first 28 days of life

neural tube defect: The neural tube is the part of the developing embryo that will eventually become the brain and the spinal cord. It forms at about four weeks after conception. Disorders such as spina bifida are neural tube defects.

nuchal ultrasound scan: Nuchal means neck, so a nuchal scan looks at the baby's neck. This scan can be performed at around 10–14 weeks. This test helps screen for Down's syndrome because Down's syndrome babies have a thicker pad of tissue at the back of their neck than babies without Down's syndrome.

occipito-anterior position: See position.

occipito-posterior position: See position.

occipito-transverse position: See position.

oedema: Swelling of the soft tissues, such as round the ankles, due to fluid retention.

oestriol: A type of oestrogen made by the placenta.

oestrogen: A female hormone important for controlling the growth of the lining of the womb (the endometrium).

opiates: Medications of the morphine family. They are very potent painkillers. The best known and most widely used are morphine, diamorphine and pethidine.

ovarian cyst: A fluid-filled or solid growth on the ovary.

ovaries: The female organs that produce eggs.

ovulation: Release of a mature egg from the ovary.

ovulation prediction kit: A test that can help establish when ovulation occurs in the menstrual cycle.

oxytocin: A natural hormone that your body makes. It stimulates the womb to contract and is used to induce or speed up labour. It is given through a drip in your arm. The amount you get is carefully controlled with a pump to ensure you do not get too much or too little. Oxytocin will make the womb contract more strongly.

palmer erythema: Over half of all women will develop red palms in pregnancy. This is called palmer erythema. It is a normal feature of pregnancy.

palpating the uterus: When the doctor or midwife examines your abdomen by moving their hands over it to determine the size, lie and presentation of the baby.

parvovirus: Infection with human parvovirus is relatively common in children. It causes a condition called *erythema infectiosum*. It is sometimes called 'slapped cheek' syndrome due to the characteristic rash on the face that looks like a slapped cheek. It is unusual for parvovirus to cause a problem in pregnancy, but infection in early pregnancy has been linked to miscarriage and in late pregnancy infection can cause severe anaemia in about 3 in every 100 babies infected. It does not appear to cause any congenital abnormality.

pelvic diastasis: Softening of the ligaments holding the bones of the pelvis together during pregnancy leading to excessive mobility of the pelvic bones, in particular at the joint at the front of the pelvis, called the symphysis pubis. This leads to pain on movement.

pelvic examination: An internal examination of the pelvic organs carried out by the doctor by placing usually two fingers in the vagina and a hand on the abdomen.

pelvic floor: A sheet of muscle and fibrous tissue lying across the bottom of the pelvis. It supports the pelvic organs including the bladder, part of the bowel and the womb. The vagina, bowel and urethra (the tube that takes urine from the bladder to the outside) all pass through it. The pelvic floor therefore helps control of your bladder and bowel function.

pelvic floor exercises: Exercises to strengthen the pelvic floor during pregnancy and following delivery.

perineum: The area of skin between the vagina and anus.

pethidine: See opiates.

phenylketonuria: A genetic disorder found in only about 1 in every 16,000 babies. Babies with this condition are not able to metabolise properly a substance called phenylalanine. This is a serious condition as it causes an accumulation of this substance in the bloodstream, which in turn can lead to brain damage. This damage can be prevented with a special diet that can allow affected babies to develop normally.

pinard stethoscope: A trumpet-like device held against the abdomen to listen to the baby's heartbeat.

placenta: The placenta is a disc-shaped organ that is essentially a rich network of blood vessels derived from the foetus. It implants into the wall of the womb in very early pregnancy and is linked to the foetus by the umbilical cord. The placenta is able to extract oxygen and nutrients from the mother's blood. The oxygen and nutrients are then transported to the foetus through its bloodstream. Waste products produced by the foetus are transferred from the placenta to the mother's blood and the mother then excretes these for the foetus through her lungs and kidneys.

placenta praevia: Placenta praevia is the situation where the afterbirth lies wholly or partly in the lower part of the womb close to or sometimes covering the cervix or neck of the womb.

placental abruption: See abruption.

placental insufficiency: Damage to the afterbirth that prevents it from providing enough nutrients to the developing baby.

polyhydramnios: Excess amniotic fluid round the baby.

position: Position describes the way that the baby's head is facing. Doctors always indicate where the back of the baby's head is relative to the mother's back. The most posterior part of the baby's skull is called the occiput. So if the back of the baby's head points to your abdomen, this is called occipito-anterior position. This is the most common position of the head for delivery. If the back of the baby's head is towards your back this is the occipito-posterior position. If the back of the baby's head is towards your side this is the occipito-transverse position.

postnatal: The period after the birth of the baby.

postnatal depression (PND): Severe or persistent form of depression that occurs after delivery of the baby.

post-partum haemorrhage: Heavy bleeding from the womb or vagina that occurs after delivery.

pre-eclampsia: A complication of pregnancy where high blood pressure is combined with abnormally high levels of protein in the urine. This disorder can also affect other organs such as the liver and placenta.

premature labour: Labour starting before 37 completed weeks of pregnancy.

premature pre-labour rupture of the membranes (PROM): When the waters break before 37 weeks completed weeks of pregnancy and before labour starts.

presentation: The presentation is the part of the foetus that is leading into the mother's pelvis. The most common presentation is cephalic, where the baby enters the mother's pelvis head first. Sometimes this is called a vertex presentation, which indicates that the neck is bent forwards and the top of the baby's head – the so-called vertex – is leading. When the baby is coming bottom first this is known as a breech presentation.

primigravida: A woman in her first pregnancy.

progesterone: A female hormone important in regulating the growth of the lining of the womb (the endometrium) and which makes it suitable for the fertilised egg to implant.

prostaglandin: A natural substance produced prior to and during labour that causes the cervix to soften and the womb to contract. It can also be given as a medication to induce labour.

protein level in urine: See proteinuria.

proteinuria: Protein in the urine. This is easily diagnosed on 'dipstick' testing of the urine. The dipsticks give a reading for protein in the urine of 'none, trace, +, ++, +++, or ++++'. Small amounts of protein can be found in the urine with a bladder infection or if a small amount of vaginal discharge gets into the urine specimen. If the reading is '++' or more and the blood pressure is elevated this usually indicates pre-eclampsia. Sometimes the doctor will send a urine specimen to the laboratory to get an accurate measure of the amount of protein in the urine.

puerperium: The first six weeks after the delivery.

quickening: The first movements of the baby usually felt at about 18–20 weeks.

recurrent miscarriage: A series of spontaneous pregnancy losses before 24 weeks of pregnancy.

rhesus blood group: There are two main parts to blood group typing. The first is the ABO type. This can be group A, B, AB or O. The second major type is rhesus. You can be rhesus negative or positive. Some 85% of people are rhesus positive and 15% are rhesus negative.

respiratory distress syndrome (RDS): A syndrome that occurs in premature babies as their lungs have not developed fully through to maturity. With RDS the baby's lungs do not make enough of a substance called surfactant. Surfactant is in the fluid that forms a very thin layer over the inside surface of the lung and is important in keeping the lungs open. This allows easy entry of air into the lungs. A baby with RDS will have difficulty breathing, taking rapid breaths – usually more than 60 breaths a minute – grunting as it breaths with flaring of the nostrils.

rubella: Rubella, better known as German measles, is a very common infection in children. It is usually a mild condition with a transient rash, and swelling of the lymph glands behind the ears. It is caught by airborne droplet spread when infected peoples cough or sneeze. German measles if caught, particularly in the first three months of pregnancy, can cause malformations in the baby. These may include deafness, blindness and heart problems. It can only be caught if the mother is not immune to it. Most women have either had rubella in childhood or been immunised against it and so are immune.

ruptured membranes: The membranes form the bag of amniotic fluid in which the baby grows and develops. The membranes tend to break or rupture when the neck of the womb opens. This is due to weakening of the membranes after the cervix opens, coupled with the force of the contractions which cause the membranes to burst and the amniotic fluid to be released. Sometimes the membranes rupture before labour starts and sometimes the labour may be quite advanced before the membranes rupture. The membranes can also be ruptured or broken by the doctor or midwife when doing an internal examination. This can speed up the labour.

scans: See ultrasound scan.

show: A show is the plug of thick mucus, like jelly, that 'seals' the cervix during pregnancy. When the cervix thins-out and starts to dilate (open) as labour approaches, the plug falls out. The release of this plug of mucus, which is usually blood stained, into your vagina is called the show.

sickle-cell anaemia: An inherited condition that affects the red blood cells and is most commonly found in people of African origin. It is so-called because the red blood cells, which carry oxygen around the body, are crescent-shaped instead of disc-shaped, as they would be normally. When there is a shortage of oxygen or when there is an infection in the body, these red blood cells clump together and so prevent the smooth flow of blood. As well as causing chronic anaemia, the condition can give rise to bone pain, kidney upset and lung problems.

slapped cheek syndrome: See parvovirus.

slow progress in labour: An insufficient rate of cervical dilatation and/or descent of the head through the pelvis in labour.

small-for-dates baby: The size of the baby is smaller than would be expected for the stage in pregnancy.

special care baby unit (SCBU): Specialist units that offer a range of care for the baby from observation for minor problems through to intensive care of the small number of babies who are seriously ill. These units have specialist nurses and doctors, with particular expertise in the treatment of newborn babies.

spina bifida: A defect in which part of one or more vertebrae, the bones making up the spine, fails to develop completely, leaving a portion of the nervous tissue in the spinal cord exposed, which leads to damage of the nerves. This defect can occur anywhere in the baby's spine but is most commonly seen in the lower back. The condition varies in severity and much depends on where the defect is and how much of the nervous tissue is exposed.

station: A description of how far into the pelvis the baby's head has descended. It is assessed during a vaginal examination. The level of the head is gauged relative to a bony prominence on either side of the pelvis called the ischial spines. These are easily felt during the examination.

steroid injections: Medication (usually either Betamethasone or Dexamethasone) given by injections to the mother before a premature delivery to accelerate the maturity of the baby's lungs and so reduce the risk of complications.

stillbirth: Delivery of a baby after 24 weeks of pregnancy where the baby has not shown any sign of life after delivery.

systemic lupus erythematosis (SLE): A connective tissue disease affecting the joints, skin, kidneys and other organs.

TENS machine: a battery-operated device about the size of a cigarette packet connected to two pairs or pads (electrodes) that are taped to a woman's back in early labour. The first pair is placed about halfway up the back on either side of the spine and the second pair is taped on either side of the bottom of the woman's back, just above the buttocks. The device sends electrical impulses through the skin to the nerves. This blocks the perception of pain from the womb by the brain.

thalassaemia: A genetic condition in which there is an abnormality in the gene controlling the production of red blood cells, leading to varying degrees of anaemia.

threatened miscarriage: Painless vaginal bleeding from the site of the placenta in early pregnancy. The bleeding is often not severe enough to trouble the pregnancy. It can settle spontaneously and the pregnancy will continue normally.

thrush: Thrush is caused by an overgrowth of a fungal organism called candida. It causes a thick, white and curd like vaginal discharge. It is sometimes described as looking like cottage cheese. It does not usually have any odour. A vulval itch is very common. Thrush is easily treated with a course of anti-fungal pessaries and creams that are safe to use in pregnancy.

toxoplasma: Toxoplasma is an organism called a protozoan that usually lives in cats. It is excreted in cat faeces so litter trays are potentially a source of infection. Contaminated meat and soiled vegetables are also a source of infection. This infection has many features in common with rubella and cytomegalovirus infection. Toxoplasma infection in adults is usually symptomless or mild. Overall about 70% of infected babies have no problem, around 10% will have eye problems, and the remainder will have similar problems to those seen with rubella.

transient tachypneoa: A temporary problem with rapid breathing in a newborn baby. This condition is due to there being too much fluid on the lungs after the baby is born.

transverse lie: The baby lies across the womb so that its feet are on one side of the abdomen and its head is on the other side. This means that the shoulder is often leading the way into the birth canal. It is impossible for the baby to be delivered vaginally when lying this way.

triple test: Blood test to screen for the risk of problems such as Down's syndrome and spina bifida in the baby by measuring the levels of three chemicals in the mother's blood (sometimes done by the 'double test' where only two chemicals are measured.

twin-to-twin transfusion syndrome: This can occur when twins share the same placenta, and blood vessels from each twin merge in the placenta in such a way that one twin loses blood from its circulation while the other gains it. The 'donor' twin will usually have impaired growth and anaemia as it is giving a lot of its blood to the other twin. The 'recipient' twin may have problems from overload of its circulation and high blood pressure.

ultrasound scan: A technique using very high frequency sound waves that can provide accurate images of the baby while in the womb.

umbilicus: The navel. This is the site where the umbilical cord attaches to the baby.

unstable lie: Where the baby does not settle head or bottom down, but keeps changing. It might be transverse one day, head down the next and breech the next. This can cause problems if labour starts, especially if the baby is lying transversely at the time, as it is impossible for a baby to deliver vaginally when it is lying this way.

vaginal examination: Examination performed during labour to asses how dilated the cervix is and how low in the pelvis the baby's head is. It is performed before labour to assess how 'ripe'the cervix is for labour.

venous thrombosis: A blood clot in a vein, usually in the deep veins of the leg.

ventouse delivery: A ventouse is an instrument that uses suction to assist vaginal delivery of the baby. A suction cup is inserted into the vagina and placed over the crown of the baby's head. The cup is attached by a piece of tubing to a vacuum machine. The machine is switched on and the suction cup becomes firmly applied to the baby's head because of the vacuum. The doctor gently pulls on the suction cup while the mother pushes with contractions.

vernix: A white, greasy substance that protects the skin of the baby while in the womb surrounded by fluid.

vertex: The crown of the baby's head.

vitamin K: A vitamin important for the production of clotting factors from the liver.

Wharton's jelly: a jelly-like substance encasing the blood vessels in the umbilical cord.

Useful addresses

Health in pregnancy

Action on Pre-eclampsia (APEC)
31–33 College Road
Harrow
Middlesex
HA1 1EJ
Tel: 020 8427 4217

Acupuncture
The British Acupuncture Council
Park House
206–208 Latimer Road
London W10 6RE
Tel: 020 8735 0400
(Putting you in touch with qualified practitioners.)

The Anaphylaxis Campaign
Tel: 01252 542029

Antenatal Results and Choices (ARC)
73 Charlotte Street
London W1T 4PN
Helpline: 020 7631 0285
Email: arcsatfa@aol.com
Website: www.arc-uk.org
(A national charity providing non-directive support and information to parents throughout the antenatal testing process, aimed at helping parents arrive at the most appropriate decision for them in the context of their family life.)

Aromatherapy
The International Society of Professional Aromatherapists
Tel: 01455 637987
The Register of Qualified Aromatherapists
Tel: 01235 227957
(Putting you in touch with qualified practitioners.)

The British Allergy Foundation
Tel: 020 8303 8525
(Both these organisations give support and guidance to people faced with allergy problems.)

Diabetes UK
(formerly The British Diabetic Association)
Careline:
Tel: 020 7636 6112 (Monday to Friday, 9am–4pm)
Text: 020 7462 2757
Email: careline@diabetes.org.uk
Website: www.diabetes.org.uk
(The leading charity working for people with diabetes, funding research and campaigning for and helping people to live with the condition.)

Epilepsy Action
Freephone Helpline from the UK:
0808 800 5050
Website: www.epilepsy.org.uk
(Offers advice and information over the phone.)

Family Planning Association (FPA)
2–12 Pentonville Road
London N1 9FP
Tel: 020 7837 5432
Helpline: 0845 310 1334
Mon–Fri, 9am–7pm
www.fpa.org.uk
(Trained staff providing confidential advice.)

General Osteopathic Council
Tel: 020 7357 6655
For further information about osteopathy and details of osteopaths in your area.
(Putting you in touch with qualified practitioners.)

Homoeopathy
The British Homoeopathic Association
27a Devonshire Street
London W1N 1RJ
Tel: 020 7935 2163
(Putting you in touch with qualified practitioners.)

mom-e.com
Website: www.mom-e.com
(Mom-e is your access to 'knowledge'. The aim of the site is to inform couples about pregnancy in a medically accurate and easily digestible way. Mom-e presents a dynamic approach to the subject with topical issues and features being added to the existing large base of knowledge.)

Royal College of Midwives
15 Mansfield Street
London W1G 9NH.
Website: www.rcm.org.uk
(The voice of midwifery, providing excellence in professional leadership, education, influence and representation for and on behalf of midwives.)

Royal College of Obstetricians and Gynaecologists
27 Sussex Place
Regent's Park
London NW1 4RG
Tel: 020 7772 6200
Website: www.rcog.org.uk
(Putting you in touch with qualified practitioners.)

Stopping smoking/Quitline
Tel: 0800 0022 00
Website:
www.healthnet.org.uk/quit/guide
(Telephone counselling for those who are trying to stop smoking. Puts you in touch with local support groups.)

Toxoplasma infection
Tel: 020 7593 1150
(Up-to-date information, plus advice for women who may have been infected with toxoplasma infection during pregnancy.)

Wellbeing
27 Sussex Place
Regent's Park
London NW1 4SP
Tel: 020 7772 6400
Mon–Fri, 9am–5pm
Sainsbury's/Wellbeing Eating for
Pregnancy Helpline: 0845 130 3646
Mon–Fri, 10am–4pm
www.wellbeing.org.uk
(For advice on what to eat during
pregnancy and while breast-feeding.)

Infertility

National Infertility Support Network
(CHILD)
Tel: 01424 732361
Website: www.child.org.uk
(A registered charity offering support
to couples undergoing infertility
treatments or facing infertility.)

Human Fertilisation and Embryo
Authority (HFEA)
Paxton House
30 Artillery Lane
London E1 7LS
Tel: 0207 377 5077 (9.30am to
5.30pm, Monday to Friday)
Email: admin@hfea.gov.uk
Website: www.hfea.gov.uk
(A statutory body that regulates,
licenses and collects data on fertility
treatments such as IVF and donor
insemination, as well as human
embryo research, in the UK.)

UK National Fertility Association
(iSSUE)
114 Lichfield St
Walsall
WS1 1SZ
Tel: 01922 722888
Information line: 09050 280 300
(Premium Rate Line, all calls cost
25p per minute)
Website: www.issue.co.uk
(iSSUE helps people through the
infertility maze by providing
information, counselling and
support.)

Planning the birth

Active Birth Centre
25 Bickerton Road
London N19 5JT
Tel: 020 7482 5554
Mon–Fri, 9.30am–5.30pm
Sat, 10am–4pm
www.activebirthcentre.com
(Pre- and postnatal yoga classes,
preparation for birth and waterbirth
pool hire.)

Independent Midwives Association
The Wessex Maternity Centre
Mansbridge Road
West End
Southampton
SO18 3HW
www.independentmidwives.org.uk
(Enclose an A5 SAE to receive a
register of all independent midwives
in the UK.)

National Childbirth Trust (NCT)
Alexandra House
Oldham Terrace
Acton
London W3 6NH
Tel: 0870 444 8707
Mon–Thurs, 9am–5pm
Fri, 9am–4pm
Breast-feeding Helpline: 0870 444
8708
Every day, 8am–10pm
www.nctpregnancyandbabycare.com
(Organises antenatal classes. Offers
breast-feeding advice. Postnatal
depression counsellors.)

NHS Direct
Tel: 0845 4647 (24-hours)
www.nhsdirect.nhs.uk
(Providing nurse advice and
confidential health information.)

Pregnancy Crisis Centre
Tel: 01474 534 404
(Offering support and advice for
those who are thinking about an
abortion or have had one.)

Twins and multiple births

Multiple Births Foundation
Tel: 020 8383 3519
(Telephone counselling.)

Twins and Multiple Births
Association (TAMBA)
2 The Willows
Gardner Road
Guildford
Surrey GU1 4PG
Tel: 0870 770 3305
Mon–Fri, 9am–4pm
Helpline: 01732 868 000
Mon–Fri, 7–11pm
Weekends, 10am–11pm
www.tamba.org.uk
(Provides information and support
networks for families of twins,
triplets and more.)

Maternity rights at work

Daycare Trust
Shoreditch Town Hall Annexe
380 Old Street
London EC1V 9LT
Tel: 020 7739 2866
(National charity campaigning to
improve conditions for working
parents.)

Maternity Alliance
45 Beech Street
London EC2P 2XL
Tel: 020 7588 8582
Mon and Thurs, 10.30am–12.30pm
Tues, 6pm–8pm
Wed, 9.30–11.30am
www.maternityalliance.org.uk
(Information on maternity services,
benefits and rights at work.)

Parents at Work
45 Beech Street
London EC2Y 8AD
Tel: 020 7628 3565 (answer machine)
(For advice and information on
childcare and employment issues
relating to pregnancy and working
parents.)

Useful addresses

Premature babies

Baby Life Support Systems (BLISS)
68 South Lambeth Road
London SW8 1RL
Tel: 0870 770 0337
Mon–Fri, 9am–5.30pm
Helpline: 0500 618 140
Mon–Fri, 10am–5pm
www.bliss.org.uk
(A national charity offering support
and information for the families of
sick newborn babies.)

Tommy's The Baby Charity
1 Kennington Road
London SE1 7RR
Tel: 020 7620 0188
Mon–Fri, 9am–5.30pm
www.tommys.org
(A charity that raises funds for
research into prematurity and
provides advice on pregnancy and
premature birth.)

Baby loss

The Miscarriage Association
Clayton Hospital
Northgate
Wakefield
West Yorkshire
WF1 3JS
Tel: 01924 200799
Mon–Fri, 9am–4pm
www.miscarriageassociation.org.uk
(Advice and support for women who
have had or are experiencing a
miscarriage. Contact with other local
groups.)

Scottish Care and Information on
Miscarriage (SCIM)
41 Merryland Street
Govan
Glasgow G51 2QG
Tel: 0141 445 3727 (9.30am to
4.30pm, Monday–Friday)
Email: scim@scim.fsworld.co.uk
Website:
www.connectedscotland.org.uk/
scimnet
(Offers person-centred counselling
and telephone support from March
2004.)

Scottish Cot Death Trust
Royal Hospital for Sick Children
Yorkhill
Glasgow G3 8SJ
Scotland
Tel: 0141 357 3946
Website:
www.gla.ac.uk/departments/
childhealth/SCDT
(Parent support is the most
important element of the Trust's
work. The Trust has a wide national
network of 'befrienders' – parents
who have suffered a cot death in the
past and who are now willing to
provide comfort and encouragement
to newly bereaved parents.)

Stillbirth and Neonatal Death Scoiety
(SANDS)
28 Portland Place
London W1N 4DE
Tel: 020 7436 5881
Mon–Fri, 10am–5pm
Information and support groups.

Foundation for the Study of Infant
Deaths
Artillery House
11–19 Artillery Row
London SW1P 1RT
Helpline: 0870 787 0554
(9am–11pm)
www.sids.org.uk/fsid
(Support for bereaved parents and
contact with local groups of other
bereaved parents.)

Special care and special needs

Association for Spina Bifida and
Hydrocephalus
ASBAH House
42 Park Road
Peterborough
PE1 2UQ
Tel: 01733 555988

Birth Defects Foundation
Martindale
Hawksgreen
Cannock
Staffordshire
WS11 2XN

Tel: 01543 464800
Mon–Fri, 9.30am–3pm
Enquiries@birthdefects.co.uk
www.birthdefects.co.uk
(Support and information.)

Caesarean Support Network
55 Cooil Drive
Douglas
Isle of Man
IM2 2HF
Tel: 01624 661269
Every day, 6pm–10pm

Cleft Lip and Palate Association
(CLAPA)
235-237 Finchley Road
London NW3 6LS
Tel: 020 7431 0033

Contact-a-Family
Tel: 020 7383 3555
(Helping families of children with
'special needs'.)

Disabled Parents Network
PO Box 5876
Towcester
NN12 7ZN
(Supporting pregnancy and
parenthood for people with
disabilities.)

Down's Syndrome Association
155 Mitcham Road
London SW17 9PG
Tel: 020 8682 4001
(Support and information.)

The Osteopathic Centre For Children
109 Harley Street
London W1G 6AN
Tel: 020 7486 6160
www.occ.uk.com
(Tries to help provide paediatric
osteopathy for all children.)

SCOPE
6 Market Road
London N7 9PW
Tel: 020 7619 7100 or 0808 800 3333
Mon–Fri, 9am–9pm
Sat–Sun, 2pm–6pm
(Support and information for children
with cerebral palsy.)

Sickle Cell Society
54 Sattion Road
Harlesden
London NW10 4UA
Tel: 020 8691 7795 or 020 8961 4006
(A national charity for sufferers of
sickle cell.)

Parent support

Association for Post-Natal Illness
(APNI)
25 Jerdan Place
Fulham
London SW6 1BE
Tel. 020 7000 0068

Cry-sis
See Serene, below

Fathers Direct
Tel: 020 7920 9491 (Mon–Fri,
10am–6pm)
www.fathersdirect.com
(The national information centre for
fatherhood.)

Gingerbread Association for One-
Parent Families
1st Floor
7 Sovereign Close
Sovereign Court
London E1W 3HW
Tel: 020 7488 9300
Helpline: 0800 018 4318
Mon–Fri, 9am–5pm
www.gingerbread.org.uk
(Help, advice and contact with other
lone parents.)

Home-Start
2 Salisbury Road
Leicester
LE1 7QR
Tel: 0116 233 9955
(Trained volunteers give support if
you've just had a baby and are
under stress.)

The National Childbirth Trust
(see above)
(Runs local postnatal groups in all
areas where new parents can get to
know each other.)

Meet-a-Mum Association
Waterside Centre
25 Avenue Rd
London SE25 4DX
Tel: 020 8768 0123
Weekdays, 7–10pm
www.mama.org.uk
(Concerned with helping mothers
who feel depressed and isolated
when their babies are born.)

National Council for One Parent
Families
255 Kentish Town Road
London NW5 2LX
Tel: 0800 018 5026
Mon–Fri, 9am–5pm
www.oneparentfamilies.org.uk
(Provides free information and advice
for people bringing up children on
their own.)

Parentline Plus
520 Highgate Studios
53 79 Highgate Road
Kentish Town
London NW5 1TL
Tel: 0808 800 2222
www.parentlineplus.org.uk
(Help and information for parents
concerning a range of topics.)

Positively Women
347-349 City Road
London EC1V 1LR
Tel: 020 7713 0222
(Support for women with HIV and
AIDS and their families.)

Serene (formerly known as Cry-sis)
Helpline: 020 7404 5011
Every day, 8am–11pm
www.our-space.co.uk/serene.htm
(Provides emotional support and
practical advice to parents dealing
with excessive crying, demanding
behaviour and sleep problems.)

Breast-feeding

Association of Breastfeeding
Mothers
PO Box 207
Bridgewater TA6 7YT
Tel: 020 7813 1481 (24-hours)
(Counsellors offering
advice/information over the phone.)

Breastfeeding Network
Supporterline
Tel: 0870 900 8787
Every day, 9.30am–9.30pm
www.breastfeeding.co.uk/bfn
(Independent support and
information about breast-feeding.)

La Leche League
BM3424
London WC1N 3XX
Tel: 020 7242 1278
Mon Fri, 9am– 6pm, answering
machine at weekends
www.laleche.org.uk
(Breast-feeding advice, breast pump
hire.)

The National Childbirth Trust
(see above)
(Can put you in touch with a local
NCT breast-feeding counsellor. You
don't need to join the NCT to get
this help.)

Index

Page numbers in *italic* refer to the illustrations

abbreviations, medical 116–19
abdomen: baby's 126–7, *126*
    mother's 101, 266, *269*
abruption, placental 142–3, *143*, 146
acne 70
acupuncture 205, 212
afterbirth *see* placenta
afterpains 265–6
age, and fertility problems 52, 59
AIDS 50, 153–4
ailments 165–8
air travel 92–3
alcohol 15–16, 67, 89
allergies 30–1, 186, 259
alpha-fetoprotein (AFP) blood test 120, 122
amniocentesis 120, 122–3
amniotic fluid 75, *115*
    excess fluid 135
    meconium staining 201, 214
    ruptured membranes 199, 201–2, 231
    twin pregnancies 157
anaemia 30, 32, 33, 67, 95, 108, 109, 147, 171–2, 183
anaesthetics: Caesarean section 241, 242
    epidurals 208–11
animals, toxoplasma 90, 152
antenatal care 106–19
anti-D immunoglobulin 81, 143, 146, 147
antibiotics 81, 148, 149, 153, 154, 173, 236, 263
antibodies 146–7, 177, 259, 260
anticoagulants 187–8, 192–3
antiphospholipid antibodies 83, 176, 177–8
anus: piles 166
    tears 222, 223, 224
Apgar score 247–9
areola 66, 258
aromatherapy 91, 205, 212
aspirin 129, 140–1, 177–8, 189
assisted conception 56–9, *57*, *58*, 155
assisted vaginal delivery 237–40
asthma 31, 46, 172–3, 259

baby: delivery 220–4, *220*
    distress during birth 201, 214
    monitoring in labour 213–17, 228, 231
    newborn baby, 246–64
    second trimester 162–3
    special care 277–85
    third trimester 194–5
    see also foetus
baby blues 271–2
baby clothes 202–3
backache 103, 210–11, 270
baths: after birth 268
    baby 253, *253*
BCG vaccination 255

beta-carotene 29, 34
biophysical profiles 133–5
birth *see* labour; delivery
birth canal 220–2, *220*
birth partners 204–5, 219, 227, 242–3
birth plans 200–1, 227–8
birth positions 218–19, 228
birth weight 124, *125*, 169, 252
birthmarks 285
bladder: catheters 210, 227, 238, 242, 268
    infections 69, 109, 139, 148, 178, 268, 275
bleeding: after delivery 225, 227, 267
    in early pregnancy 76
    ectopic pregnancy 85
    intraventricular haemorrhage 280, 284–5
    in later pregnancy 142–6
    miscarriage 81
    premature labour 235
blighted ovum 77–9, 80
blood: increased volume of 164
    placental insufficiency 128–9, *128*
    transfusions 147, 280
    twin-to-twin transfusion syndrome 157
blood cells 30, 49, 95, 139–40, 146–7, 164
blood clots: intrauterine growth restriction 129
    miscarriage 83, 159
    overweight mothers 170
    the pill and 270–1
    thrombosis 46, 68, 93, 191–3, 275
blood groups 81, 146–7
blood pressure: epidurals 208
    measuring 111, 136
    see also high blood pressure
blood sugar levels, newborn baby 284
blood tests 108, 109, 112, 122, 139, 217
blood vessels: pre-eclampsia 138, 140
    umbilical cord 75
body mass index (BMI) 40–1, 42, 168–9
bottle-feeding 256, 260, 263–4
bowel movements: after delivery 267, 268–70
    baby's 252, 260
bowel problems 173–4, 284
    see also constipation
brain: baby's development 127
    eclampsia 141–2
    hydrocephalus 31, 32, 285
    intraventricular haemorrhage 280, 284–5
bras 66–7
Braxton-Hicks contractions 130, 195, 197, 198
breast-feeding 249, 255–63, *258*
    contraception and 270–1

dieting and 170
    epilepsy and 185
    premature babies 280
breasts: engorgement 259–60
    mastitis 263
    newborn baby's 251
    signs of pregnancy 66–7
breathing: asthma 172–3
    during contractions 205
    during pregnancy 165
    premature babies 160, 181, 194, 236, 279, 280–1
breech presentation 135, 226, 232–3, *233*
    Caesarean section 232, 234
    episiotomy 223
    placenta praevia 144
    recurrence of 159–60
    twin pregnancies 158
brittle bone disease 18
bronchopulmonary dysplasia (BPD) 282–3
brow presentation 234

Caesarean section 240–3
    after effects 274–5
    anaesthetics 241
    birth plans 228
    breech presentation 232, 234
    brow presentation 234
    cord prolapse 237
    diabetic mothers 180–1
    elective 241
    emergency 241
    incision *240*, 242, 243
    overweight mothers 170
    placenta praevia 145–6
    pre-eclampsia 140
    slow labour 232
    twin pregnancies 158–9
    vaginal delivery after 243
caffeine 14, 88–9
calcium 29, 36, 38, 95, 97
candida 70, 149
car travel 94, *94*
carbohydrates 36, 38–9, 97
cardiotocography (CTG) 130–4, *131*, *132*, 214–16
carpal tunnel syndrome 166
catheters, urine 210, 227, 238, 242, 268
cats, toxoplasma 90, 152
cell division 25–7, *26*
cephalic presentation 226
cephalo-pelvic disproportion 232
cervix: dilatation 198, 200, 201, 218, 226
    effacement 197, *197*, 200, 226
    first stage of labour 196–201, *197*
    incompetence 78, 83, 102, 159
    induction of labour 230
    membrane sweep 230–1
    miscarriage 78, 79, 80

placenta praevia 143–6, *145*
  ripening 230, 231
  second stage of labour 196
  smear tests 108, 110, 276
cheese, listeria risk 37, 149
chest infections 173
chicken pox 150–1
childbirth *see* labour; delivery
chloasma 70
chromosomes 17, 25
  disorders 13, 17–20
cleft lip 120, 121, 124, 183, 285
cleft palate 178, 183, 285
clinics, antenatal 106–19
clothes: baby 202–3
  in labour 202
club foot 183
coffee 14, 67, 88–9
coil 22–3, 84, 186, 271
cold sores 151
colitis, ulcerative 174
colostrum 259, 260
complete miscarriage 79, 80
computers 90
conception 12–17, 25–7, *26*, 51–2
  assisted conception 56–9, *57*, *58*
condoms 271
congenital abnormalities 285
  epilepsy and 183–4
  genetic conditions 18–20, 78, 83, 120
  German measles and 150
  twin pregnancies 157
conjoined twins 156
connective tissue disease 174–8
constipation 96, 165–6, 173, 267
contraception 22–3, 270–1, 276
contraction stress CTG test 133
contractions: afterpains 265–6
  Braxton-Hicks 130, 195, 197, 198
  coping with 203, 205
  first stage 196–200
  foetal monitoring 131–3, *132*
  frequency 200
  induction of labour 231
  premature labour 235–6
  second stage 218
  slow labour 232
  third stage 225
convenience foods 38
convulsions *see* fits
cord *see* umbilical cord
cordocentesis 120, 123
corpus luteum cysts 22, 86–7
cot death 90, 254–5, 260
counselling, genetic 19
cracked nipples 262–3
Crohn's disease 174
crowning 221–2
crying, newborn baby 247
CVS (chorionic villus sampling) 120, 123
cystic fibrosis 18, 109, 122
cystitis 69, 148, 268
cysts, ovarian 22, 86–7, 109
cytomegalovirus 152

death: cot death 90, 254–5, 260
  miscarriage 76–83
  stillbirth 285–6

dehydration 217, 267
delivery 220–4, *220*
  assisted vaginal delivery 237–40
  delivery room 204, *204*
  diabetes and 180–1
  overweight mothers 170
  placenta 224–7
  see also Caesarean section; labour
dental care 70–1
depression 82, 271–4
diabetes 109
  effect on baby 284
  gestational diabetes 159, 169–70, 175, 181–3
  and pre-eclampsia 138
  pre-existing 45–6, 178–81, *180*
diamorphine 205, 206
diaphragm, contraceptive 271
diarrhoea 173, 174
diet: breast-feeding 259
  eating in labour 217
  foods to avoid 37, 96, 149
  pre-pregnancy 30–1, 34–9
  in pregnancy 95–9
dieting 42–3, 99, 169, 170
dilatation, cervix 198, 200, 201, 218, 226
disability, premature babies 281
discharges, vaginal 69–70, 148–9, 266, 274–5
DNA 17
doctors, antenatal care 107–9
donor insemination (DI) 58–9
Doppler ultrasound *115*, 128–9, *128*
double test 120
Down's syndrome 13, 18, 20, 52, 120, 121–2, 124
drinking, in labour 217
driving 94, *94*
drugs: opiates 205, 206–7, 209, 213, 217, 247
  prescription drugs 16, 44–5, 90
  street drugs 90
  see also individual medical conditions
due date, calculating 71–2
DVT (deep vein thrombosis) 191–3
dwarfism 19

eclampsia 137, 140, 141–2
ectopic pregnancy 76, 80, 83–6, *84*, 160
effacement, cervix 197, *197*, 200, 226
egg: assisted conception 57–8
  chromosomes 17
  conception 25–7, *26*, 52
  ovulation 13, 21–5, *22*, *24*, 27, 53, 55
  twin pregnancy 155, 156, *156*
electronic monitoring 213–16, 228, 231
embryo 73, 104
emergency Caesarean section 241
emotions: death of a baby 286
  miscarriage 81–2
endometriosis 59–61
endometrium 13
endorphins 207, 208, 212
engagement, baby's head 194, 200, 226
engorgement, breasts 259–60
Entonox 205–6
epidurals 203, 205, 208–11, 238, 241

epilepsy 47–8, 183–6
episiotomy 222–3, *223*, 238, 268–70
ergometrine 225
erythema infectiosum 150
essential fatty acids 36–7, 96
essential oils, massage 91
estimated date of delivery (EDD) 71–2
evacuation of the uterus 80–1
exercise 43, 99–103, 169
expressing breast milk 260–2, *261*
external cephalic version (ECV) 160, 233
eyes, colour 18–19

face: changes in pregnancy 70
  swollen 137, 138, 139
face presentation 233–4
faintness 101, 166–7
fallopian tubes: conception 25, *26*
  ectopic pregnancy 83–6, *84*, 160
  fertility problems 13, 52, 54–6, *54*, 60
family history 107, 108
fat, in diet 36, 39
feeding: premature babies 279–80
  see also bottle-feeding; breast-feeding
feet, club 183
fertilisation 25, *26*, 27
fertility 12–13, 23, 27
fertility problems 51–61, 85
fibre 96–8, 173, 182
fibroids 13–14
fish 36–7, 96
fits: eclampsia 141–2
  epilepsy 183, 184–5
fluid intake 96
fluid retention 166
flying 92–3
foetal alcohol syndrome 89
foetus: development 73
  first trimester 105
  heartbeat 110
  miscarriage 76–83
  monitoring 130–5, *131*, *132*
  movements 133–4
  second trimester 162
  small babies 124–30, *125*, *126*
  ultrasound scans 72–5, *74*, *114–15*
  see also baby
folic acid 29–33, 164
  anaemia 171
  epilepsy and 48, 183
  neural tube defects and 31–2
  placental abruption 142
  supplements 31–3, 46, 69, 95, 169, 172
  twin pregnancy 158
food *see* diet
food poisoning 38
forceps delivery 210, 211, 223, 237–40, *238*, 242
formula milk 256, 257, 264
fraternal twins 155
fruit 39, 97
fundal height, measuring 112–13, *112*

gas and air 205–6
general anaesthetics 241
genetic conditions 18–20, 78, 83, 120

Index

genetics 17–20
genital herpes 151–2
genitals, newborn baby 250, 251
German measles 20–1, 108, 109, 149–50, 276
gestational diabetes 159, 175, 181–3
glucose: diabetes 178–82
  in urine 109
grasp reflex 250–1
gums, bleeding 70–1
Guthrie test 251

haemoglobin 34–5, 171
haemophilia 19
haemorrhage see bleeding
hands: pins and needles 166
  reddening of palms 71
  swollen 137, 138, 139
hay fever 31, 186, 259
head (baby's) 126, 127
  after birth 246–7
  assisted vaginal delivery 238–9, 238
  delivery 220–2, 220
  engagement 194, 200, 226
  measuring 249–50, 249
  presentation 233–4
  slow labour 232
headaches 189, 211
health care 44–50
heart: defects 47, 183
  heart disease 41, 47, 102, 141, 186–8
  increased volume of blood 164
heart rate (baby's) 110, 250
  cardiotocography 130–3, 131, 132, 214–16
  monitoring in labour 213–16, 228, 231
heartburn 95, 96, 165
HELLP syndrome 139–40
heparin 170, 177, 187–8, 192–3, 275
hepatitis 50, 108, 109, 154–5
herpes simplex 151–2
high blood pressure 13, 40, 41–2, 46, 136–40, 188–9
hips, dislocation 250
HIV 50, 108, 153–4, 280
home birth 229
hormones: assisted conception 57, 57, 58
  breast-feeding 256–7
  endometriosis 60–1
  menstrual cycle 21
  miscarriage 78
  morning sickness 67, 68
  ovulation 22, 24, 25, 53, 55
  pregnancy tests 65, 66
hospital birth 202–3, 229
hot tubs 100
hCG (human chorionic gonadotrophin) 65–8, 86, 122
Huntington's chorea 18
hydrocephalus 31, 32, 121, 124, 285
hyperemesis gravidarum 68
hypertension see high blood pressure
hyperthyroidism 190
hypoglycaemia 180
hypothyroidism 190–1

identical twins 155
immune system: HIV 153–4
  rubella 20–1, 150
immunisation 254, 255
immunoglobulin, anti-D 143, 146, 147
in vitro fertilisation (IVF) 20, 55–6, 57, 57, 59, 155
incomplete miscarriage 79, 80, 81
incontinence 102, 268
incubators 278, 278
indigestion 95
induction of labour 230–2, 237
inevitable miscarriage 79
infections: after Caesarean 274, 275
  breast-feeding and 260
  miscarriage 78, 80, 81
  in pregnancy 148–55
  premature labour 235, 236
infertility 13, 14, 51–61
inflammatory bowel disease 174
inherited disorders 17, 18–20
injections, oxytocin 224–5, 228
insulin 45–6, 178–82, 180
internal examinations 109–10, 200, 201, 206
intracytoplasmic sperm injection (ICSI) 58, 58, 59
intrauterine contraceptive device (coil) 22–3, 84, 186, 271
intrauterine growth restriction (IUGR) 126–30
iron 29, 34–6, 49, 95, 164–5
  anaemia 171
  in breast milk 260
  supplements 69, 95, 158, 171–2
  vegetarian diet 38
irritable bowel syndrome (IBS) 173

jaundice 181, 251, 280
jogging 101

kick charts 133
kidney problems 78, 109, 137, 138, 148, 179
Kliehauer test 147

labour 196–243
  birth plans 200–1, 227–8
  eating and drinking in 217
  first stage 196, 197–217, 197, 198
  home birth 229
  induction of 230–2, 237
  length of 200
  monitoring baby 213–17, 228, 231
  overweight mothers 170
  pain relief 203–13, 227
  placenta praevia 145
  positions 218–19, 228
  premature labour 235–7
  presentation 226, 232–5
  pushing 210, 218–19
  second stage 196, 198, 217–24
  signs of 197–9
  slow progress 232
  third stage 196, 198, 224–6
  transition stage 218
  triggers 91–2
  twin pregnancy 157

lactoferrin 260
laparoscopy 54–5, 60, 85
large for dates babies 135
legs: epidurals 209
  swollen 137, 138, 139
  varicose veins 166
  venous thrombosis 93, 191–3, 275
lie 226, 234–5
lifestyle 88–103
lifting, safety 103
ligaments, softening 101, 165, 167–8, 270
lightening 194
linea nigra 70
lip, cleft 120, 121, 124, 183, 285
listeria 37, 149
liver, baby's 126–7
lochia 266, 274–5
lungs: premature babies 160, 181, 194, 236, 279, 280–1
  pulmonary thromboembolism 191
  surfactant 194
lupus see SLE

macrosomia 135
'mask' of pregnancy 70
massage 91, 205, 211–12, 224
mastitis 263
meat, toxoplasma 152
meconium 201, 214, 252
  aspiration 283
medical conditions 44–50, 78, 101–2, 170–93
membranes: premature rupture 236–7
  ruptured 199, 201–2, 231
  sweeping 230–1
menstrual cycle 21–5, 22, 71–2
mercury, in fish 37, 96
midwives 204, 229
migraine 189
milk: bottle-feeding 256, 257
  breast-feeding 255–63, 280
minerals 29, 34–6, 95
miscarriage 42, 52, 60, 76–83, 87
  after amniocentesis 123
  and diabetes 178
  recurrent 82–3, 159
  twin pregnancy 156
  VDUs and 90
missed miscarriage 79, 80, 81
Mittelschmerz 22, 53
monitoring: baby in womb 130–5, 131, 132
  special care babies 278
Montgomery's tubercles 66
morning sickness 67–9, 179, 184
Moro reflex 250
morphine 205, 206, 247
movements, foetal 133–4
mucus: 'show' 198–9, 231, 235
  vaginal 25
multiple sclerosis 48–9
muscles, abdominal 101, 269

Naegele's formula 72
nappy rash 252
nausea 67–9, 207
necrotising enterocolitis (NEC) 236, 284

nerves: epidurals 208–9
  pins and needles 166
  TENS 205, 207–8
neural tube defects 30, 31–2, 120, 121,
  122, 169, 178, 183, 184
nipples: breast-feeding 258
  cracked 262–3
  signs of pregnancy 66
  thrush 263
non-stress CTG test 133, 134
NSAIDS (non-steroidal anti-inflammatory
  drugs) 175
nuchal scans 120, 121–2
nutrition see diet

obesity 168
occipito-anterior position 226
occipito-posterior position 221, 226
oedema 137, 138, 139
oestrogen 21, 186
  endometriosis 60, 61
  oral contraceptives 186, 189, 193,
    270–1
oligohydramnios 157
operating theatres 242
opiates 205, 206–7, 209, 213, 217, 247
oral contraceptives 23, 136, 186, 189,
  193, 270–1
orgasm 91, 92
ovaries 26, 54, 55
  assisted conception 57, 57
  cysts 22, 86–7, 109
  endometriosis 59–61
overdue babies 230
overweight mothers 14, 40–3, 99, 168–70,
  182–3
ovulation 13, 21–5, 22, 24, 27, 53, 55, 271
oxytocin: breast-feeding 257, 266
  delivery of afterbirth 225, 228
  induction of labour 231, 237
  slow labour 232

pain: afterpains 265–6
  ectopic pregnancy 85
  endometriosis 59, 60
  miscarriage 79
  ovulation 22, 53
  pain relief 203–13, 227, 238
  pelvic diastasis 168
  stitches 268–70
panting 222
paracetamol 175, 189
partogram 201
parvovirus 150
pelvic floor exercises 102, 268
pelvic infections 13, 55, 84
pelvis: engagement 194, 200, 226
  ligaments 101, 165, 167–8
  pelvic diastasis 167–8, 167
  size of 109–10
  slow labour 232
perineum: episiotomy 222–3, 223
  tears 219, 222, 223
periods 13, 21, 65, 271
pethidine 205, 206
pets, toxoplasma 90, 152
phenylketonuria 251
phototherapy 251, 280

pigment changes 70
piles 166
the pill see oral contraceptives
Pinard stethoscope 213–14
pins and needles 166
placenta 75
  abruption 142–3, 143, 146
  delivery 224–7
  insufficiency 125–30, 138
  monitoring in labour 213
  placenta praevia 143–6, 145
  and pre-eclampsia 137–8
  retained afterbirth 227, 267
  twin pregnancy 156
platelets 139–40
polyhydramnios 135
polyps 76, 146
post-partum haemorrhage 267
postnatal check 276
postnatal depression (PND) 271–4
pre-eclampsia 40, 41–2, 47, 109, 137–41,
  188–9
pre-labour rupture of the membranes
  (PROM) 236–7
pre-pregnancy care 12–43
pregnancy-induced diabetes see
  gestational diabetes
pregnancy-induced hypertension (PIH) 137
pregnancy tests 65–6, 66, 85
premature babies 125, 160–1, 279–82
  breathing problems 160, 181, 194, 236,
    279, 280–1
premature labour 140, 235–7
premature rupture of the membranes
  (PPROM) 236
presentation, baby in womb 226, 232–5
previous pregnancies, complications
  159–61
processed foods 38
progesterone 21
  oral contraceptives 186, 193, 271
  ovulation 22, 24, 53, 55
prolactin 257
prolapse, cord 237
prostaglandins 81, 91–2, 198, 201, 231,
  237
protein 36, 95, 97
  in urine 109, 137, 139
pumps, breast 262
pushing, in labour 210, 218–19

quadruplets 157

recurrent miscarriage 82–3, 159
red blood cells 30, 49, 95, 139–40, 146–7,
  164
reflexes 250–1, 257
respiratory distress syndrome (RDS) 282
resuscitaire 248
rhesus disease 81, 112, 146–7
rheumatoid arthritis 165, 174–5
ripening cervix 230, 231
risk factors 110–11
rooting reflex 251, 257
rubella 20–1, 108, 109, 149–50, 276
ruptured membranes 199, 201–2, 231,
  236–7

salmonella 38
salt 38, 39
saunas 100
scars, Caesarean 243, 274, 275
seat belts 94, 94
sexual intercourse 27, 91–2, 270
shingles 150–1
shoulder dystocia 170, 181
shoulders, delivery of 221
'show' 198–9, 231, 235
Siamese twins 156
sickle-cell anaemia 18, 49–50, 108, 109
signs of pregnancy 64–5
skin: changes in pregnancy 70, 71
  nappy rash 252
  newborn baby's 246
skull see head (baby's)
'slapped cheek' syndrome 150
SLE (systemic lupus erythematosis) 49,
  109, 174, 175–8
sleep, newborn baby 253–4
slow labour 232
small babies 124–30, 125, 126
small-for-dates babies 32, 40, 283–4
smear tests 108, 110, 276
smoking 14–15, 40, 88–90, 142, 255
spacing pregnancies 14
special care baby units 277–85
sperm: assisted conception 58–9
  chromosomes 17
  conception 25–7, 52
  fertility problems 53–4, 56
'spiders', vascular 71
spina bifida 31, 120, 121, 122, 124, 178,
  183, 184
squatting, in labour 218, 219
'startle' reflex 250
'station of the head' 226
sterilising bottles 263–4
steroids 140, 172, 173, 174–5, 176, 236
stillbirth 285–6
stitches: Caesarean section 274
  cervical incompetence 83, 159
  episiotomy 223, 268–70
stockings, support 93, 166, 275
stork marks 285
stress 14
stress incontinence 102, 268
sugar 36, 38, 39
sun protection 70
supplements 31, 32–3, 35, 95, 169, 171–2
surfactant 194, 282
surgery: ectopic pregnancy 86
  evacuation of the uterus 80–1
  ovarian cysts 87
  see also Caesarean section
swimming 100
syphilis 108, 109

tampons 266
tears, perineum 219, 222, 223–4
teats, bottle-feeding 264
temperature: after Caesarean 275
  ovulation 23–5, 24
TENS 205, 207–8
termination of pregnancy 124
tests, antenatal 108, 109, 120–4

tetracycline 148, 173
thalassaemia 18, 108, 109
thermometers 24
threatened miscarriage 79, 80
thrombophilia 192, 193
thrombosis 46, 68, 93, 170, 188, 191–3, 275
thrush 69–70, 148–9, 178, 252, 263
thyroid problems 55, 78, 109, 179, 190–1
tiredness 67, 171
tooth care 70–1
toxoplasma 37, 90, 152–3
transient tachypnoea 282, 283
transition stage, labour 218
transverse lie 234–5
travel 92–4
trimesters: first 104–5
    second 162–3
    third 194–5
triple test 120, 122
triplets 55, 155, 157
tuberculosis 255
twins 55, 135, 155–9
    anaemia 171
    epidural analgesia 211
    placenta praevia 144
    premature labour 235
    twin-to-twin transfusion syndrome 157, 158
    ultrasound scans 113

ultrasound scans: biophysical profiles 133–5
    early pregnancy 71–5, 74, 108, 110
    ectopic pregnancy 85
    later pregnancy 113, 113–15
    miscarriage 77–80
    placenta praevia 144
    screening for abnormalities 120, 121
    small babies 125, 126, 128–9, 128
    twin pregnancies 156, 157

umbilical cord 75, 115
    breech presentation 233
    cordocentesis 120, 123
    cutting 224
    delivery of baby 222
    prolapse 237
    stump 252
    twin pregnancy 156
    water birth 220
unstable lie 235
urinary tract infections (UTI) 148, 170
urination 69, 267–8
urine: catheters 210, 227, 238, 242, 268
    newborn baby 251–2
    protein in 109, 137, 139
    stress incontinence 102, 268
    tests 108, 109, 111
uterus see womb

vaccination 254, 255
vacuum delivery see ventouse delivery
vagina 54
    bleeding see bleeding
    discharges 69–70, 266, 274–5
    episiotomy 222–3, 223
    internal examinations 109–10, 200, 201, 206
    tears 219, 222, 223–4
'vanishing twin' 156–7
varicose veins 166
VDUs (visual display units) 90
vegan diet 35, 38
vegetables 39, 97
vegetarian diet 35, 38, 98
veins, varicose 166
ventouse (vacuum) delivery 210, 211, 223, 237, 239–40
vernix 246
vertex presentation 226
viral infections 149–55
vitamins 28–34, 95

vitamin A 29, 34, 35, 95
vitamin B complex 29–33, 38, 95, 171
vitamin C 29, 33, 95, 129, 141, 172
vitamin D 29, 33, 38, 95
vitamin E 95, 129, 141
vitamin K 183, 249
vomiting 67–9

waist measurements 41–2
walking 100, 167
walking reflex 251
warfarin 187–8, 192–3
water, drinking 36, 96, 217
water birth 205, 212–13, 219–20, 229
waters: breaking 199, 201–2, 231
    premature rupture 236–7
weight: birth weight 124, 125, 169, 252
    gain during pregnancy 98–9
    pre-pregnancy care 40–3
    small babies 124, 125
wind 264
winter, pre-eclampsia in 141
womb 54
    adenomyosis 59
    after delivery 266
    Caesarean section 240–3
    delivery of placenta 224–7
    fibroids 13–14
    first stage of labour 197
    implantation 27
    induction of labour 231
    measuring 111–13, 112
    miscarriage 78–81
    placenta praevia 143–6, 145
    placental abruption 142–3, 143, 146
    twin pregnancies 158–9
    see also contractions
work 16, 90, 260

yoga 100

zinc 29

Acknowledgements

Writing the text of a book like this is the easy part for the author. Delivering the completed work is much more difficult and requires a great deal of team work. I am grateful to many people for their advice, help and support in bringing this book to fruition and I would like to acknowledge my appreciation of their various contributions. Lauren, as always, inspired me and made sure that I got the style just right. David McCusker and Jean Long spawned the website that made this book possible. Dr Alan Mathers, my friend and colleague at the Princess Royal Maternity Unit in Glasgow, provided me with the excellent ultrasound images that light up the book. I am indebted to Ellen Green and Elsevier for allowing me to reproduce some artworks from Mosby's *Color Atlas and Text of Obstetrics and Gynaecology*, which I coauthored. The Medical Illustration Department at Glasgow Royal Infirmary kindly provided the photographs of the delivery unit. Peggy McLellan organised the positive and negative tests, proving that anything is possible! Karen Whitty organised the embryology photographs that show how it all starts. Peter Altman gave me sound advice on publishing. I have also enjoyed interacting with the team at Harper Collins who put together the final product. Angela Newton, managing editor, was there from conception to delivery. Emma Callery patiently managed and coordinated the project while stretching time. Alastair Laing made sure we got everything together. Kate Parker asked all the questions that put the final polish on the text. Bob Vickers turned the bare text into a splendid layout and Amanda Williams's artworks put life on the pages.

Credits

The following artworks are reprinted from *Mosby's Color Atlas and Text of Obstetrics and Gynecology*, Greer *et al*, © 2000, with permission from Elsevier Science: pp. 125, 126, 143, 145, 156, 197, 221, 233, 238

Photographs on pp. 246, 265, 277 © NCT Publishing Photo Library

Ultrasound scans by Dr Alan Mathers, © Professor Ian Greer

Photographs on pp. 66, 204, 242, 248, 278 taken by the Medical Illustration Department at Glasgow Royal Infirmary, © Professor Ian Greer